'One day we met a boy about the same age as my two-year-old in the park, wearing the same cap. But that boy was a little rowdy. When my son approached him with a big smile, happy to see a cap like his, he slapped my son with a full swing, as if saying, "Stay away!"

They were toddlers. It wasn't a problem as long as no one got hurt. But thinking the boy's parents might be upset if they saw what was going on, I grabbed my son's hand, saying, "Let's go play over there."

My two-year-old flung off my hand, and with a look that said, "I am going to teach that boy the most important lesson of his life," he went running toward the other boy.

Well done, two-year-old!

—Hiroyuki Asada, 2013'

Hiroyuki Asada made his debut in *Monthly Shonen Jump* in 1986. He's best known for his basketball manga *I'll*. He's a contributor to artist Range Murata's quarterly manga anthology *Robot*. *Tegami Bachi: Letter Bee* is his most recent series.

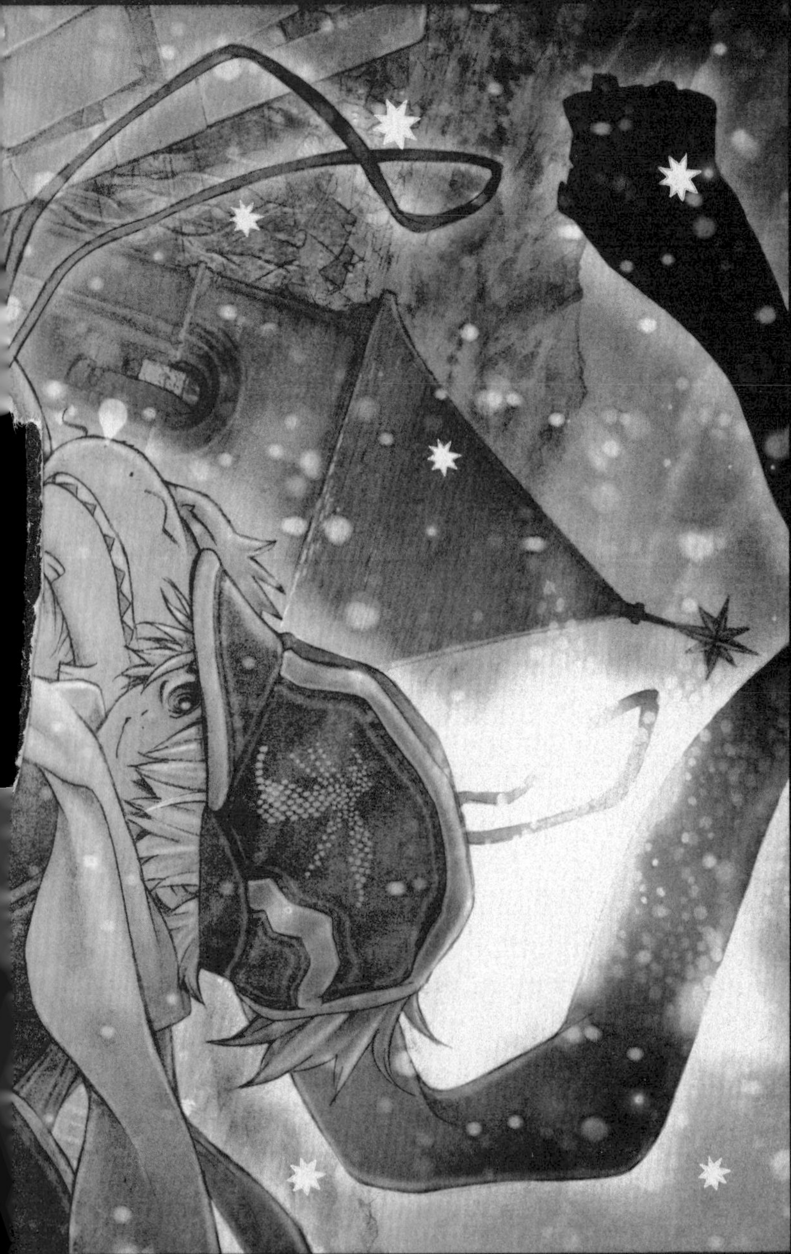

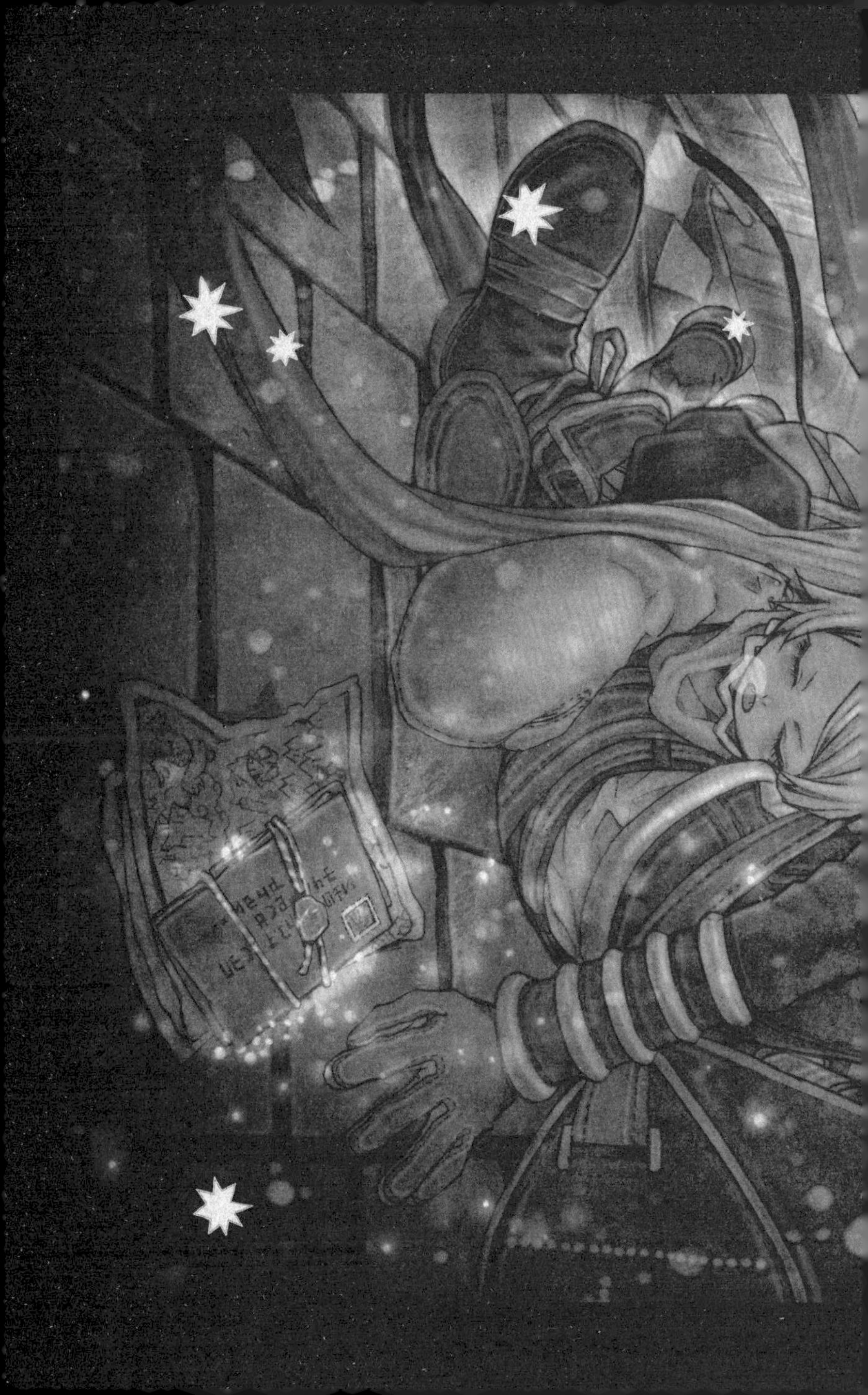

Volume 17
SHONEN JUMP Manga Edition

Story and Art by Hiroyuki Asada

English Adaptation/Rich Amtower
Translation/JN Productions
Touch-up & Lettering/Annaliese Christman
Design/Amy Martin
Editor/Shaenon K. Garrity

TEGAMIBACHI © 2006 by Hiroyuki Asada. All rights reserved.
First published in Japan in 2006 by SHUEISHA Inc., Tokyo. English
translation rights arranged by SHUEISHA Inc.

The stories, characters and incidents mentioned in this publication are
entirely fictional.

Printed in Canada

Published by VIZ Media, LLC
P.O. Box 77010
San Francisco, CA 94107

10 9 8 7 6 5 4 3 2 1
First printing, November 2014

www.viz.com

THE WORLD'S
MOST POPULAR MANGA
SHONEN JUMP
www.shonenjump.com

Tegami Bachi
LETTER BEE

VOLUME 17

LATE HIRE
CHICO

STORY AND ART BY
HIROYUKI ASADA

This is a country known as Amberground, where night never ends.

Its capital, Akatsuki, is illuminated by a man-made sun. The farther one strays from the capital, the weaker the light. The Yuusari region is cast in twilight; the Yodaka region survives only on pale moonlight.

Letter Bee Gauche Suede and young Lag Seeing meet as a postal worker and the "letter" he must deliver. Five years later, Lag sets out for Yuusari to become a Letter Bee like Gauche. But Gauche is no longer there, having lost his *heart* and vanished.

In time Lag becomes a Letter Bee, delivering letters while searching for Gauche. He and Gauche are unexpectedly reunited–but Gauche, now calling himself Noir, has become a Marauder working for the rebel organization Reverse. Reverse plots an attack on the Amberground government by unleashing a powerful Gaichuu called Cabernet. The Bees launch an all-out effort to block the attack and manage to stop Cabernet on the verge of breaking into the capital.

After finding a message from his mother Anne inside Noir's *heart*, Lag returns to his hometown to seek the truth about Amberground. There, he discovers that his mother is the Empress of Amberground and learns the secret of his birth. Meanwhile, Letter Bee Zazie tracks Laphroaig, the Gaichuu that devoured his parents' *hearts*. He finds that Emil, a young innkeeper, has been controlling Laphroaig with spirit amber. With the help of his fellow Bees, Zazie defeats the Gaichuu and learns of his parents' feelings for him.

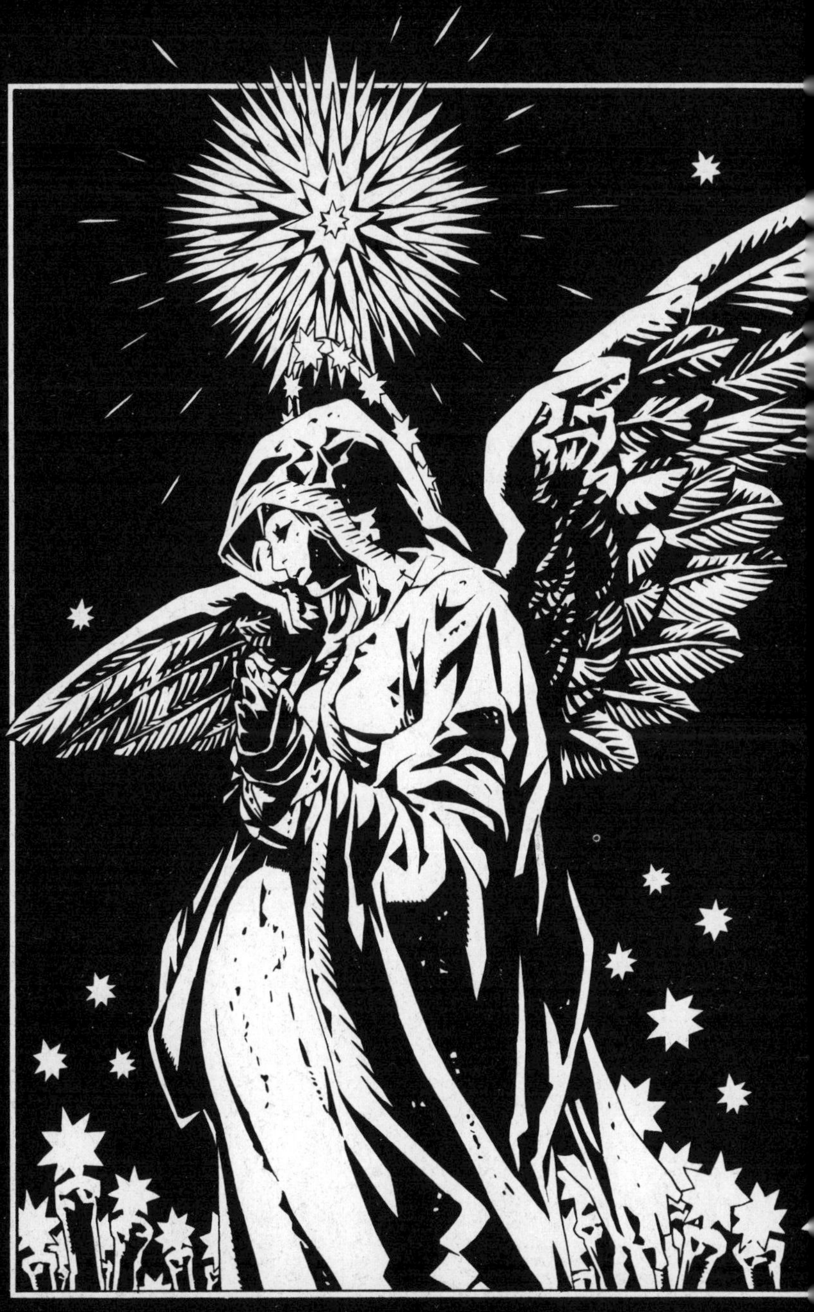

List of Characters

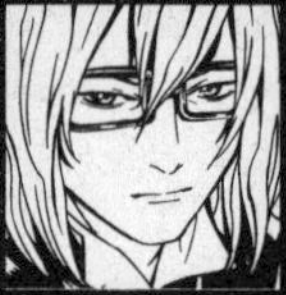

LARGO LLOYD
Ex-Beehive Director

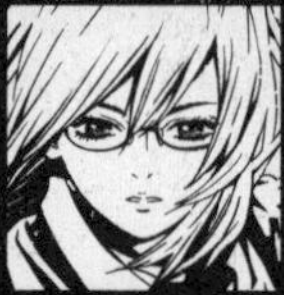

ARIA LINK
Section Chief of the Dead Letter Office

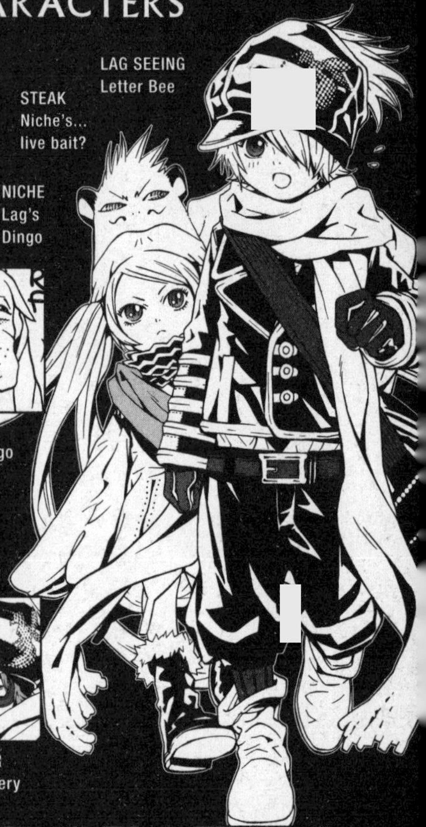

LAG SEEING
Letter Bee

STEAK
Niche's... live bait?

NICHE
Lag's Dingo

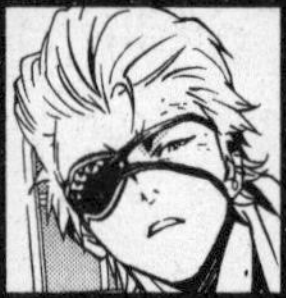

DR. THUNDERLAND, JR.
Member of the AG Biological Science Advisory Board, Third Division and head doctor at the Beehive

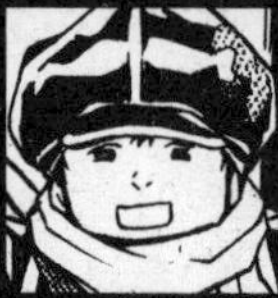

CONNOR KLUFF
Letter Bee

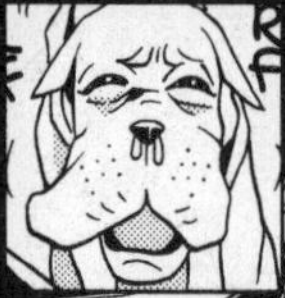

GUS
Connor's Dingo

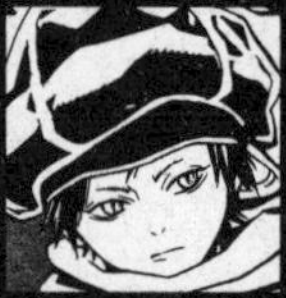

ZAZIE
Letter Bee

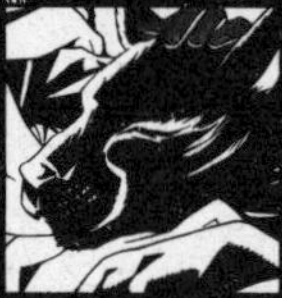

WASIOLKA
Zazie's Dingo

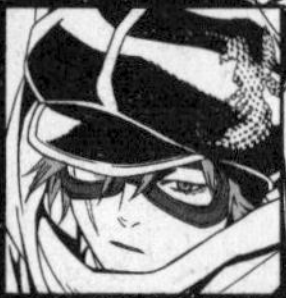

JIGGY PEPPER
Express Delivery Letter Bee

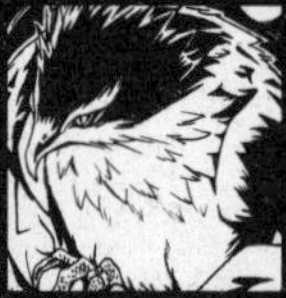

HARRY
Jiggy's Dingo

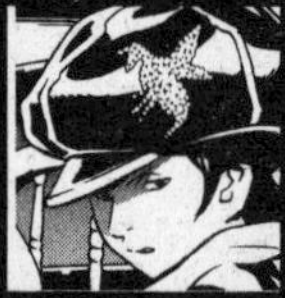

MOC SULLIVAN
Letter Bee

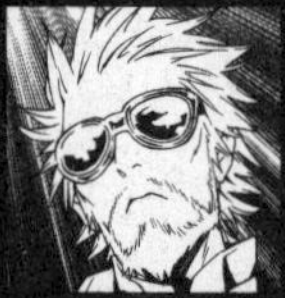

CHALYBS GARRARD
Inspector and ex-Letter Bee

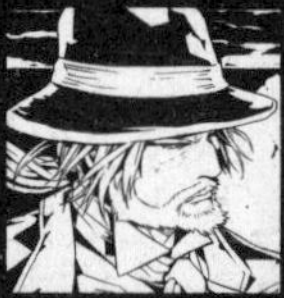

HAZEL VALENTINE
Inspector and Garrard's ex-Dingo

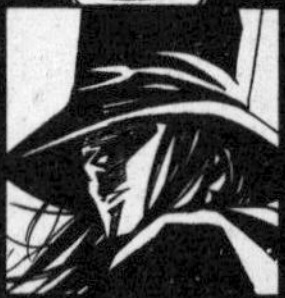

LAWRENCE
The ringleader of Reverse

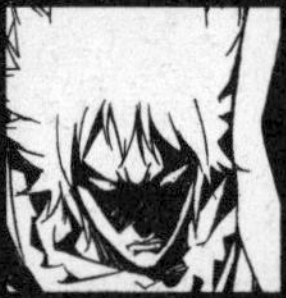

ZEAL
Marauder for Reverse

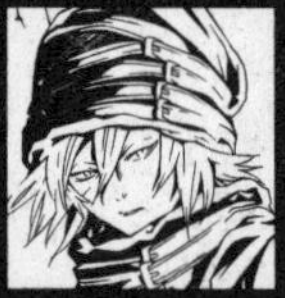

NOIR (FORMERLY GAUCHE SUEDE)
Marauder for Reverse and an ex–Letter Bee

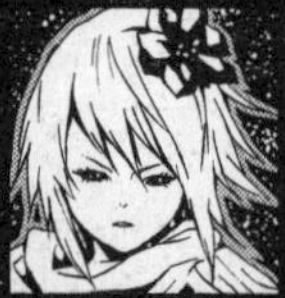

RODA
Noir's Dingo

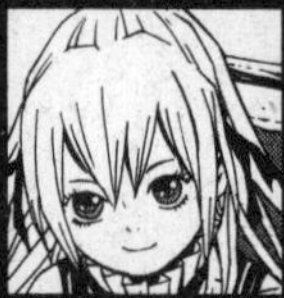

SYLVETTE SUEDE
Gauche's Sister

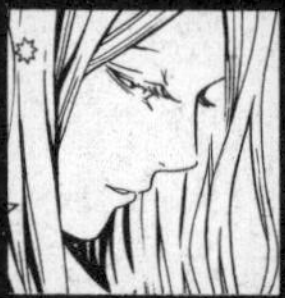

ANNE SEEING
Lag's Mother (Missing)

Tegami Bachi

LETTER · BEE

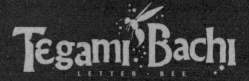

VOLUME 17

Late Hire Chico

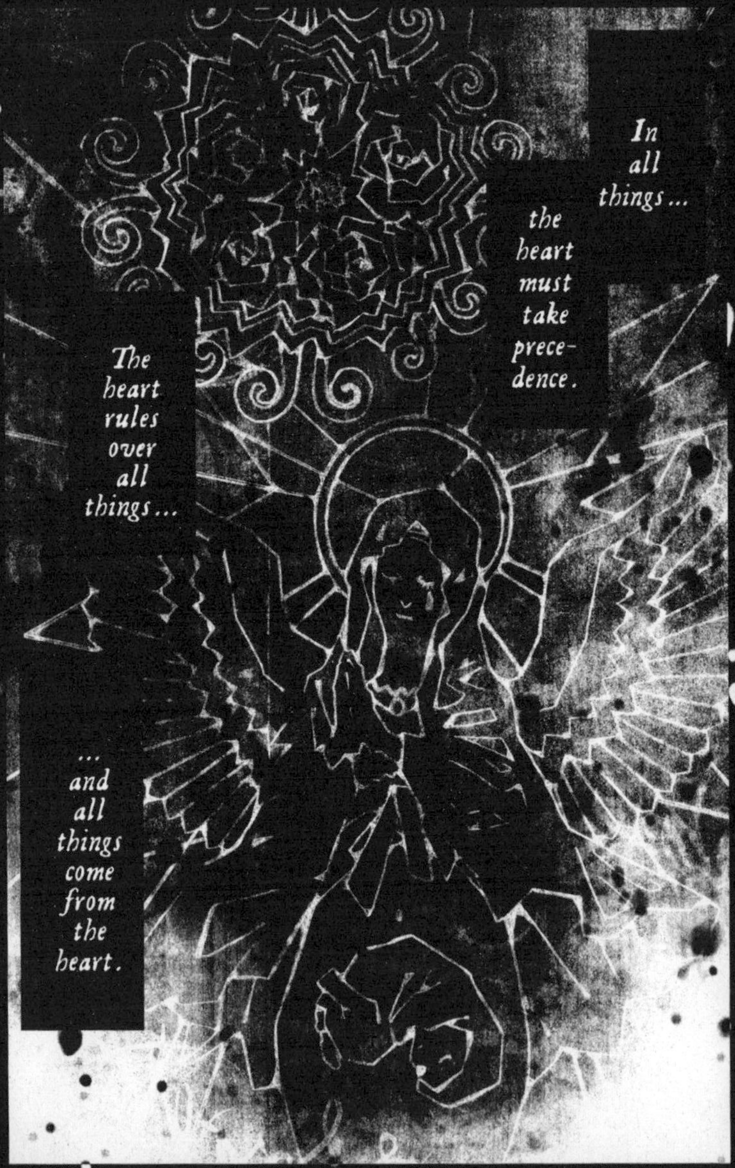
In all things...
the heart must take precedence.
The heart rules over all things...
... and all things come from the heart.

–THE SCRIPTURES OF AMBERGROUND, 1st verse

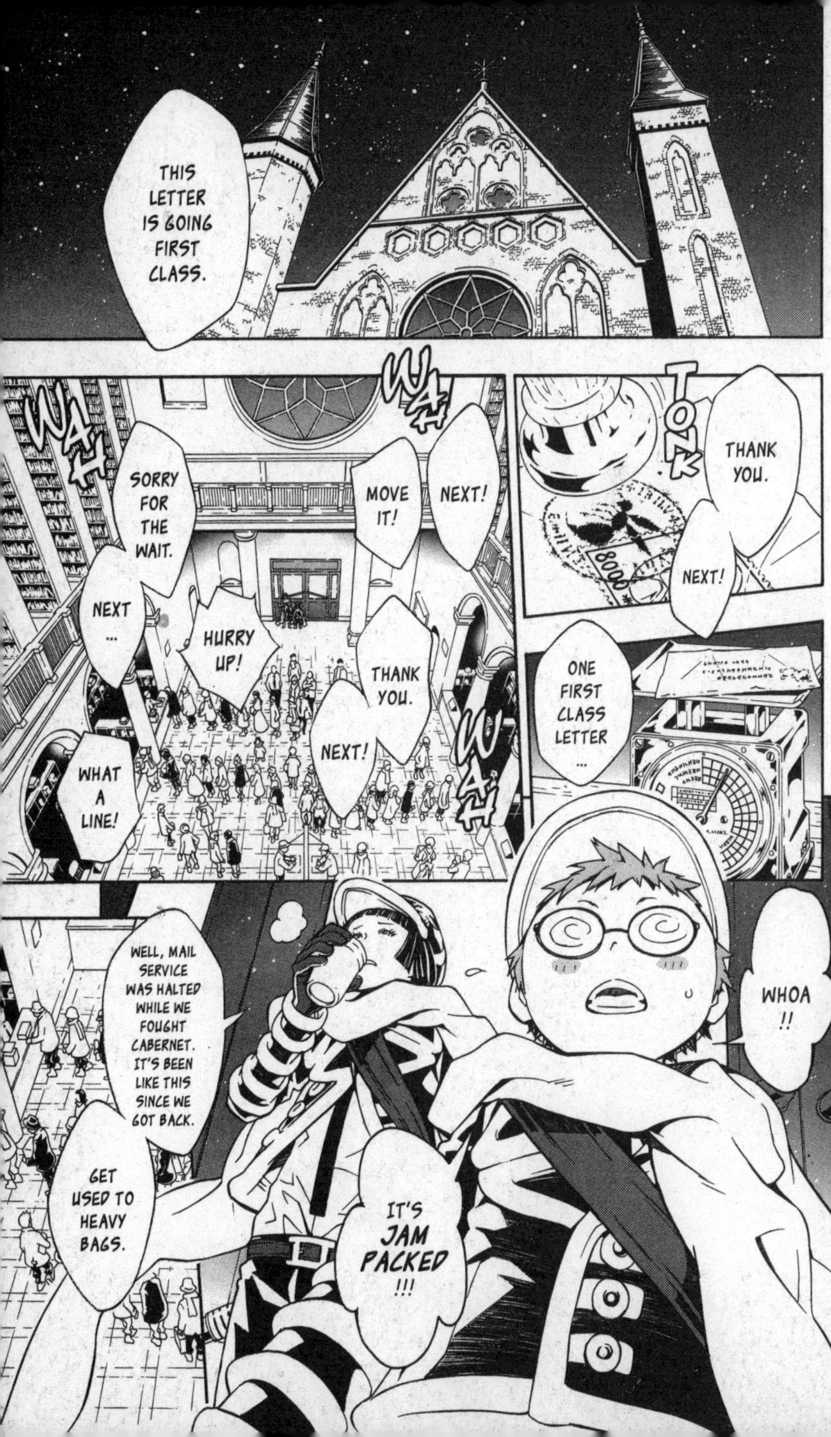
THIS LETTER IS GOING FIRST CLASS.
TONK
THANK YOU.
NEXT!
ONE FIRST CLASS LETTER ...
WAH
NEXT!
MOVE IT!
WAH
SORRY FOR THE WAIT.
NEXT ...
HURRY UP!
THANK YOU.
NEXT!
WAH
WHAT A LINE!
WHOA !!
WELL, MAIL SERVICE WAS HALTED WHILE WE FOUGHT CABERNET. IT'S BEEN LIKE THIS SINCE WE GOT BACK.
IT'S JAM PACKED !!!
GET USED TO HEAVY BAGS.

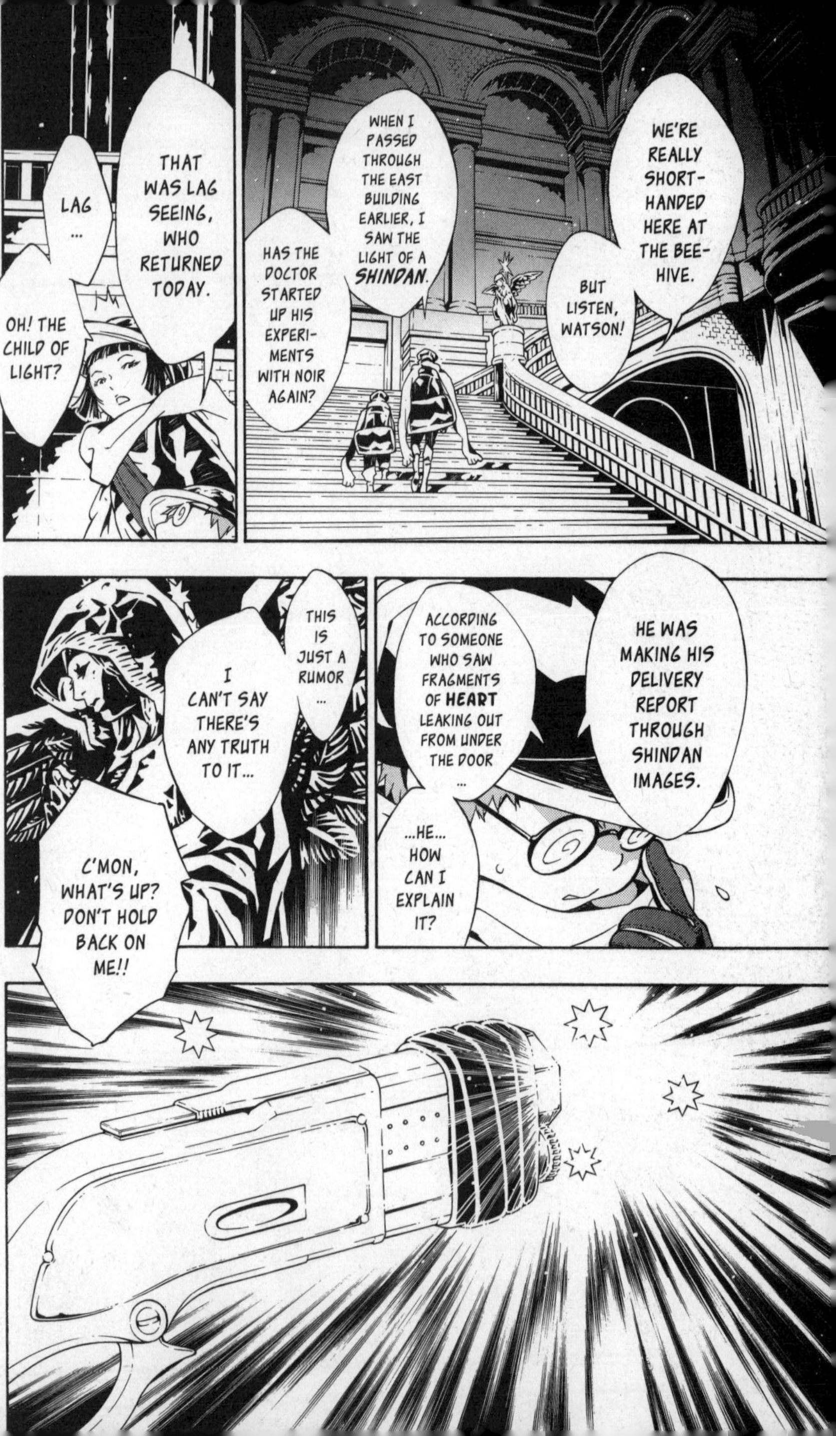
WE'RE REALLY SHORT-HANDED HERE AT THE BEE-HIVE.
BUT LISTEN, WATSON!
WHEN I PASSED THROUGH THE EAST BUILDING EARLIER, I SAW THE LIGHT OF A *SHINDAN*.
HAS THE DOCTOR STARTED UP HIS EXPERIMENTS WITH NOIR AGAIN?
THAT WAS LAG SEEING, WHO RETURNED TODAY.
LAG ...
OH! THE CHILD OF LIGHT?
HE WAS MAKING HIS DELIVERY REPORT THROUGH SHINDAN IMAGES.
ACCORDING TO SOMEONE WHO SAW FRAGMENTS OF **HEART** LEAKING OUT FROM UNDER THE DOOR ...
...HE... HOW CAN I EXPLAIN IT?
THIS IS JUST A RUMOR ...
I CAN'T SAY THERE'S ANY TRUTH TO IT...
C'MON, WHAT'S UP? DON'T HOLD BACK ON ME!!

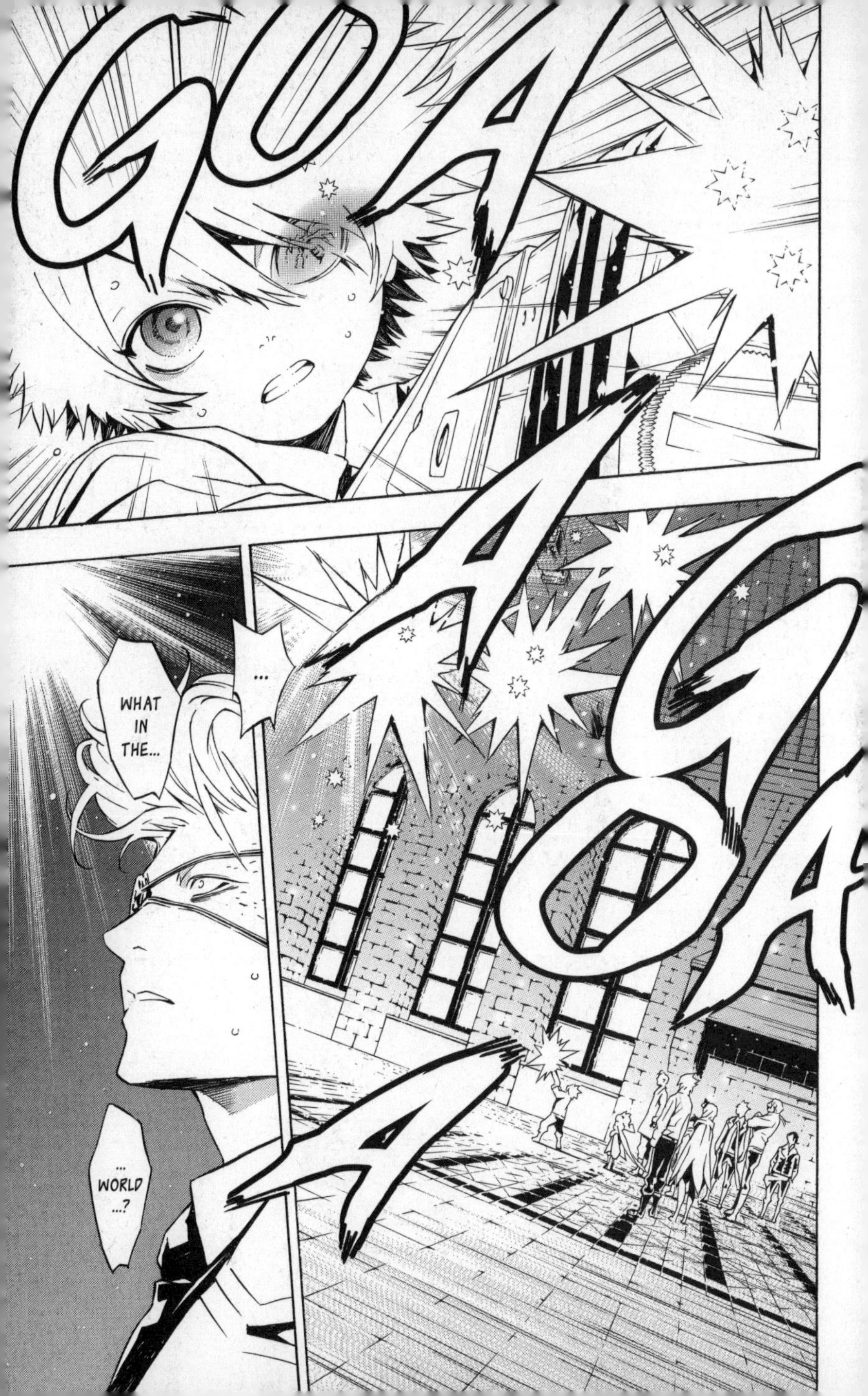
GUA
A
GOA
A
...
WHAT IN THE...
... WORLD ...?

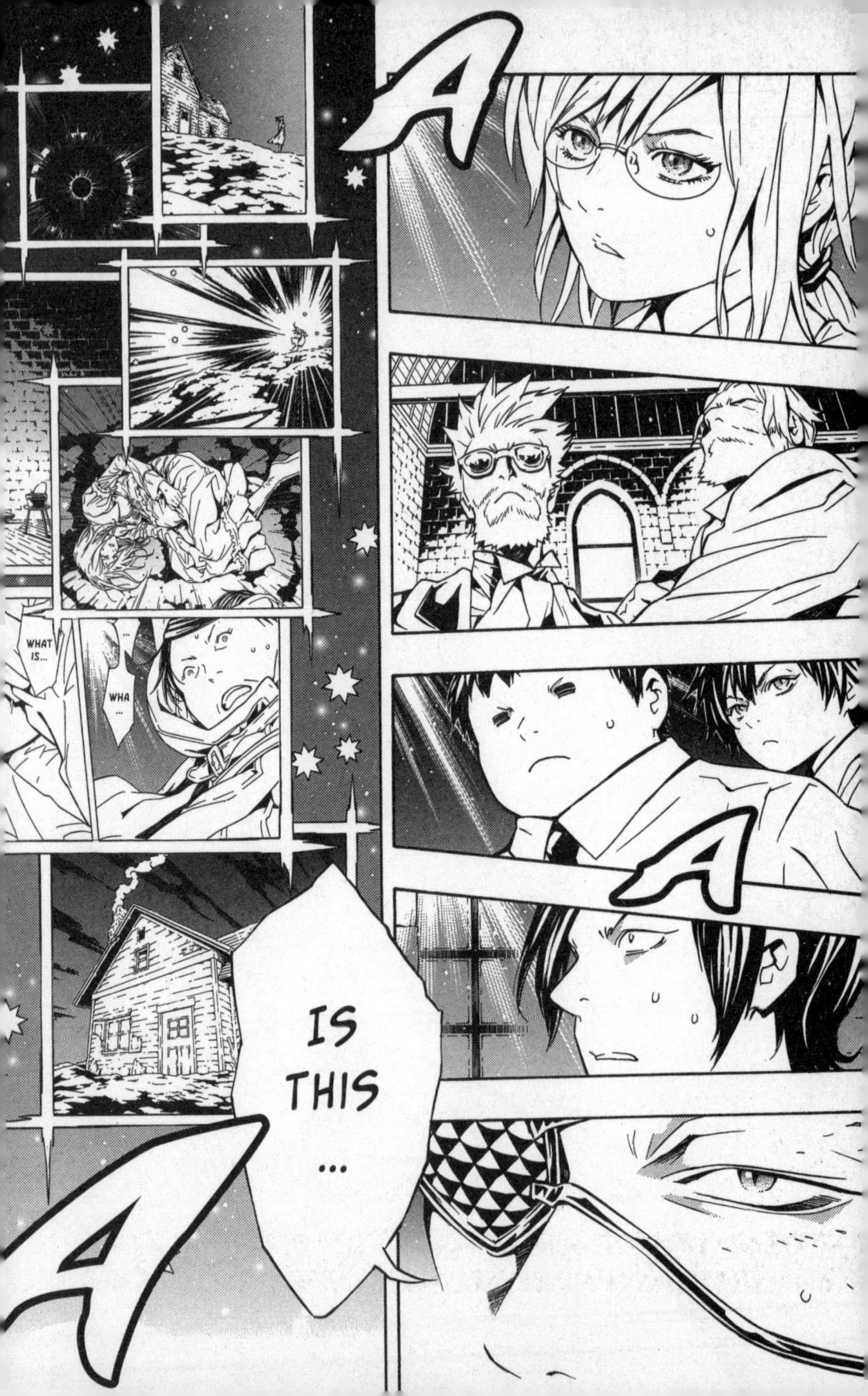

A
A
WHAT IS...
... WHA ...
IS THIS ...
A

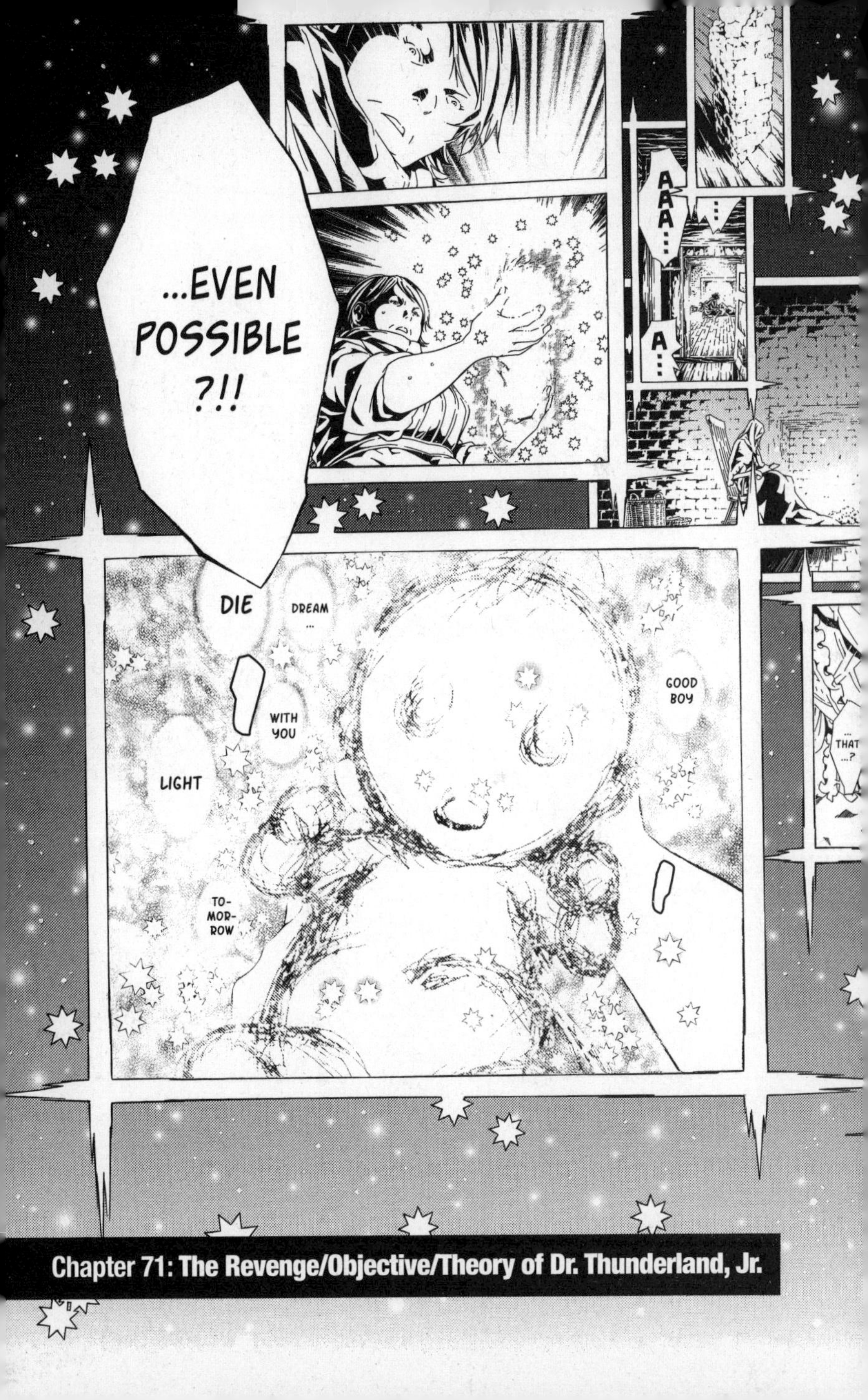
AAA...
...
A...
...EVEN POSSIBLE ?!!
...THAT ...?
GOOD BOY
!
DREAM ...
DIE
!
WITH YOU
LIGHT
TO-MOR-ROW

Chapter 71: The Revenge/Objective/Theory of Dr. Thunderland, Jr.

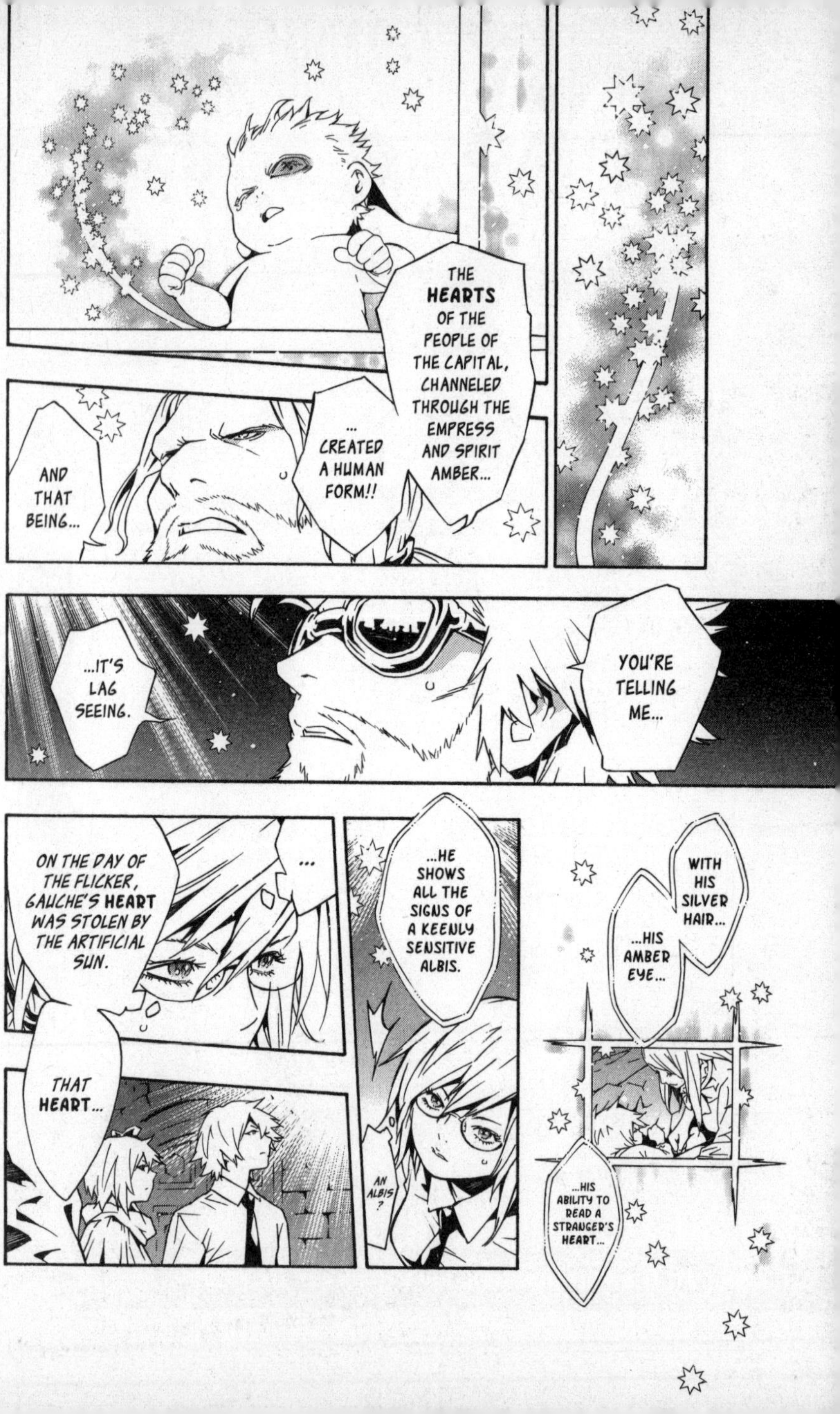
THE HEARTS OF THE PEOPLE OF THE CAPITAL, CHANNELED THROUGH THE EMPRESS AND SPIRIT AMBER...
... CREATED A HUMAN FORM!!
AND THAT BEING...
YOU'RE TELLING ME...
...IT'S LAG SEEING.
WITH HIS SILVER HAIR...
...HIS AMBER EYE...
...HIS ABILITY TO READ A STRANGER'S HEART...
...HE SHOWS ALL THE SIGNS OF A KEENLY SENSITIVE ALBIS.
AN ALBIS?
...
ON THE DAY OF THE FLICKER, GAUCHE'S HEART WAS STOLEN BY THE ARTIFICIAL SUN.
THAT HEART...

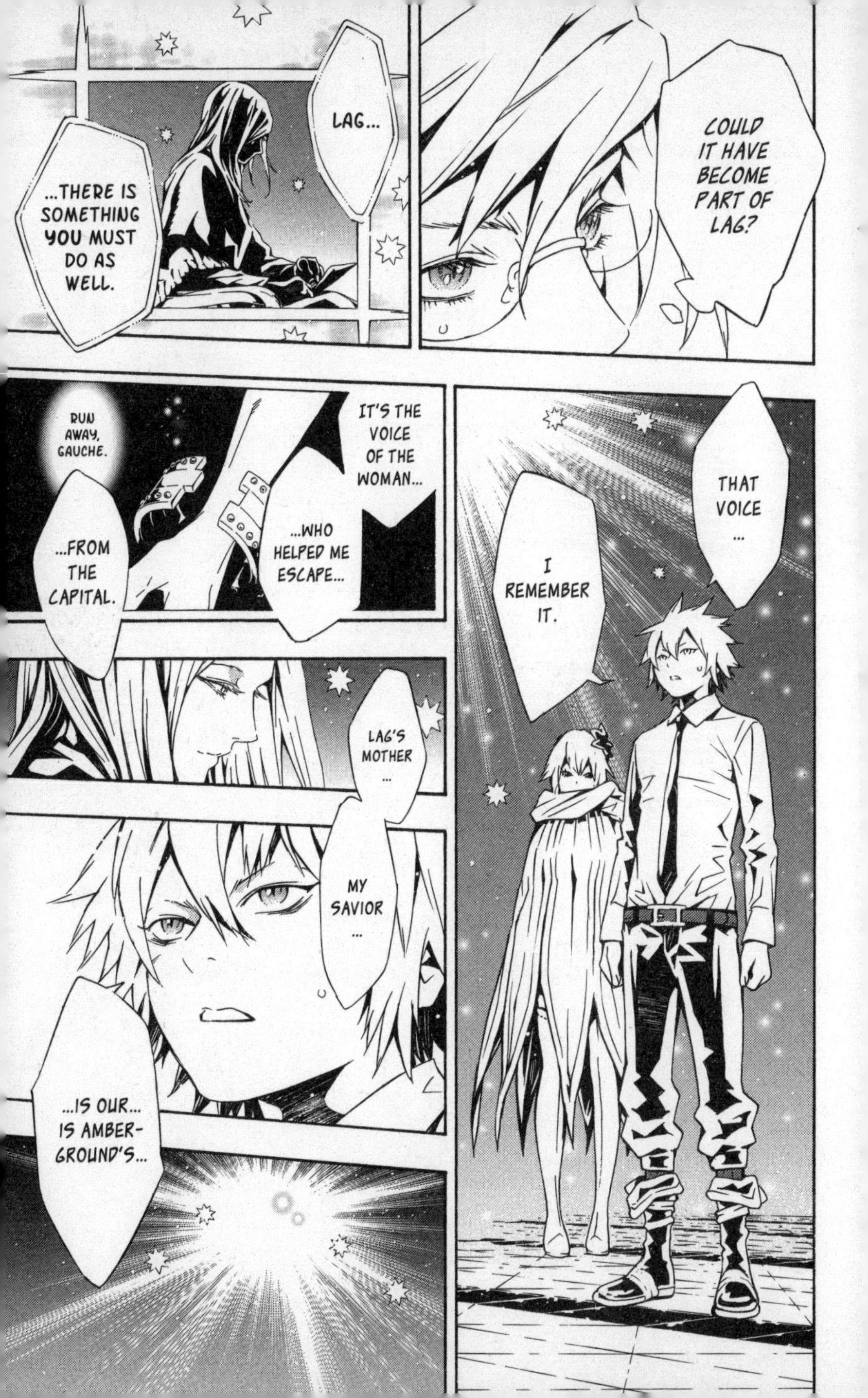
COULD IT HAVE BECOME PART OF LAG?
LAG...
...THERE IS SOMETHING YOU MUST DO AS WELL.
THAT VOICE...
I REMEMBER IT.
IT'S THE VOICE OF THE WOMAN...
...WHO HELPED ME ESCAPE...
RUN AWAY, GAUCHE.
...FROM THE CAPITAL.
LAG'S MOTHER...
MY SAVIOR...
...IS OUR... IS AMBER-GROUND'S...

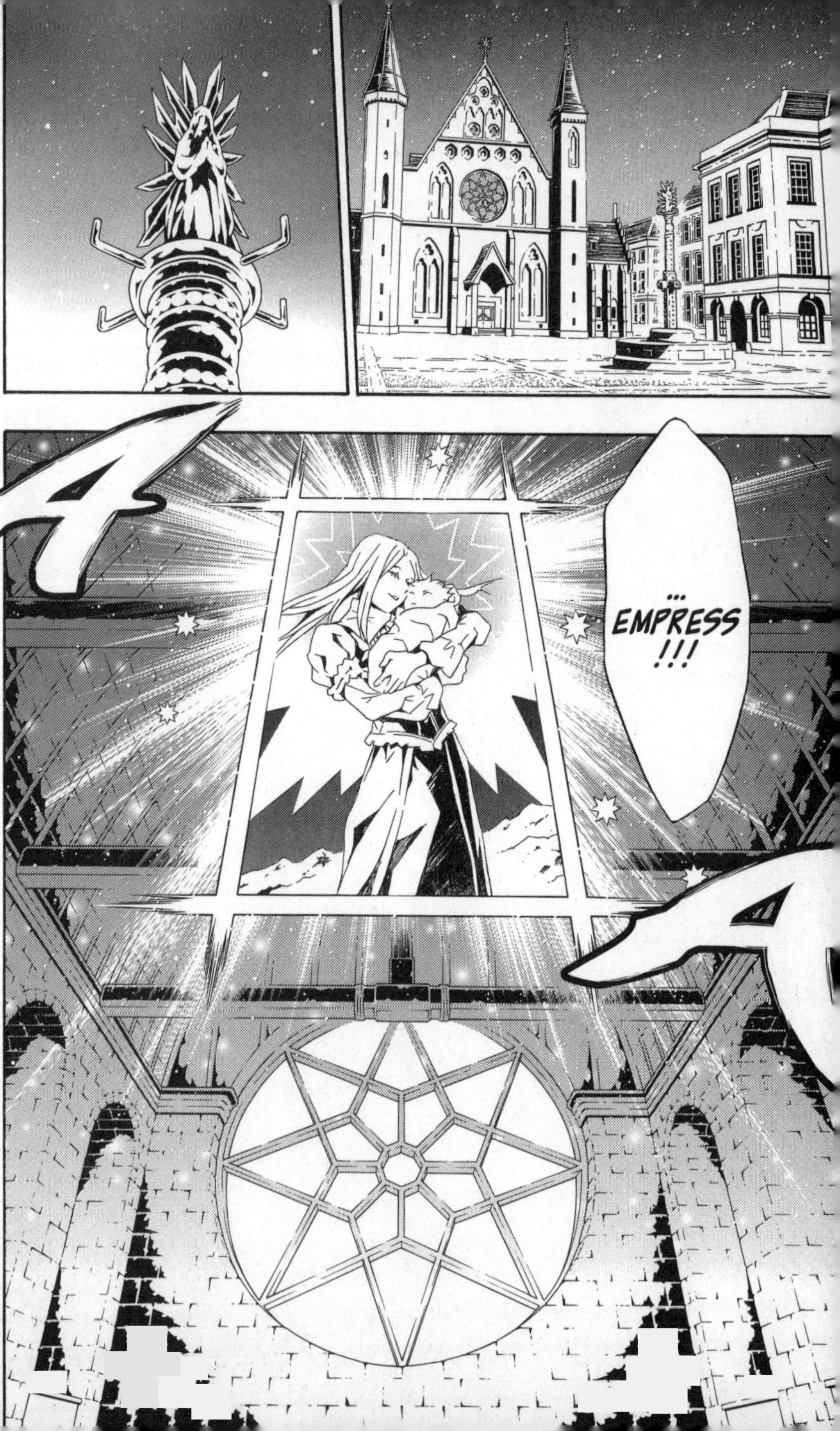
... EMPRESS !!!

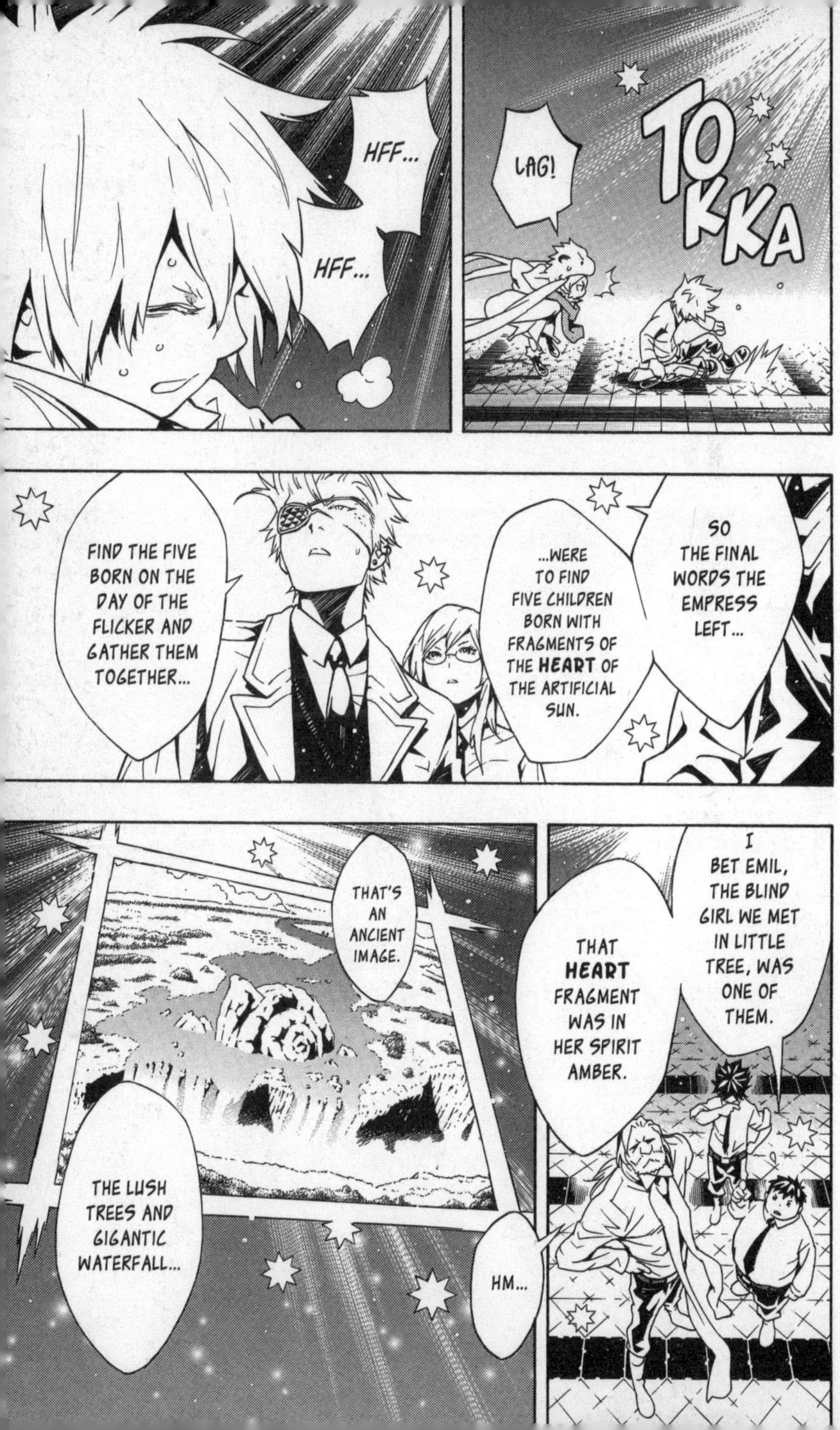
TOKKA
LAG!
HFF...
HFF...
SO THE FINAL WORDS THE EMPRESS LEFT...
...WERE TO FIND FIVE CHILDREN BORN WITH FRAGMENTS OF THE **HEART** OF THE ARTIFICIAL SUN.
FIND THE FIVE BORN ON THE DAY OF THE FLICKER AND GATHER THEM TOGETHER...
I BET EMIL, THE BLIND GIRL WE MET IN LITTLE TREE, WAS ONE OF THEM.
THAT **HEART** FRAGMENT WAS IN HER SPIRIT AMBER.
HM...
THAT'S AN ANCIENT IMAGE.
THE LUSH TREES AND GIGANTIC WATERFALL...

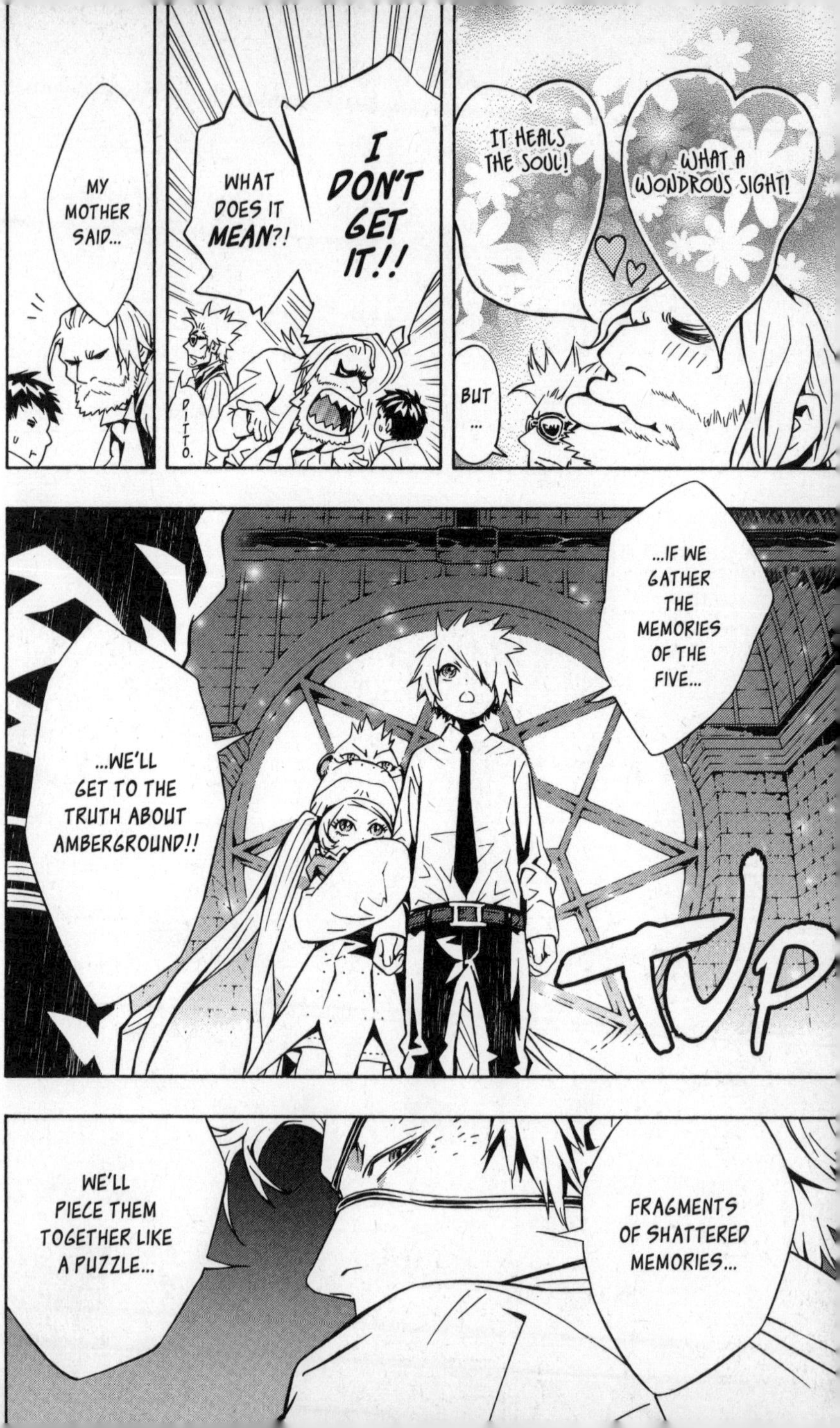
WHAT A WONDROUS SIGHT!
IT HEALS THE SOUL!
BUT...
I DON'T GET IT!!
WHAT DOES IT MEAN?!
DITTO.
MY MOTHER SAID...
...IF WE GATHER THE MEMORIES OF THE FIVE...
TUP
...WE'LL GET TO THE TRUTH ABOUT AMBERGROUND!!
FRAGMENTS OF SHATTERED MEMORIES...
WE'LL PIECE THEM TOGETHER LIKE A PUZZLE...

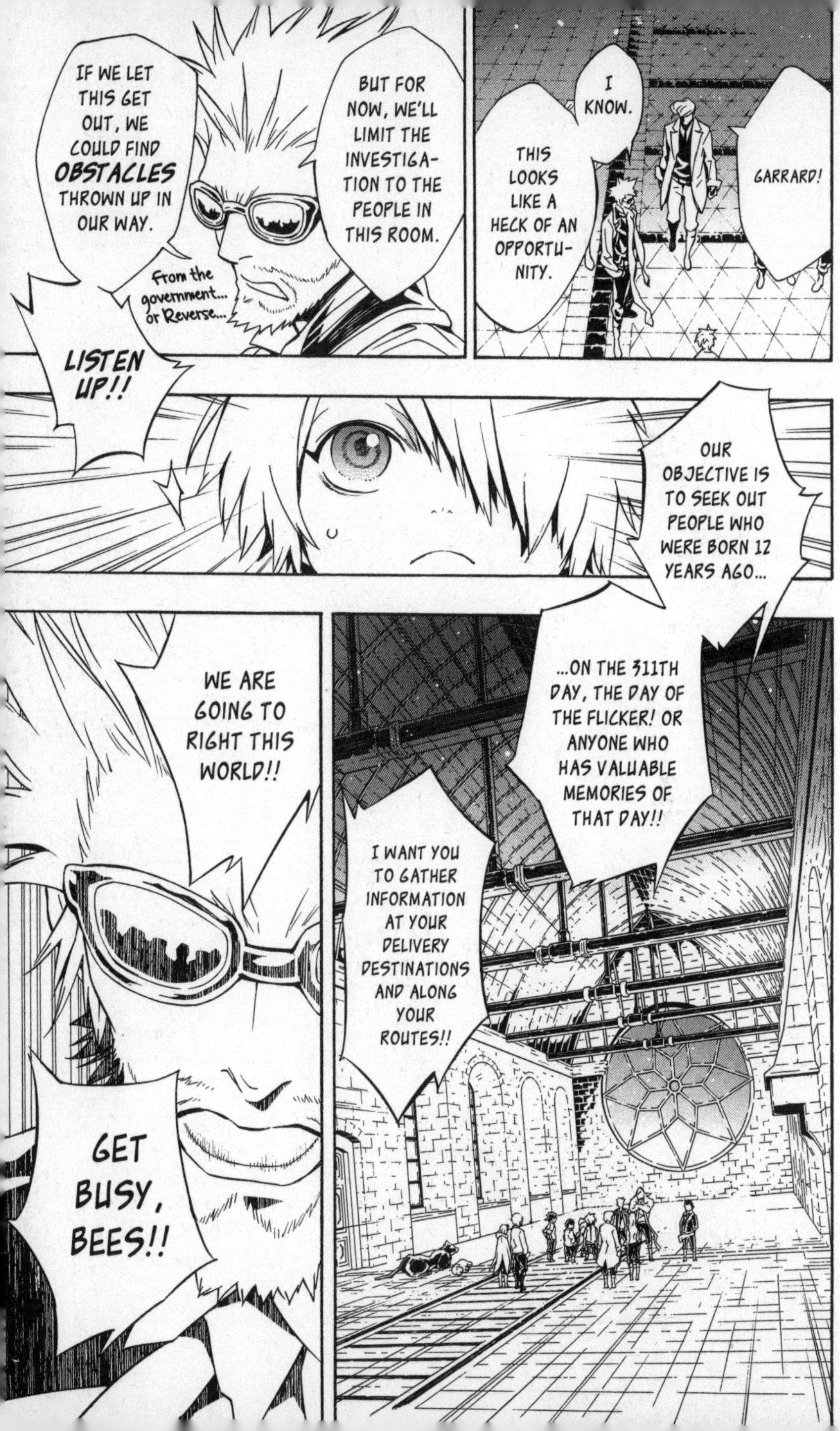
GARRARD!
I KNOW.
THIS LOOKS LIKE A HECK OF AN OPPORTU-NITY.
BUT FOR NOW, WE'LL LIMIT THE INVESTIGA-TION TO THE PEOPLE IN THIS ROOM.
IF WE LET THIS GET OUT, WE COULD FIND OBSTACLES THROWN UP IN OUR WAY.
From the government... or Reverse...
LISTEN UP!!
OUR OBJECTIVE IS TO SEEK OUT PEOPLE WHO WERE BORN 12 YEARS AGO...
...ON THE 311TH DAY, THE DAY OF THE FLICKER! OR ANYONE WHO HAS VALUABLE MEMORIES OF THAT DAY!!
I WANT YOU TO GATHER INFORMATION AT YOUR DELIVERY DESTINATIONS AND ALONG YOUR ROUTES!!
WE ARE GOING TO RIGHT THIS WORLD!!
GET BUSY, BEES!!

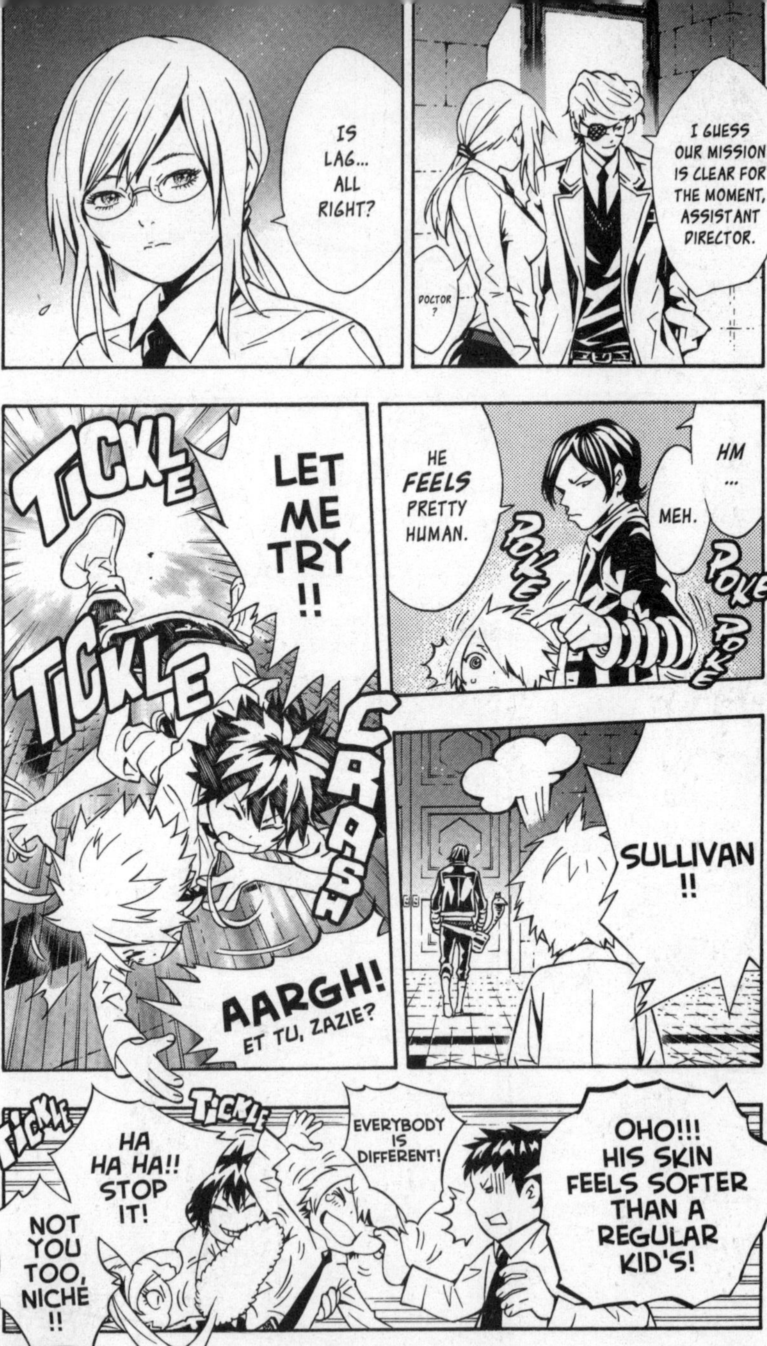
I GUESS OUR MISSION IS CLEAR FOR THE MOMENT, ASSISTANT DIRECTOR.
DOCTOR?
IS LAG... ALL RIGHT?
HM ... MEH.
POKE POKE
POKE
HE FEELS PRETTY HUMAN.
SULLIVAN!!
LET ME TRY!!
TICKLE
TICKLE
CRASH
AARGH! ET TU, ZAZIE?
OHO!!! HIS SKIN FEELS SOFTER THAN A REGULAR KID'S!
EVERYBODY IS DIFFERENT!
TICKLE
HA HA HA!! STOP IT!
TICKLE
NOT YOU TOO, NICHE!!

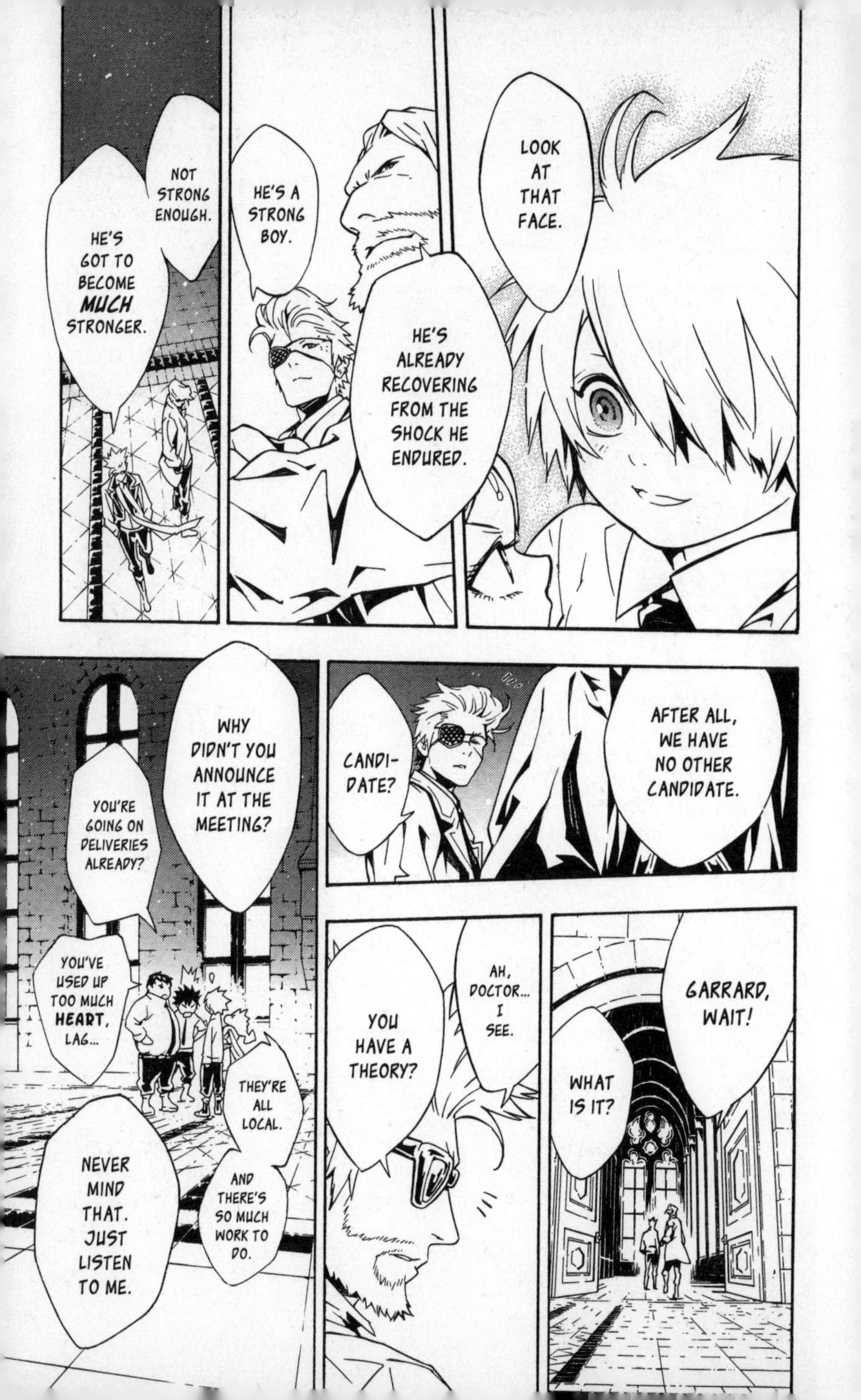
LOOK AT THAT FACE.
HE'S ALREADY RECOVERING FROM THE SHOCK HE ENDURED.
HE'S A STRONG BOY.
NOT STRONG ENOUGH.
HE'S GOT TO BECOME **MUCH** STRONGER.
AFTER ALL, WE HAVE NO OTHER CANDIDATE.
CANDI-DATE?
GARRARD, WAIT!
WHAT IS IT?
AH, DOCTOR... I SEE.
YOU HAVE A THEORY?
WHY DIDN'T YOU ANNOUNCE IT AT THE MEETING?
YOU'RE GOING ON DELIVERIES ALREADY?
YOU'VE USED UP TOO MUCH **HEART**, LAG...
THEY'RE ALL LOCAL.
AND THERE'S SO MUCH WORK TO DO.
NEVER MIND THAT. JUST LISTEN TO ME.

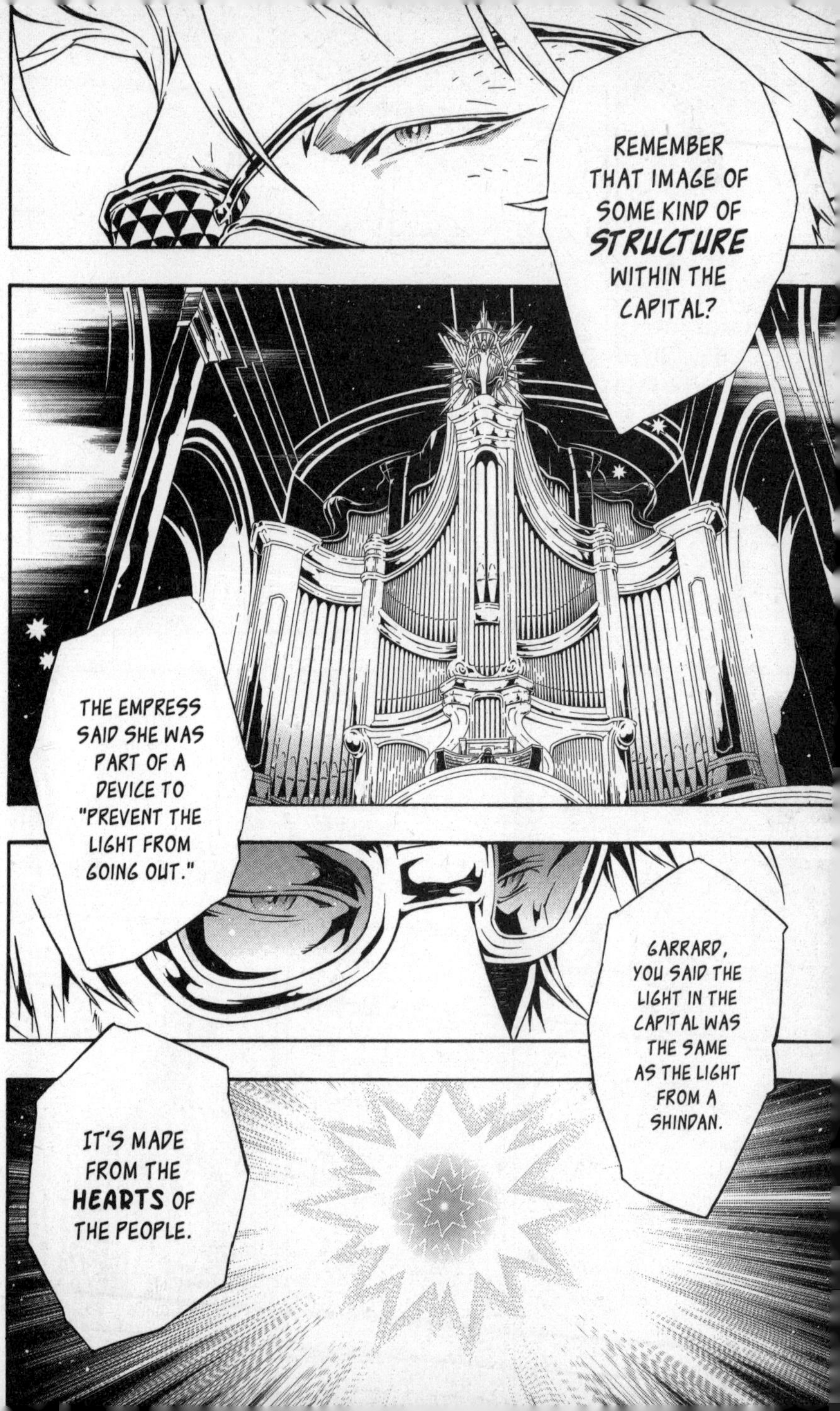
REMEMBER THAT IMAGE OF SOME KIND OF STRUCTURE WITHIN THE CAPITAL?
THE EMPRESS SAID SHE WAS PART OF A DEVICE TO "PREVENT THE LIGHT FROM GOING OUT."
GARRARD, YOU SAID THE LIGHT IN THE CAPITAL WAS THE SAME AS THE LIGHT FROM A SHINDAN.
IT'S MADE FROM THE HEARTS OF THE PEOPLE.

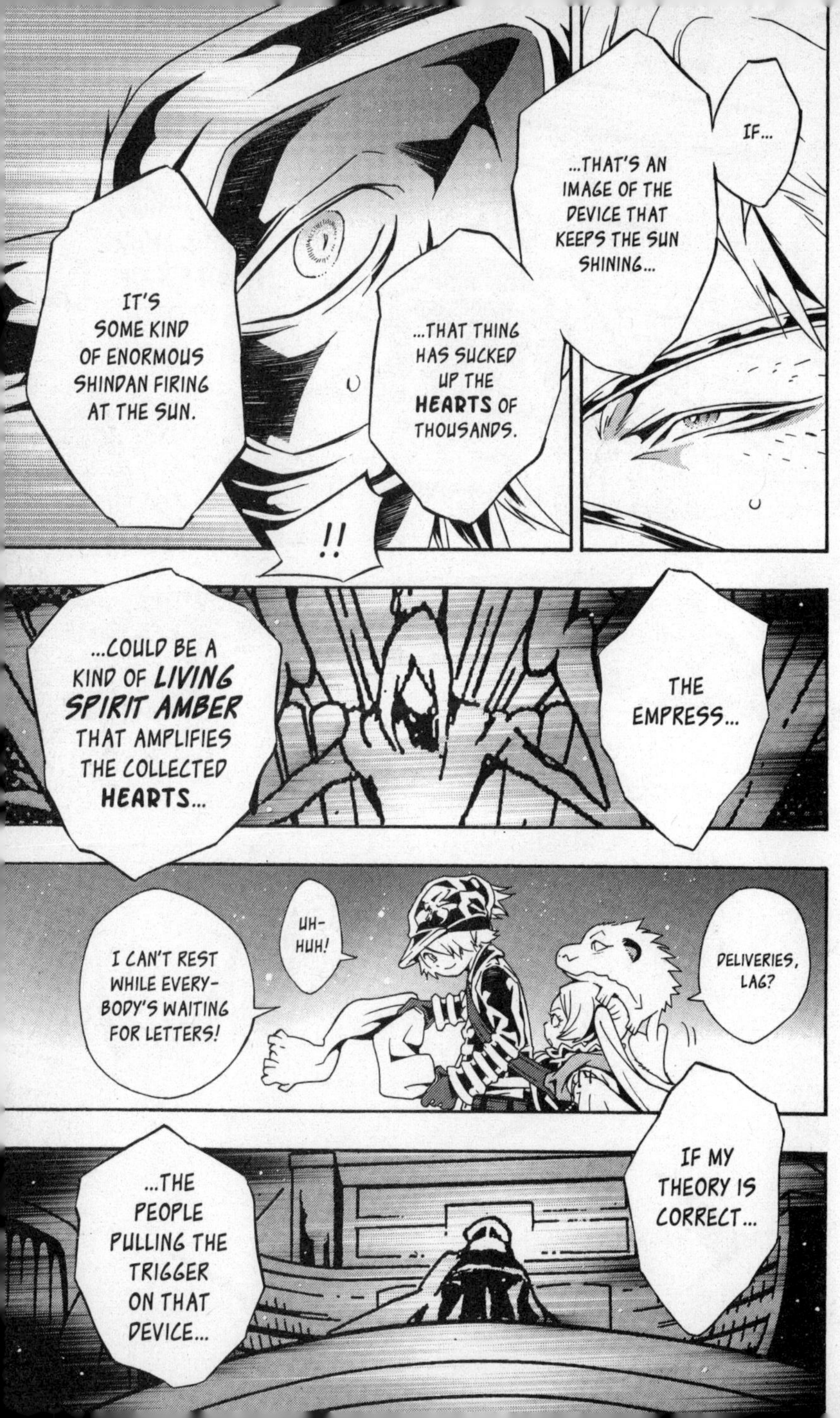
IF...
...THAT'S AN IMAGE OF THE DEVICE THAT KEEPS THE SUN SHINING...
...THAT THING HAS SUCKED UP THE HEARTS OF THOUSANDS.
IT'S SOME KIND OF ENORMOUS SHINDAN FIRING AT THE SUN.
!!
THE EMPRESS...
...COULD BE A KIND OF LIVING SPIRIT AMBER THAT AMPLIFIES THE COLLECTED HEARTS...
DELIVERIES, LAG?
UH-HUH!
I CAN'T REST WHILE EVERY-BODY'S WAITING FOR LETTERS!
IF MY THEORY IS CORRECT...
...THE PEOPLE PULLING THE TRIGGER ON THAT DEVICE...

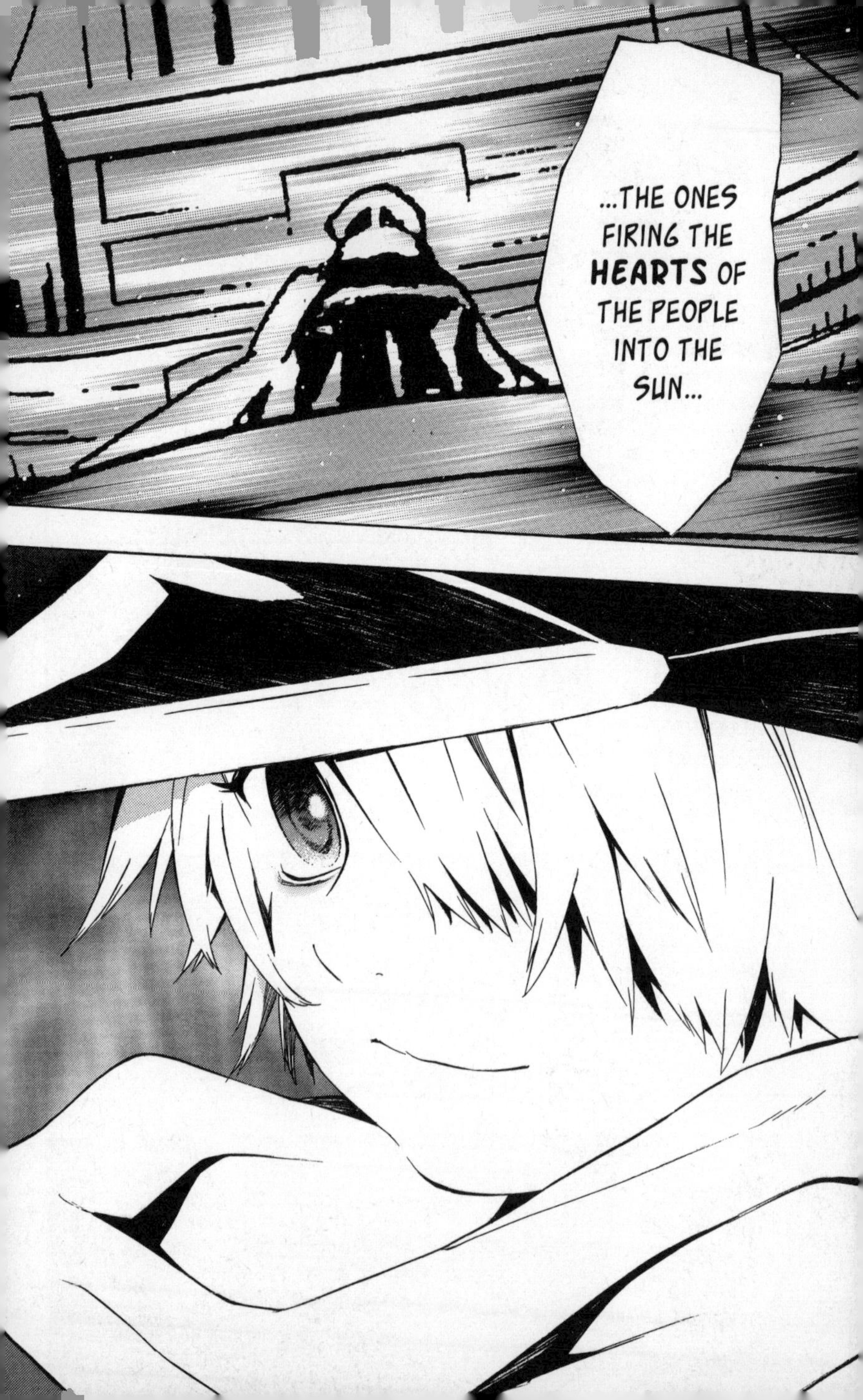
...THE ONES FIRING THE **HEARTS** OF THE PEOPLE INTO THE SUN...

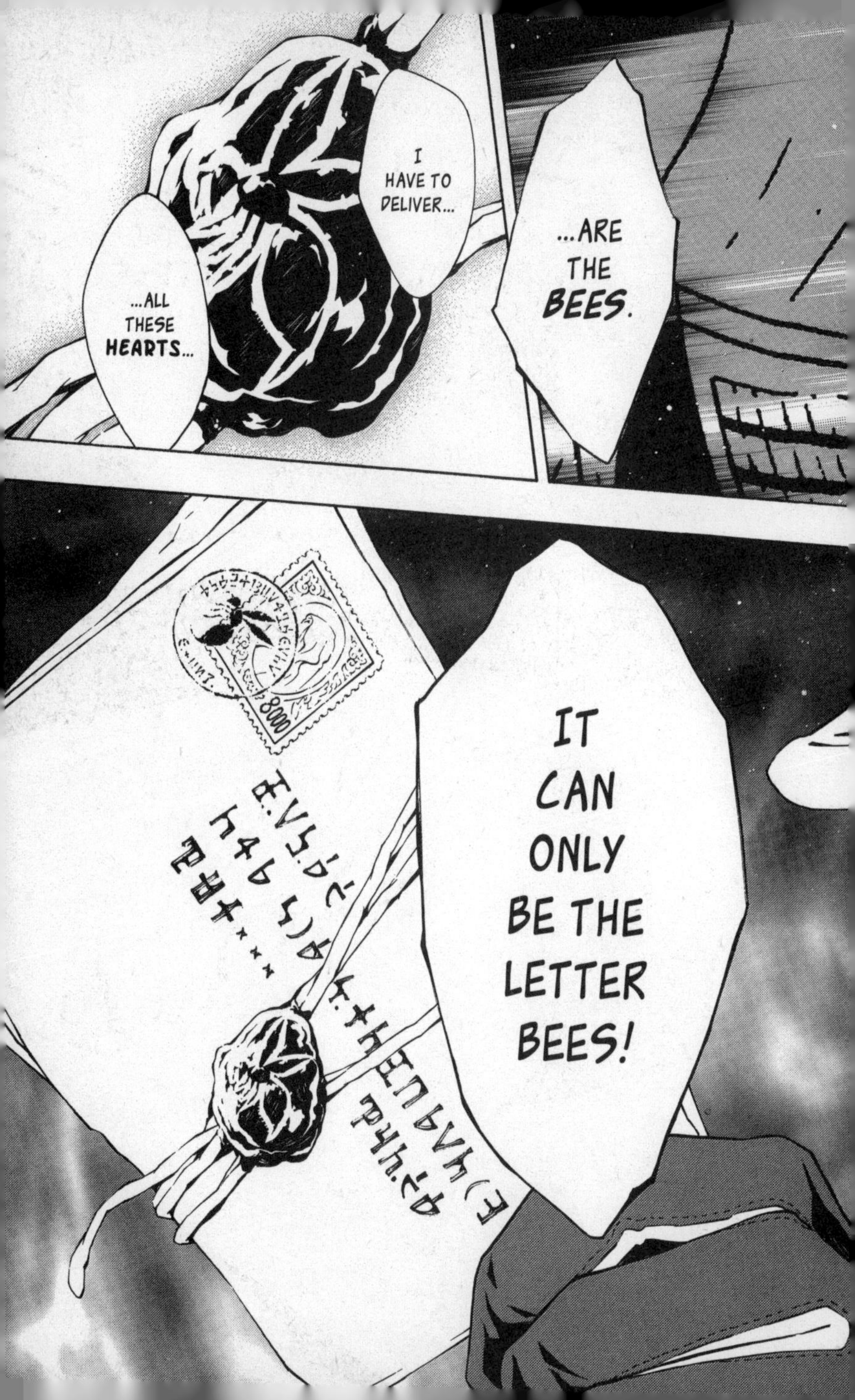
...ARE THE BEES.
I HAVE TO DELIVER...
...ALL THESE HEARTS...
IT CAN ONLY BE THE LETTER BEES!

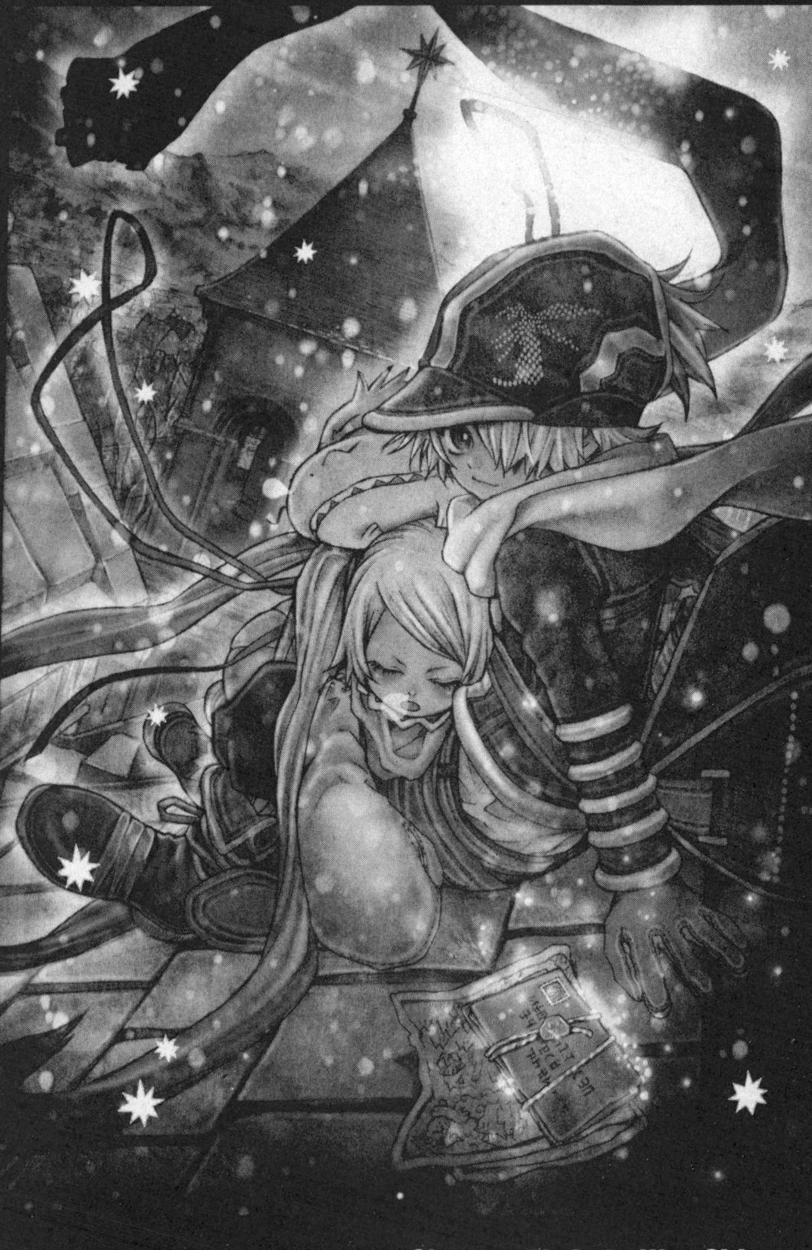

Chapter 72: Late Hire Chico

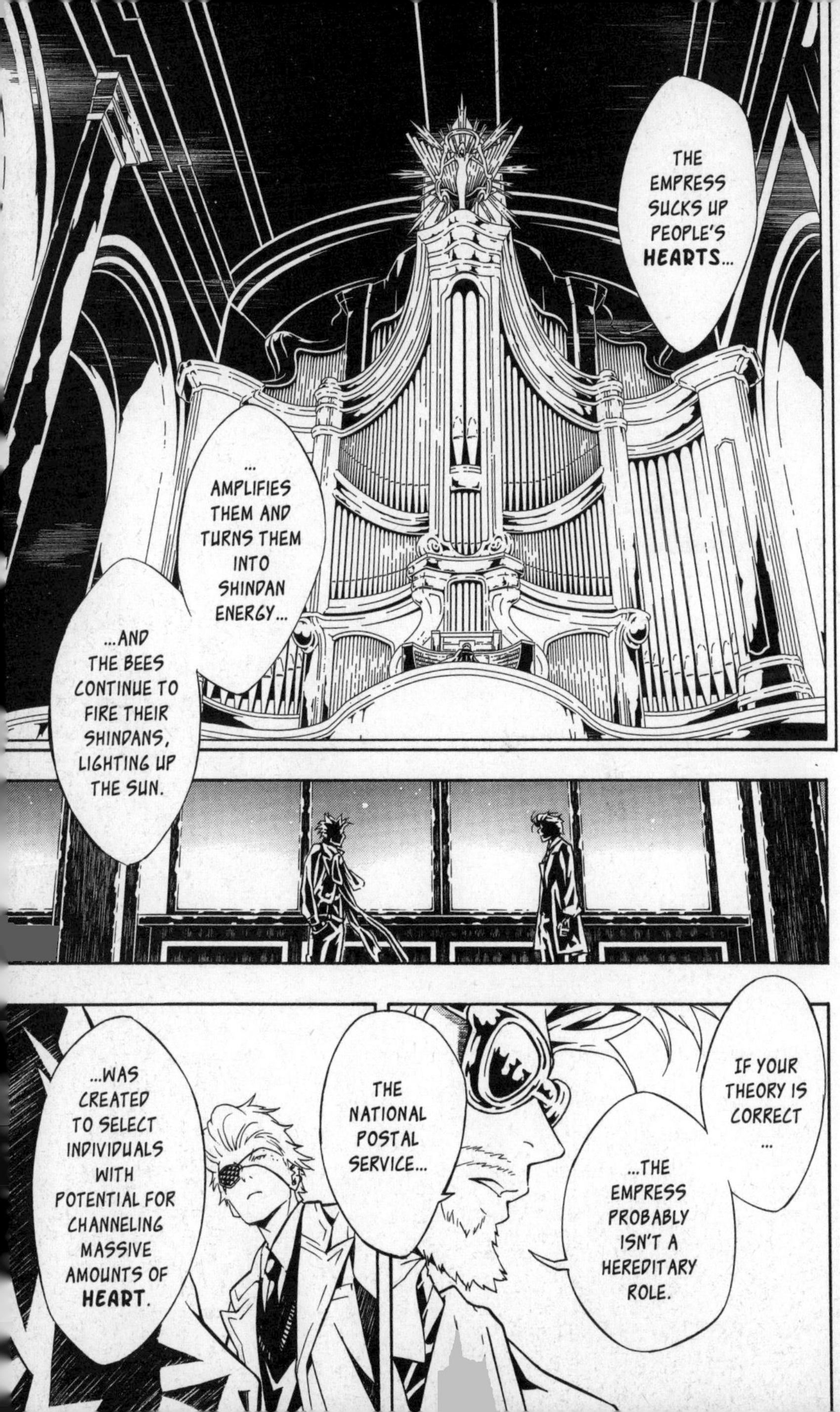
THE EMPRESS SUCKS UP PEOPLE'S **HEARTS**...
... AMPLIFIES THEM AND TURNS THEM INTO SHINDAN ENERGY...
...AND THE BEES CONTINUE TO FIRE THEIR SHINDANS, LIGHTING UP THE SUN.
IF YOUR THEORY IS CORRECT ...
...THE EMPRESS PROBABLY ISN'T A HEREDITARY ROLE.
THE NATIONAL POSTAL SERVICE...
...WAS CREATED TO SELECT INDIVIDUALS WITH POTENTIAL FOR CHANNELING MASSIVE AMOUNTS OF **HEART**.

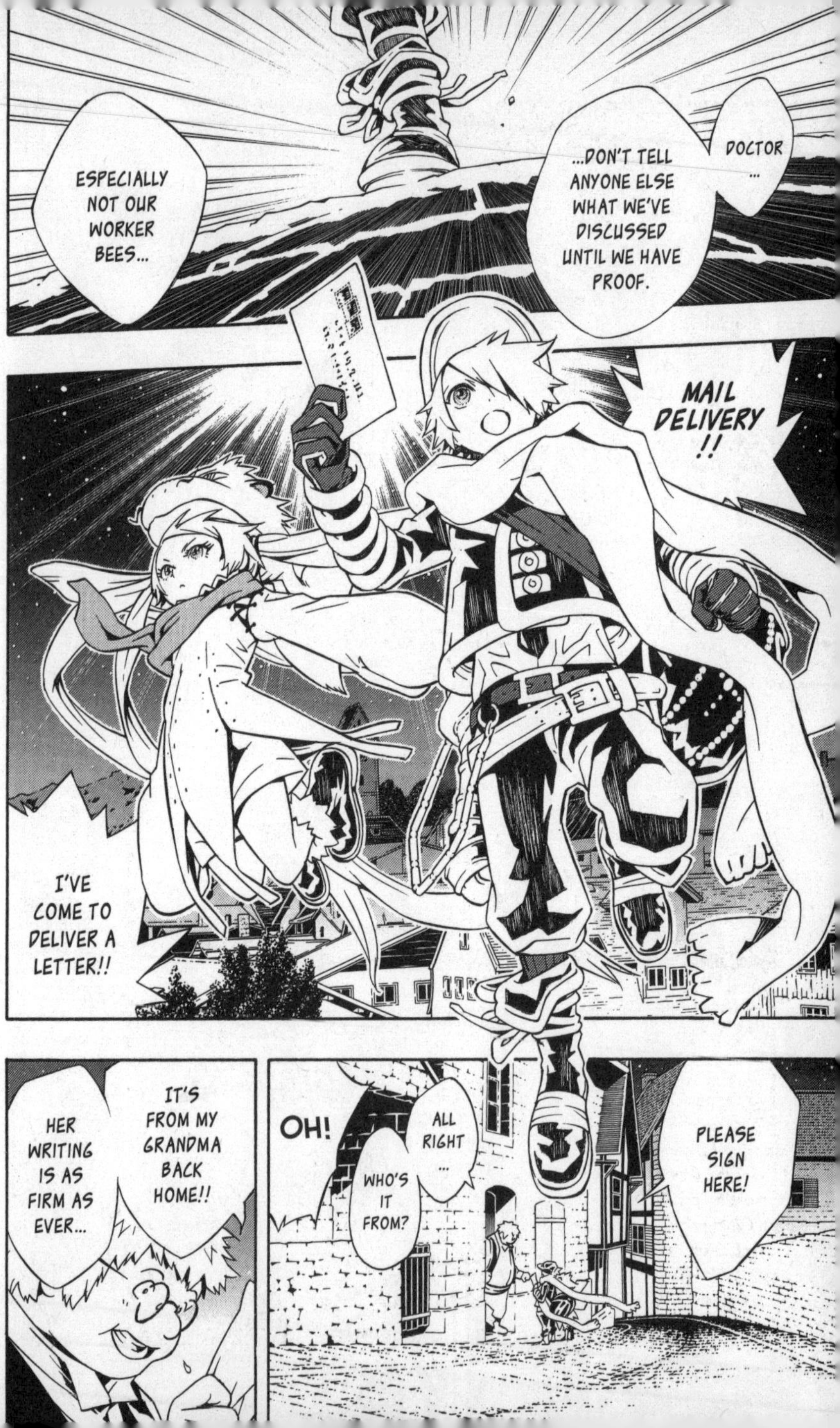
DOCTOR...
...DON'T TELL ANYONE ELSE WHAT WE'VE DISCUSSED UNTIL WE HAVE PROOF.
ESPECIALLY NOT OUR WORKER BEES...
MAIL DELIVERY!!
I'VE COME TO DELIVER A LETTER!!
PLEASE SIGN HERE!
ALL RIGHT...
OH!
WHO'S IT FROM?
IT'S FROM MY GRANDMA BACK HOME!!
HER WRITING IS AS FIRM AS EVER...

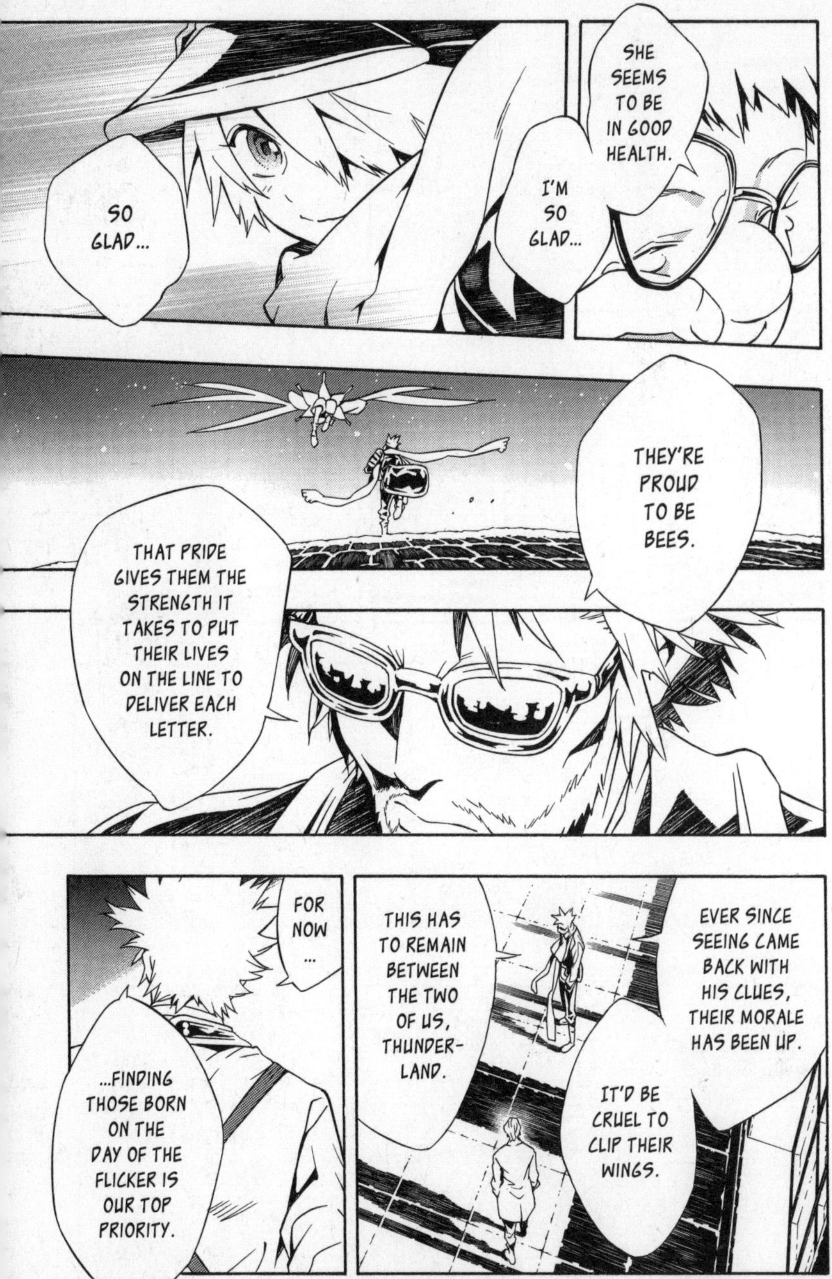
SHE SEEMS TO BE IN GOOD HEALTH.
I'M SO GLAD...
SO GLAD...
THEY'RE PROUD TO BE BEES.
THAT PRIDE GIVES THEM THE STRENGTH IT TAKES TO PUT THEIR LIVES ON THE LINE TO DELIVER EACH LETTER.
EVER SINCE SEEING CAME BACK WITH HIS CLUES, THEIR MORALE HAS BEEN UP.
IT'D BE CRUEL TO CLIP THEIR WINGS.
THIS HAS TO REMAIN BETWEEN THE TWO OF US, THUNDER-LAND.
FOR NOW ...
...FINDING THOSE BORN ON THE DAY OF THE FLICKER IS OUR TOP PRIORITY.

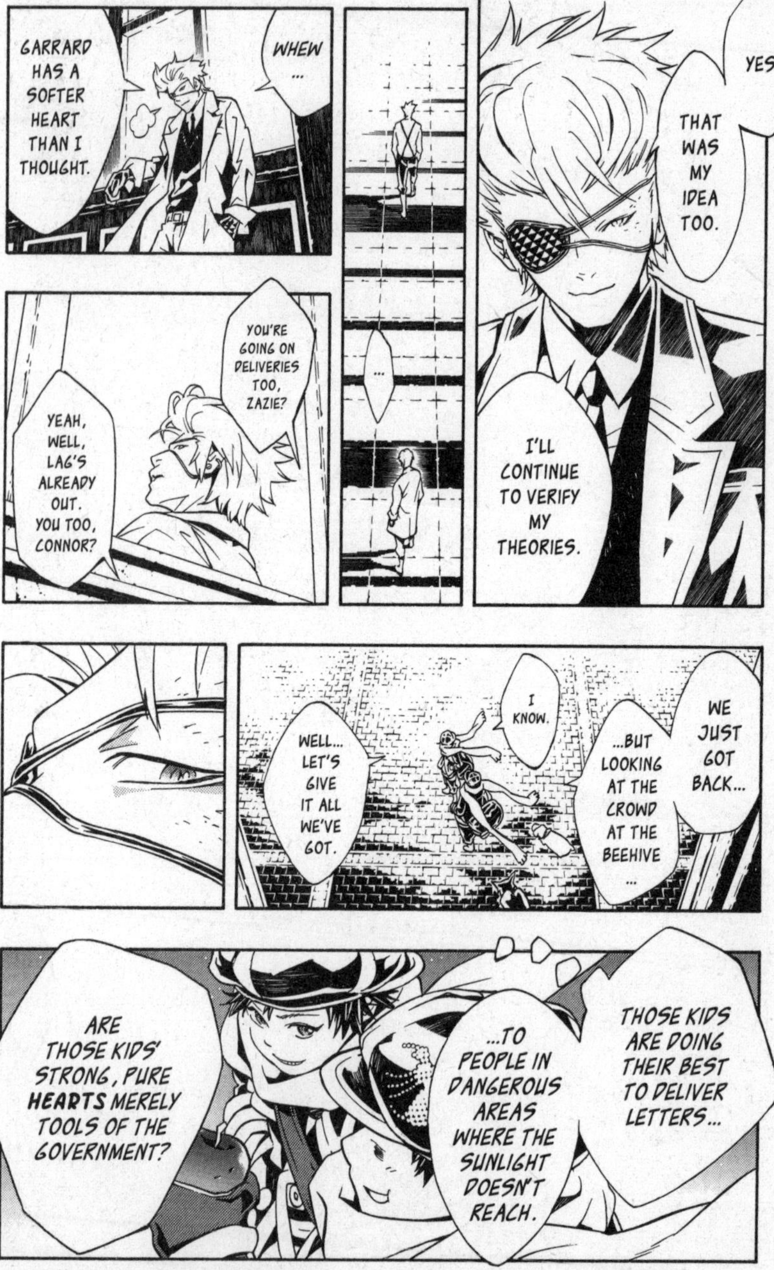
YES.
THAT WAS MY IDEA TOO.
I'LL CONTINUE TO VERIFY MY THEORIES.
...
WHEW ...
GARRARD HAS A SOFTER HEART THAN I THOUGHT.
YOU'RE GOING ON DELIVERIES TOO, ZAZIE?
YEAH, WELL, LAG'S ALREADY OUT. YOU TOO, CONNOR?
WE JUST GOT BACK...
...BUT LOOKING AT THE CROWD AT THE BEEHIVE ...
I KNOW.
WELL... LET'S GIVE IT ALL WE'VE GOT.
THOSE KIDS ARE DOING THEIR BEST TO DELIVER LETTERS...
...TO PEOPLE IN DANGEROUS AREAS WHERE THE SUNLIGHT DOESN'T REACH.
ARE THOSE KIDS' STRONG, PURE **HEARTS** MERELY TOOLS OF THE GOVERNMENT?

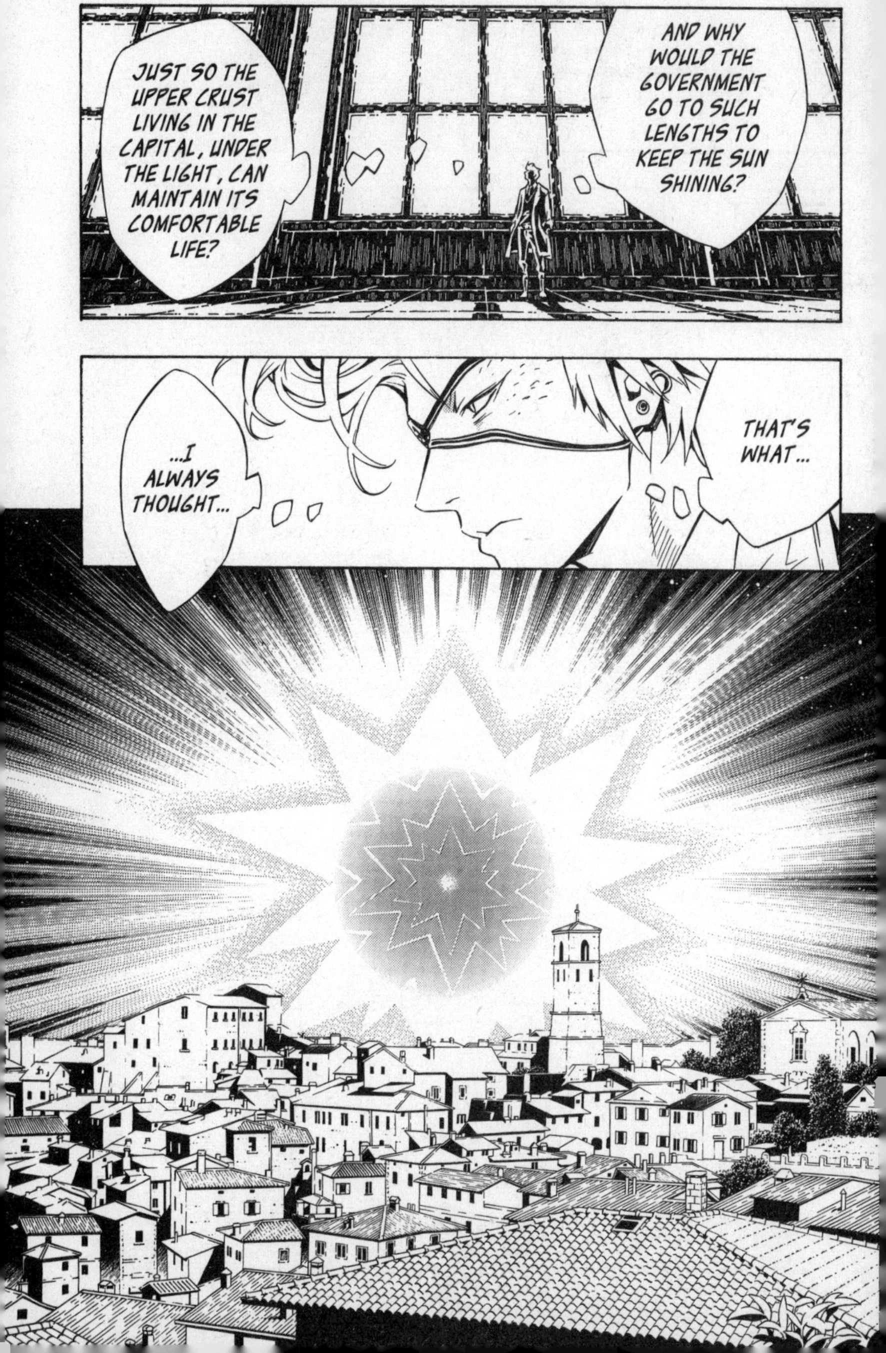
AND WHY WOULD THE GOVERNMENT GO TO SUCH LENGTHS TO KEEP THE SUN SHINING?
JUST SO THE UPPER CRUST LIVING IN THE CAPITAL, UNDER THE LIGHT, CAN MAINTAIN ITS COMFORTABLE LIFE?
THAT'S WHAT...
...I ALWAYS THOUGHT...

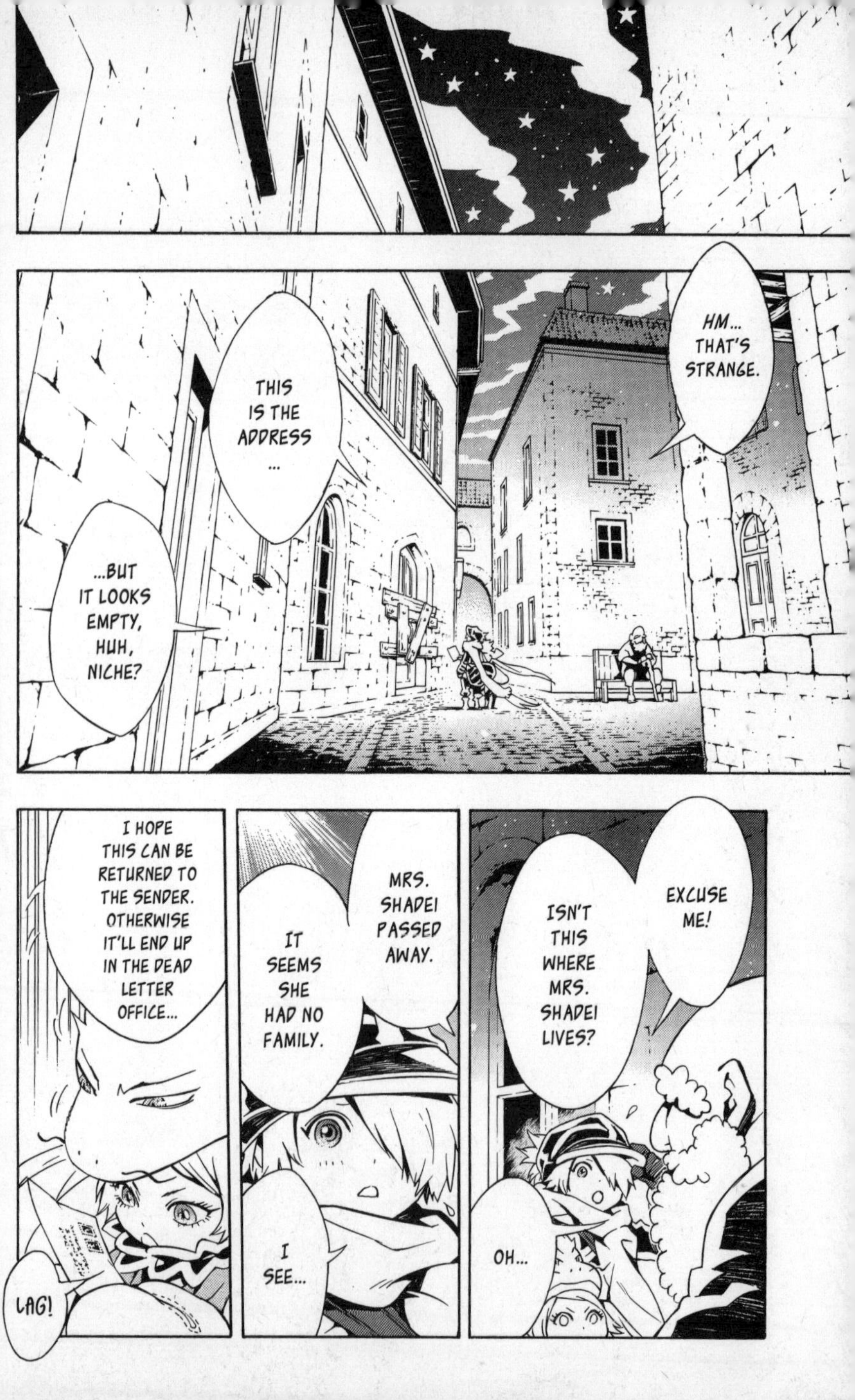
HM... THAT'S STRANGE.
THIS IS THE ADDRESS ...
...BUT IT LOOKS EMPTY, HUH, NICHE?
EXCUSE ME!
ISN'T THIS WHERE MRS. SHADEI LIVES?
OH...
MRS. SHADEI PASSED AWAY.
IT SEEMS SHE HAD NO FAMILY.
I SEE...
I HOPE THIS CAN BE RETURNED TO THE SENDER. OTHERWISE IT'LL END UP IN THE DEAD LETTER OFFICE...
LAG!

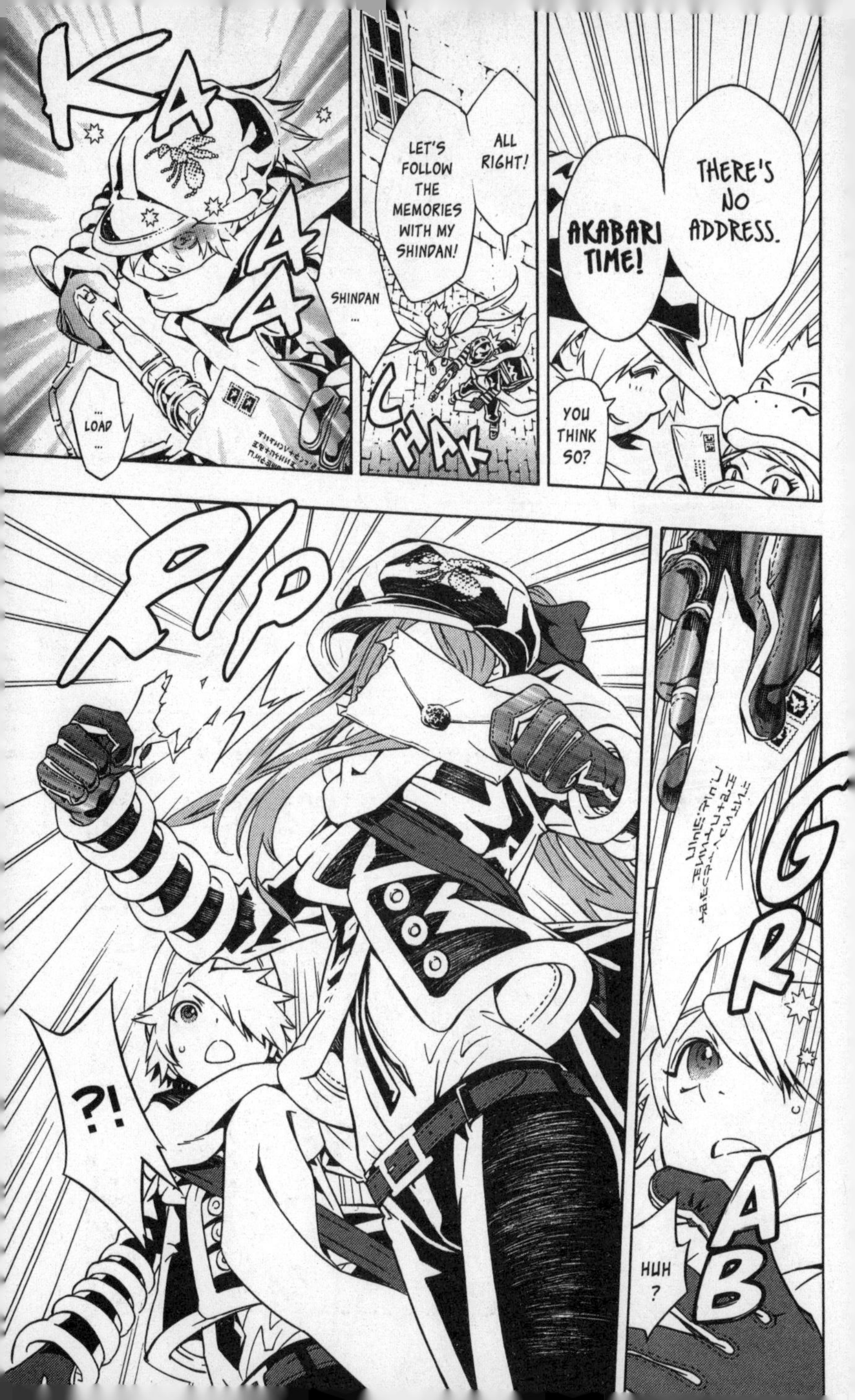
THERE'S NO ADDRESS.
AKABARI TIME!
YOU THINK SO?
ALL RIGHT!
LET'S FOLLOW THE MEMORIES WITH MY SHINDAN!
SHINDAN ...
CHAK
KAAA
... LOAD ...
GR
HUH ?
AB
RIP
?!

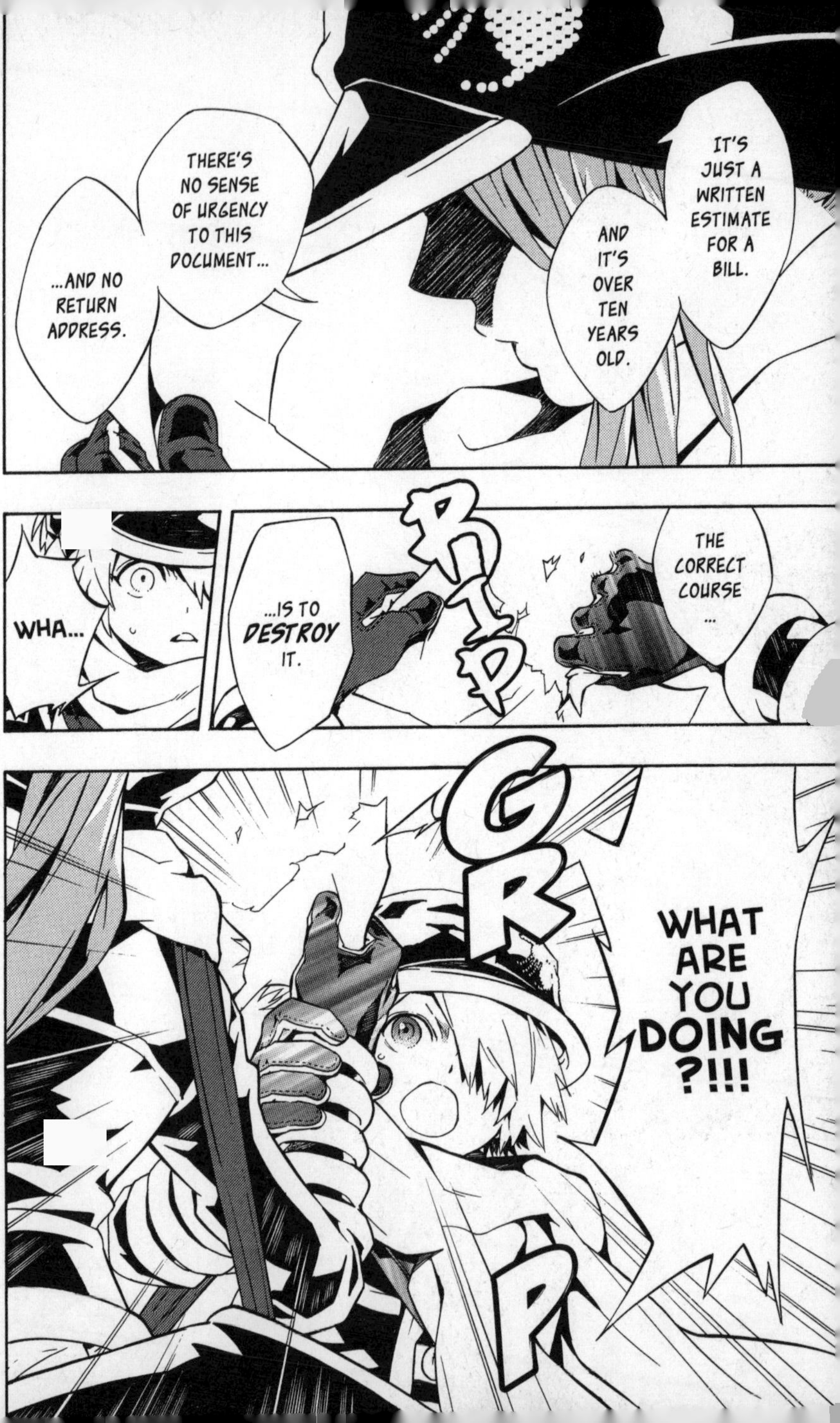
IT'S JUST A WRITTEN ESTIMATE FOR A BILL.
AND IT'S OVER TEN YEARS OLD.
THERE'S NO SENSE OF URGENCY TO THIS DOCUMENT...
...AND NO RETURN ADDRESS.
THE CORRECT COURSE ...
RIP
...IS TO DESTROY IT.
WHA...
WHAT ARE YOU DOING?!!!

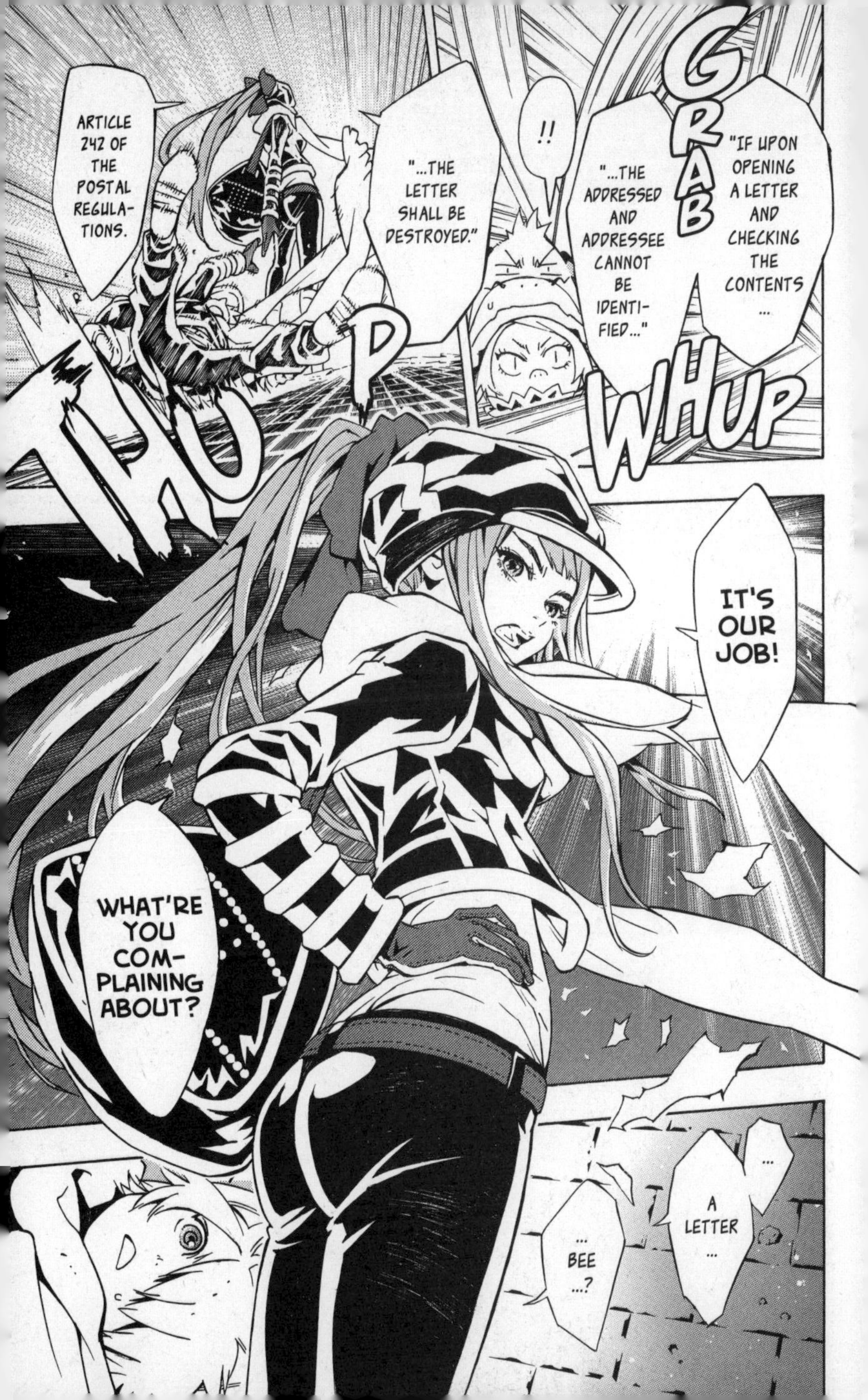

"IF UPON OPENING A LETTER AND CHECKING THE CONTENTS ...
GRAB
"...THE ADDRESSED AND ADDRESSEE CANNOT BE IDENTI-FIED..."
!!
"...THE LETTER SHALL BE DESTROYED."
ARTICLE 242 OF THE POSTAL REGULA-TIONS.
WHUP
THUD
IT'S OUR JOB!
WHAT'RE YOU COM-PLAINING ABOUT?
... A LETTER ...
... BEE ...?

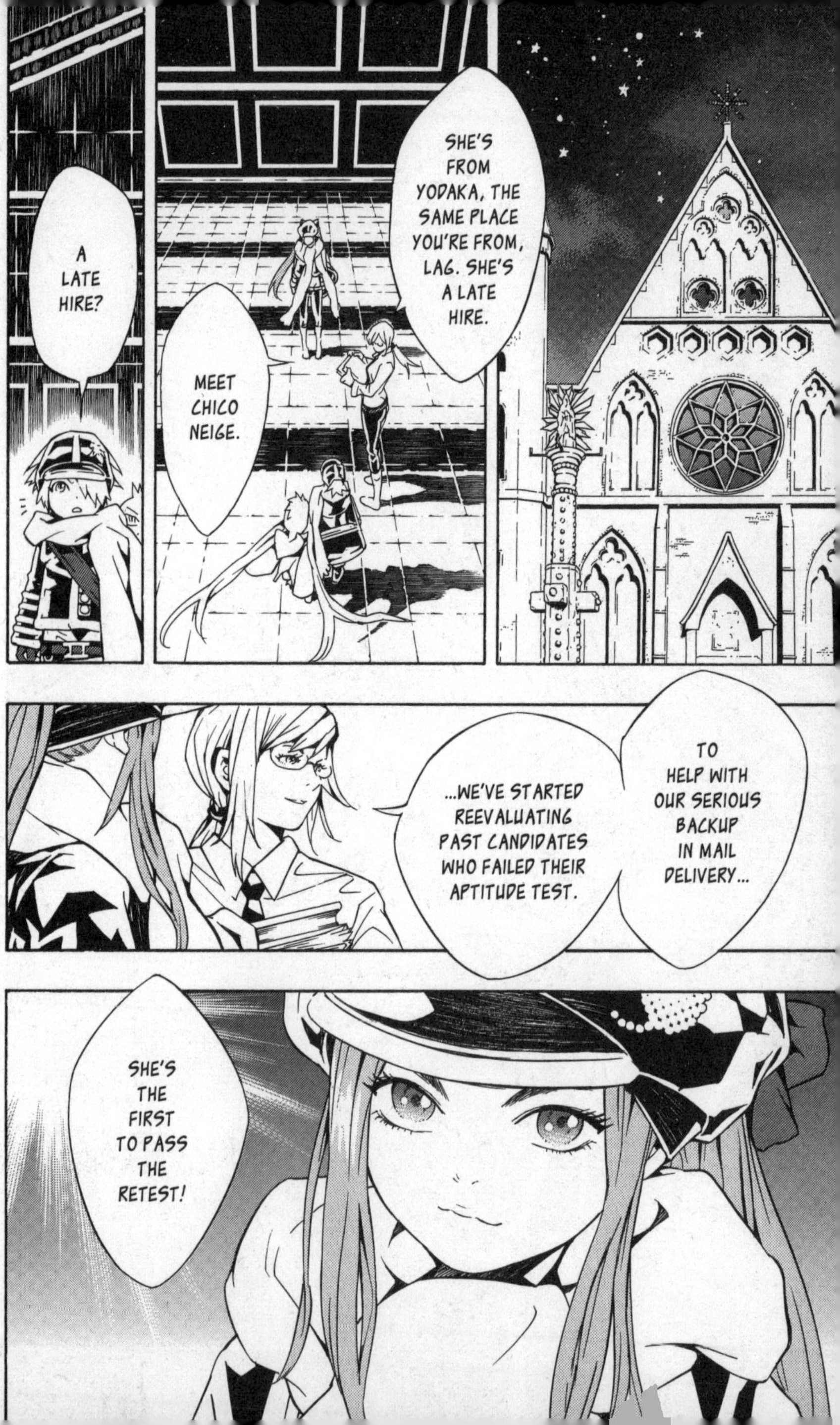
SHE'S FROM YODAKA, THE SAME PLACE YOU'RE FROM, LAG. SHE'S A LATE HIRE.
MEET CHICO NEIGE.
A LATE HIRE?
TO HELP WITH OUR SERIOUS BACKUP IN MAIL DELIVERY...
...WE'VE STARTED REEVALUATING PAST CANDIDATES WHO FAILED THEIR APTITUDE TEST.
SHE'S THE FIRST TO PASS THE RETEST!

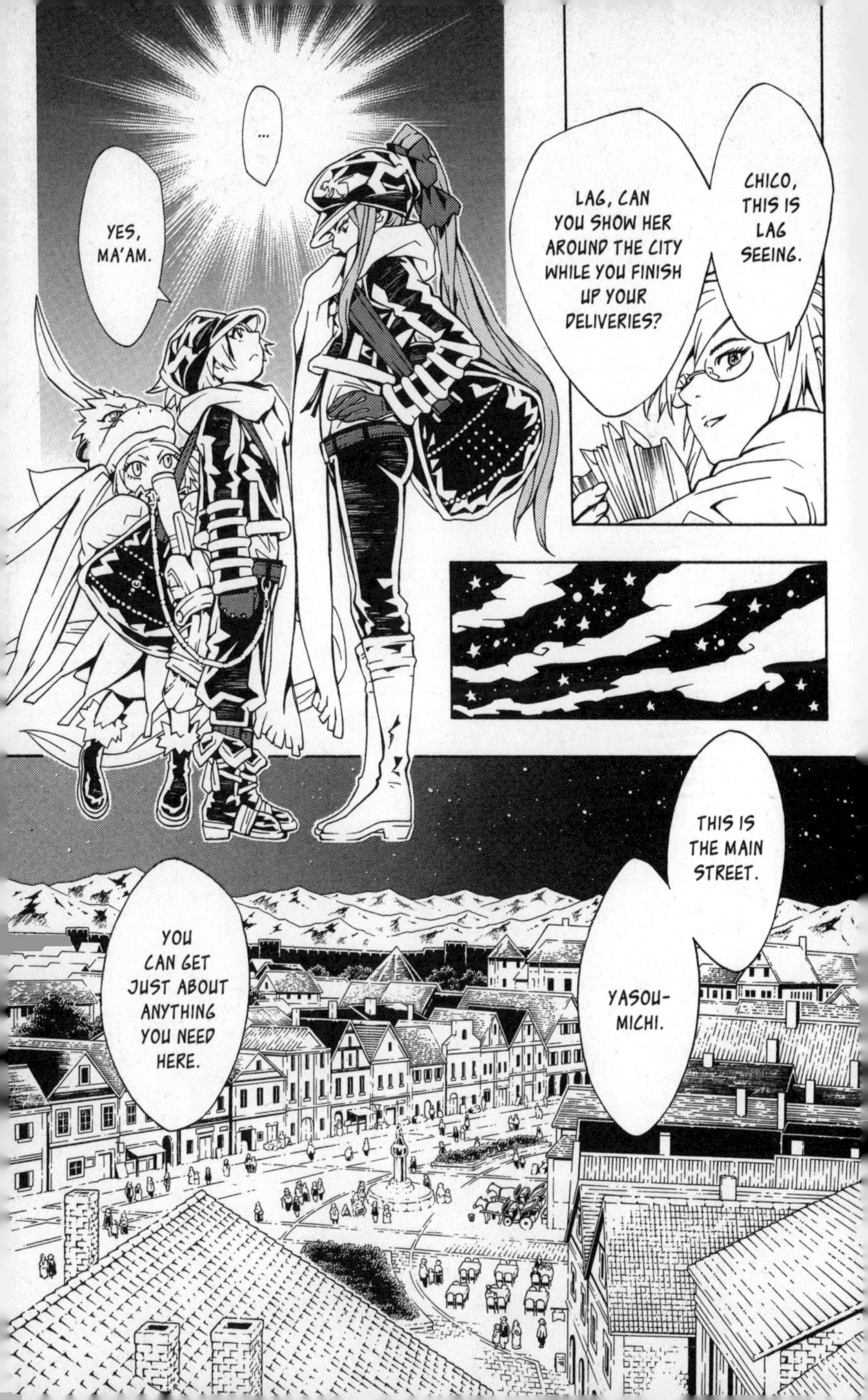
CHICO, THIS IS LAG SEEING.
LAG, CAN YOU SHOW HER AROUND THE CITY WHILE YOU FINISH UP YOUR DELIVERIES?
...
YES, MA'AM.
THIS IS THE MAIN STREET.
YASOU-MICHI.
YOU CAN GET JUST ABOUT ANYTHING YOU NEED HERE.

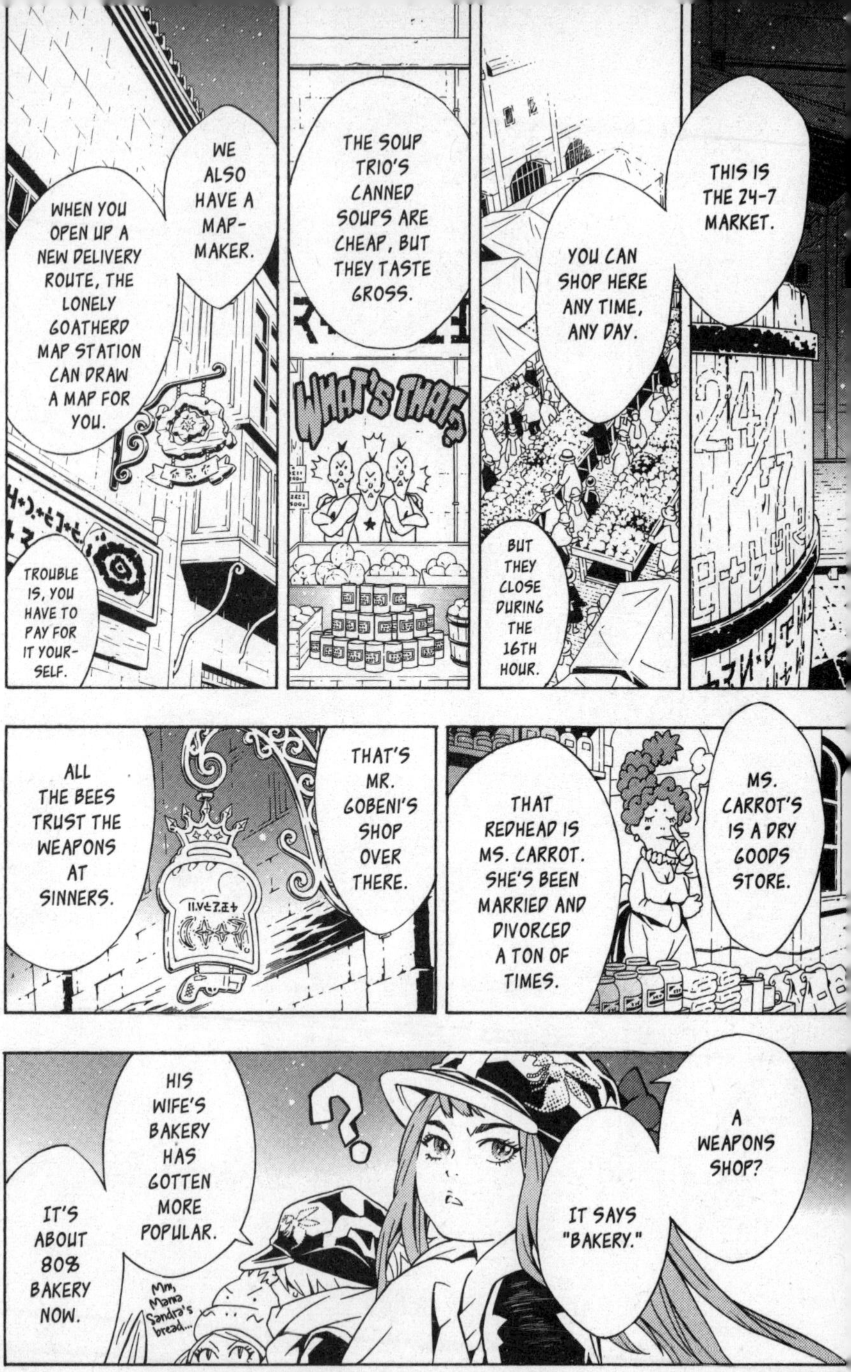
THIS IS THE 24-7 MARKET.
YOU CAN SHOP HERE ANY TIME, ANY DAY.
BUT THEY CLOSE DURING THE 16TH HOUR.
THE SOUP TRIO'S CANNED SOUPS ARE CHEAP, BUT THEY TASTE GROSS.
WHAT'S THAT?
WE ALSO HAVE A MAP-MAKER.
WHEN YOU OPEN UP A NEW DELIVERY ROUTE, THE LONELY GOATHERD MAP STATION CAN DRAW A MAP FOR YOU.
TROUBLE IS, YOU HAVE TO PAY FOR IT YOURSELF.
MS. CARROT'S IS A DRY GOODS STORE.
THAT REDHEAD IS MS. CARROT. SHE'S BEEN MARRIED AND DIVORCED A TON OF TIMES.
THAT'S MR. GOBENI'S SHOP OVER THERE.
ALL THE BEES TRUST THE WEAPONS AT SINNERS.
A WEAPONS SHOP?
IT SAYS "BAKERY."
HIS WIFE'S BAKERY HAS GOTTEN MORE POPULAR.
IT'S ABOUT 80% BAKERY NOW.
Mm, Mama Sandra's bread...

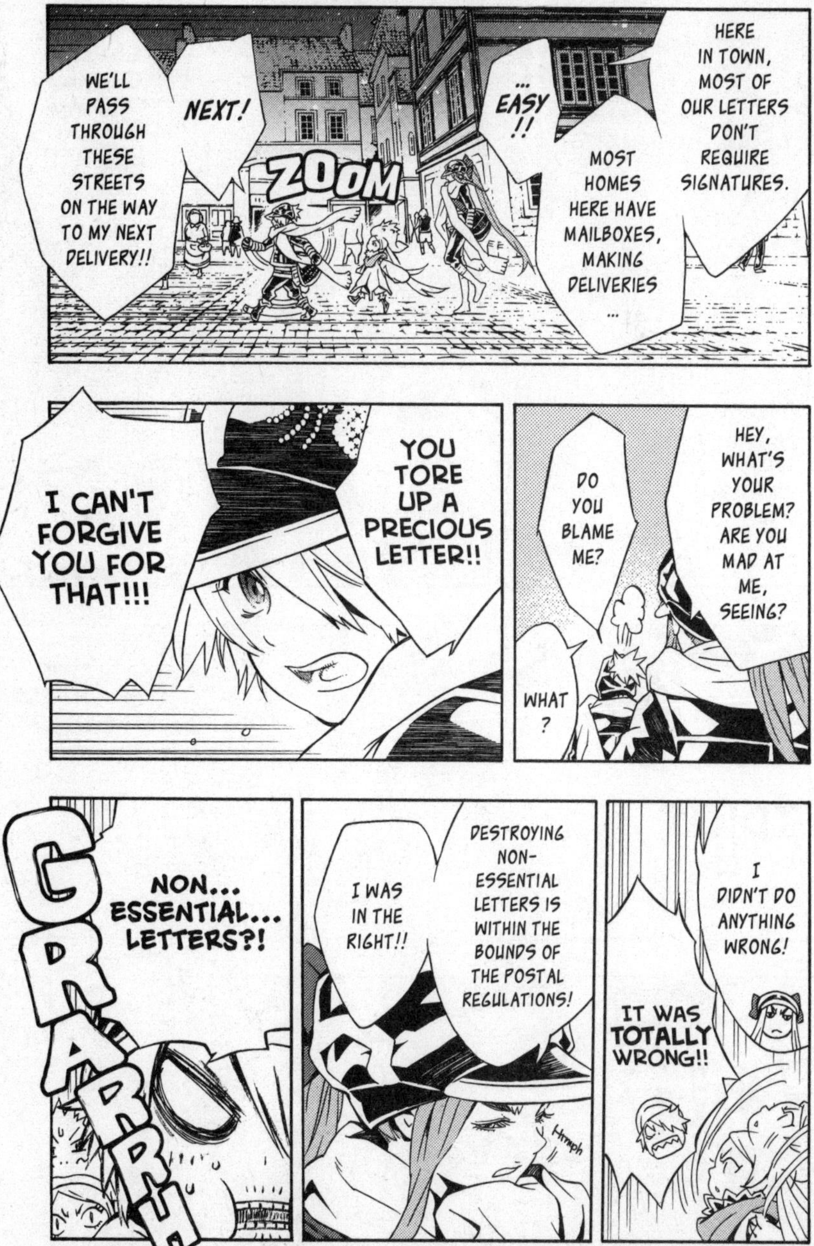
HERE IN TOWN, MOST OF OUR LETTERS DON'T REQUIRE SIGNATURES.
MOST HOMES HERE HAVE MAILBOXES, MAKING DELIVERIES ...
... EASY !!
NEXT!
ZOOM
WE'LL PASS THROUGH THESE STREETS ON THE WAY TO MY NEXT DELIVERY!!
HEY, WHAT'S YOUR PROBLEM? ARE YOU MAD AT ME, SEEING?
DO YOU BLAME ME?
WHAT ?
YOU TORE UP A PRECIOUS LETTER!!
I CAN'T FORGIVE YOU FOR THAT!!!
I DIDN'T DO ANYTHING WRONG!
IT WAS TOTALLY WRONG!!
DESTROYING NON-ESSENTIAL LETTERS IS WITHIN THE BOUNDS OF THE POSTAL REGULATIONS!
I WAS IN THE RIGHT!!
Hmph
NON... ESSENTIAL... LETTERS?!
GRARRH

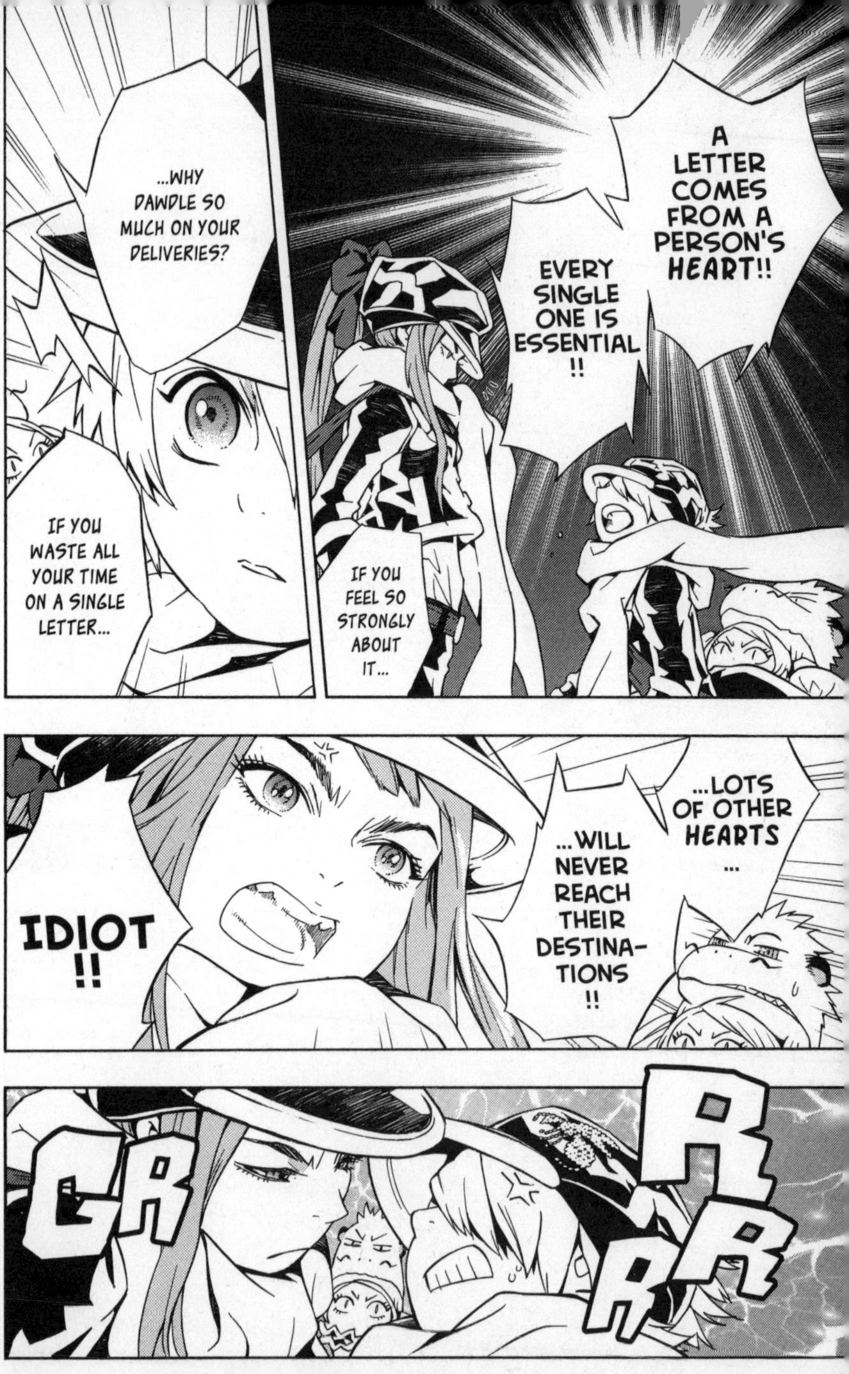
A LETTER COMES FROM A PERSON'S HEART!!
EVERY SINGLE ONE IS ESSENTIAL !!
IF YOU FEEL SO STRONGLY ABOUT IT...
...WHY DAWDLE SO MUCH ON YOUR DELIVERIES?
IF YOU WASTE ALL YOUR TIME ON A SINGLE LETTER...
...LOTS OF OTHER HEARTS ...
...WILL NEVER REACH THEIR DESTINATIONS !!
IDIOT !!
GRRRR

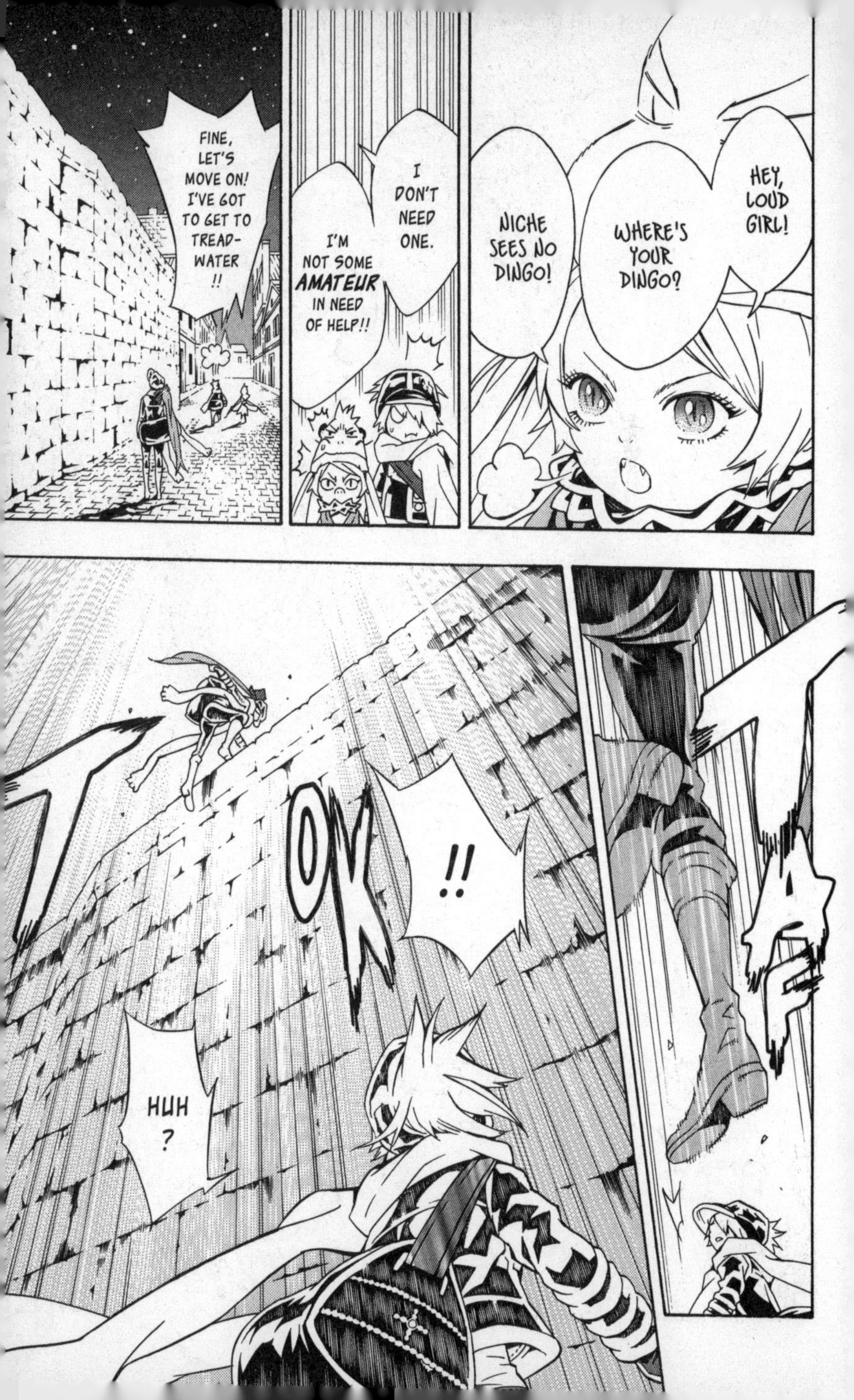
HEY, LOUD GIRL!
WHERE'S YOUR DINGO?
NICHE SEES NO DINGO!
I DON'T NEED ONE.
I'M NOT SOME AMATEUR IN NEED OF HELP!!
FINE, LET'S MOVE ON! I'VE GOT TO GET TO TREAD-WATER!!
TOK
!!
HUH?

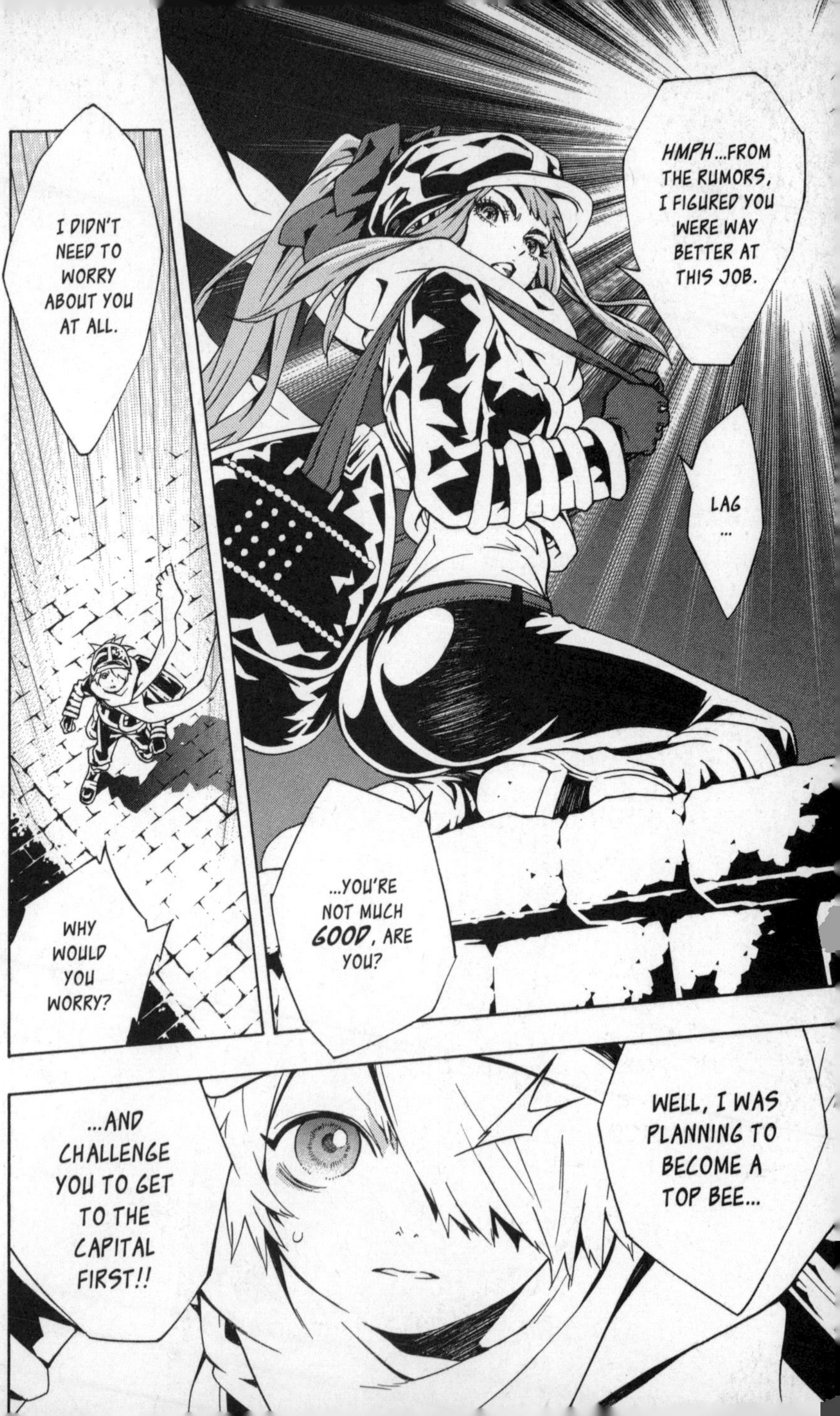
HMPH...FROM THE RUMORS, I FIGURED YOU WERE WAY BETTER AT THIS JOB.
LAG...
...YOU'RE NOT MUCH GOOD, ARE YOU?
I DIDN'T NEED TO WORRY ABOUT YOU AT ALL.
WHY WOULD YOU WORRY?
WELL, I WAS PLANNING TO BECOME A TOP BEE...
...AND CHALLENGE YOU TO GET TO THE CAPITAL FIRST!!

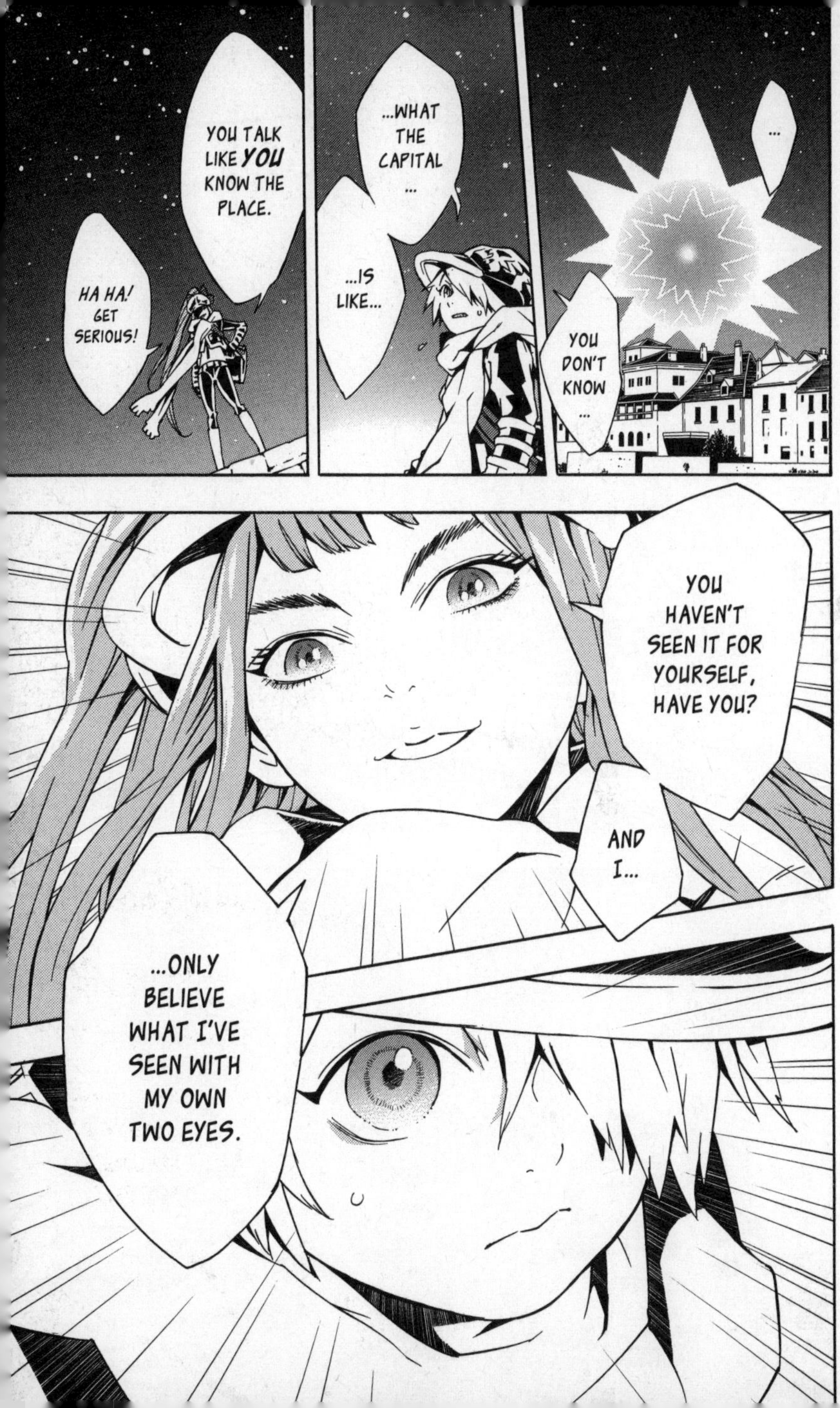
...
YOU DON'T KNOW ...
...WHAT THE CAPITAL ...
...IS LIKE...
YOU TALK LIKE YOU KNOW THE PLACE.
HA HA! GET SERIOUS!
YOU HAVEN'T SEEN IT FOR YOURSELF, HAVE YOU?
AND I...
...ONLY BELIEVE WHAT I'VE SEEN WITH MY OWN TWO EYES.

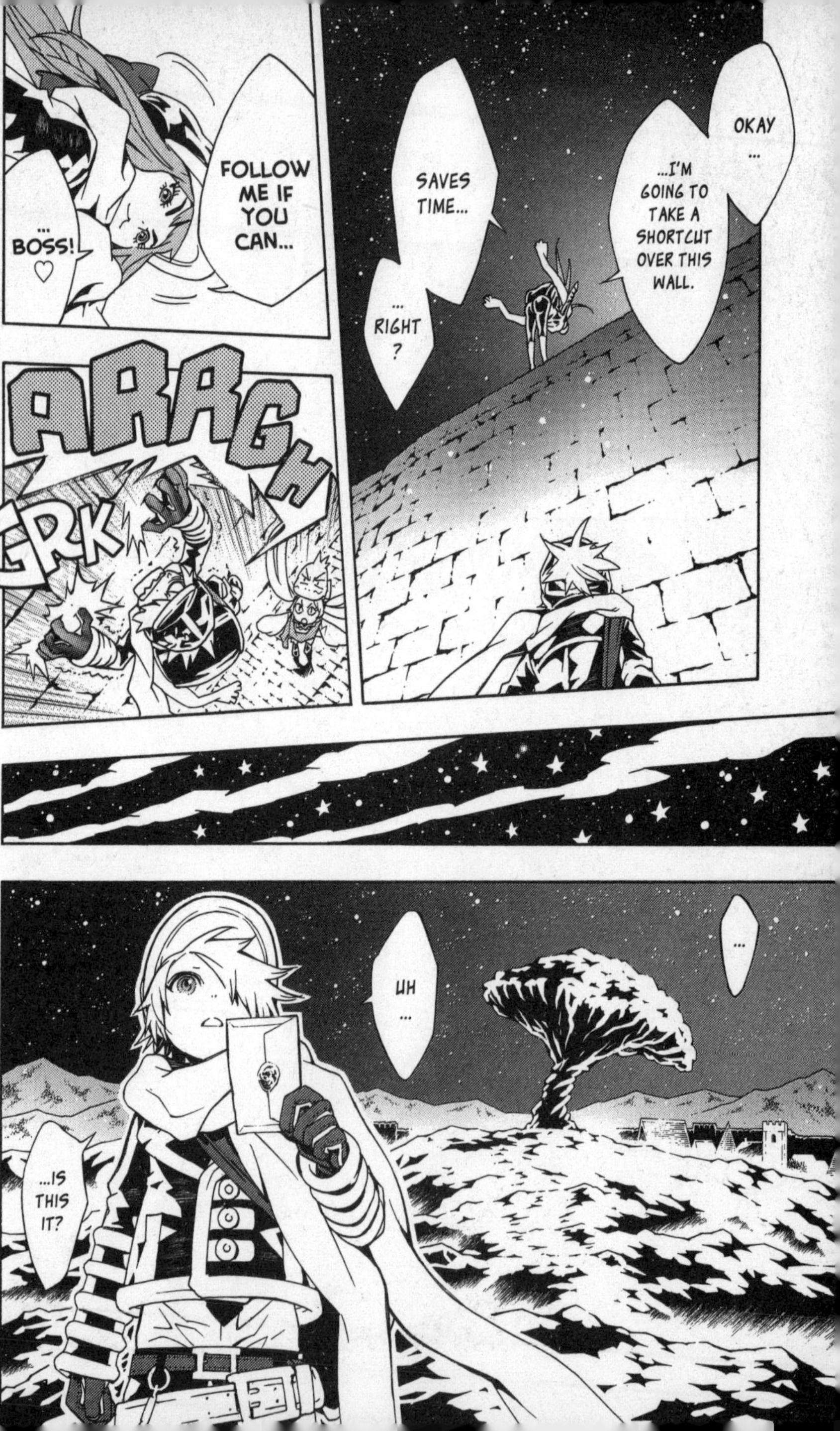
OKAY ...
...I'M GOING TO TAKE A SHORTCUT OVER THIS WALL.
SAVES TIME...
... RIGHT ?
FOLLOW ME IF YOU CAN...
... BOSS! ♡
ARRAGH
GRK
...
UH ...
...IS THIS IT?

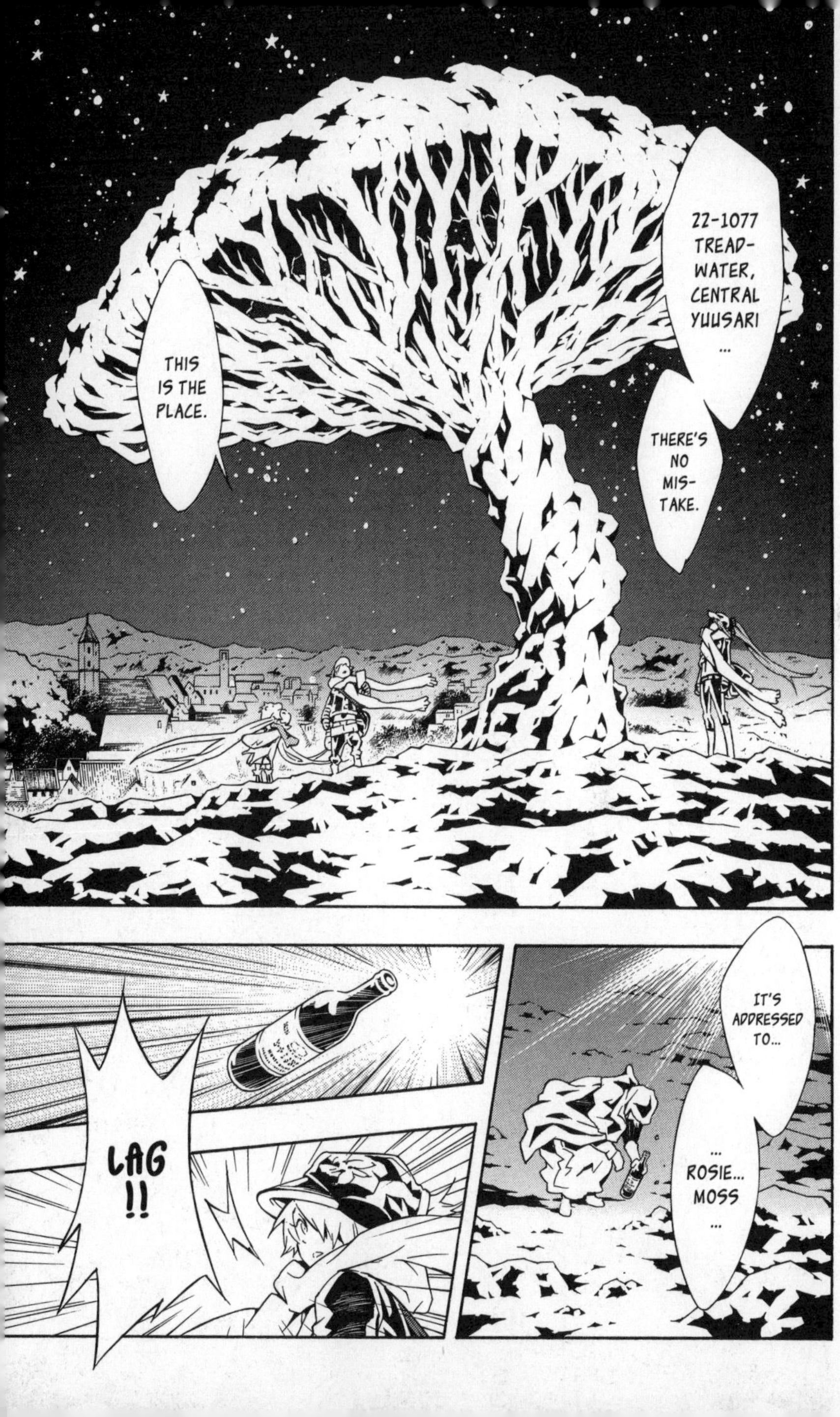
22-1077 TREAD-WATER, CENTRAL YUUSARI ...
THERE'S NO MIS-TAKE.
THIS IS THE PLACE.
IT'S ADDRESSED TO...
... ROSIE... MOSS ...
LAG !!

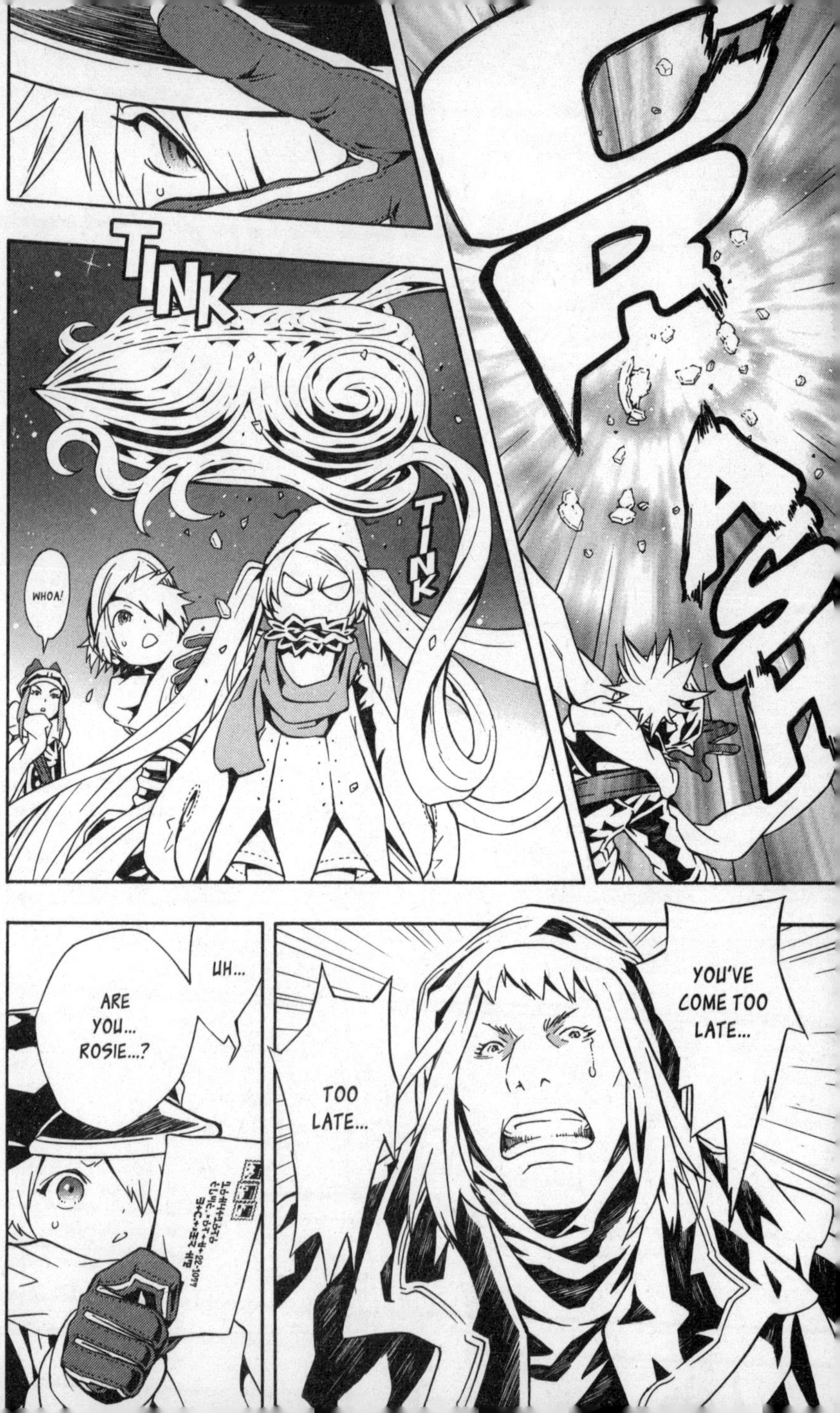
CRASH
TINK
TINK
WHOA!
YOU'VE COME TOO LATE...
TOO LATE...
UH...
ARE YOU... ROSIE...?

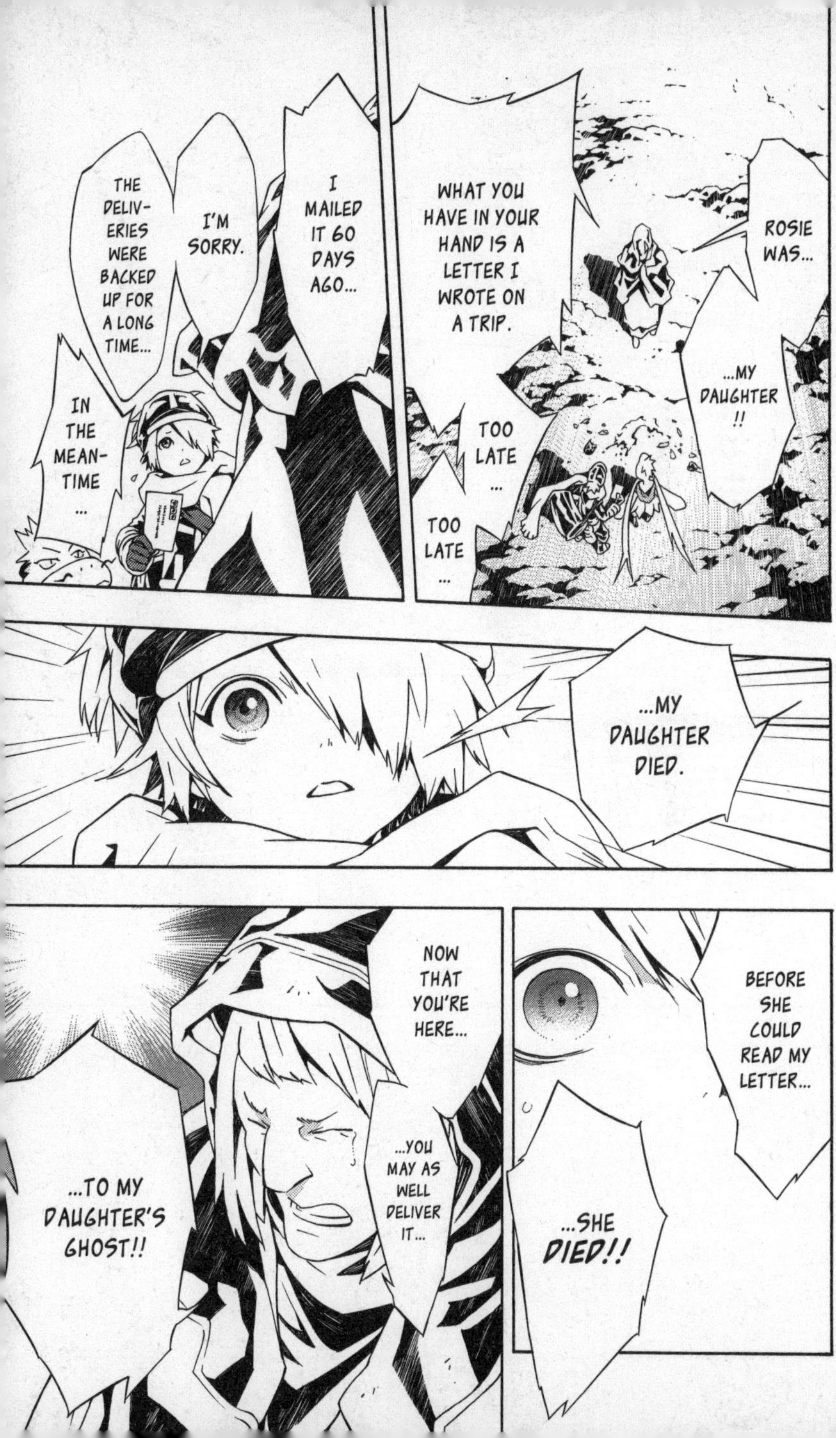
WHAT YOU HAVE IN YOUR HAND IS A LETTER I WROTE ON A TRIP.
ROSIE WAS...
...MY DAUGHTER !!
TOO LATE ...
TOO LATE ...
I MAILED IT 60 DAYS AGO...
I'M SORRY.
THE DELIV-ERIES WERE BACKED UP FOR A LONG TIME...
IN THE MEAN-TIME ...
...MY DAUGHTER DIED.
BEFORE SHE COULD READ MY LETTER...
...SHE *DIED!!*
NOW THAT YOU'RE HERE...
...YOU MAY AS WELL DELIVER IT...
...TO MY DAUGHTER'S GHOST!!

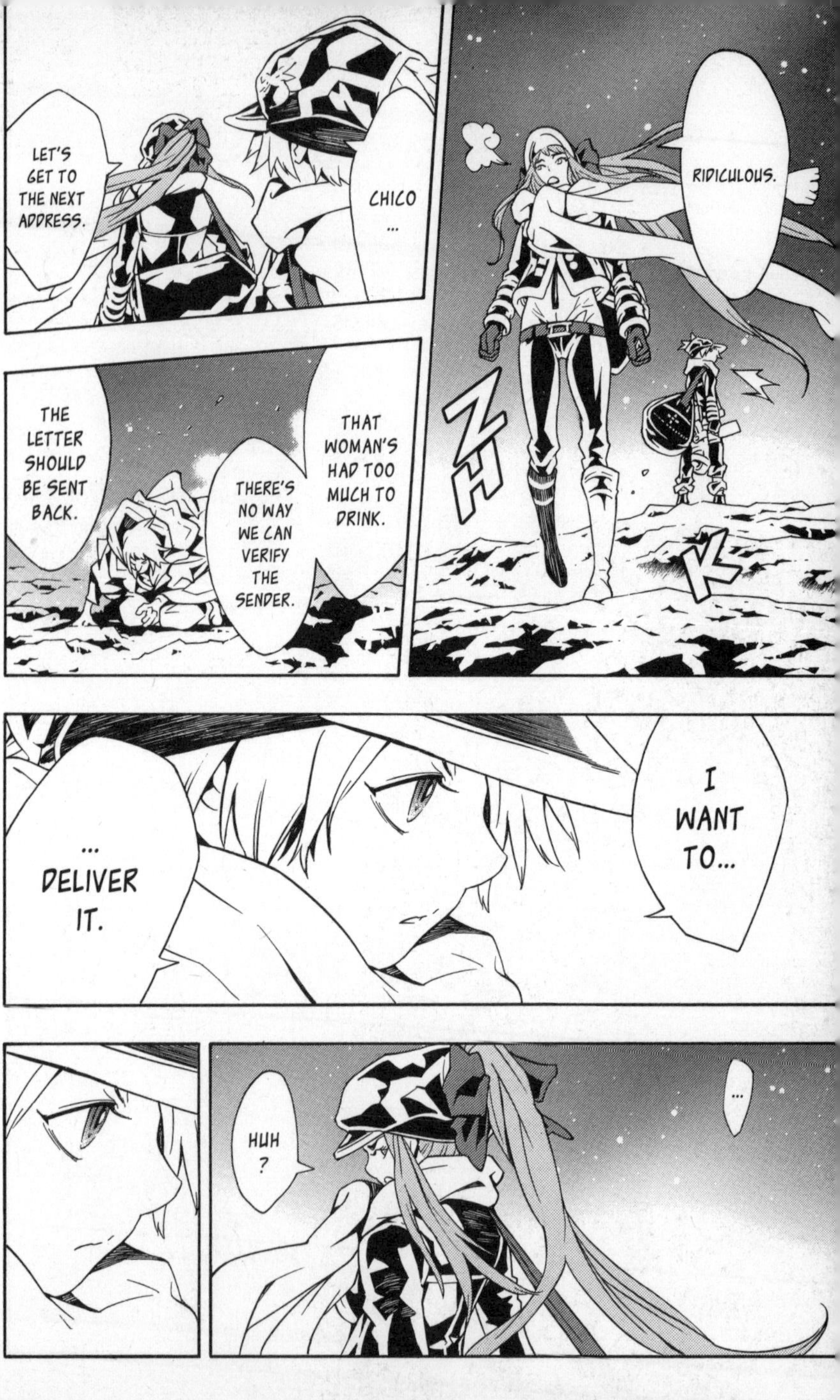
RIDICULOUS.
NH
K
CHICO...
LET'S GET TO THE NEXT ADDRESS.
THAT WOMAN'S HAD TOO MUCH TO DRINK.
THERE'S NO WAY WE CAN VERIFY THE SENDER.
THE LETTER SHOULD BE SENT BACK.
I WANT TO...
...DELIVER IT.
...
HUH?

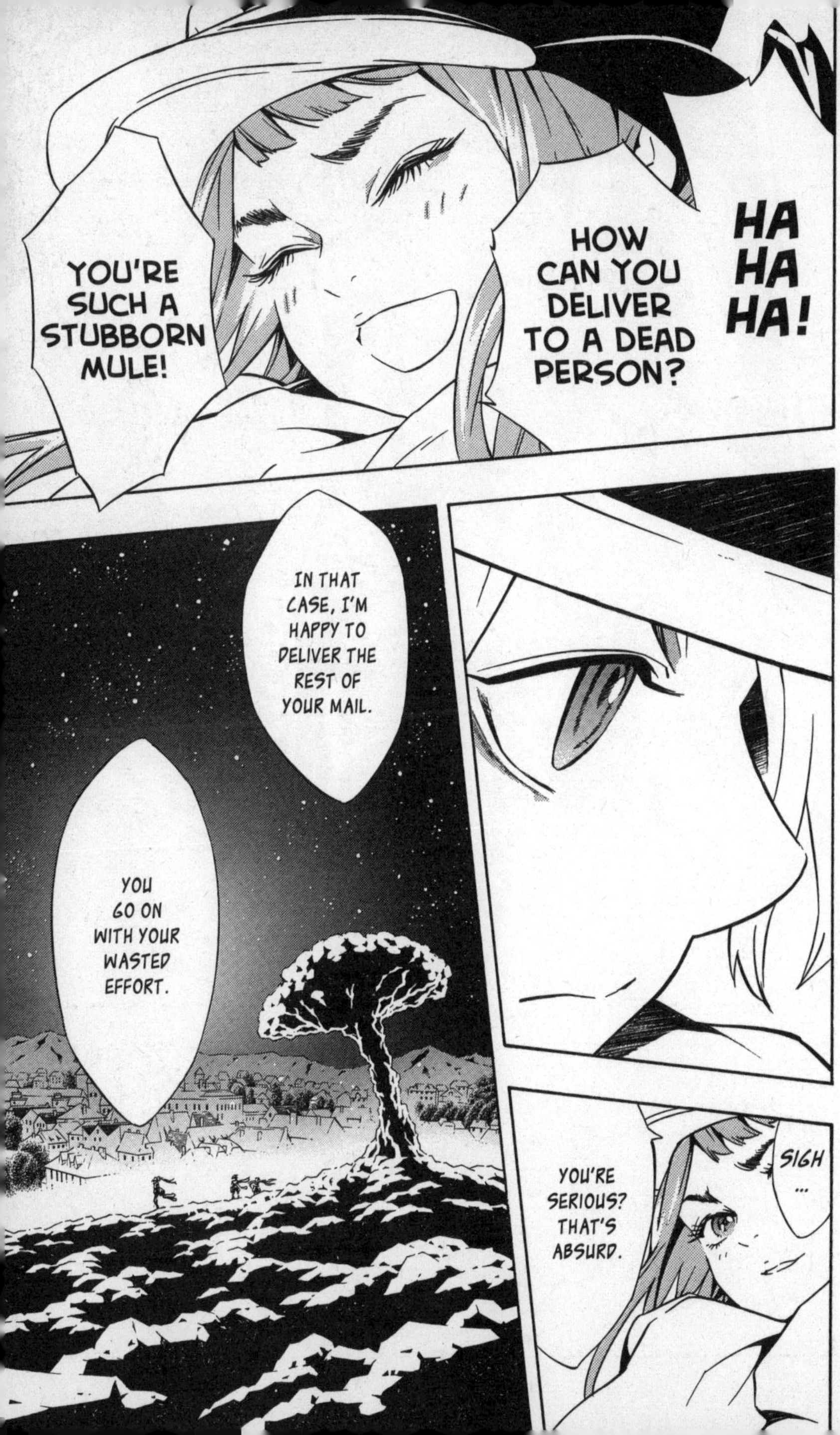
HA HA HA!
HOW CAN YOU DELIVER TO A DEAD PERSON?
YOU'RE SUCH A STUBBORN MULE!
SIGH...
YOU'RE SERIOUS? THAT'S ABSURD.
IN THAT CASE, I'M HAPPY TO DELIVER THE REST OF YOUR MAIL.
YOU GO ON WITH YOUR WASTED EFFORT.

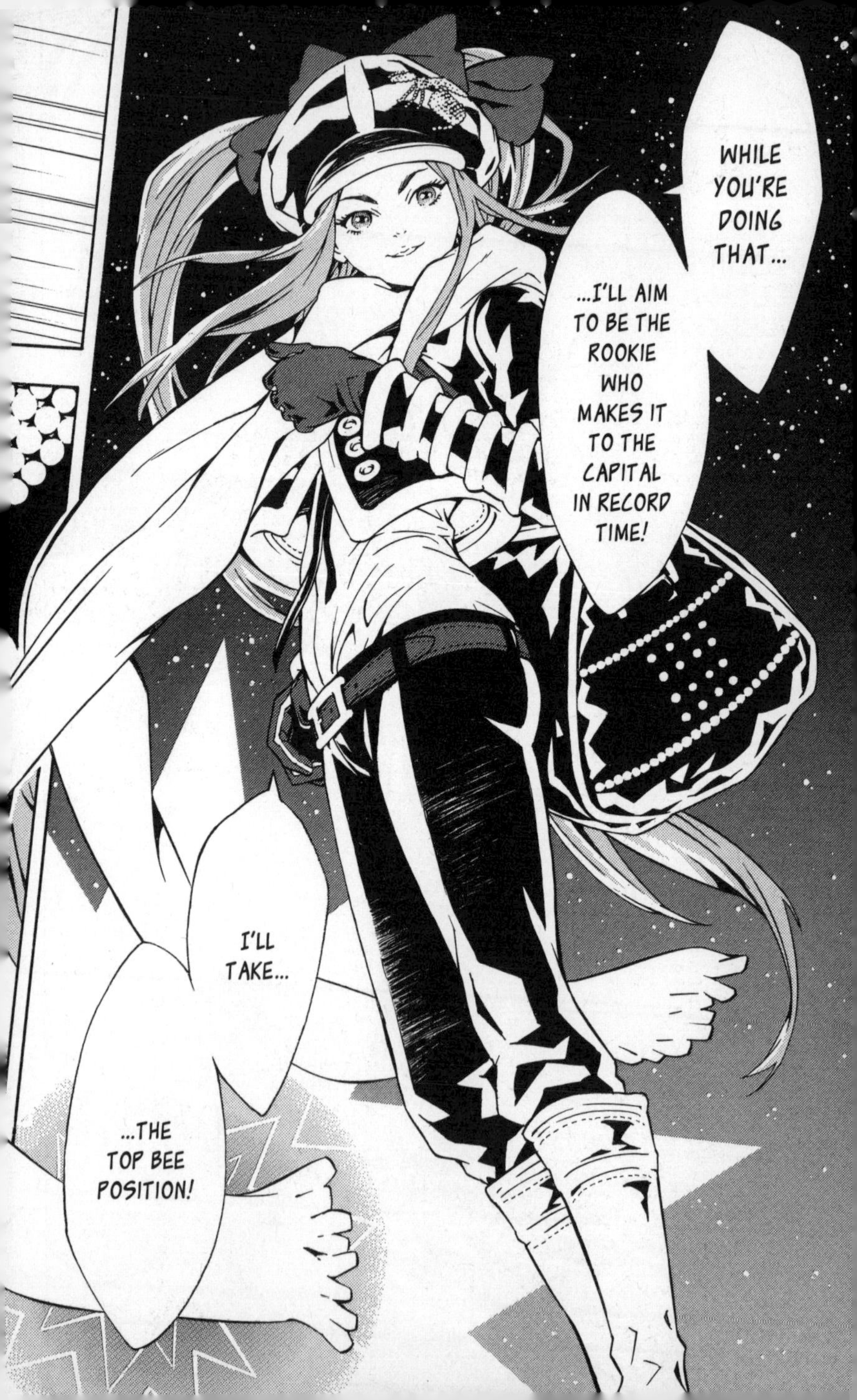
WHILE YOU'RE DOING THAT...
...I'LL AIM TO BE THE ROOKIE WHO MAKES IT TO THE CAPITAL IN RECORD TIME!
I'LL TAKE...
...THE TOP BEE POSITION!

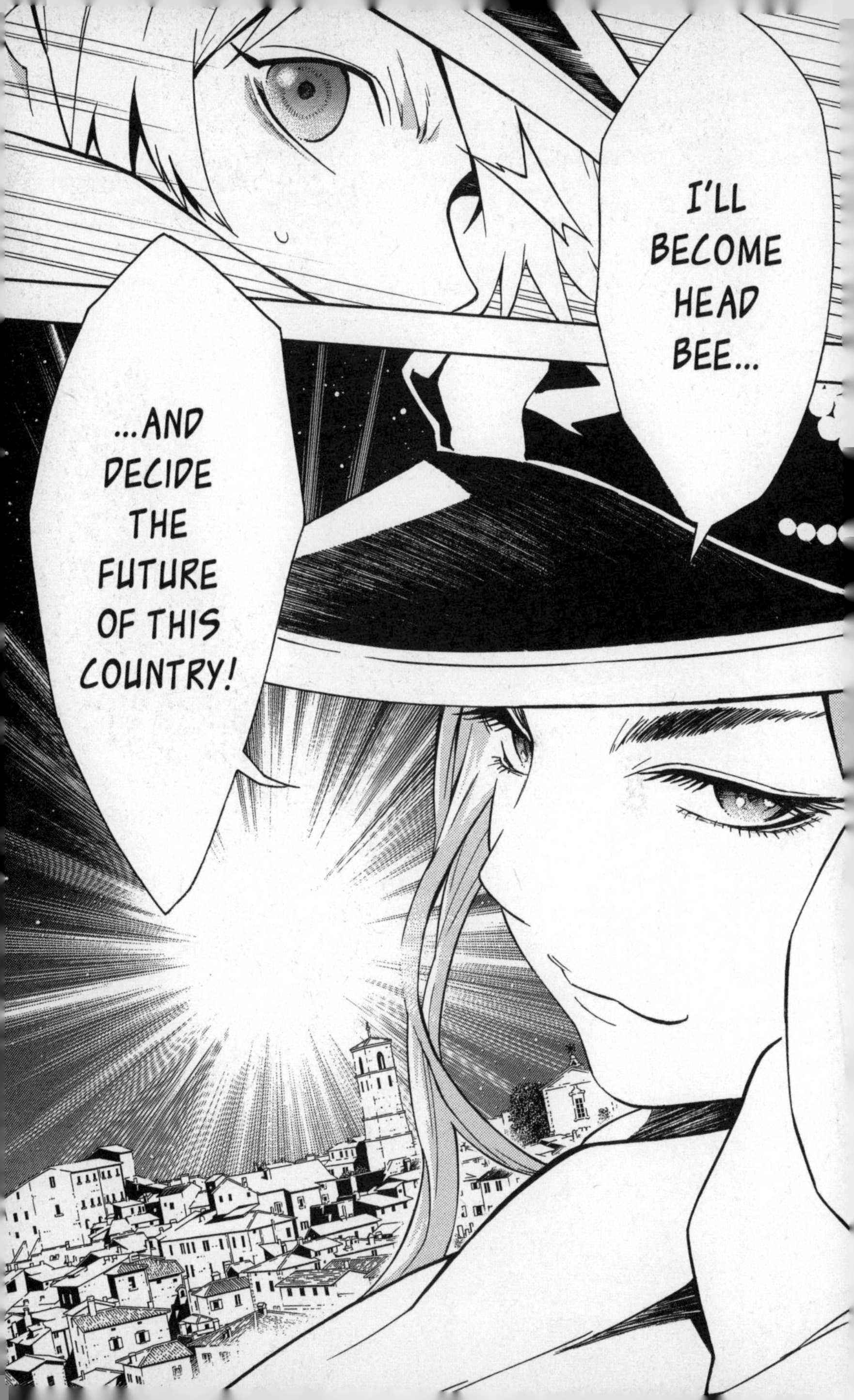
I'LL BECOME HEAD BEE...
...AND DECIDE THE FUTURE OF THIS COUNTRY!

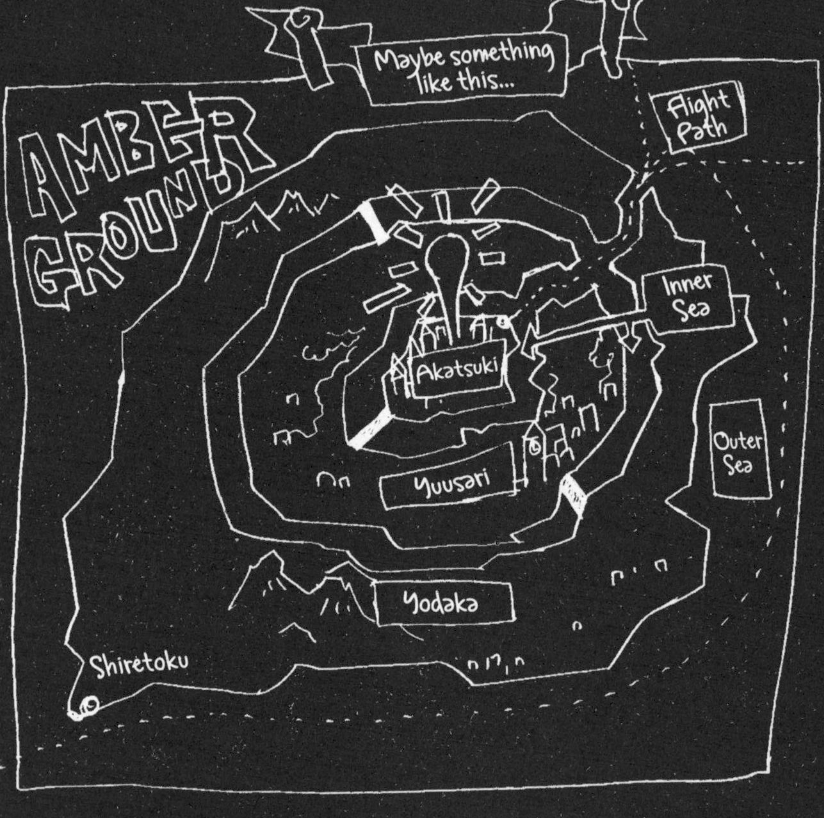
Maybe something like this...
AMBER GROUND
Flight Path
Inner Sea
Akatsuki
Outer Sea
Yuusari
Yodaka
Shiretoku

Rough sketch of Amberground I drew before the manga launched.

Chapter 73: Don't Fear the Rain

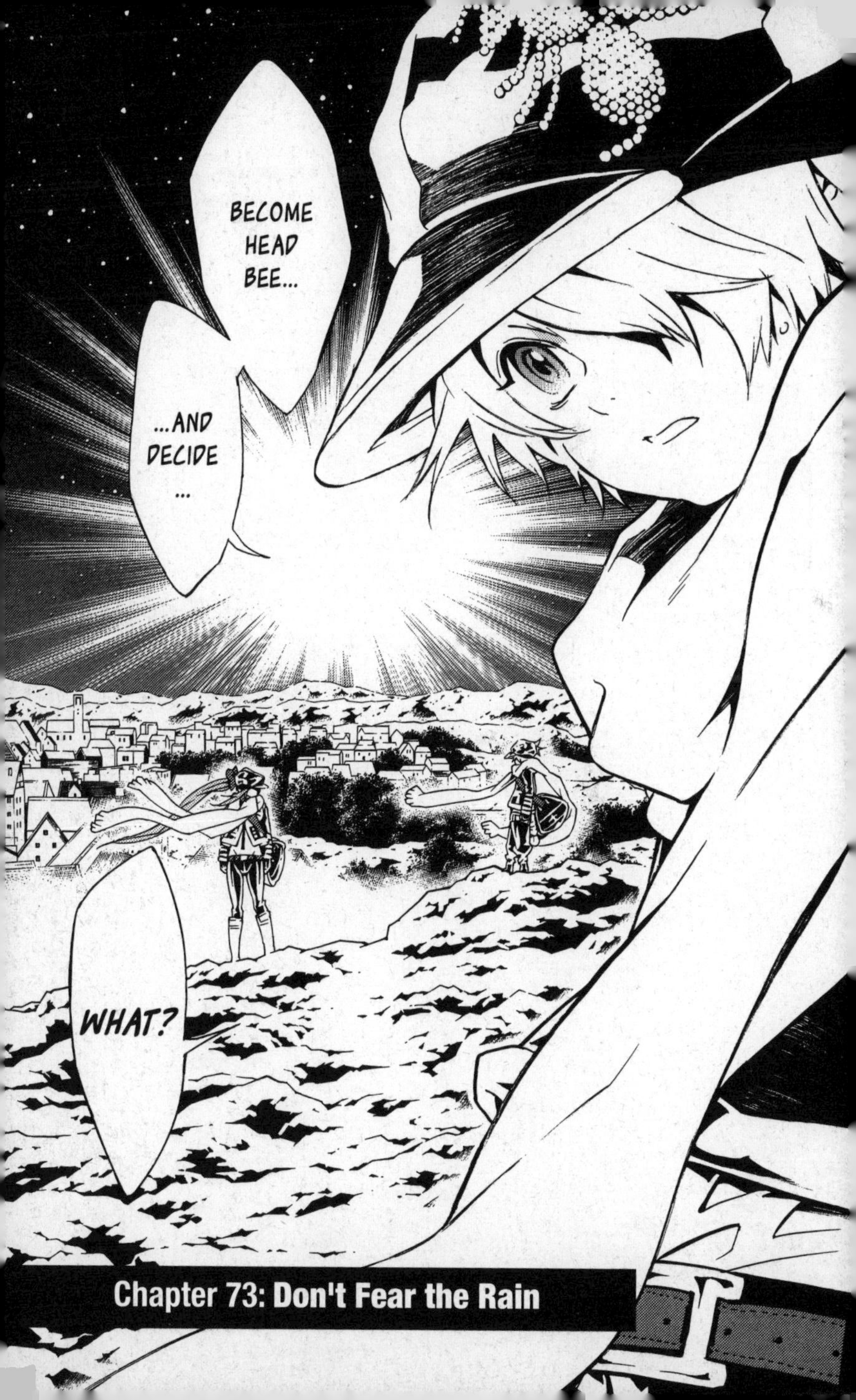
BECOME HEAD BEE...
...AND DECIDE ...
WHAT?

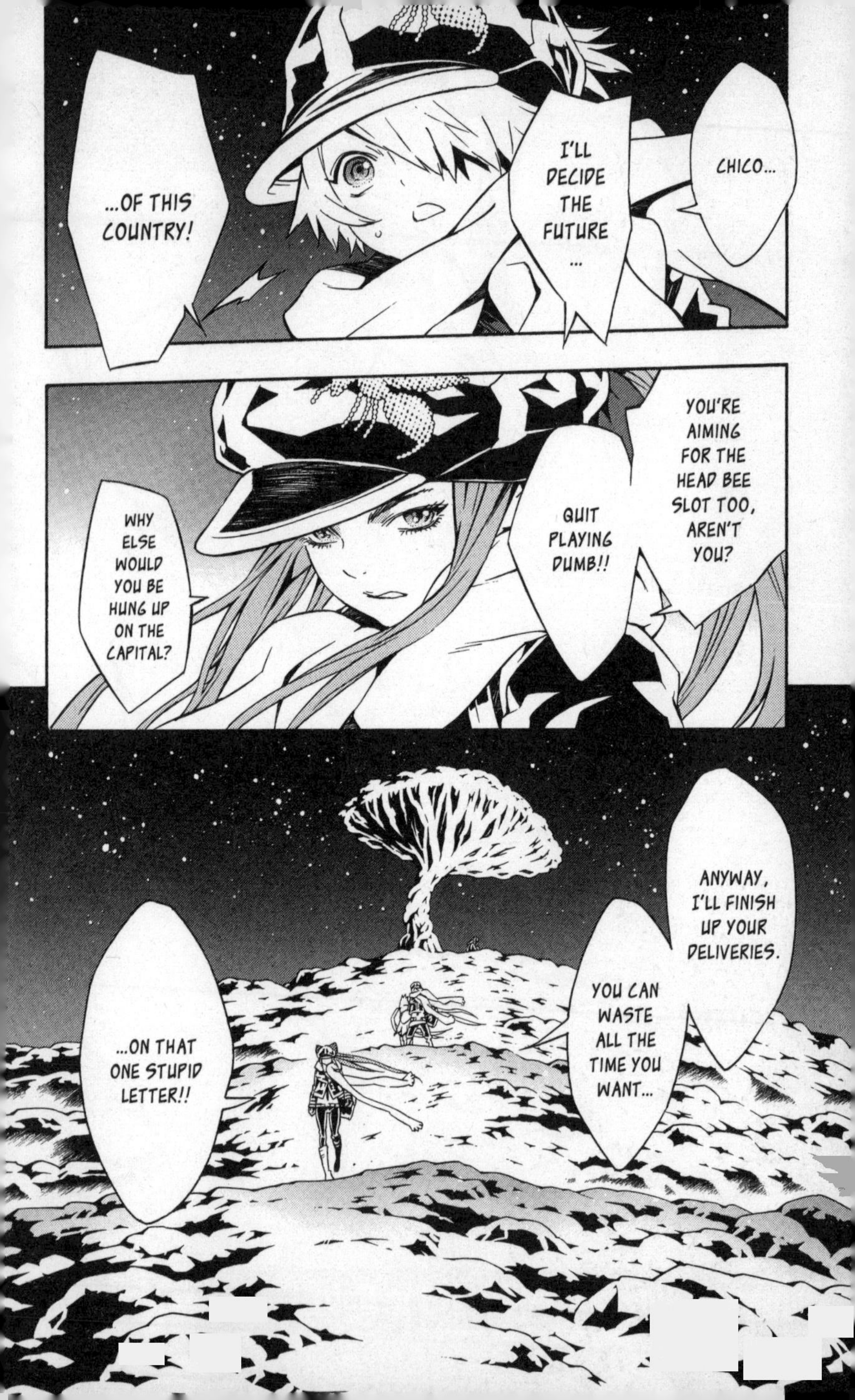
CHICO...
I'LL DECIDE THE FUTURE...
...OF THIS COUNTRY!
YOU'RE AIMING FOR THE HEAD BEE SLOT TOO, AREN'T YOU?
QUIT PLAYING DUMB!!
WHY ELSE WOULD YOU BE HUNG UP ON THE CAPITAL?
ANYWAY, I'LL FINISH UP YOUR DELIVERIES.
YOU CAN WASTE ALL THE TIME YOU WANT...
...ON THAT ONE STUPID LETTER!!

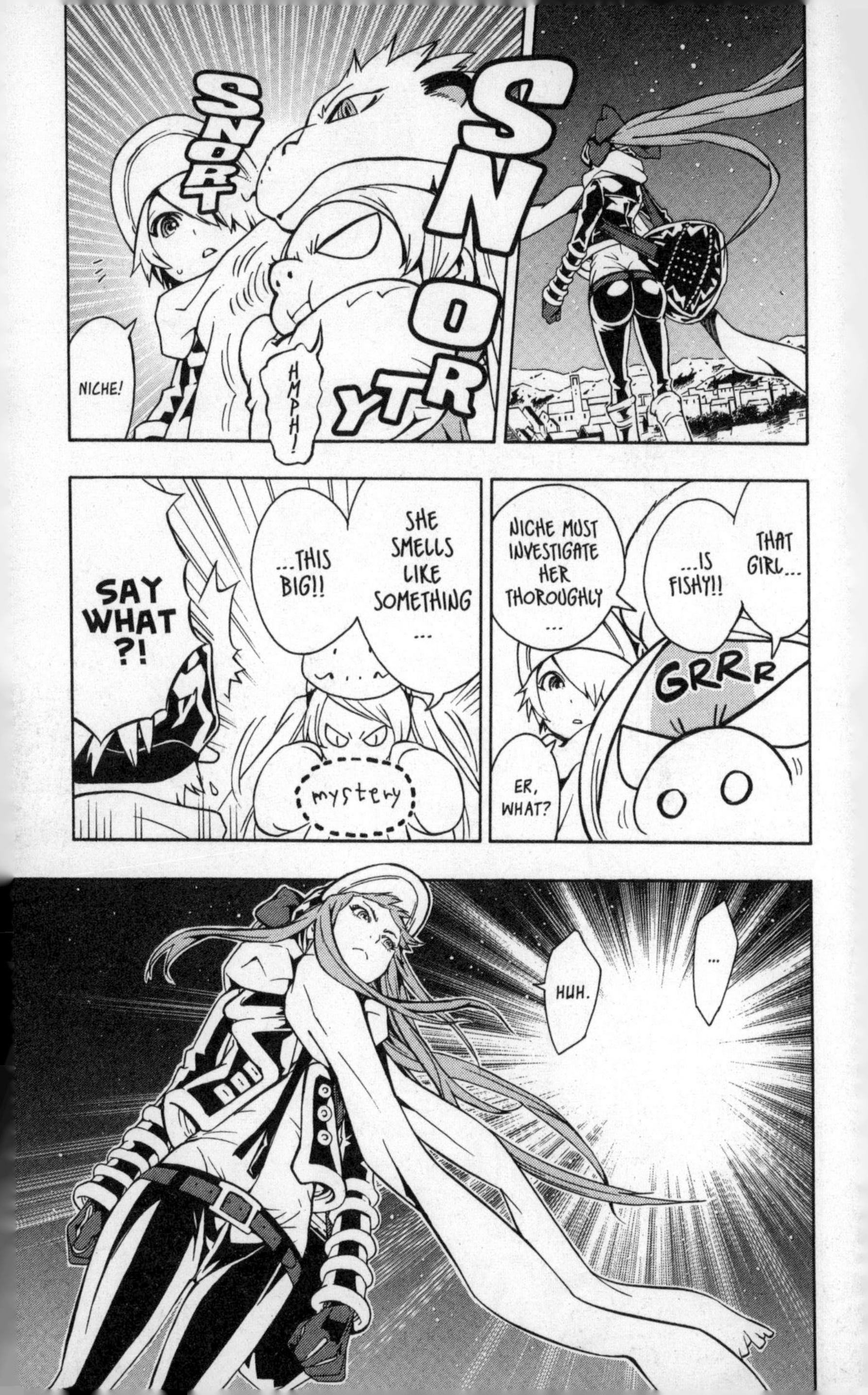
SNORTY
SNORT
HMPH!
NICHE!
THAT GIRL...
...IS FISHY!!
NICHE MUST INVESTIGATE HER THOROUGHLY...
GRRR
ER, WHAT?
SHE SMELLS LIKE SOMETHING...
...THIS BIG!!
mystery
SAY WHAT?!
...
HUH.

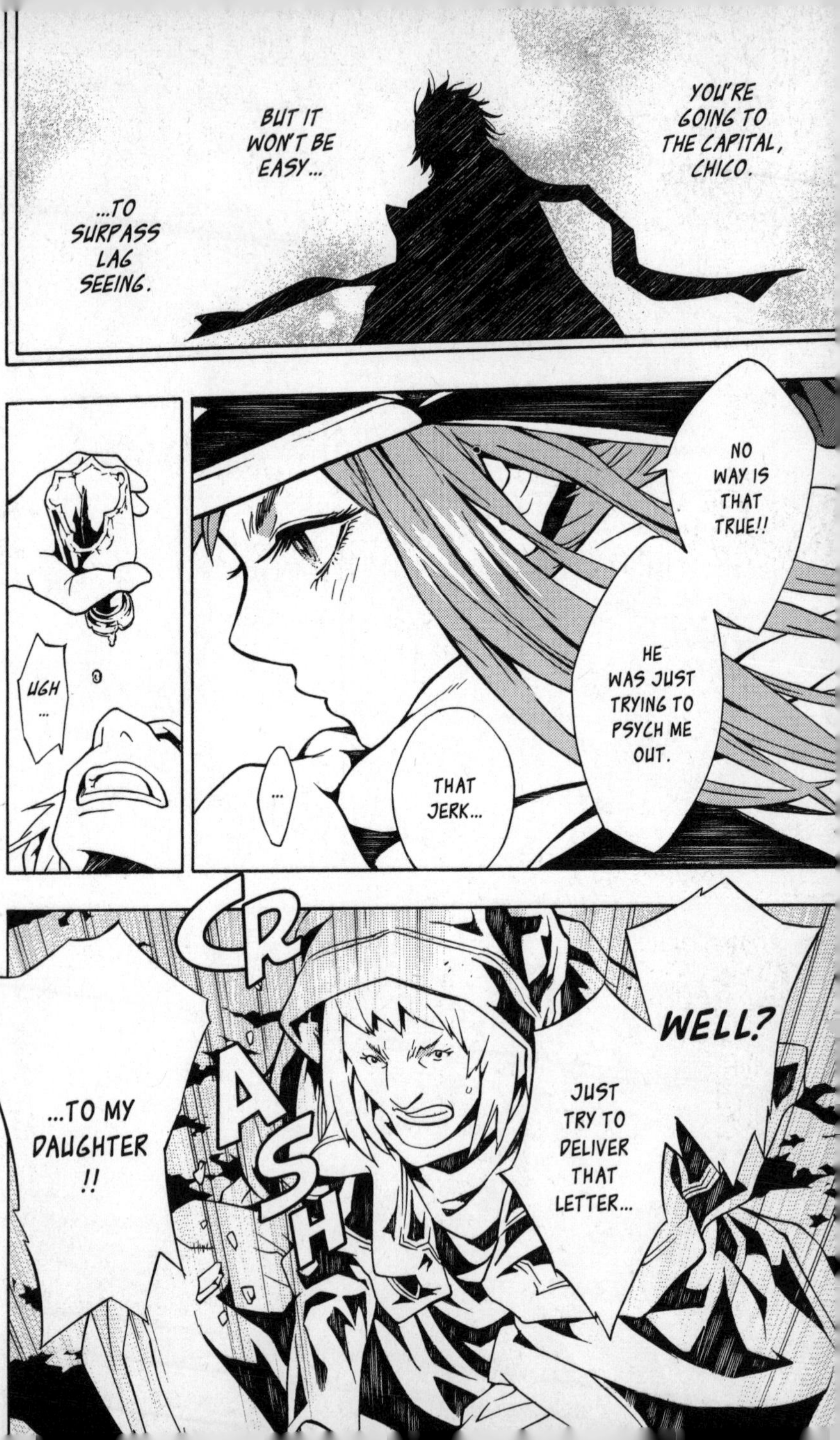
YOU'RE GOING TO THE CAPITAL, CHICO.
BUT IT WON'T BE EASY...
...TO SURPASS LAG SEEING.
NO WAY IS THAT TRUE!!
HE WAS JUST TRYING TO PSYCH ME OUT.
THAT JERK...
...
UGH ...
WELL?
JUST TRY TO DELIVER THAT LETTER...
CRASH
...TO MY DAUGHTER !!

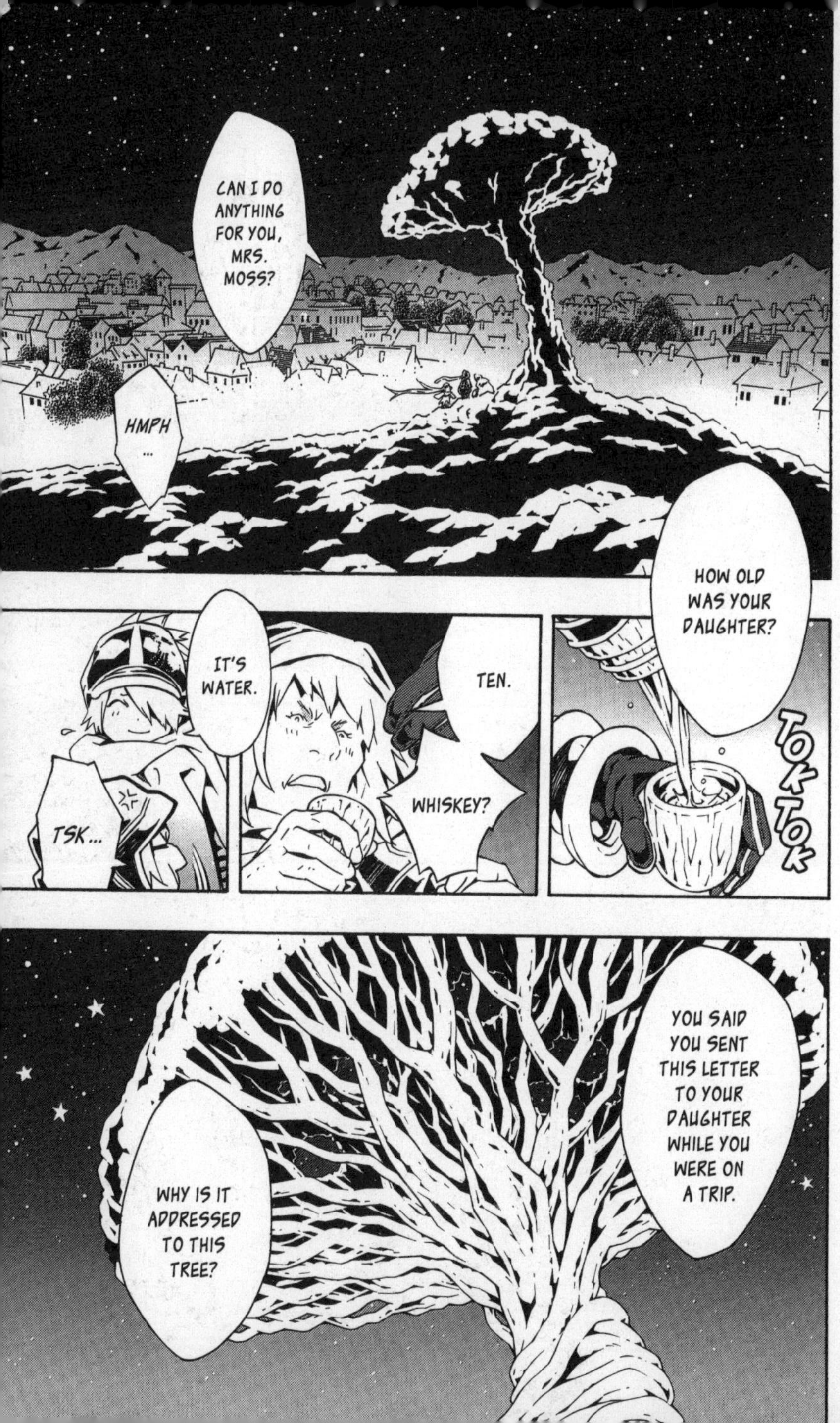
CAN I DO ANYTHING FOR YOU, MRS. MOSS?
HMPH ...
HOW OLD WAS YOUR DAUGHTER?
TOK TOK
TEN.
WHISKEY?
IT'S WATER.
TSK...
YOU SAID YOU SENT THIS LETTER TO YOUR DAUGHTER WHILE YOU WERE ON A TRIP.
WHY IS IT ADDRESSED TO THIS TREE?

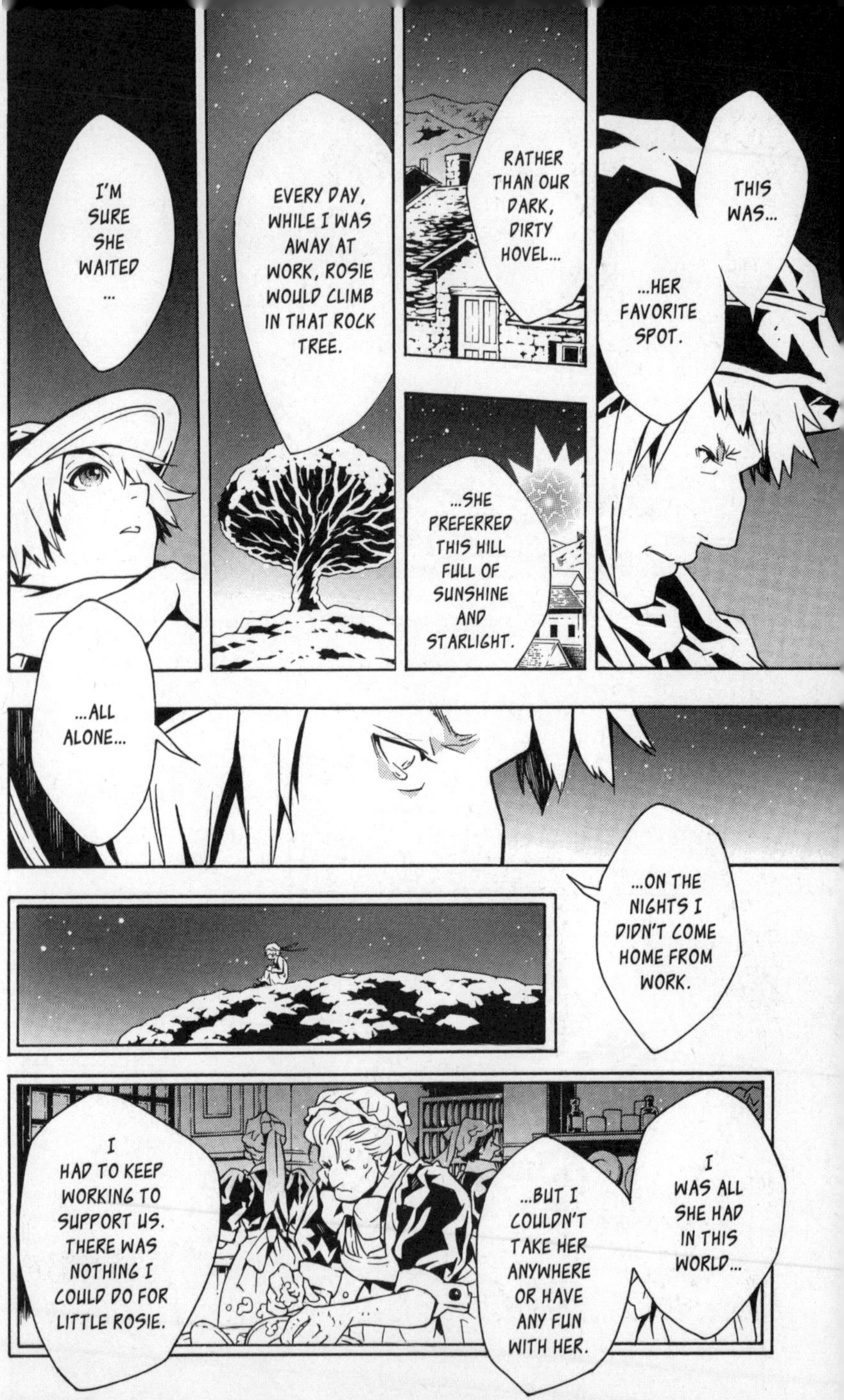
THIS WAS...
...HER FAVORITE SPOT.
RATHER THAN OUR DARK, DIRTY HOVEL...
...SHE PREFERRED THIS HILL FULL OF SUNSHINE AND STARLIGHT.
EVERY DAY, WHILE I WAS AWAY AT WORK, ROSIE WOULD CLIMB IN THAT ROCK TREE.
I'M SURE SHE WAITED ...
...ALL ALONE...
...ON THE NIGHTS I DIDN'T COME HOME FROM WORK.
I WAS ALL SHE HAD IN THIS WORLD...
...BUT I COULDN'T TAKE HER ANYWHERE OR HAVE ANY FUN WITH HER.
I HAD TO KEEP WORKING TO SUPPORT US. THERE WAS NOTHING I COULD DO FOR LITTLE ROSIE.

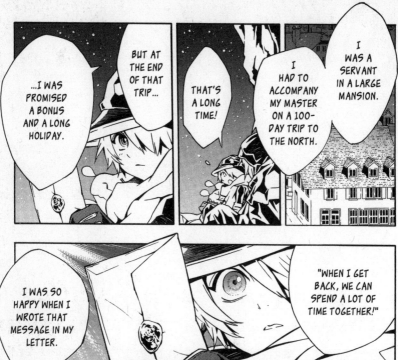

I WAS A SERVANT IN A LARGE MANSION.
I HAD TO ACCOMPANY MY MASTER ON A 100-DAY TRIP TO THE NORTH.
THAT'S A LONG TIME!
BUT AT THE END OF THAT TRIP...
...I WAS PROMISED A BONUS AND A LONG HOLIDAY.
"WHEN I GET BACK, WE CAN SPEND A LOT OF TIME TOGETHER!"
I WAS SO HAPPY WHEN I WROTE THAT MESSAGE IN MY LETTER.
I THOUGHT IT WOULD BRING HOPE...
...TO BOTH OF US.
TO THINK...
...IT NEVER EVEN REACHED HER...
ROSIE WAS KILLED IN A CARRIAGE ACCIDENT.
BUT...

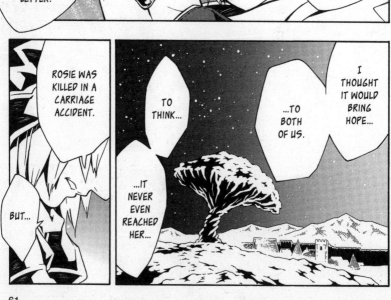

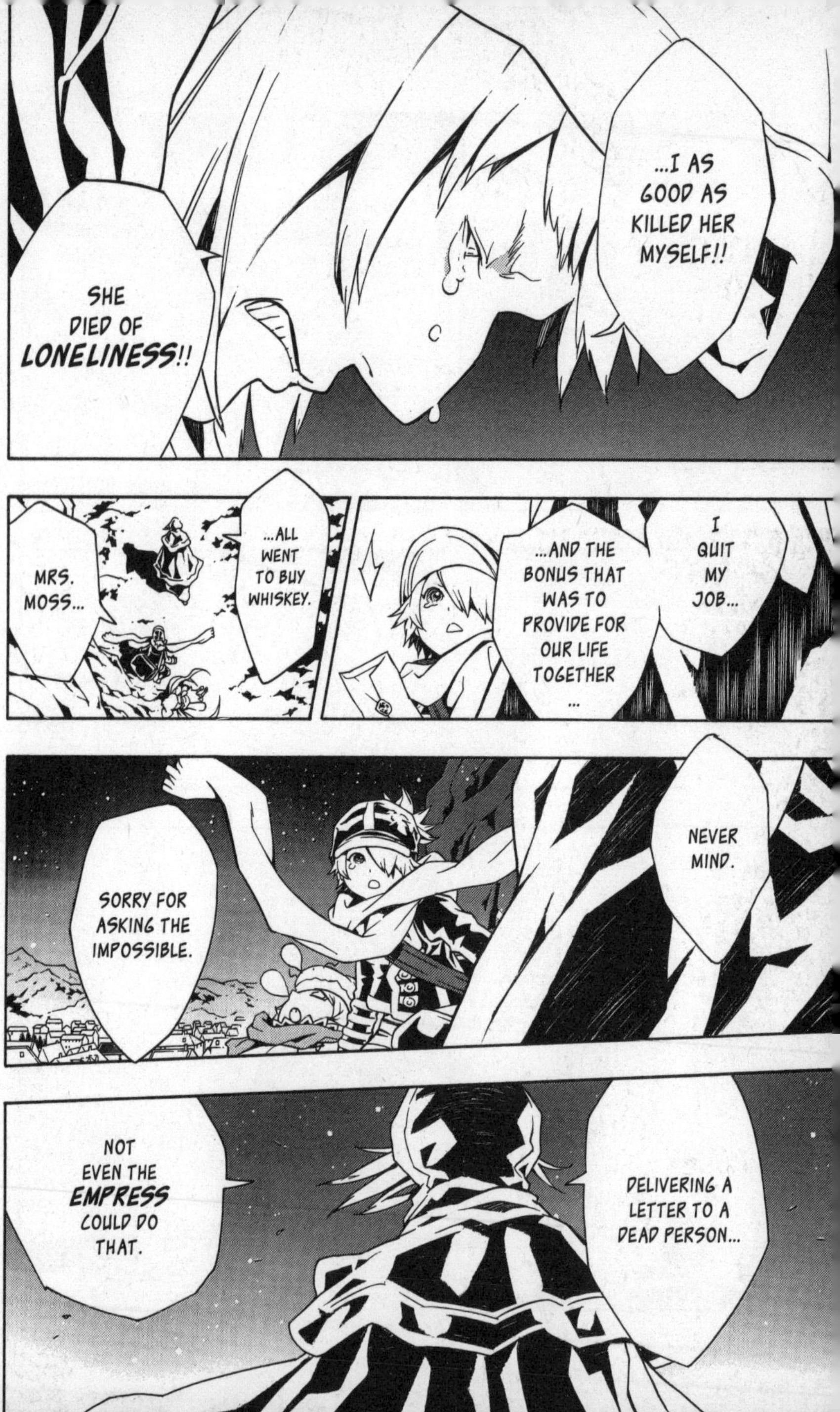
...I AS GOOD AS KILLED HER MYSELF!!
SHE DIED OF LONELINESS!!
I QUIT MY JOB...
...AND THE BONUS THAT WAS TO PROVIDE FOR OUR LIFE TOGETHER ...
...ALL WENT TO BUY WHISKEY.
MRS. MOSS...
NEVER MIND.
SORRY FOR ASKING THE IMPOSSIBLE.
DELIVERING A LETTER TO A DEAD PERSON...
NOT EVEN THE EMPRESS COULD DO THAT.

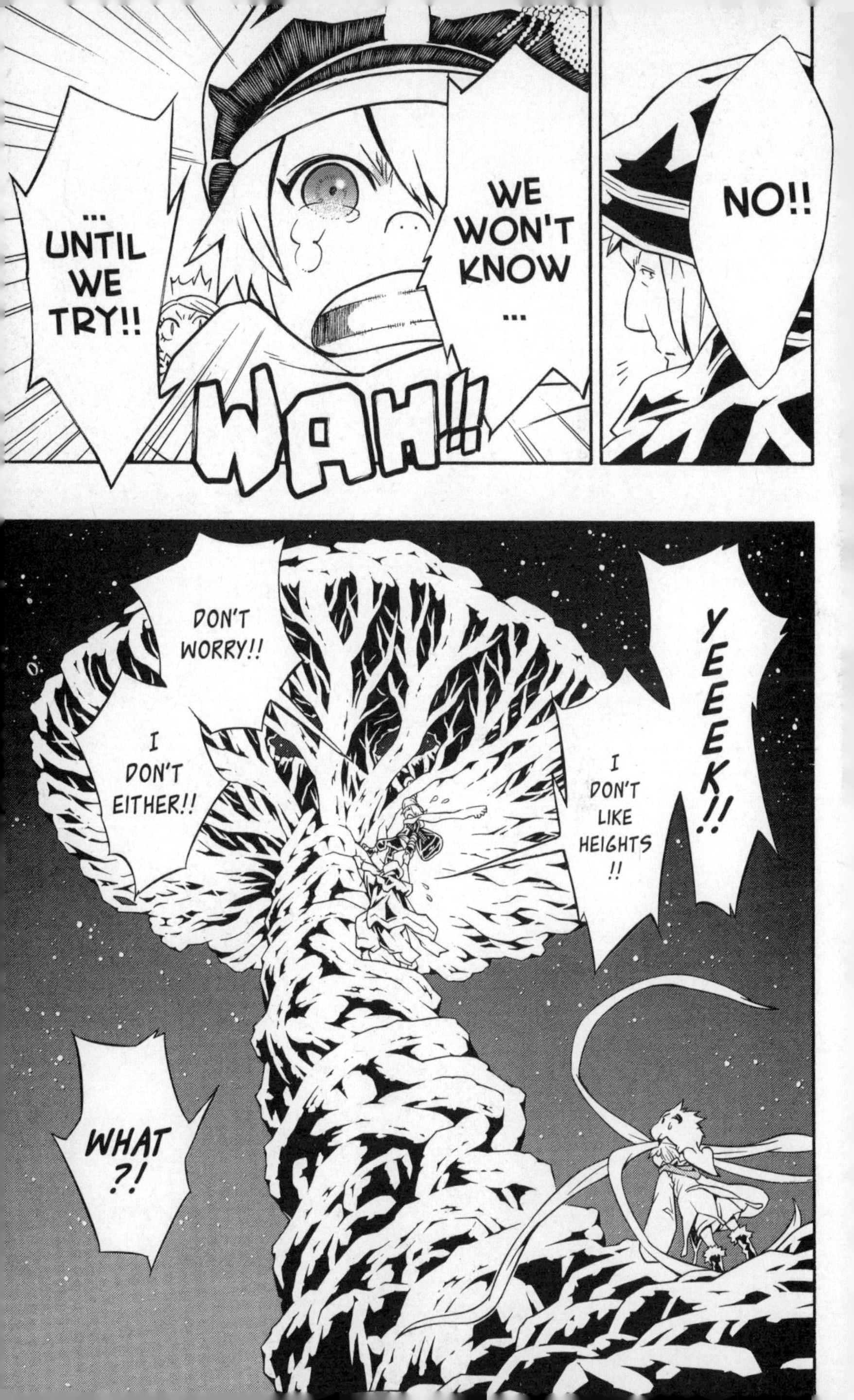
NO!!
WE WON'T KNOW ...
... UNTIL WE TRY!!
WAH!!
YEEEK!!
I DON'T LIKE HEIGHTS!!
DON'T WORRY!!
I DON'T EITHER!!
WHAT?!

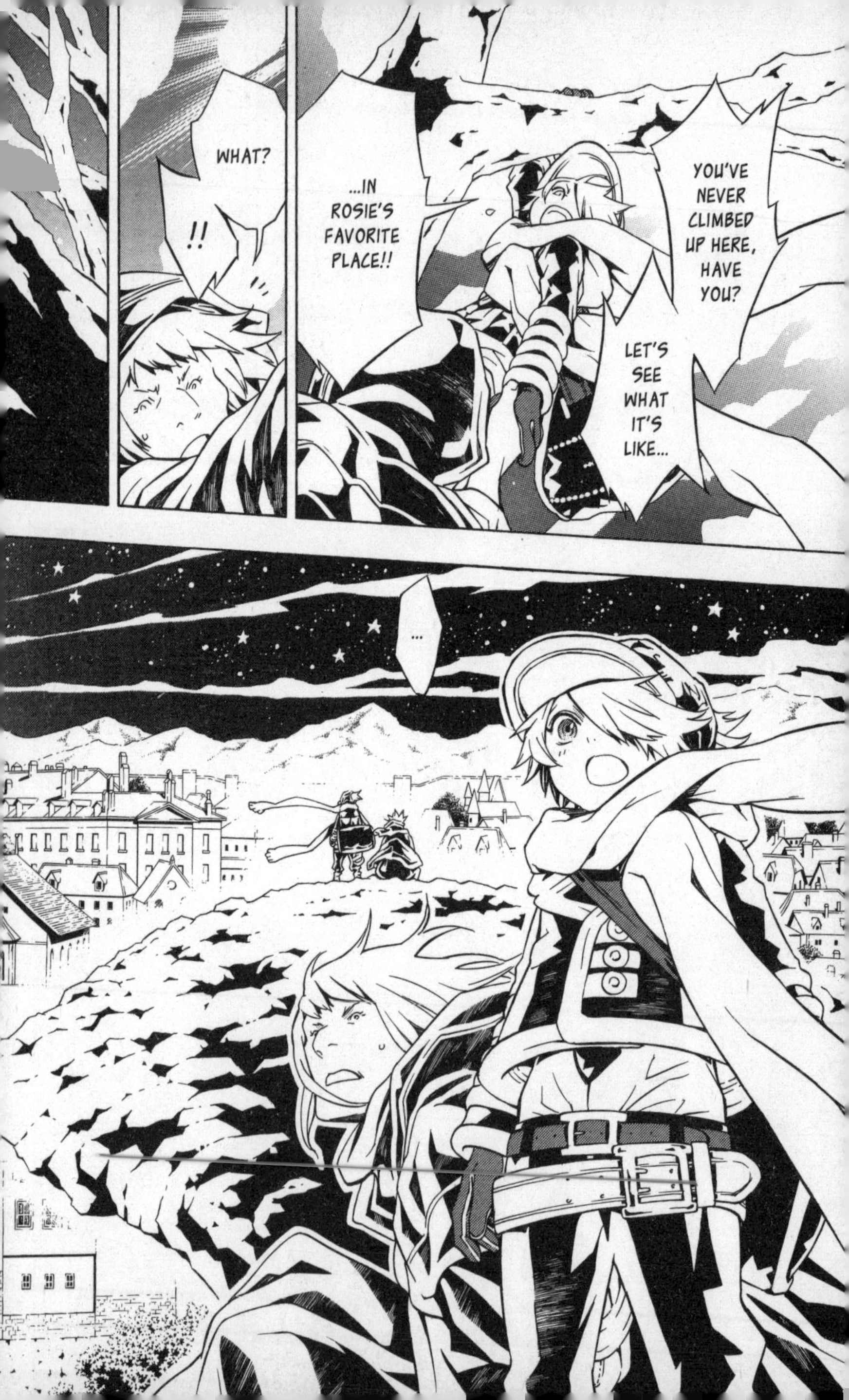
YOU'VE NEVER CLIMBED UP HERE, HAVE YOU?
LET'S SEE WHAT IT'S LIKE...
...IN ROSIE'S FAVORITE PLACE!!
WHAT?
!!
...

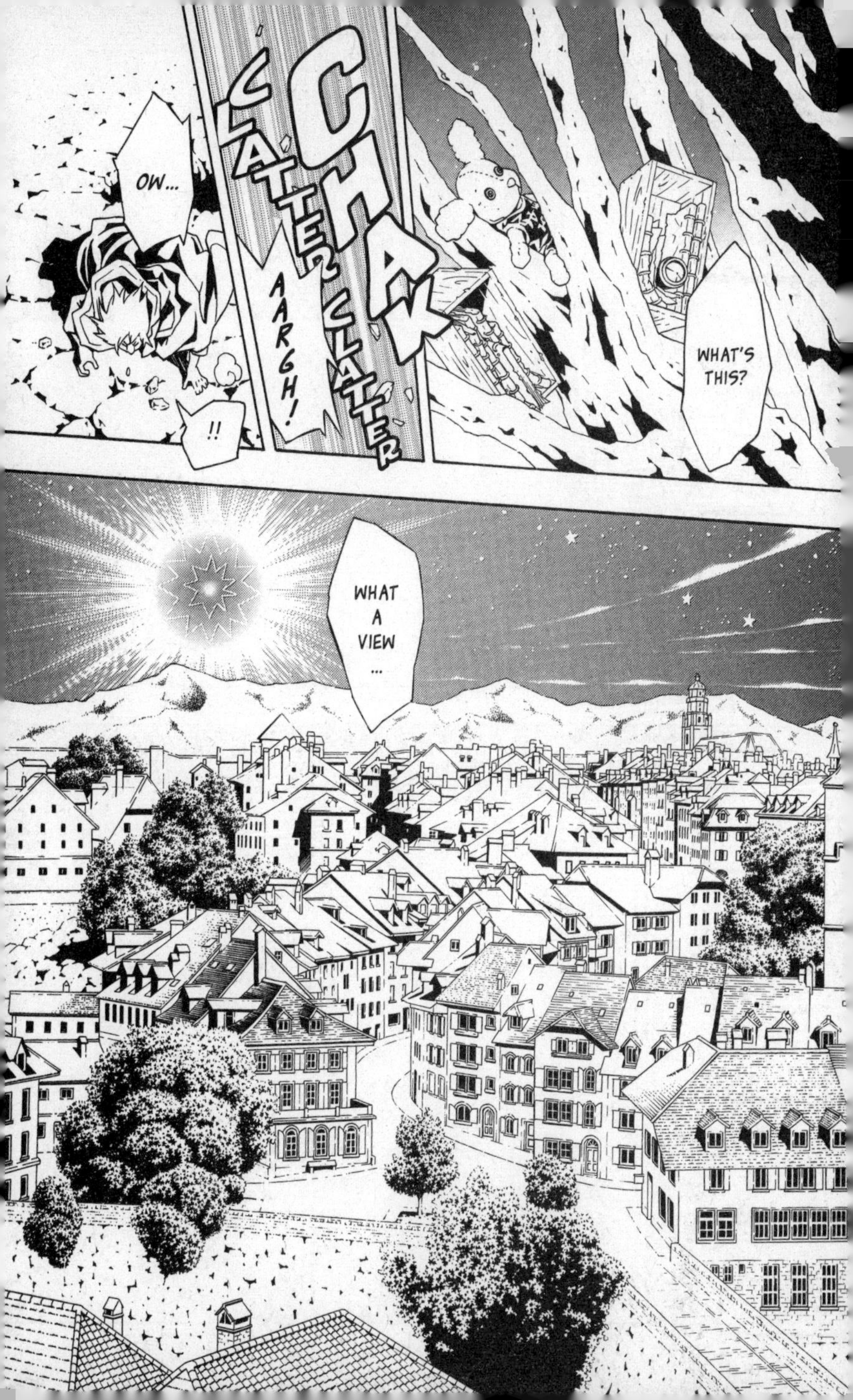
WHAT'S THIS?
CHAK
CLATTER CLATTER
AARGH!
OW...
!!
WHAT A VIEW ...

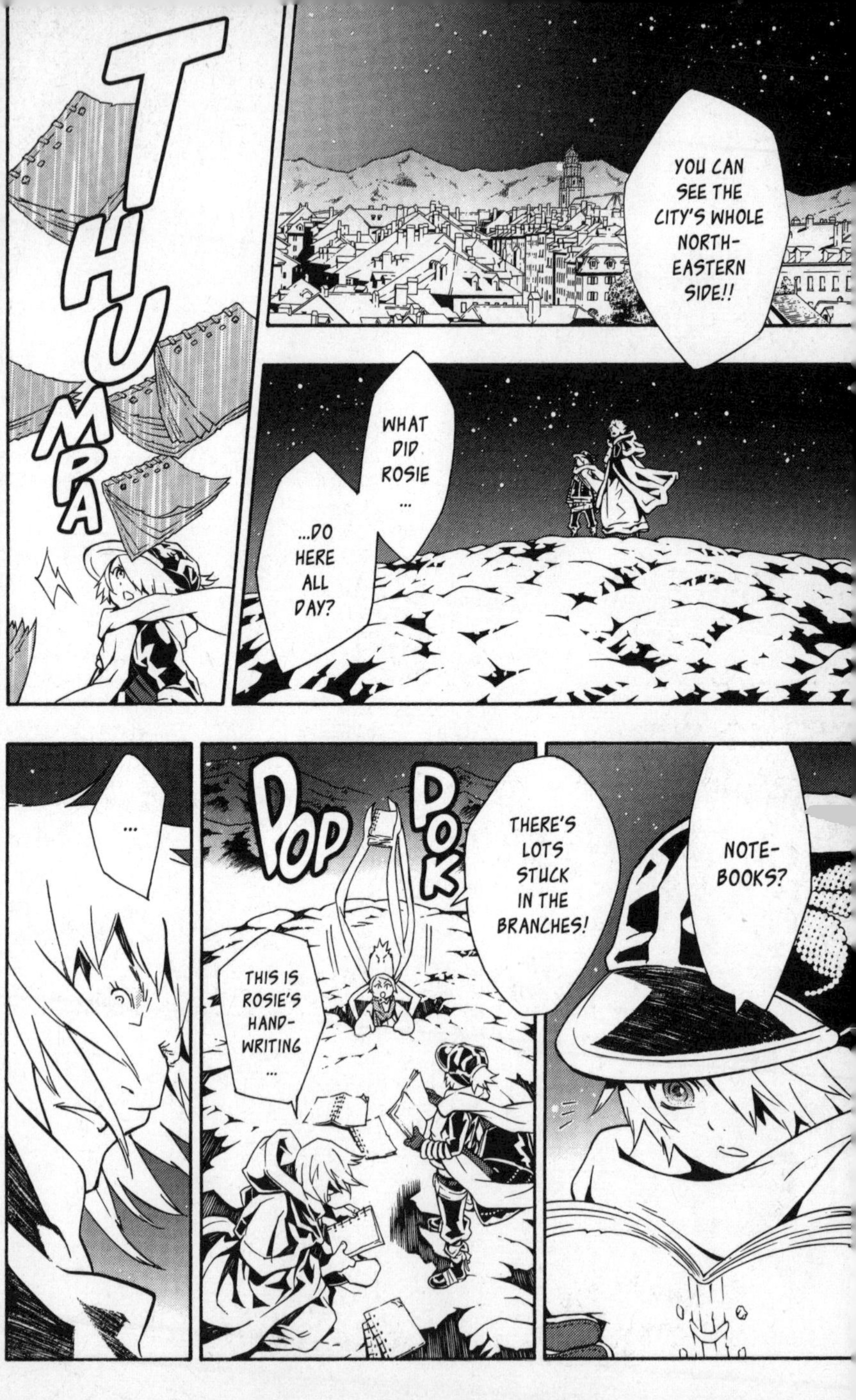
YOU CAN SEE THE CITY'S WHOLE NORTH-EASTERN SIDE!!
WHAT DID ROSIE ...
...DO HERE ALL DAY?
THUMPA
NOTE-BOOKS?
THERE'S LOTS STUCK IN THE BRANCHES!
POK
POP
THIS IS ROSIE'S HAND-WRITING ...
...

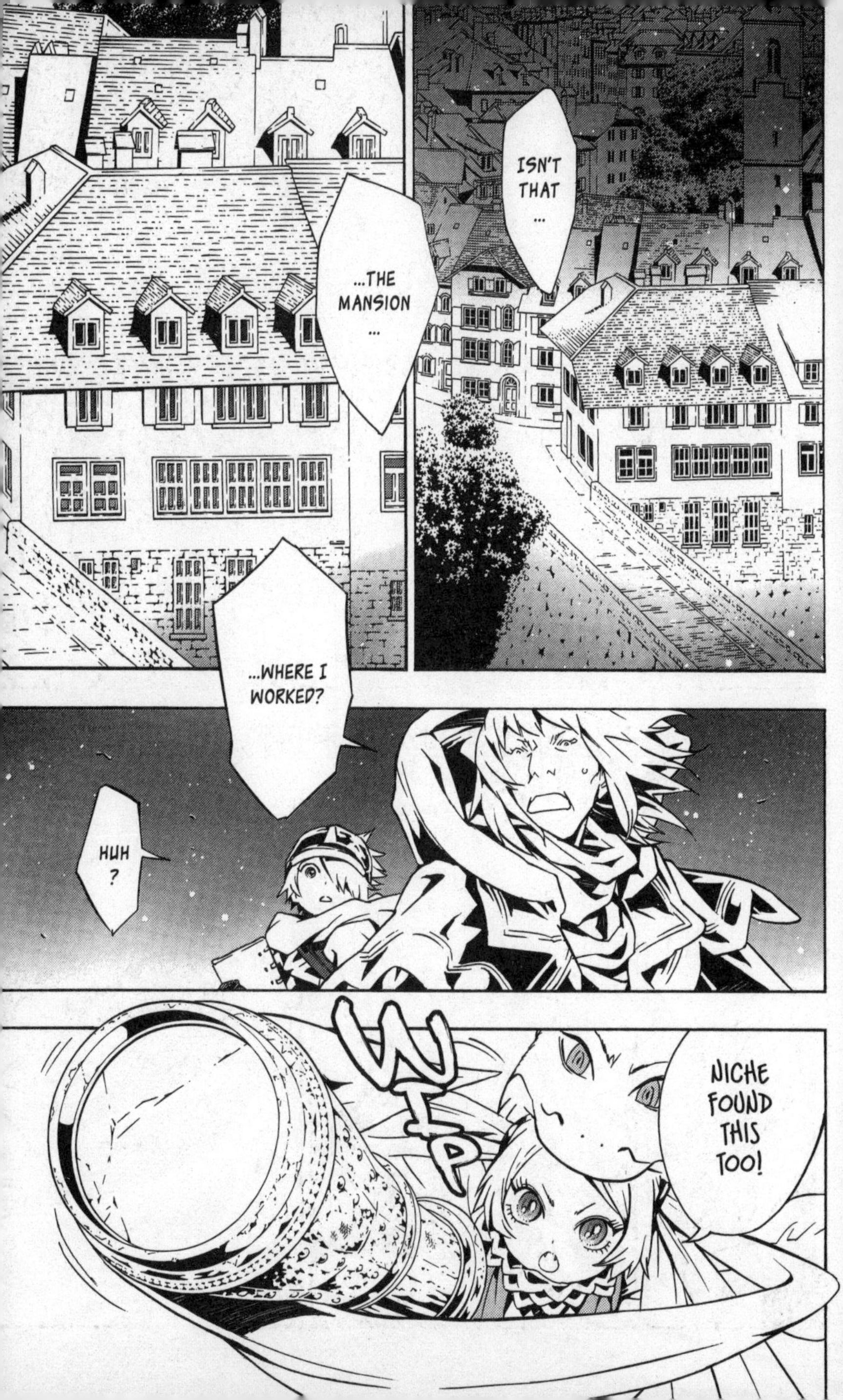
ISN'T THAT ...
...THE MANSION ...
...WHERE I WORKED?
HUH?
NICHE FOUND THIS TOO!
WIP

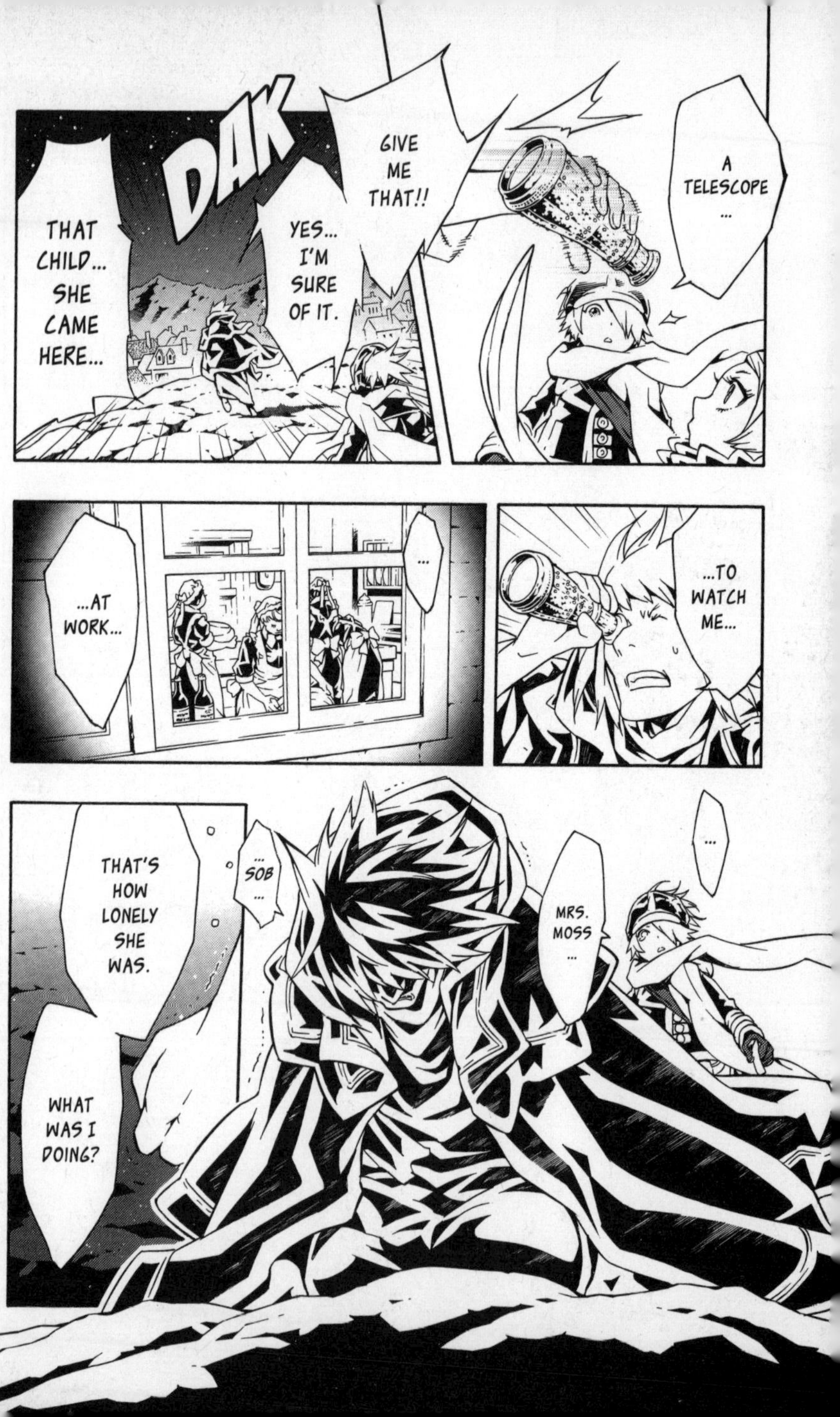
A TELESCOPE...
GIVE ME THAT!!
DAK
YES... I'M SURE OF IT.
THAT CHILD... SHE CAME HERE...
...TO WATCH ME...
...
...AT WORK...
...
MRS. MOSS...
...SOB...
THAT'S HOW LONELY SHE WAS.
WHAT WAS I DOING?

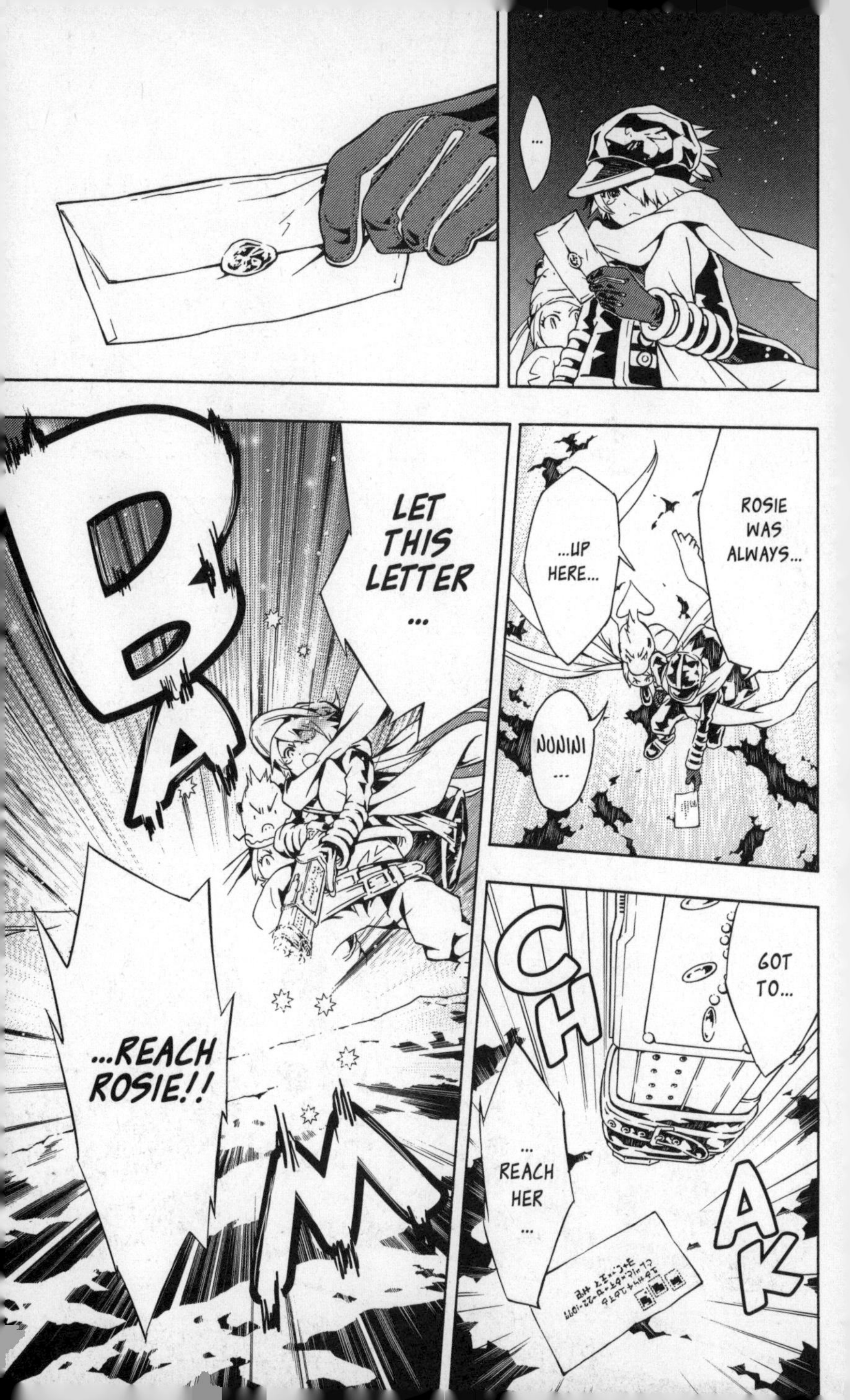
...
ROSIE WAS ALWAYS...
...UP HERE...
NUNINI ...
GOT TO...
CH
AK
... REACH HER ...
LET THIS LETTER ...
BAM
...REACH ROSIE!!

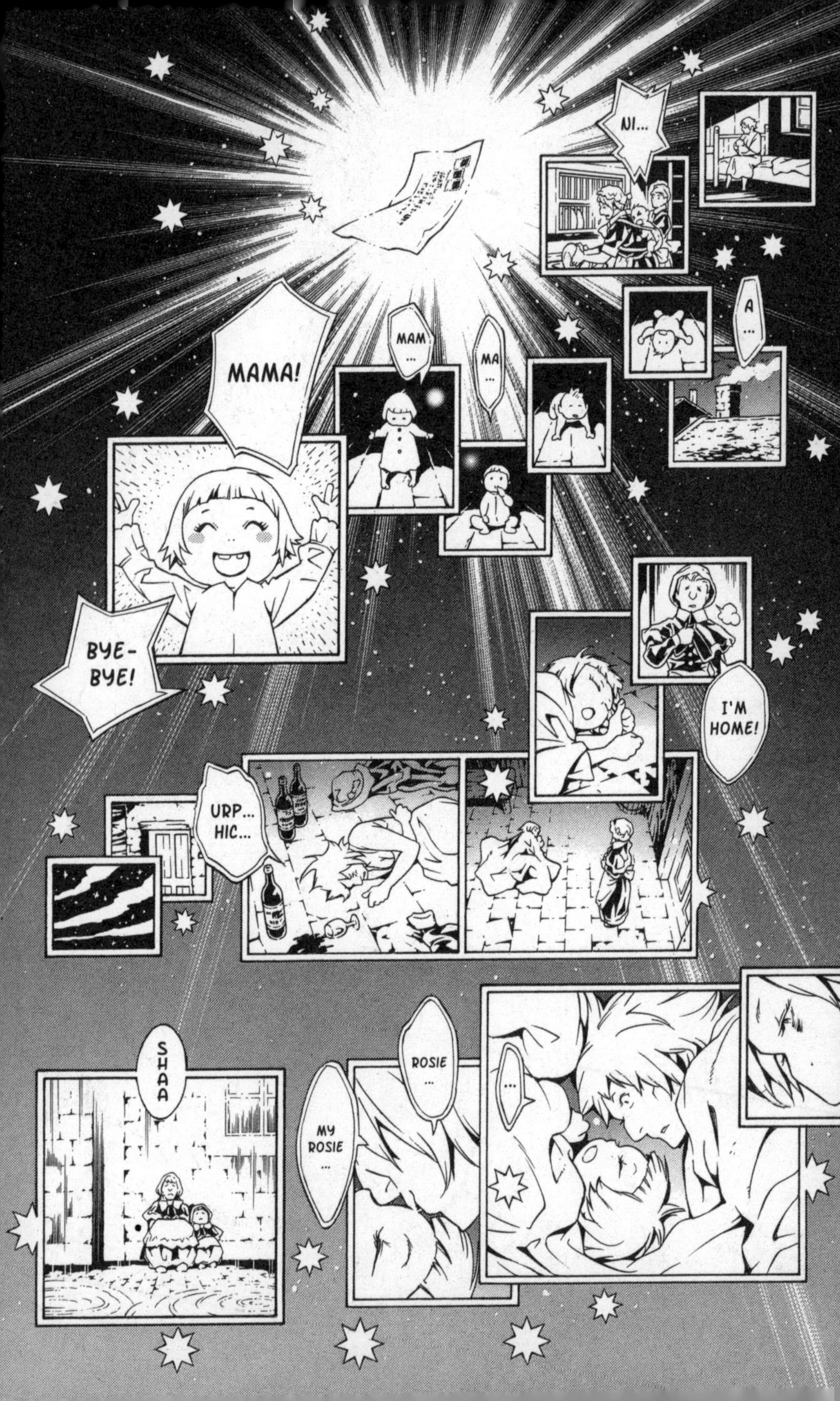
NI...
A...
MA...
MAM...
MAMA!
BYE-BYE!
I'M HOME!
URP... HIC...
...
ROSIE...
MY ROSIE...
SHAA

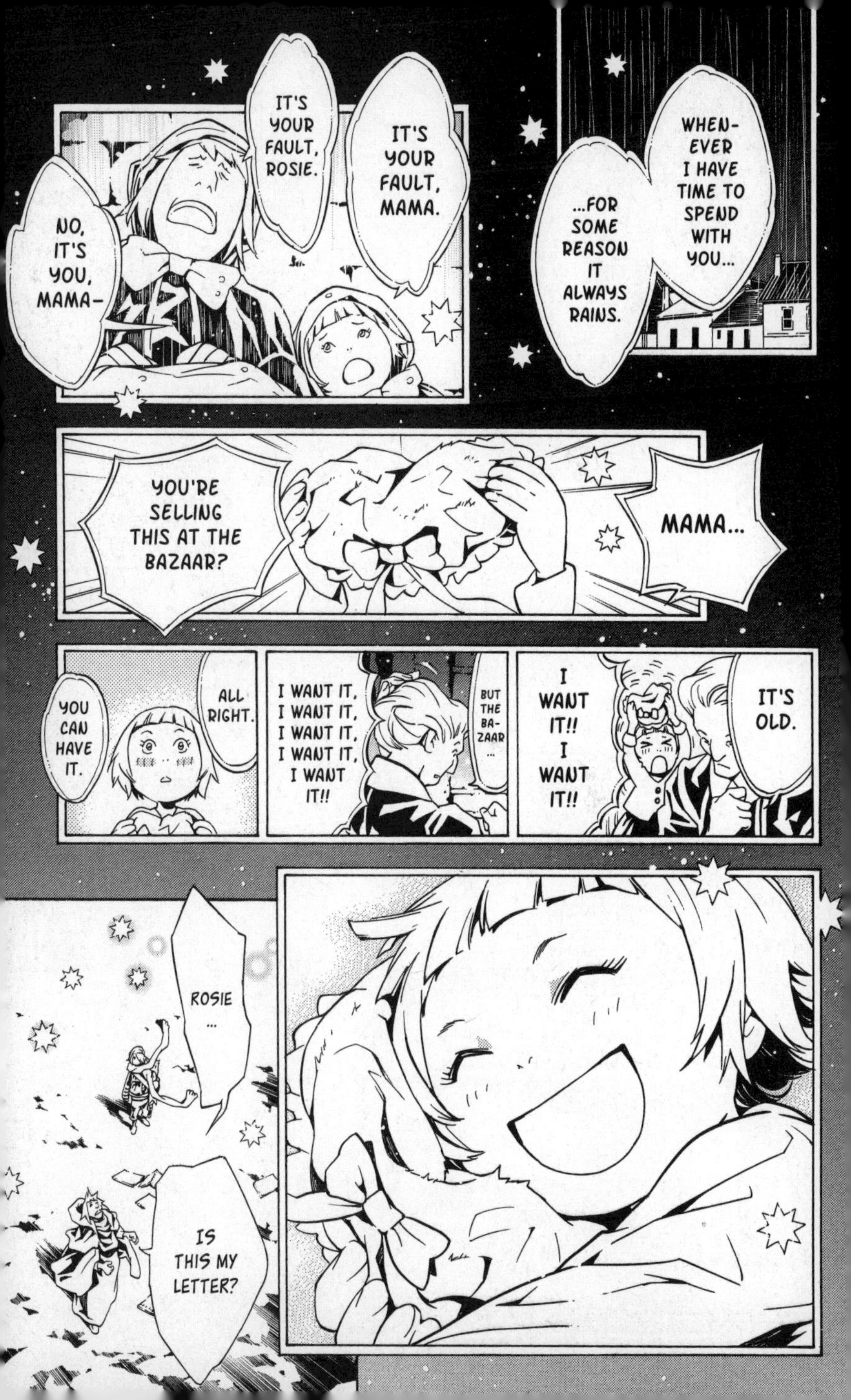
WHEN-EVER I HAVE TIME TO SPEND WITH YOU...
...FOR SOME REASON IT ALWAYS RAINS.
IT'S YOUR FAULT, MAMA.
IT'S YOUR FAULT, ROSIE.
NO, IT'S YOU, MAMA—
MAMA...
YOU'RE SELLING THIS AT THE BAZAAR?
IT'S OLD.
I WANT IT!! I WANT IT!!
BUT THE BAZAAR...
I WANT IT, I WANT IT, I WANT IT, I WANT IT, I WANT IT!!
ALL RIGHT.
YOU CAN HAVE IT.
ROSIE...
IS THIS MY LETTER?

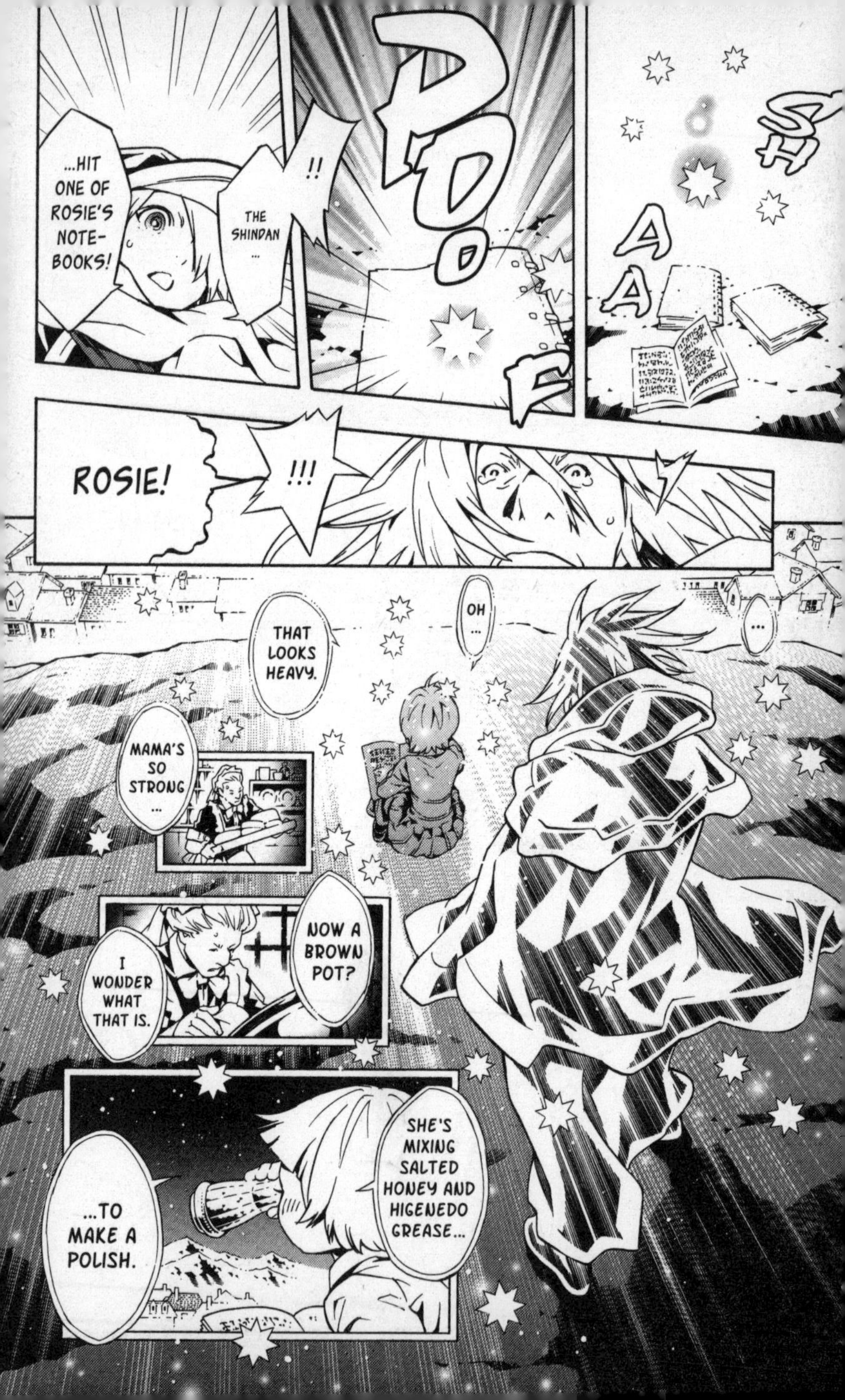
SHAAA
DOOF
!!
THE SHINDAN ...
...HIT ONE OF ROSIE'S NOTE-BOOKS!
!!!
ROSIE!
...
OH ...
THAT LOOKS HEAVY.
MAMA'S SO STRONG ...
NOW A BROWN POT?
I WONDER WHAT THAT IS.
SHE'S MIXING SALTED HONEY AND HIGENEDO GREASE...
...TO MAKE A POLISH.

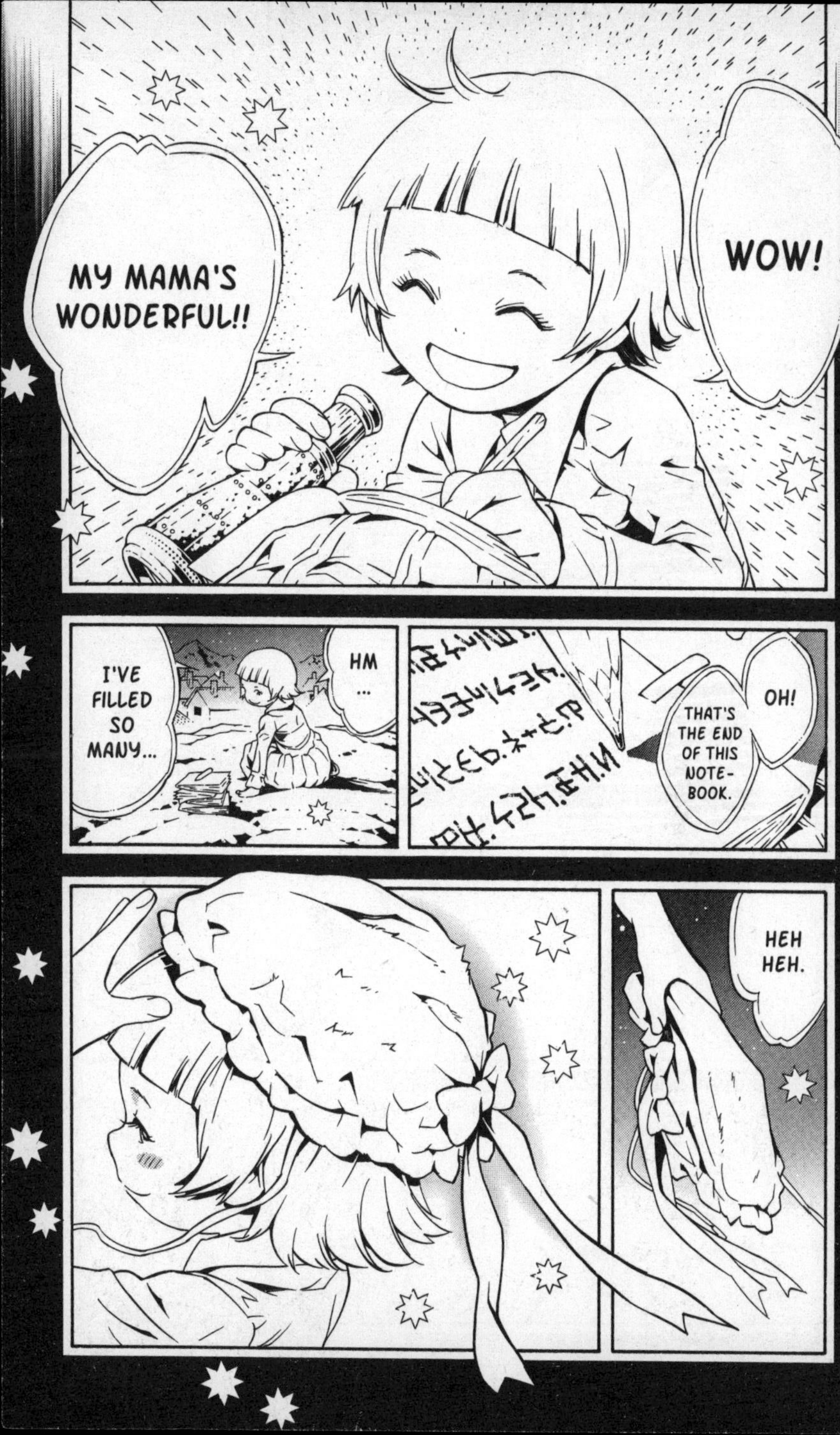
WOW!
MY MAMA'S WONDERFUL!!
OH!
THAT'S THE END OF THIS NOTE-BOOK.
HM ...
I'VE FILLED SO MANY...
HEH HEH.

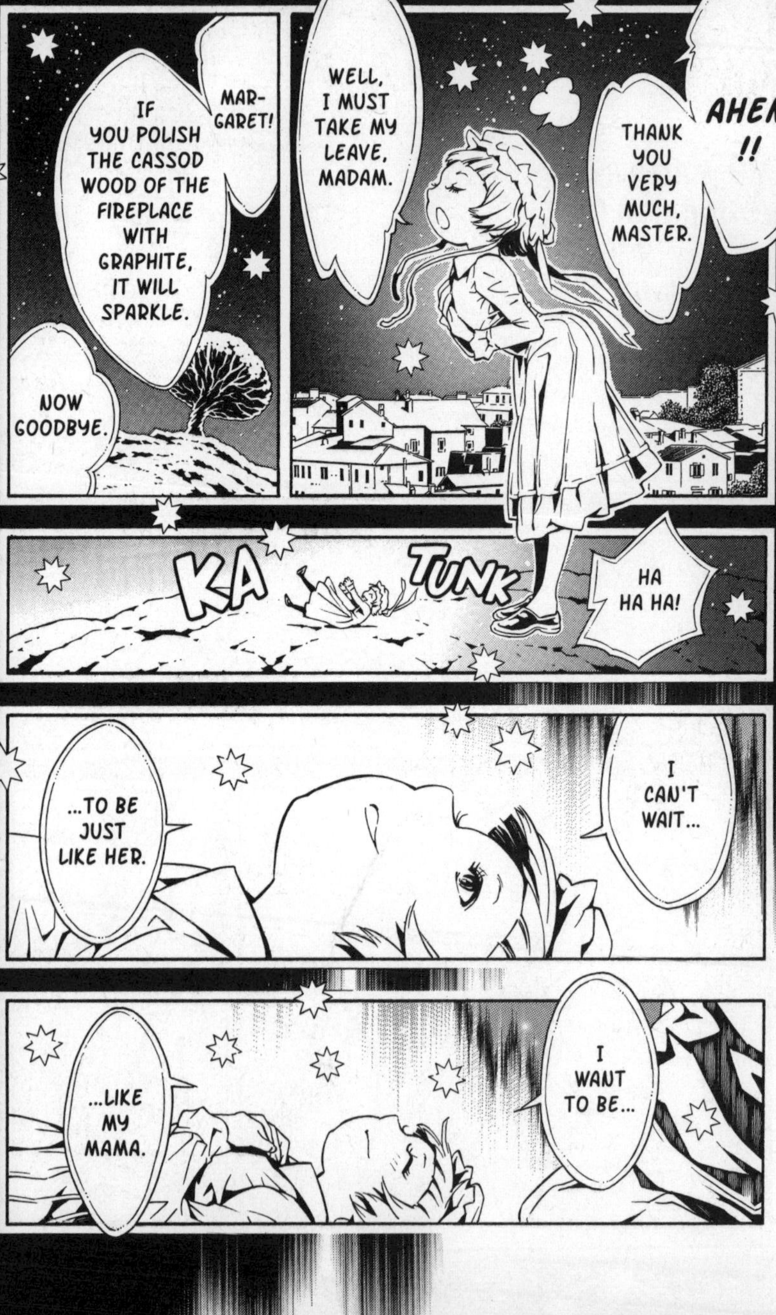
AHEM !!
THANK YOU VERY MUCH, MASTER.
WELL, I MUST TAKE MY LEAVE, MADAM.
MARGARET!
IF YOU POLISH THE CASSOD WOOD OF THE FIREPLACE WITH GRAPHITE, IT WILL SPARKLE.
NOW GOODBYE.
HA HA HA!
KA TUNK
I CAN'T WAIT...
...TO BE JUST LIKE HER.
I WANT TO BE...
...LIKE MY MAMA.

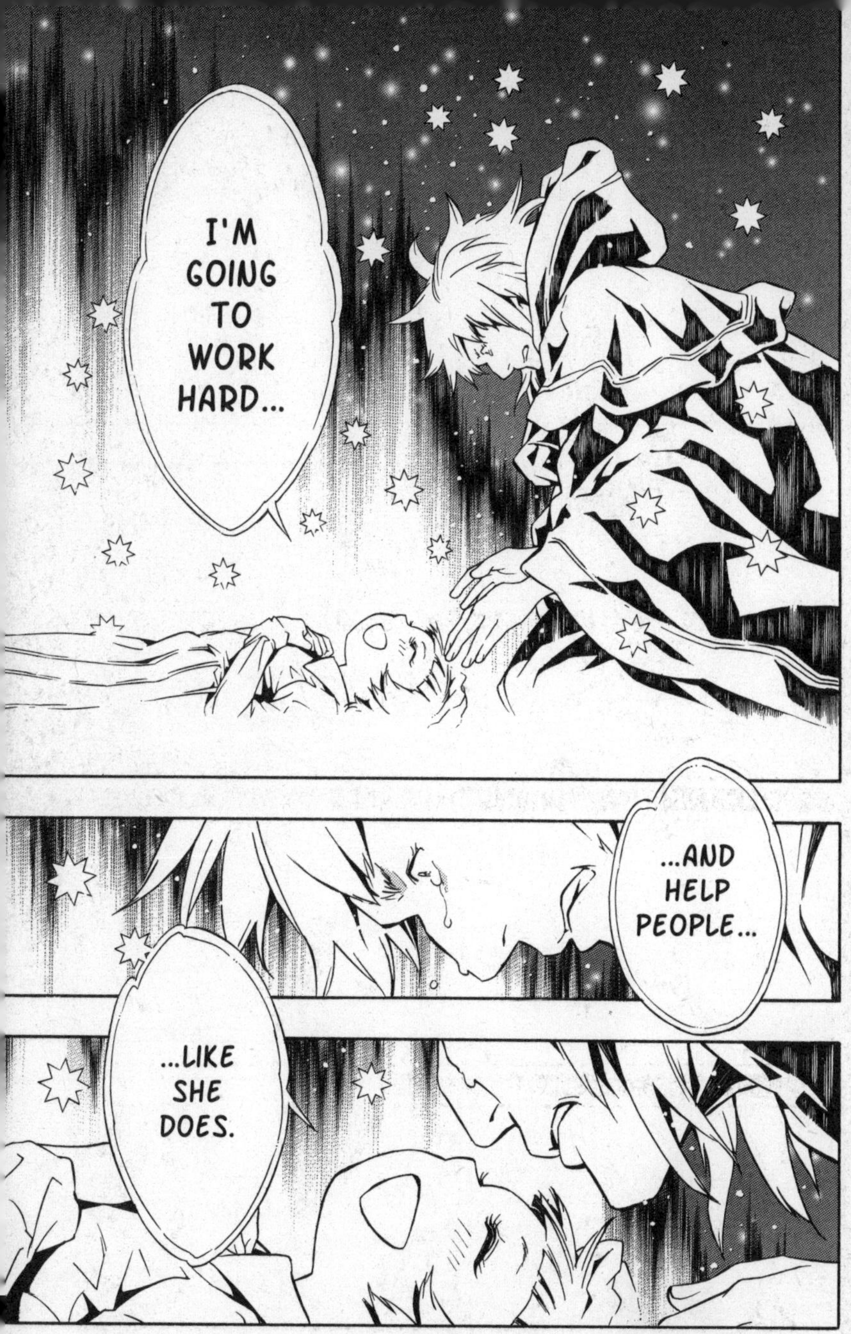
I'M GOING TO WORK HARD...
...AND HELP PEOPLE...
...LIKE SHE DOES.

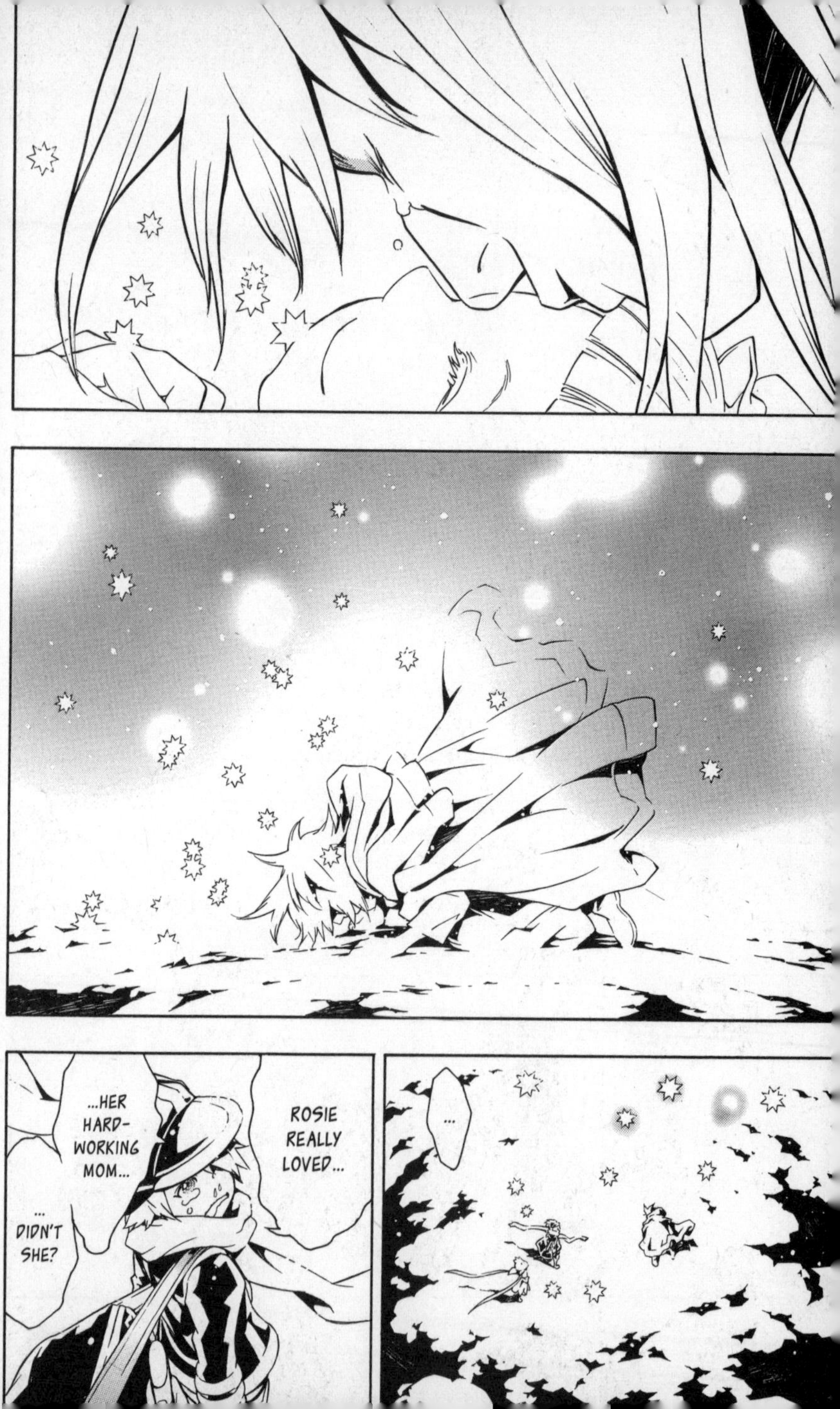
...
ROSIE REALLY LOVED...
...HER HARD-WORKING MOM...
...DIDN'T SHE?

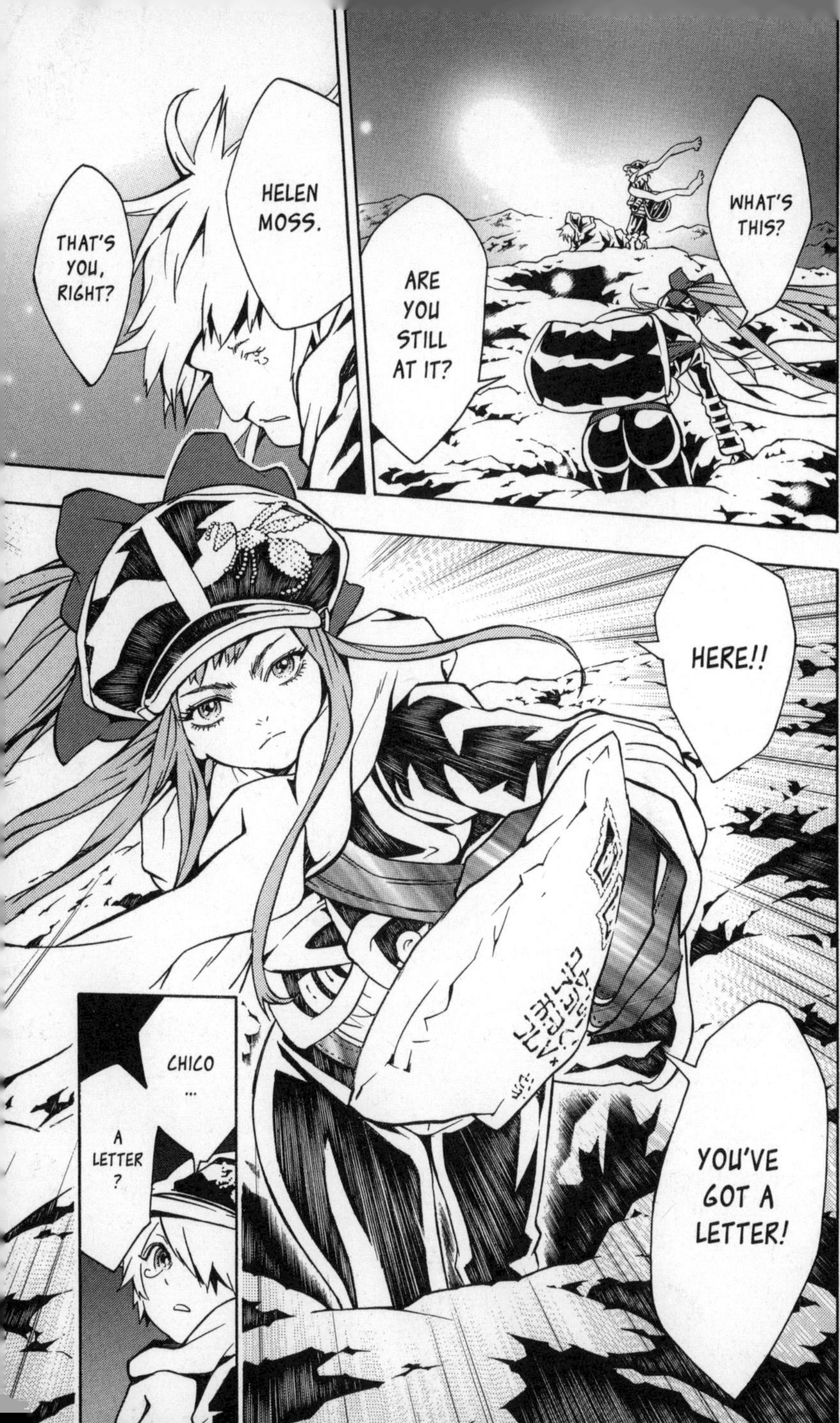

WHAT'S THIS?
ARE YOU STILL AT IT?
HELEN MOSS.
THAT'S YOU, RIGHT?
HERE!!
YOU'VE GOT A LETTER!
CHICO...
A LETTER?

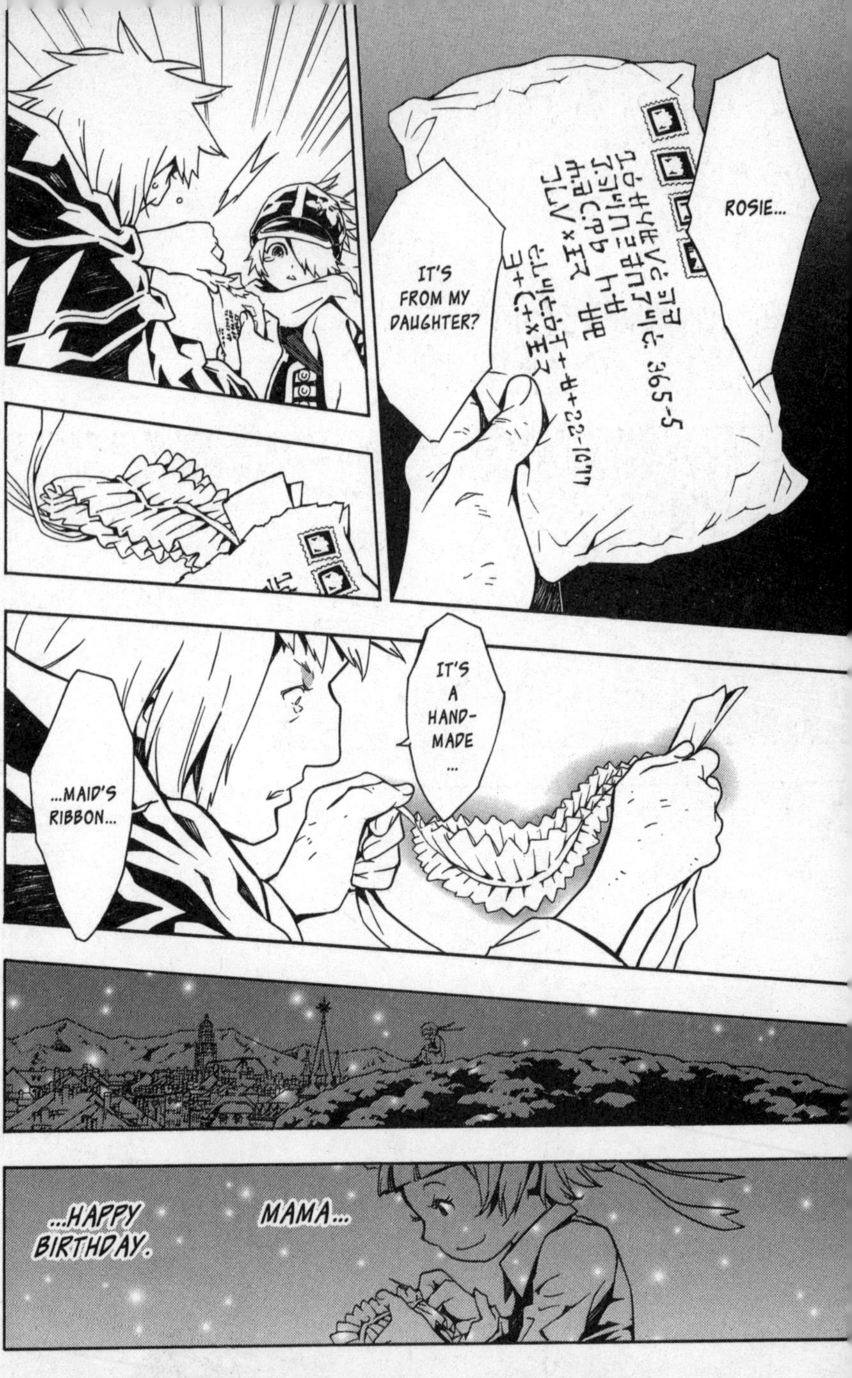
ROSIE...
IT'S FROM MY DAUGHTER?
IT'S A HAND-MADE...
...MAID'S RIBBON...
MAMA...
...HAPPY BIRTHDAY.

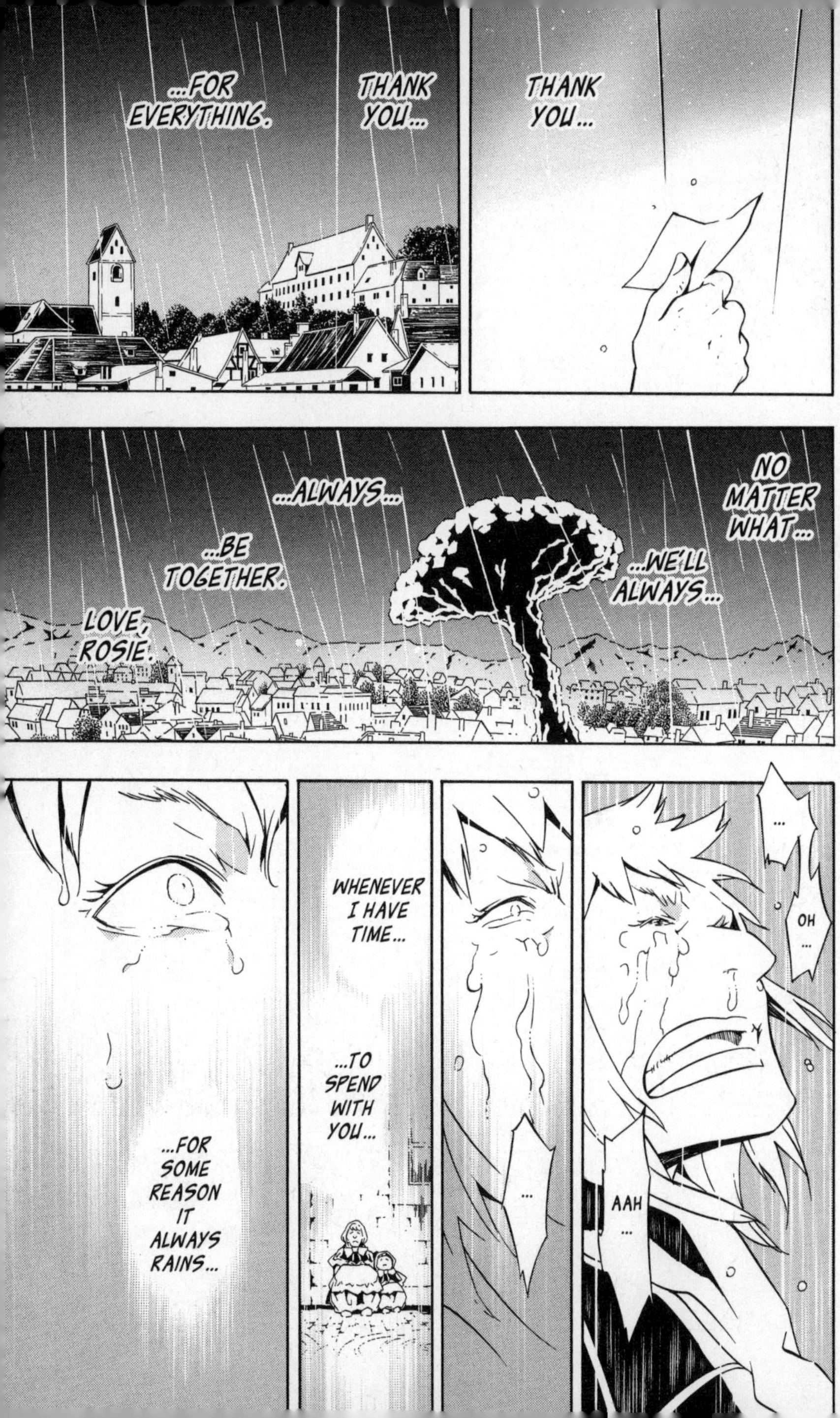
THANK YOU...
THANK YOU...
...FOR EVERYTHING.
NO MATTER WHAT...
...WE'LL ALWAYS...
...ALWAYS...
...BE TOGETHER.
LOVE, ROSIE.
...
OH ...
AAH ...
...
WHENEVER I HAVE TIME...
...TO SPEND WITH YOU...
...FOR SOME REASON IT ALWAYS RAINS...

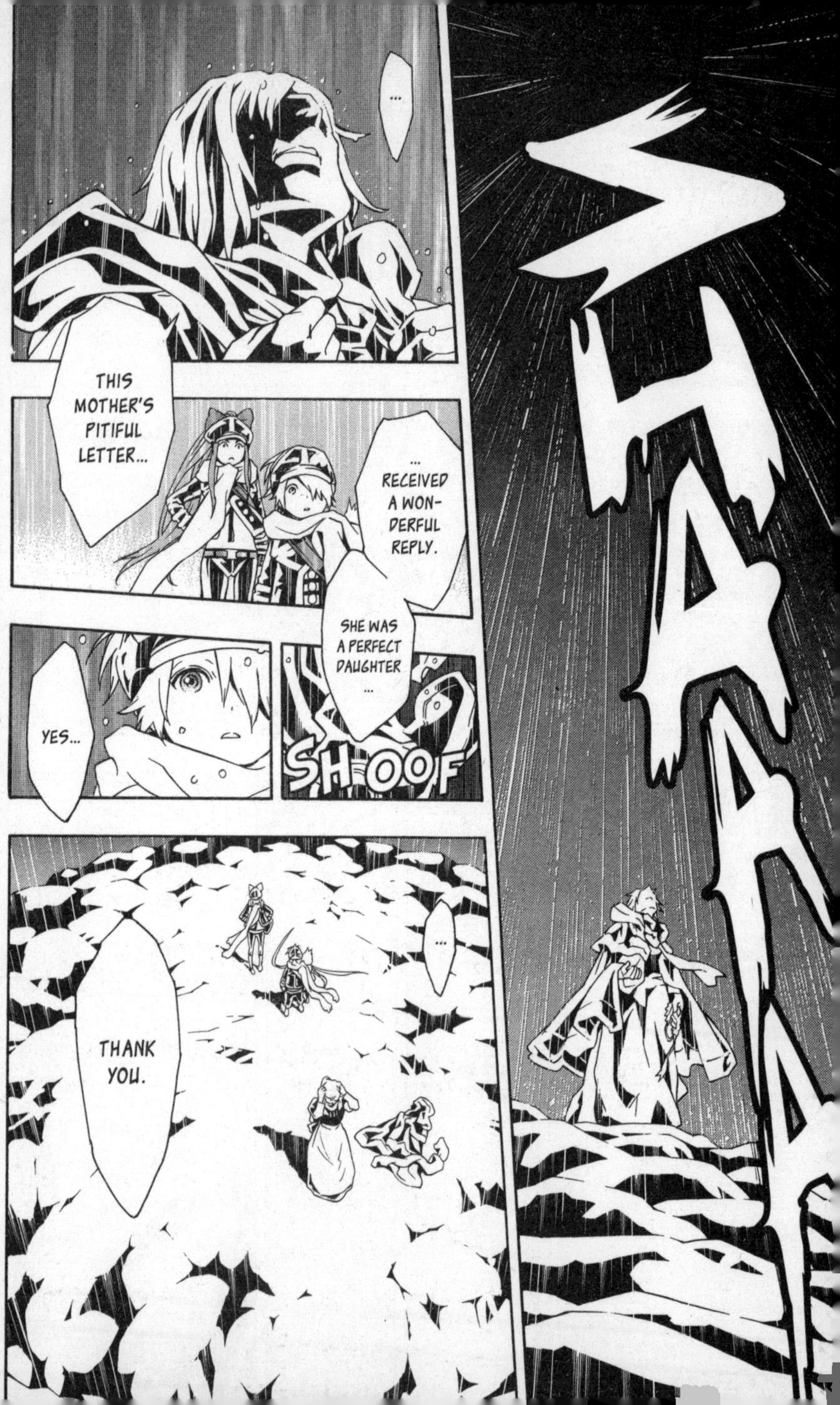
HAHA
...
THIS MOTHER'S PITIFUL LETTER...
...RECEIVED A WON-DERFUL REPLY.
SHE WAS A PERFECT DAUGHTER...
SHOOF
YES...
...
THANK YOU.

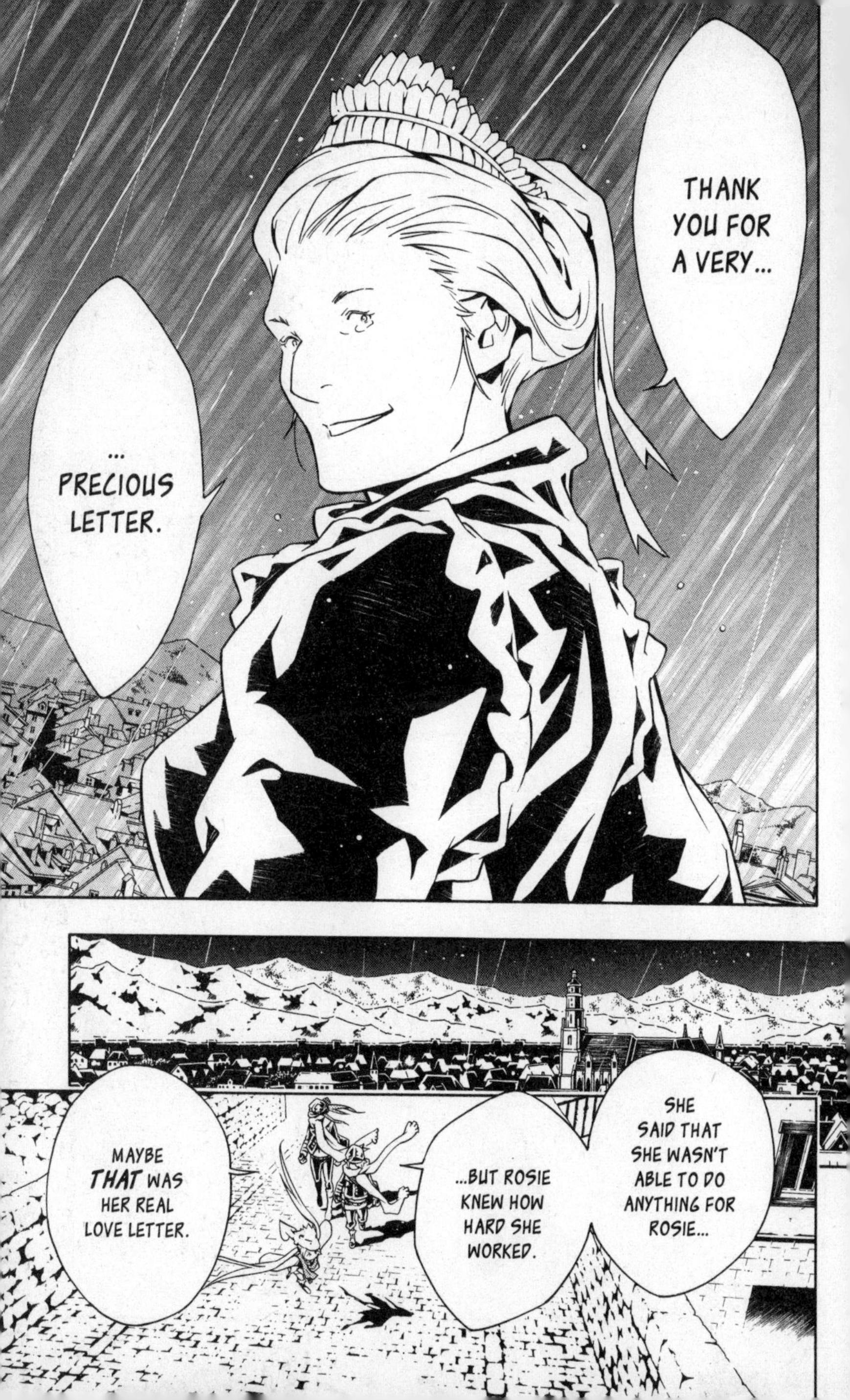
THANK YOU FOR A VERY...
...PRECIOUS LETTER.
SHE SAID THAT SHE WASN'T ABLE TO DO ANYTHING FOR ROSIE...
...BUT ROSIE KNEW HOW HARD SHE WORKED.
MAYBE THAT WAS HER REAL LOVE LETTER.

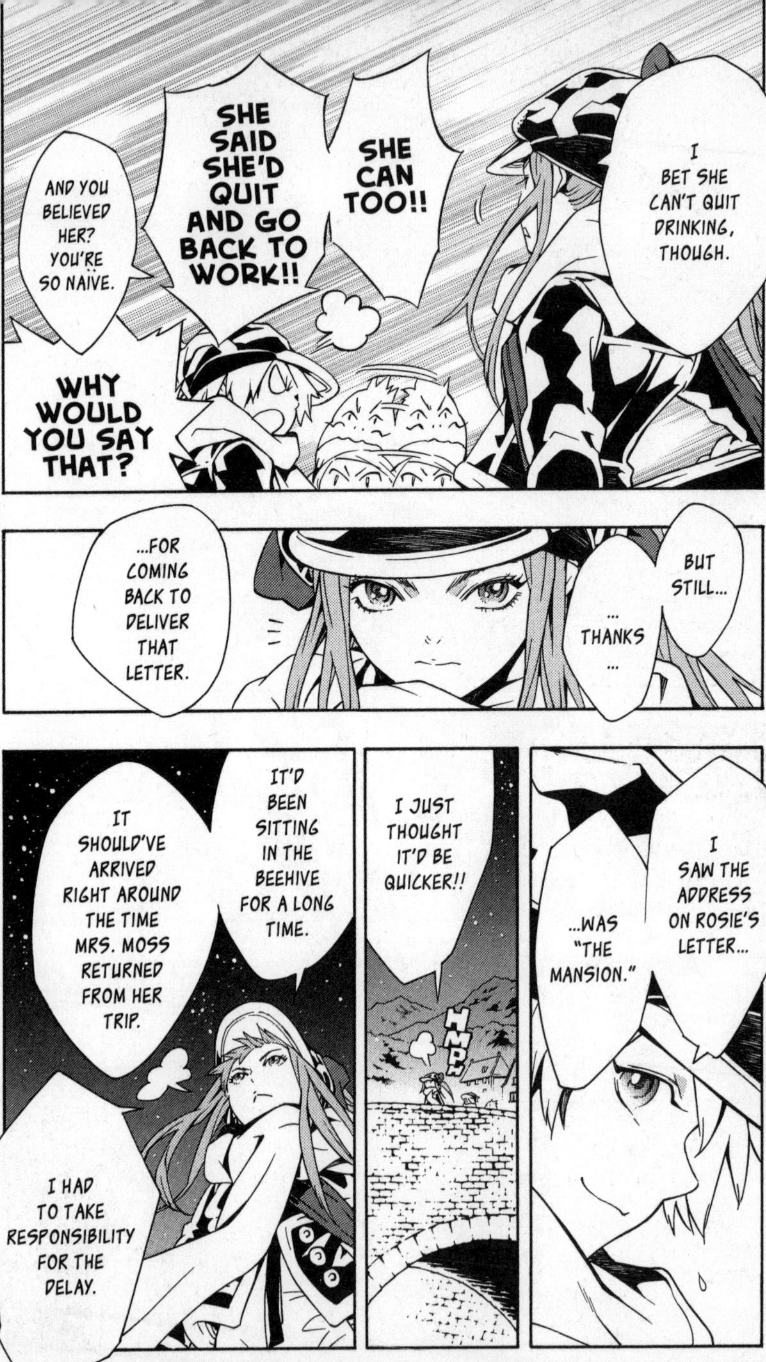
I BET SHE CAN'T QUIT DRINKING, THOUGH.
SHE CAN TOO!!
SHE SAID SHE'D QUIT AND GO BACK TO WORK!!
AND YOU BELIEVED HER? YOU'RE SO NAÏVE.
WHY WOULD YOU SAY THAT?
BUT STILL...
... THANKS ...
...FOR COMING BACK TO DELIVER THAT LETTER.
I SAW THE ADDRESS ON ROSIE'S LETTER...
...WAS "THE MANSION."
I JUST THOUGHT IT'D BE QUICKER!!
HMPH
IT'D BEEN SITTING IN THE BEEHIVE FOR A LONG TIME.
IT SHOULD'VE ARRIVED RIGHT AROUND THE TIME MRS. MOSS RETURNED FROM HER TRIP.
I HAD TO TAKE RESPONSIBILITY FOR THE DELAY.

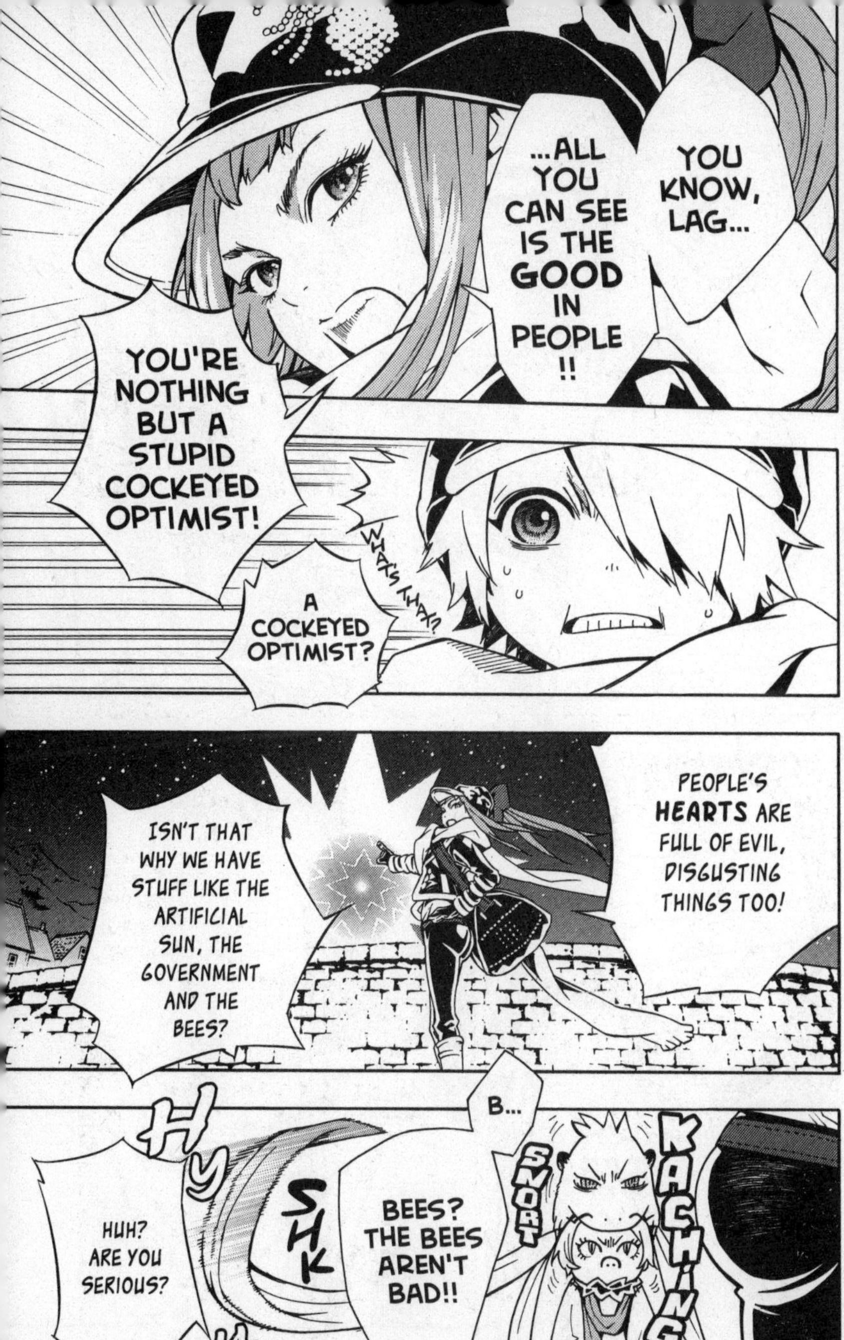
YOU KNOW, LAG...
...ALL YOU CAN SEE IS THE GOOD IN PEOPLE!!
YOU'RE NOTHING BUT A STUPID COCKEYED OPTIMIST!
WHAT'S THAT?
A COCKEYED OPTIMIST?
PEOPLE'S HEARTS ARE FULL OF EVIL, DISGUSTING THINGS TOO!
ISN'T THAT WHY WE HAVE STUFF LIKE THE ARTIFICIAL SUN, THE GOVERNMENT AND THE BEES?
KACHING
SNORT
B...
BEES? THE BEES AREN'T BAD!!
SHK
HY
UU
HUH? ARE YOU SERIOUS?

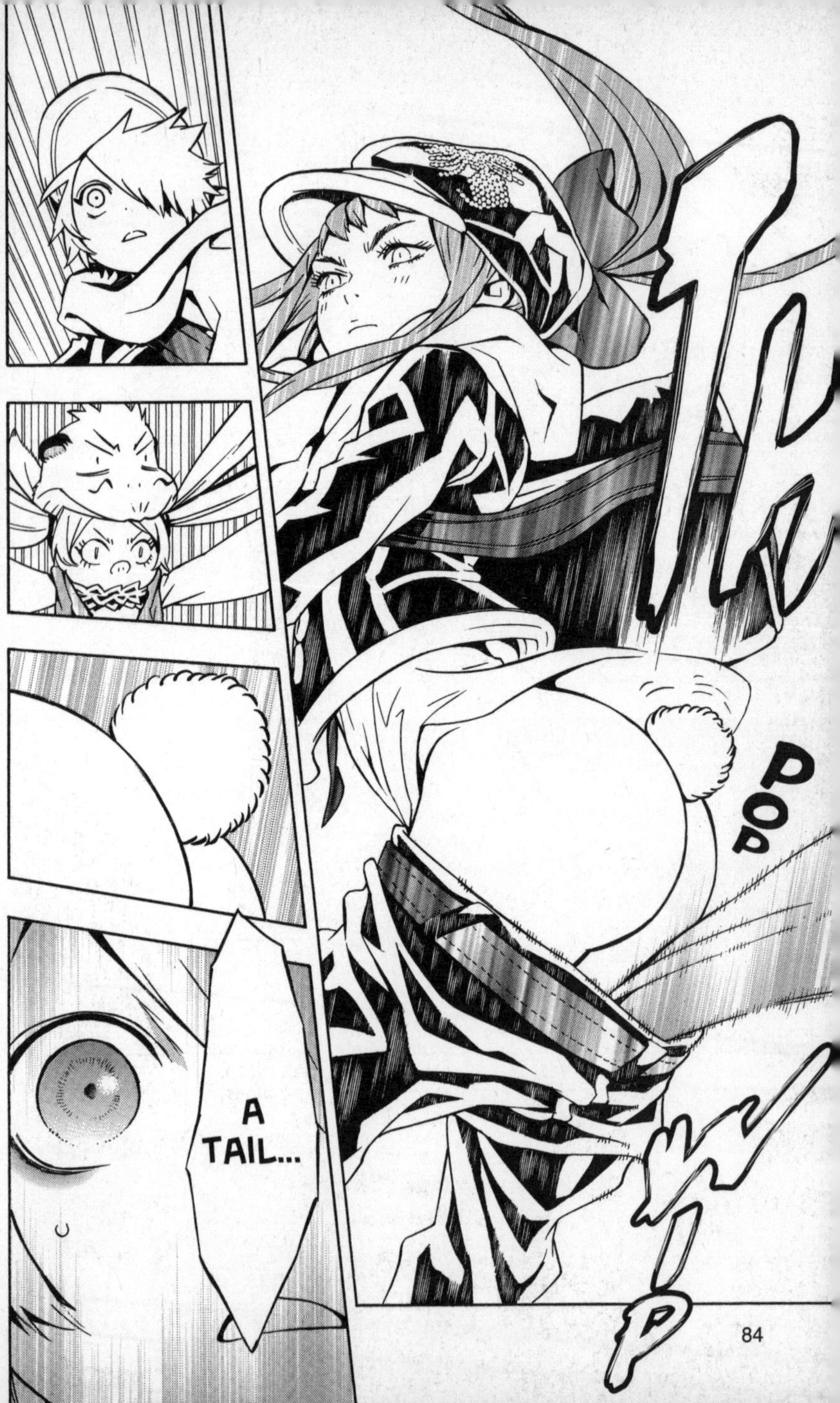
POP
A TAIL...

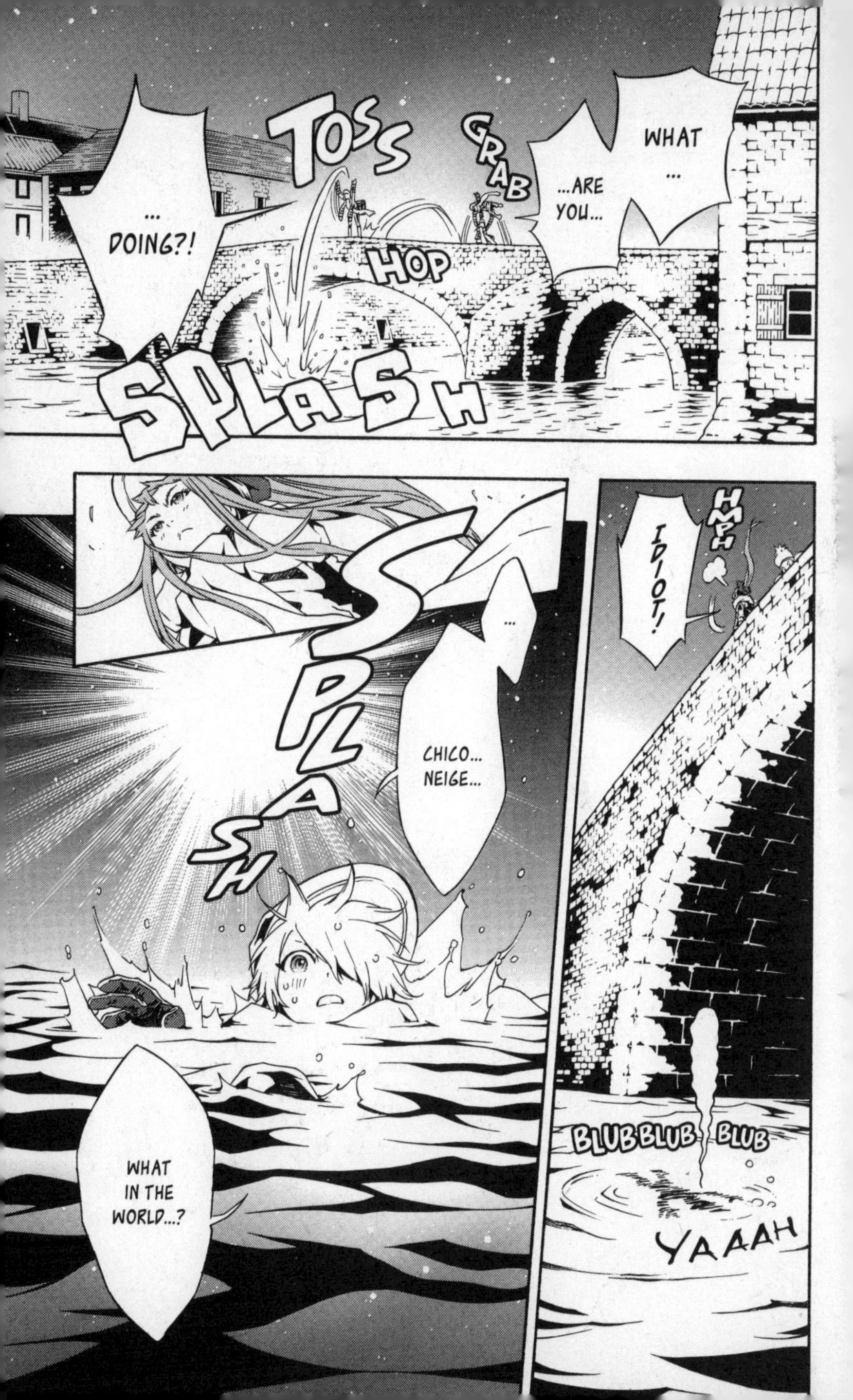
WHAT ...
...ARE YOU...
GRAB
TOSS
HOP
... DOING?!
SPLASH
HMPH
IDIOT!
BLUB BLUB BLUB
YAAAH
...
SPLASH
CHICO... NEIGE...
WHAT IN THE WORLD...?

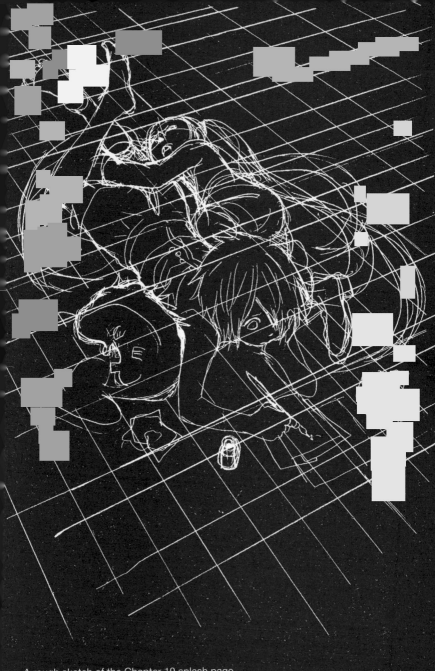

A rough sketch of the Chapter 19 splash page.

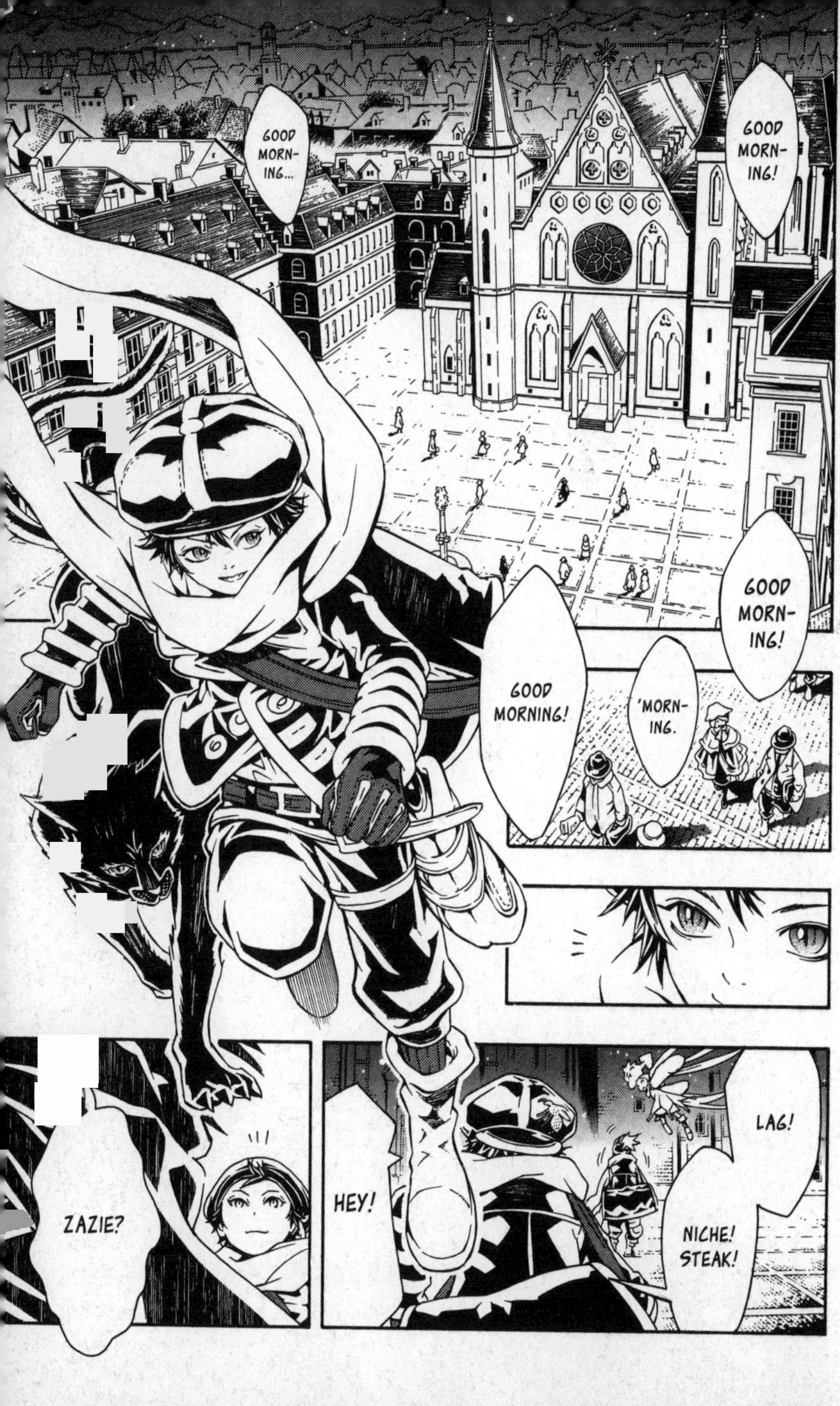
GOOD MORN-ING!
GOOD MORN-ING...
GOOD MORN-ING!
'MORN-ING.
GOOD MORNING!
LAG!
NICHE! STEAK!
HEY!
ZAZIE?

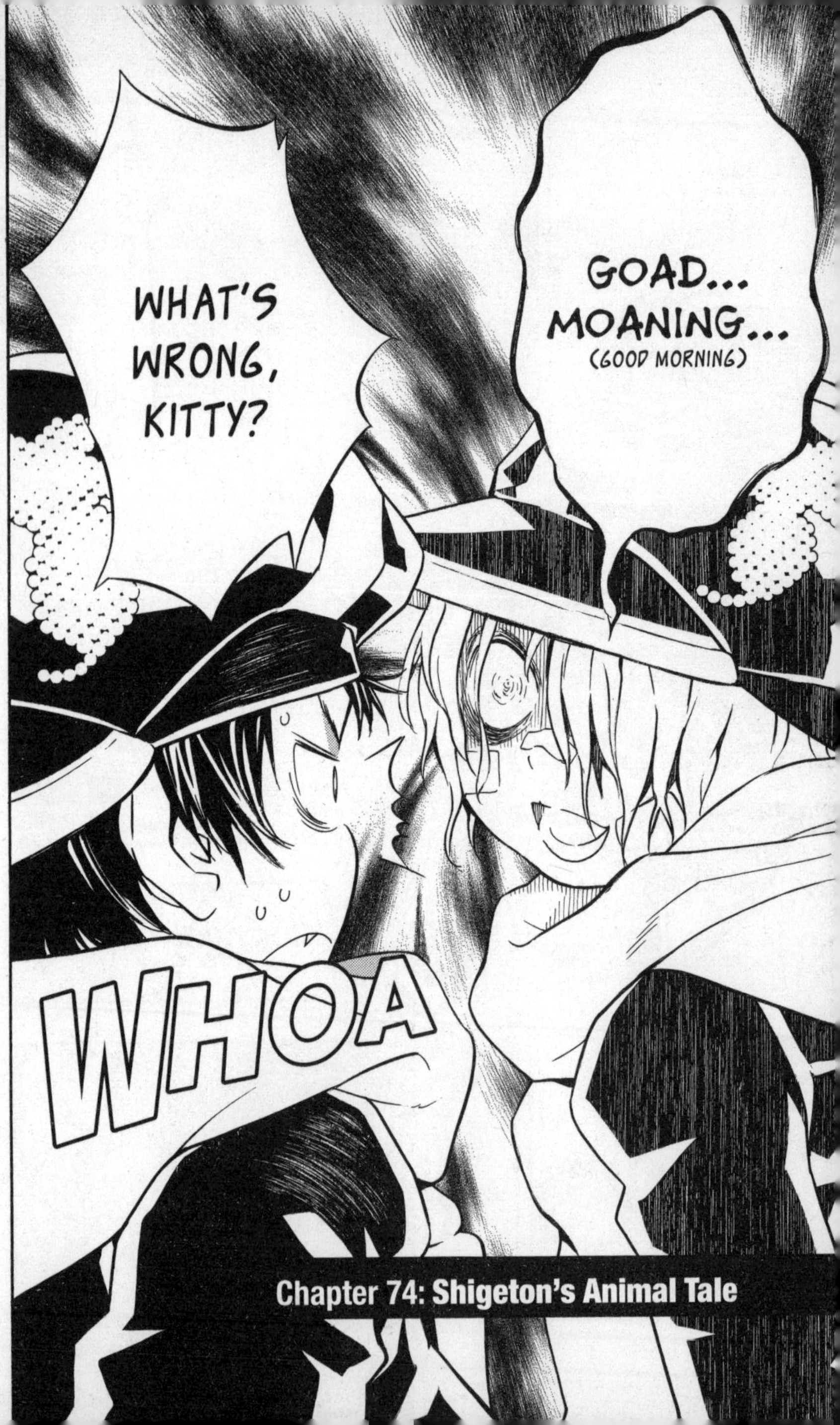
GOAD... MOANING...
(GOOD MORNING)
WHAT'S WRONG, KITTY?
WHOA

Chapter 74: Shigeton's Animal Tale

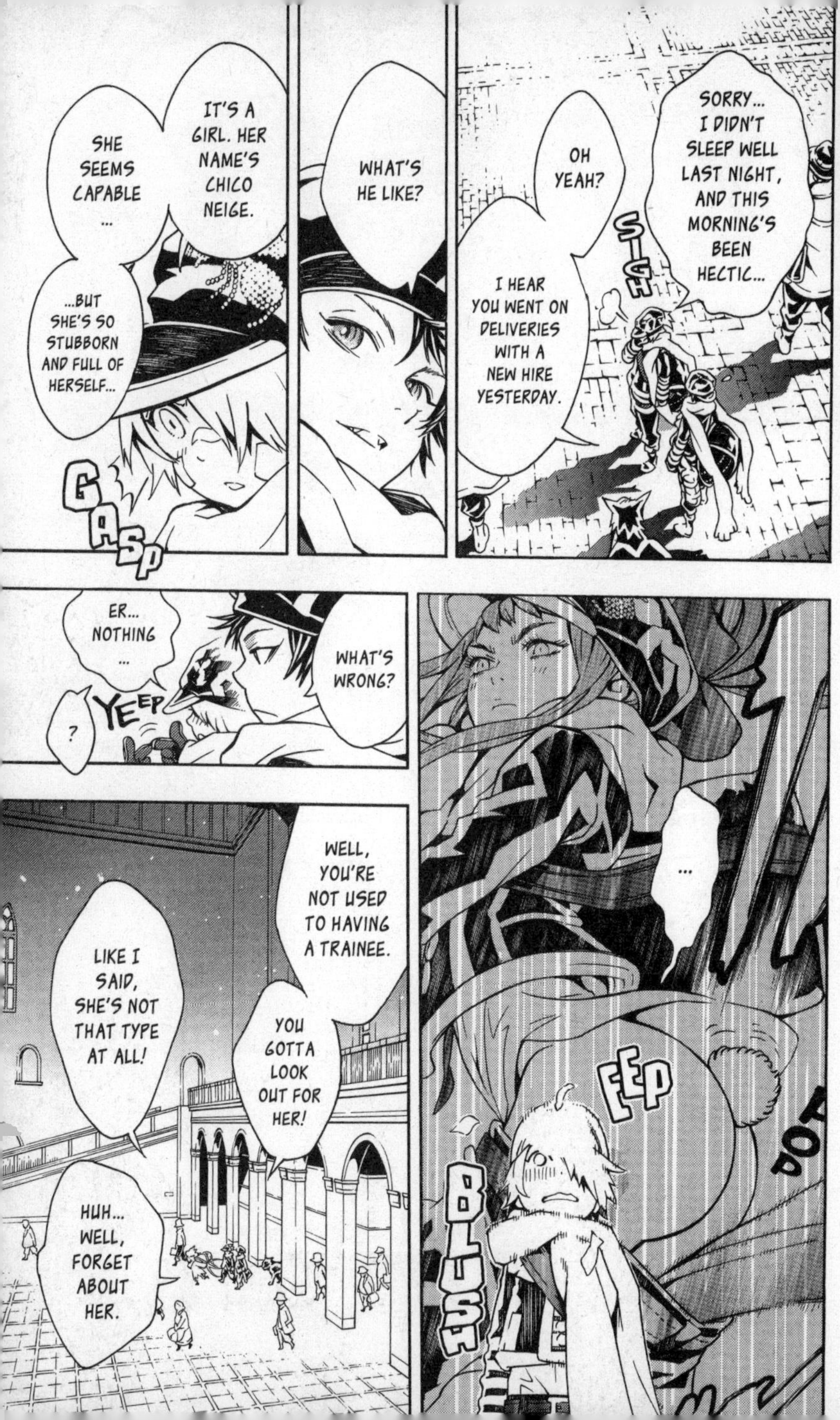
SORRY... I DIDN'T SLEEP WELL LAST NIGHT, AND THIS MORNING'S BEEN HECTIC...
SIGH
OH YEAH?
I HEAR YOU WENT ON DELIVERIES WITH A NEW HIRE YESTERDAY.
WHAT'S HE LIKE?
IT'S A GIRL. HER NAME'S CHICO NEIGE.
SHE SEEMS CAPABLE ...
...BUT SHE'S SO STUBBORN AND FULL OF HERSELF...
GASP
...
FEEP
DOT
BLUSH
WHAT'S WRONG?
ER... NOTHING ...
YEEP
?
WELL, YOU'RE NOT USED TO HAVING A TRAINEE.
YOU GOTTA LOOK OUT FOR HER!
LIKE I SAID, SHE'S NOT THAT TYPE AT ALL!
HUH... WELL, FORGET ABOUT HER.

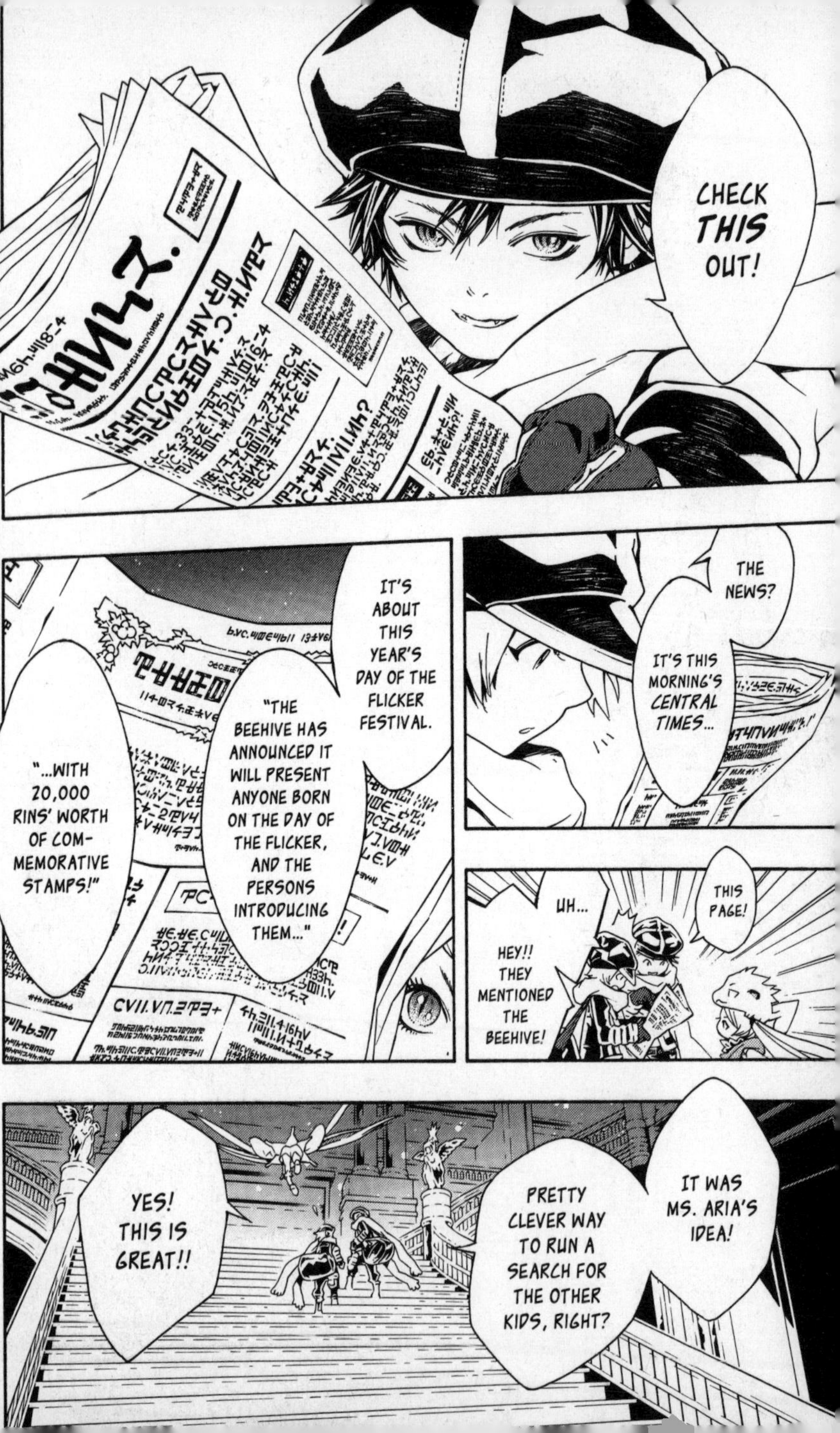
CHECK THIS OUT!
THE NEWS?
IT'S THIS MORNING'S CENTRAL TIMES...
THIS PAGE!
UH...
HEY!! THEY MENTIONED THE BEEHIVE!
IT'S ABOUT THIS YEAR'S DAY OF THE FLICKER FESTIVAL.
"THE BEEHIVE HAS ANNOUNCED IT WILL PRESENT ANYONE BORN ON THE DAY OF THE FLICKER, AND THE PERSONS INTRODUCING THEM..."
"...WITH 20,000 RINS' WORTH OF COM-MEMORATIVE STAMPS!"
IT WAS MS. ARIA'S IDEA!
PRETTY CLEVER WAY TO RUN A SEARCH FOR THE OTHER KIDS, RIGHT?
YES! THIS IS GREAT!!

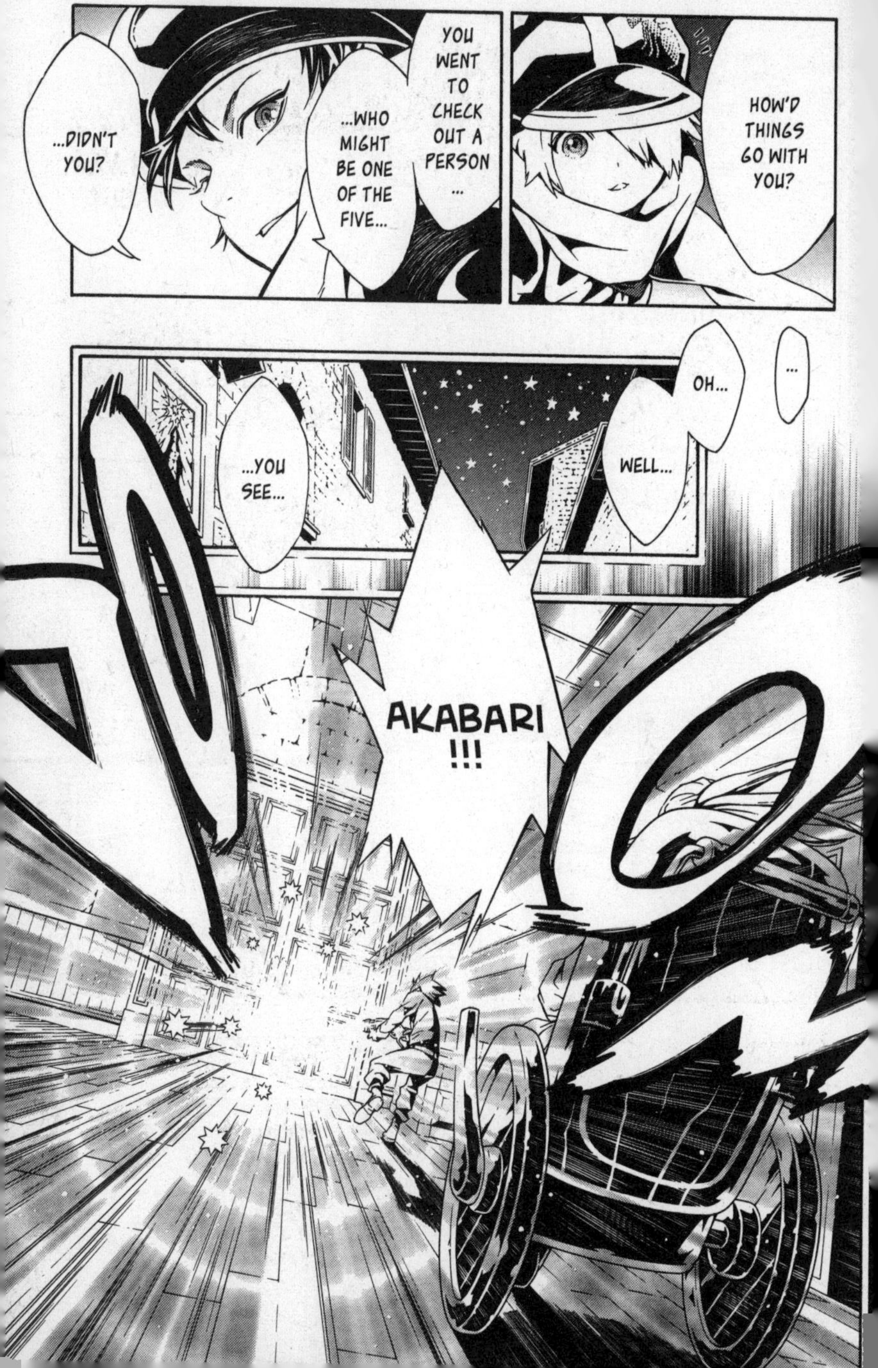
HOW'D THINGS GO WITH YOU?
YOU WENT TO CHECK OUT A PERSON...
...WHO MIGHT BE ONE OF THE FIVE...
...DIDN'T YOU?
...
OH...
WELL...
...YOU SEE...
AKABARI!!!

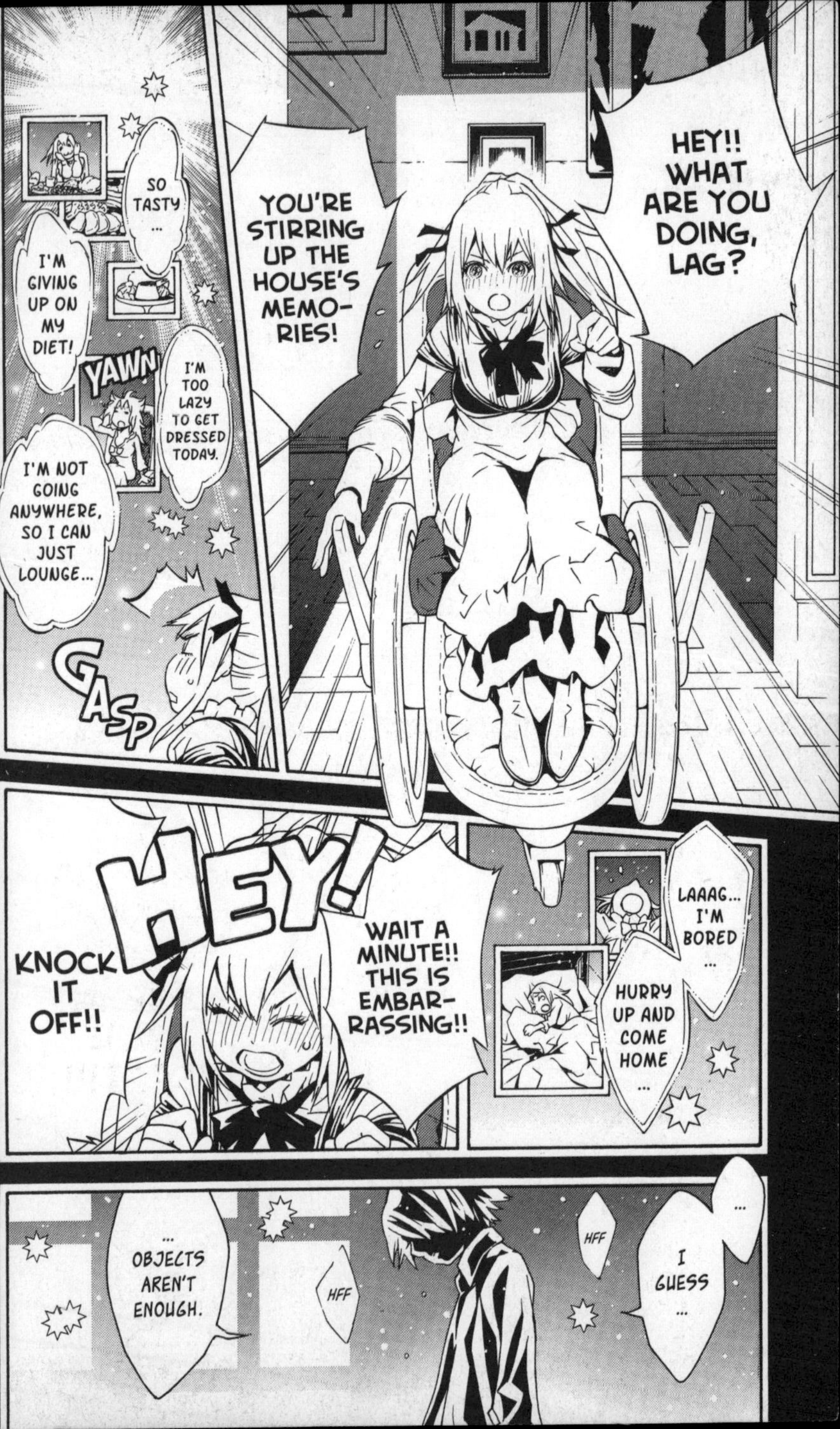
HEY!! WHAT ARE YOU DOING, LAG?
YOU'RE STIRRING UP THE HOUSE'S MEMO-RIES!
SO TASTY ...
I'M GIVING UP ON MY DIET!
YAWN
I'M TOO LAZY TO GET DRESSED TODAY.
I'M NOT GOING ANYWHERE, SO I CAN JUST LOUNGE...
GASP
LAAAG... I'M BORED ...
HURRY UP AND COME HOME ...
HEY!
WAIT A MINUTE!! THIS IS EMBAR-RASSING!!
KNOCK IT OFF!!
... I GUESS ...
HFF
HFF
... OBJECTS AREN'T ENOUGH.

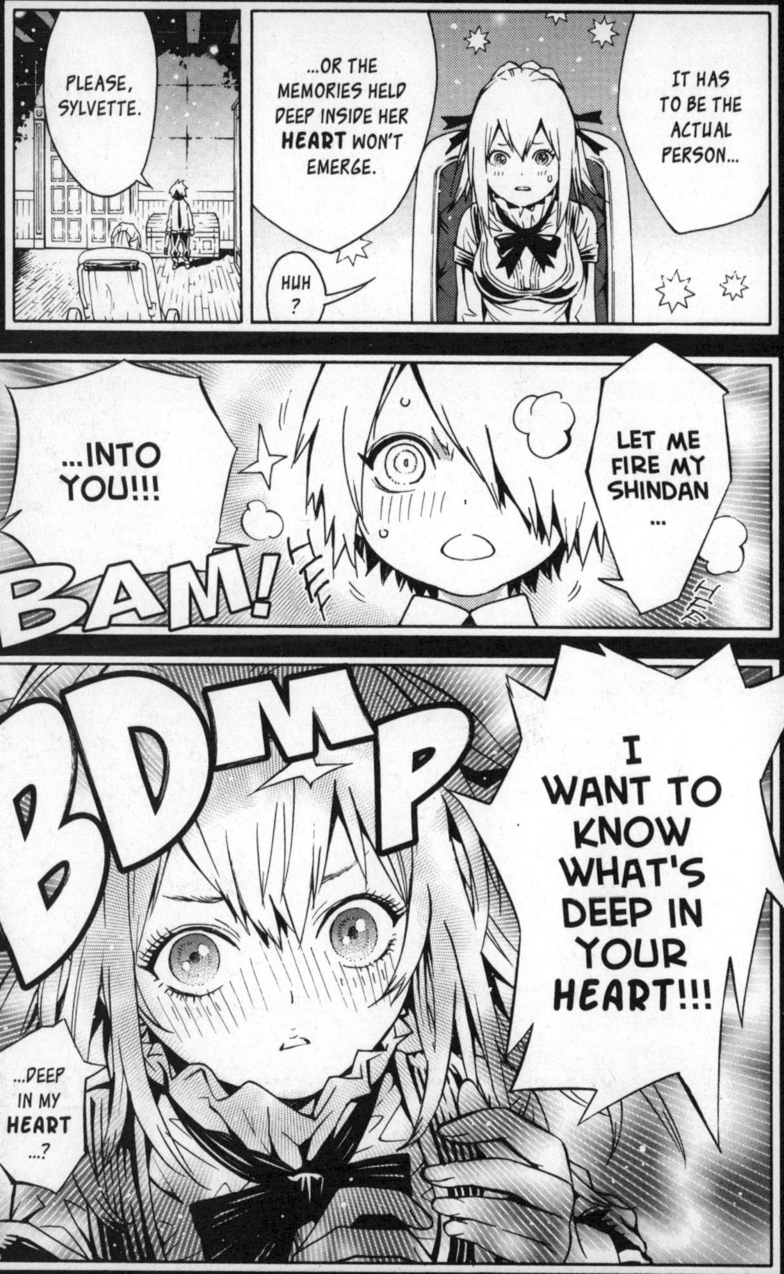
IT HAS TO BE THE ACTUAL PERSON...
...OR THE MEMORIES HELD DEEP INSIDE HER HEART WON'T EMERGE.
HUH?
PLEASE, SYLVETTE.
LET ME FIRE MY SHINDAN ...
...INTO YOU!!!
BAM!
I WANT TO KNOW WHAT'S DEEP IN YOUR HEART!!!
BDMP
...DEEP IN MY HEART ...?

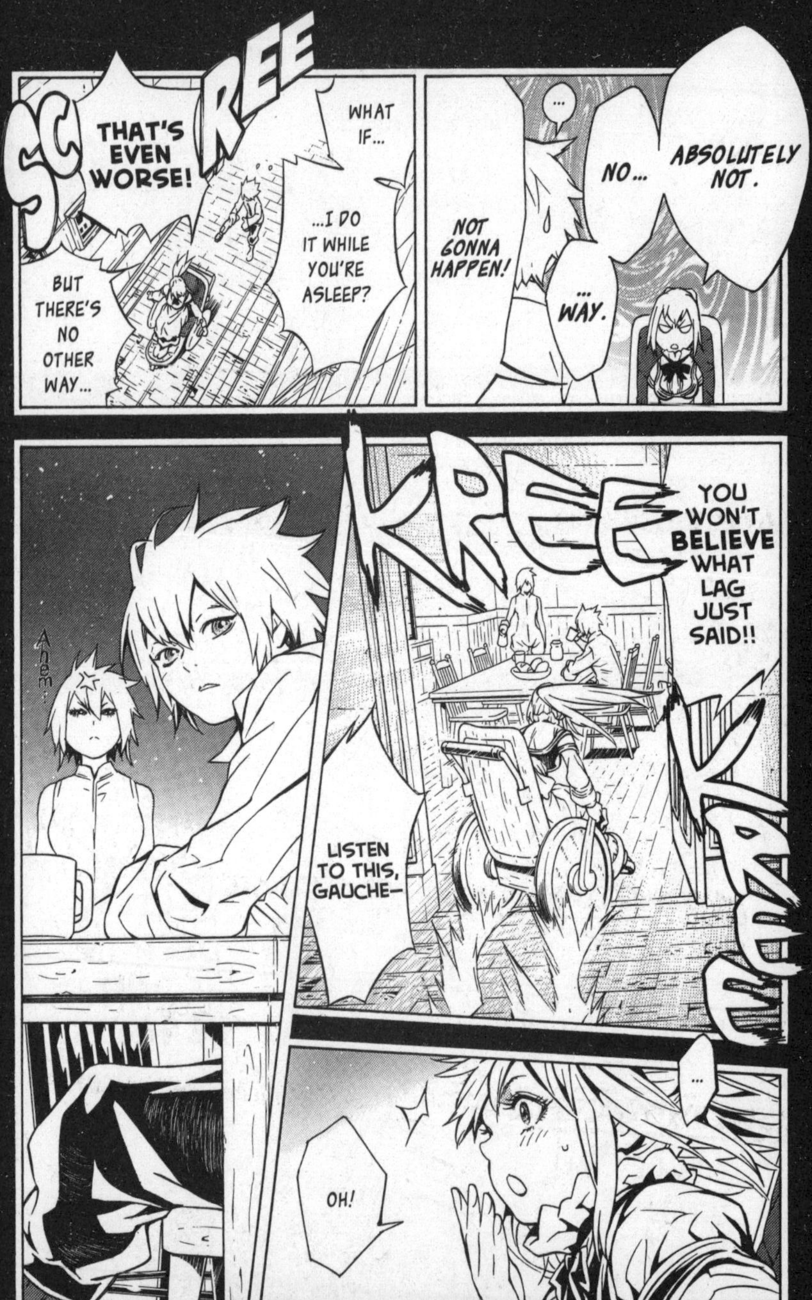
...
ABSOLUTELY NOT.
NO...
NOT GONNA HAPPEN!
... WAY.
SCREE
WHAT IF...
...I DO IT WHILE YOU'RE ASLEEP?
THAT'S EVEN WORSE!
BUT THERE'S NO OTHER WAY...
KREE
YOU WON'T BELIEVE WHAT LAG JUST SAID!!
KREEE
LISTEN TO THIS, GAUCHE—
Ahem!
...
OH!

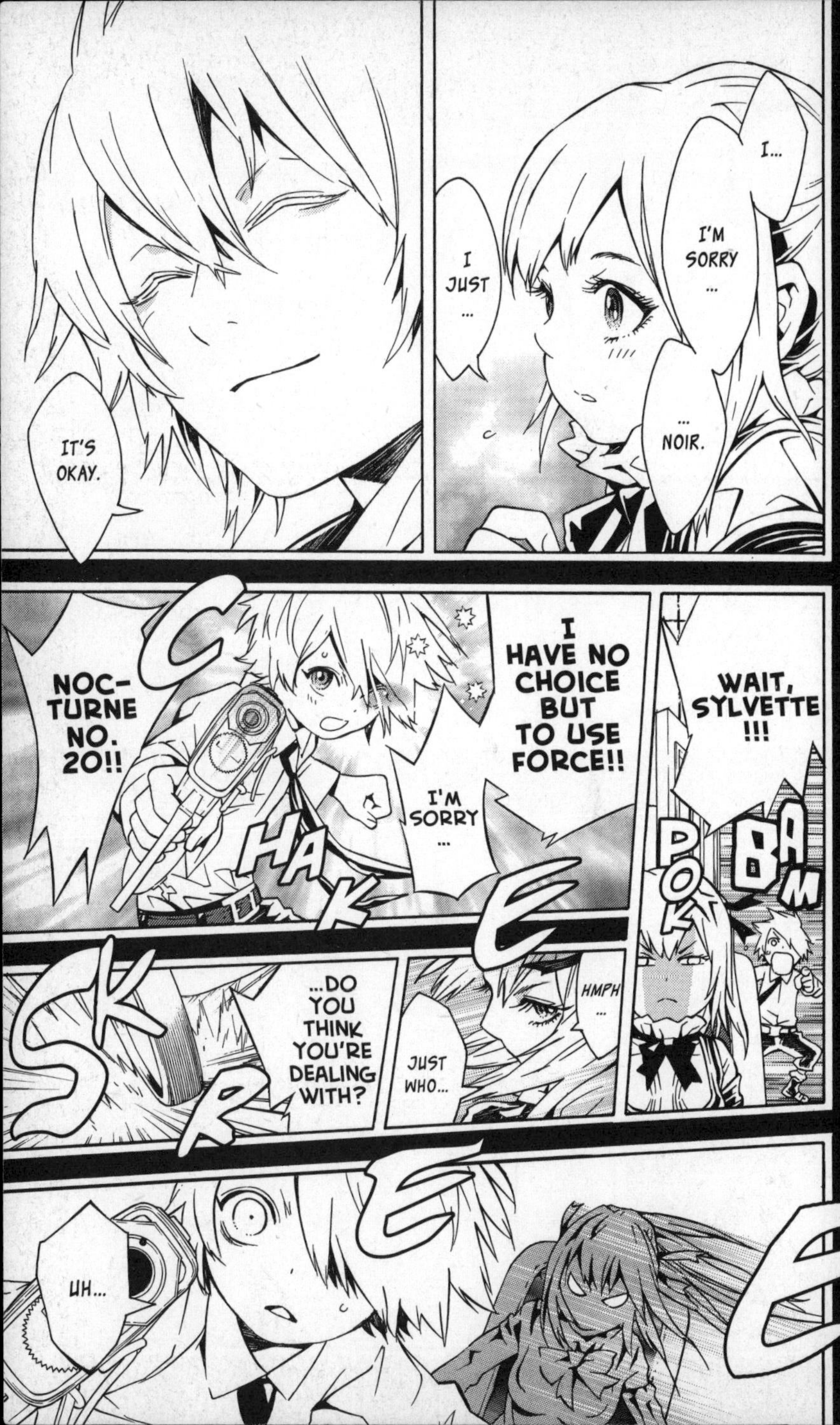
I... I'M SORRY ... ... NOIR.
I JUST ...
IT'S OKAY.
WAIT, SYLVETTE!!!
POK
BAM
I HAVE NO CHOICE BUT TO USE FORCE!!
I'M SORRY ...
NOC-TURNE NO. 20!!
HAK
HMPH ...
JUST WHO...
...DO YOU THINK YOU'RE DEALING WITH?
SKREEE
UH...

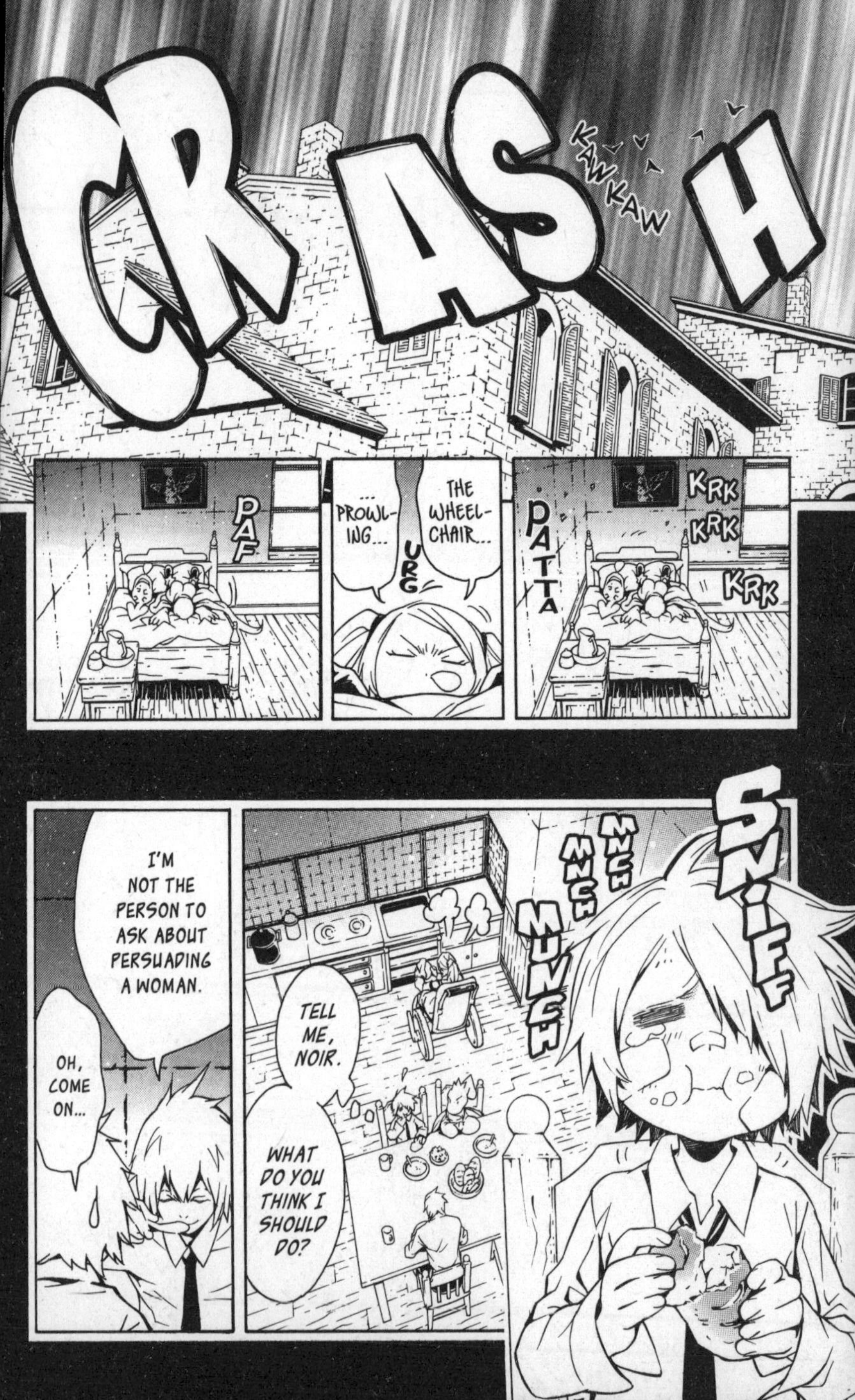
CRASH
KAW KAW
KRK KRK
KRK
PATTA
THE WHEEL-CHAIR...
...PROWLING...
URG
PAF
SNIFF
MNCH MNCH
MUNCH
TELL ME, NOIR.
WHAT DO YOU THINK I SHOULD DO?
I'M NOT THE PERSON TO ASK ABOUT PERSUADING A WOMAN.
OH, COME ON...

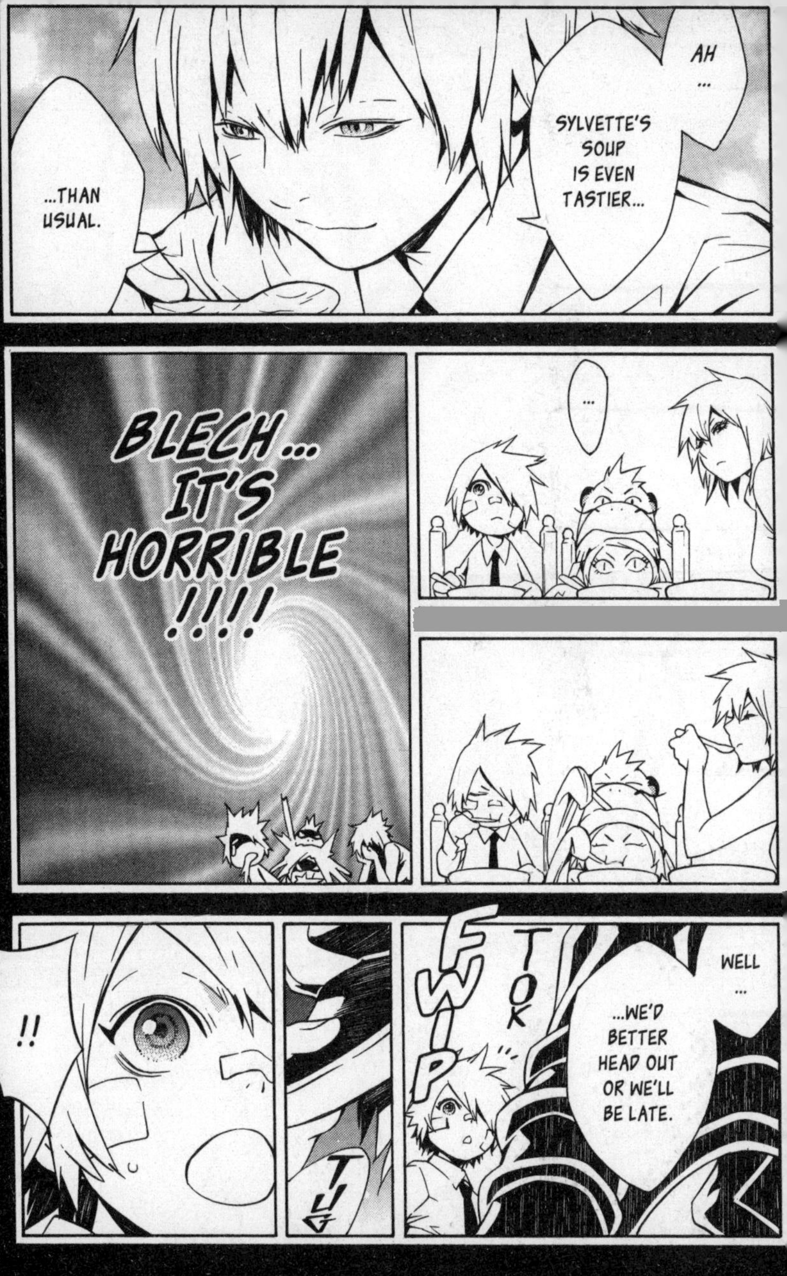
AH ...
SYLVETTE'S SOUP IS EVEN TASTIER...
...THAN USUAL.
...
BLECH... IT'S HORRIBLE !!!!
WELL ...
...WE'D BETTER HEAD OUT OR WE'LL BE LATE.
TOK
FWIP
TUG
!!

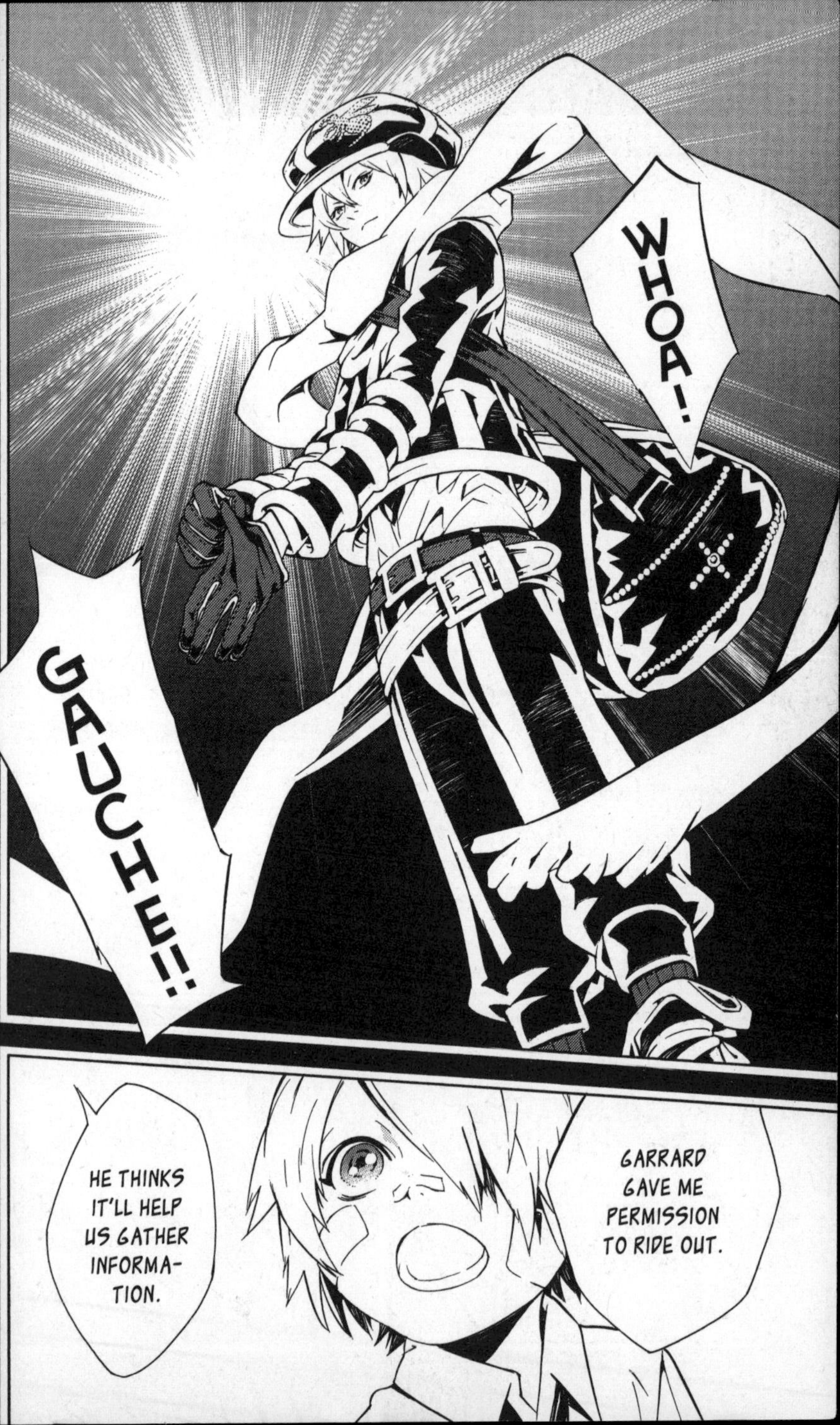
WHOA!!
GAUCHE!!
GARRARD GAVE ME PERMISSION TO RIDE OUT.
HE THINKS IT'LL HELP US GATHER INFORMATION.

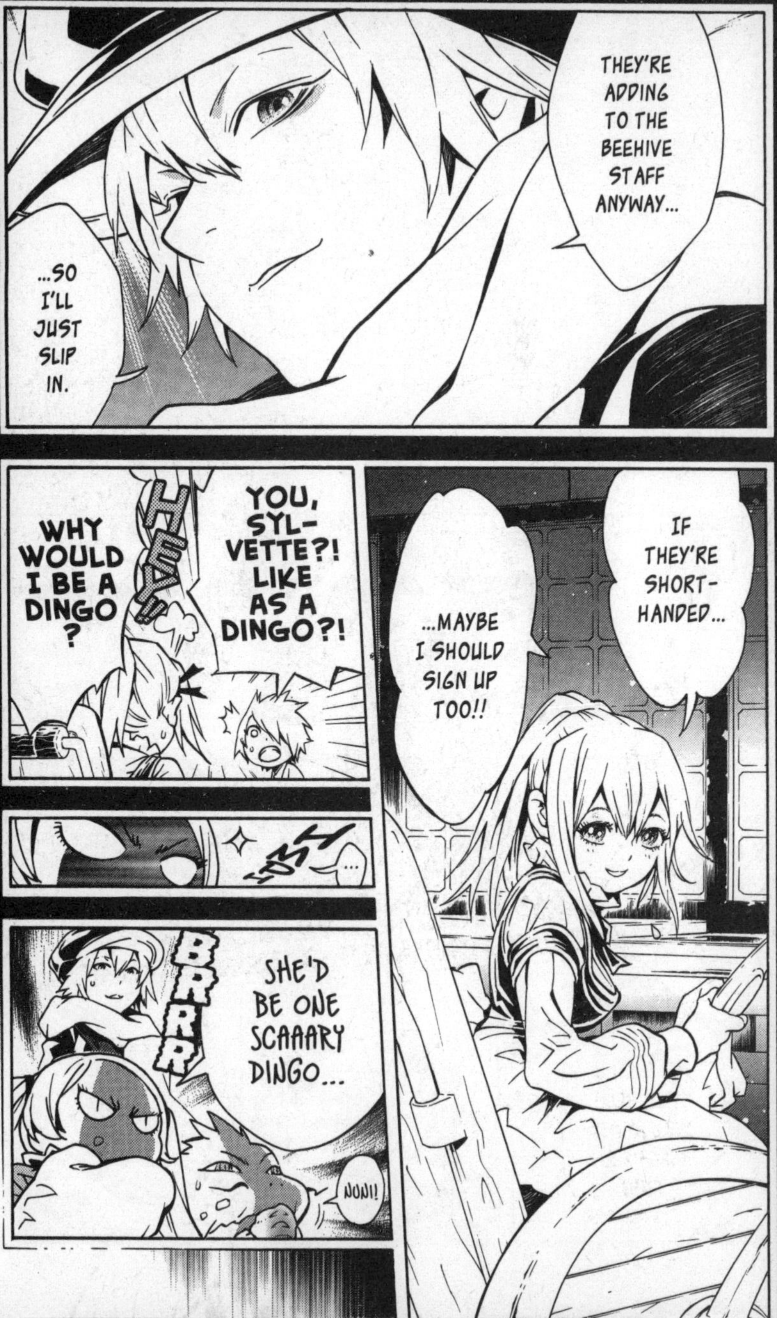
THEY'RE ADDING TO THE BEEHIVE STAFF ANYWAY...
...SO I'LL JUST SLIP IN.
IF THEY'RE SHORT-HANDED...
...MAYBE I SHOULD SIGN UP TOO!!
YOU, SYL-VETTE?! LIKE AS A DINGO?!
HEY!!
WHY WOULD I BE A DINGO?
...
SHE'D BE ONE SCAAARY DINGO...
BRRR
NUNI!

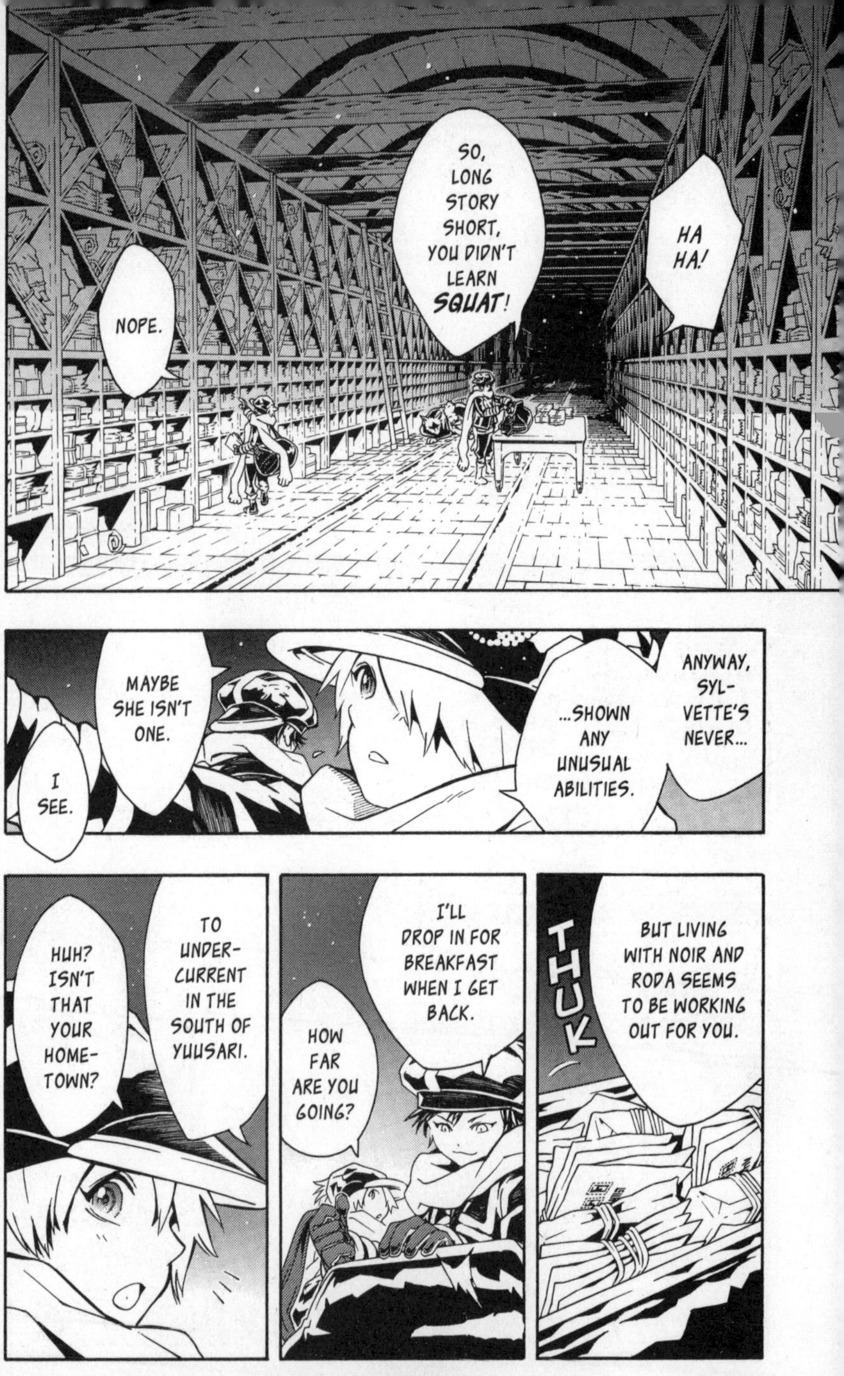
HA HA!
SO, LONG STORY SHORT, YOU DIDN'T LEARN SQUAT!
NOPE.
ANYWAY, SYLVETTE'S NEVER...
...SHOWN ANY UNUSUAL ABILITIES.
MAYBE SHE ISN'T ONE.
I SEE.
THUK
BUT LIVING WITH NOIR AND RODA SEEMS TO BE WORKING OUT FOR YOU.
I'LL DROP IN FOR BREAKFAST WHEN I GET BACK.
HOW FAR ARE YOU GOING?
TO UNDER-CURRENT IN THE SOUTH OF YUUSARI.
HUH? ISN'T THAT YOUR HOME-TOWN?

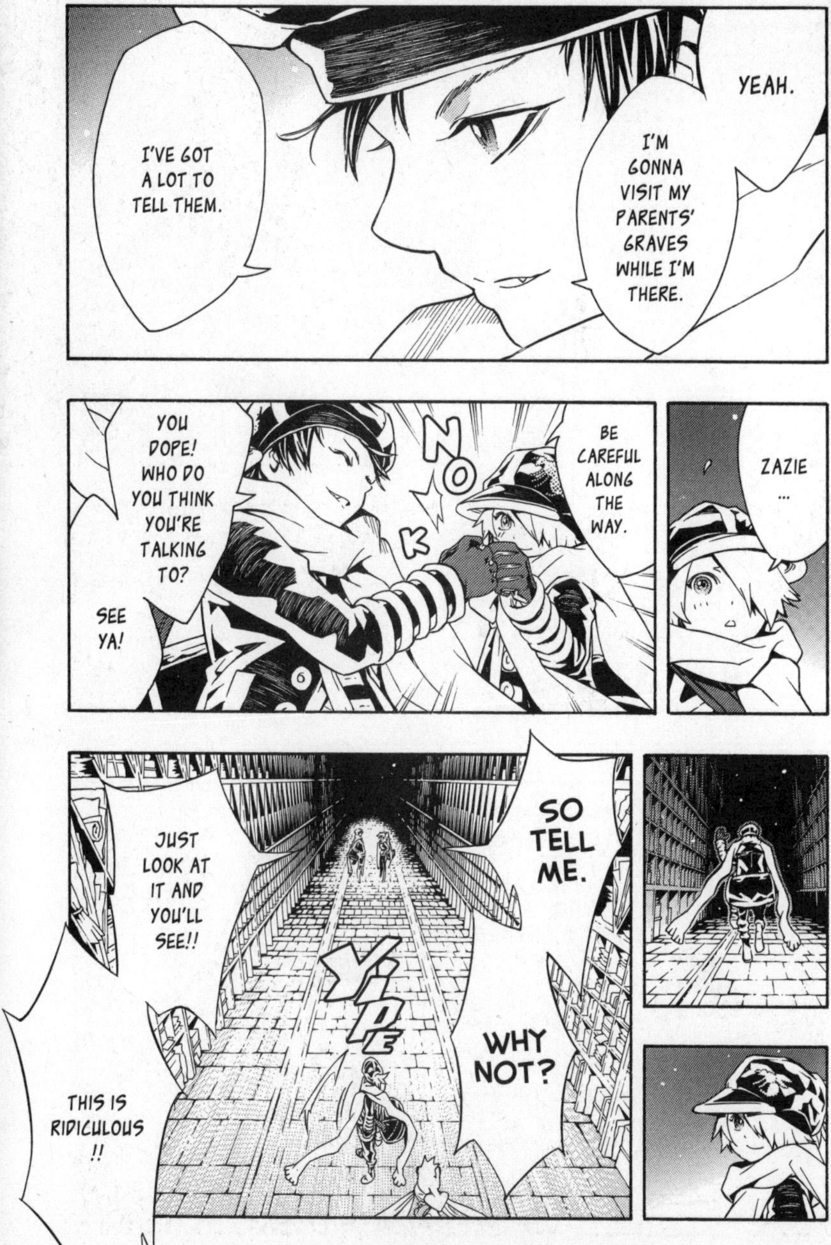
YEAH.
I'M GONNA VISIT MY PARENTS' GRAVES WHILE I'M THERE.
I'VE GOT A LOT TO TELL THEM.
ZAZIE ...
BE CAREFUL ALONG THE WAY.
NOK
YOU DOPE! WHO DO YOU THINK YOU'RE TALKING TO?
SEE YA!
SO TELL ME.
JUST LOOK AT IT AND YOU'LL SEE!!
YIPE
WHY NOT?
THIS IS RIDICULOUS!!

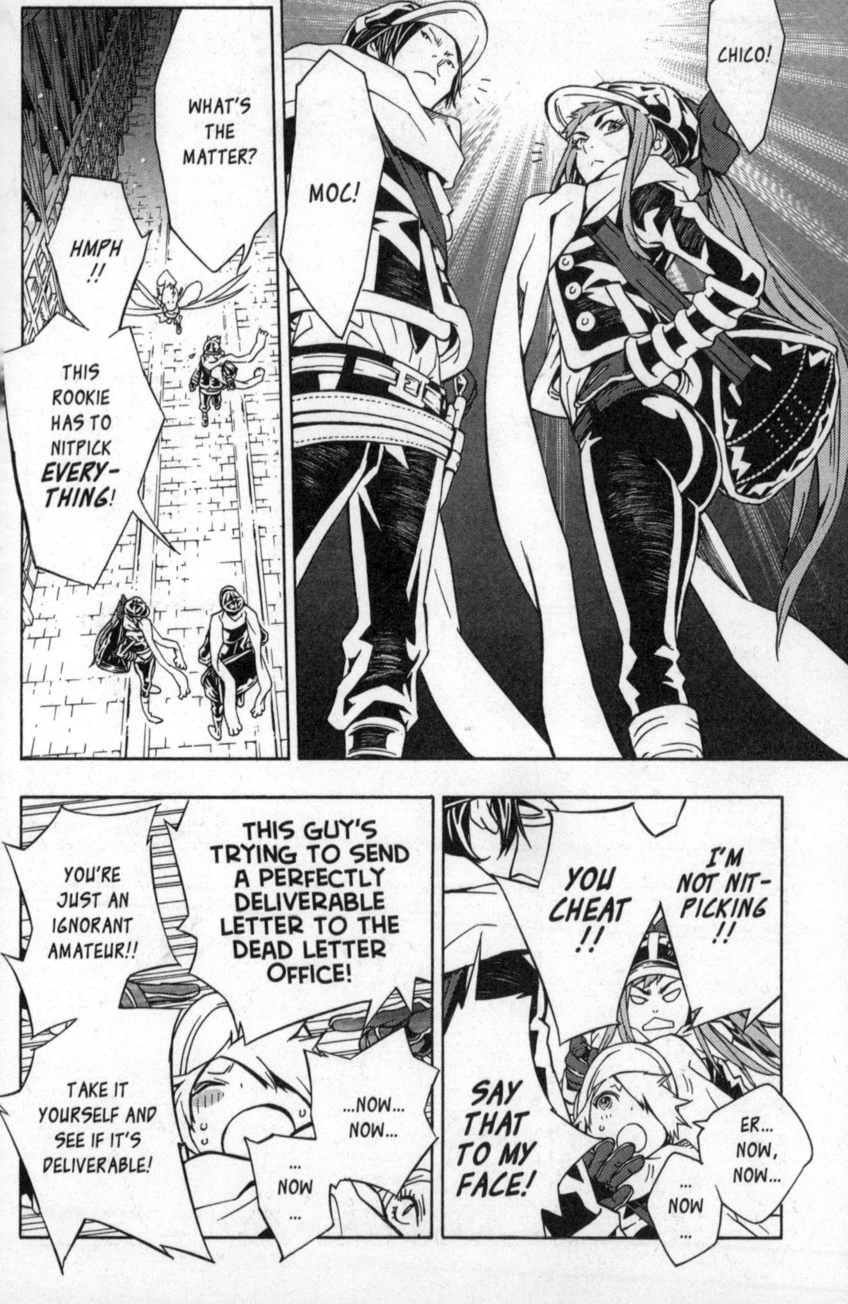
CHICO!
MOC!
WHAT'S THE MATTER?
HMPH !!
THIS ROOKIE HAS TO NITPICK EVERYTHING!
I'M NOT NIT-PICKING !!
YOU CHEAT !!
SAY THAT TO MY FACE!
ER... NOW, NOW...
... NOW ...
THIS GUY'S TRYING TO SEND A PERFECTLY DELIVERABLE LETTER TO THE DEAD LETTER OFFICE!
YOU'RE JUST AN IGNORANT AMATEUR!!
...NOW... NOW...
TAKE IT YOURSELF AND SEE IF IT'S DELIVERABLE!
... NOW ...

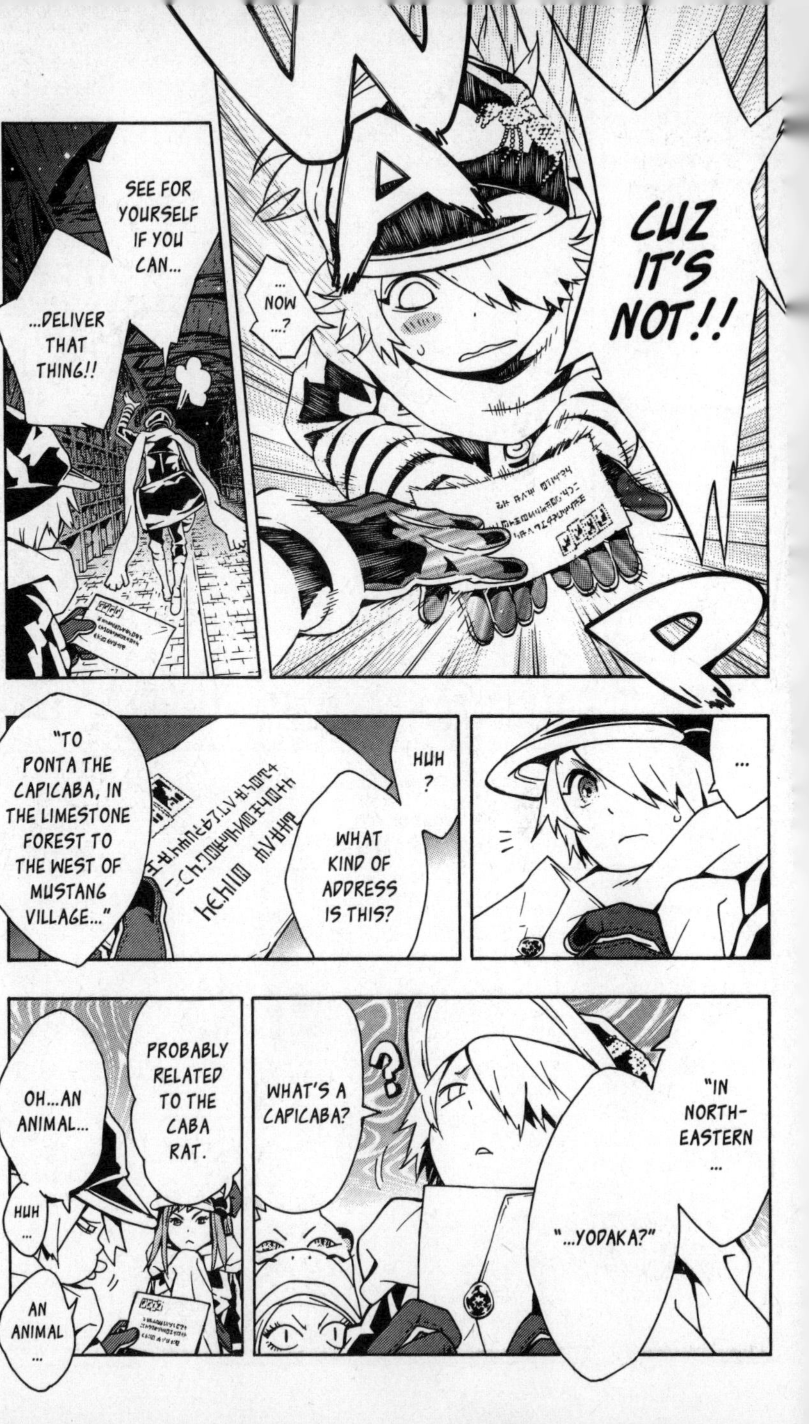
CUZ IT'S NOT!!
... NOW ...?
SEE FOR YOURSELF IF YOU CAN...
...DELIVER THAT THING!!
...
"TO PONTA THE CAPICABA, IN THE LIMESTONE FOREST TO THE WEST OF MUSTANG VILLAGE..."
HUH?
WHAT KIND OF ADDRESS IS THIS?
"IN NORTH-EASTERN ...
"...YODAKA?"
WHAT'S A CAPICABA?
PROBABLY RELATED TO THE CABA RAT.
OH...AN ANIMAL...
HUH ...
AN ANIMAL ...

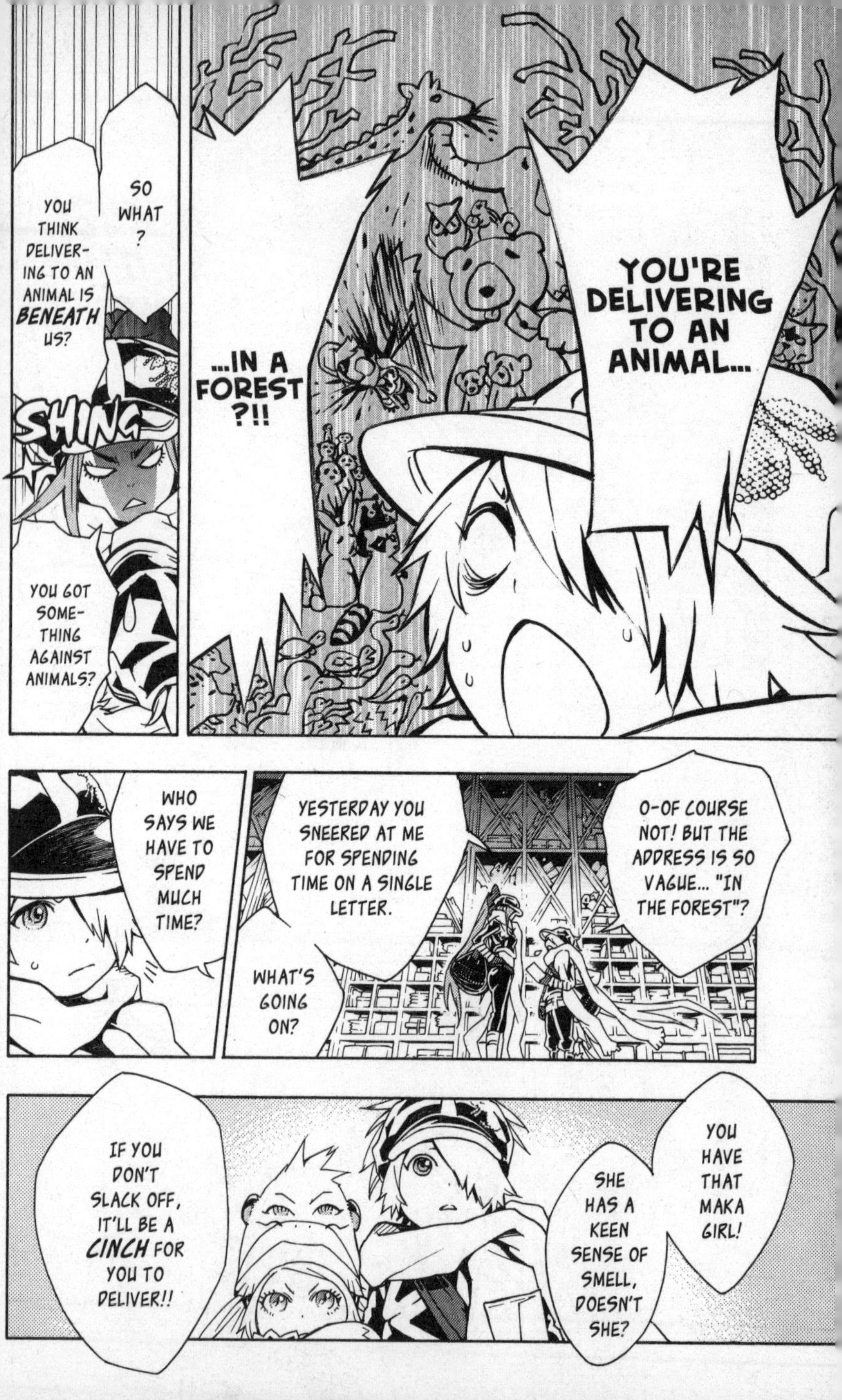
YOU'RE DELIVERING TO AN ANIMAL...
...IN A FOREST?!!
SO WHAT?
YOU THINK DELIVERING TO AN ANIMAL IS BENEATH US?
SHING
YOU GOT SOMETHING AGAINST ANIMALS?
O-OF COURSE NOT! BUT THE ADDRESS IS SO VAGUE... "IN THE FOREST"?
YESTERDAY YOU SNEERED AT ME FOR SPENDING TIME ON A SINGLE LETTER.
WHAT'S GOING ON?
WHO SAYS WE HAVE TO SPEND MUCH TIME?
YOU HAVE THAT MAKA GIRL!
SHE HAS A KEEN SENSE OF SMELL, DOESN'T SHE?
IF YOU DON'T SLACK OFF, IT'LL BE A CINCH FOR YOU TO DELIVER!!

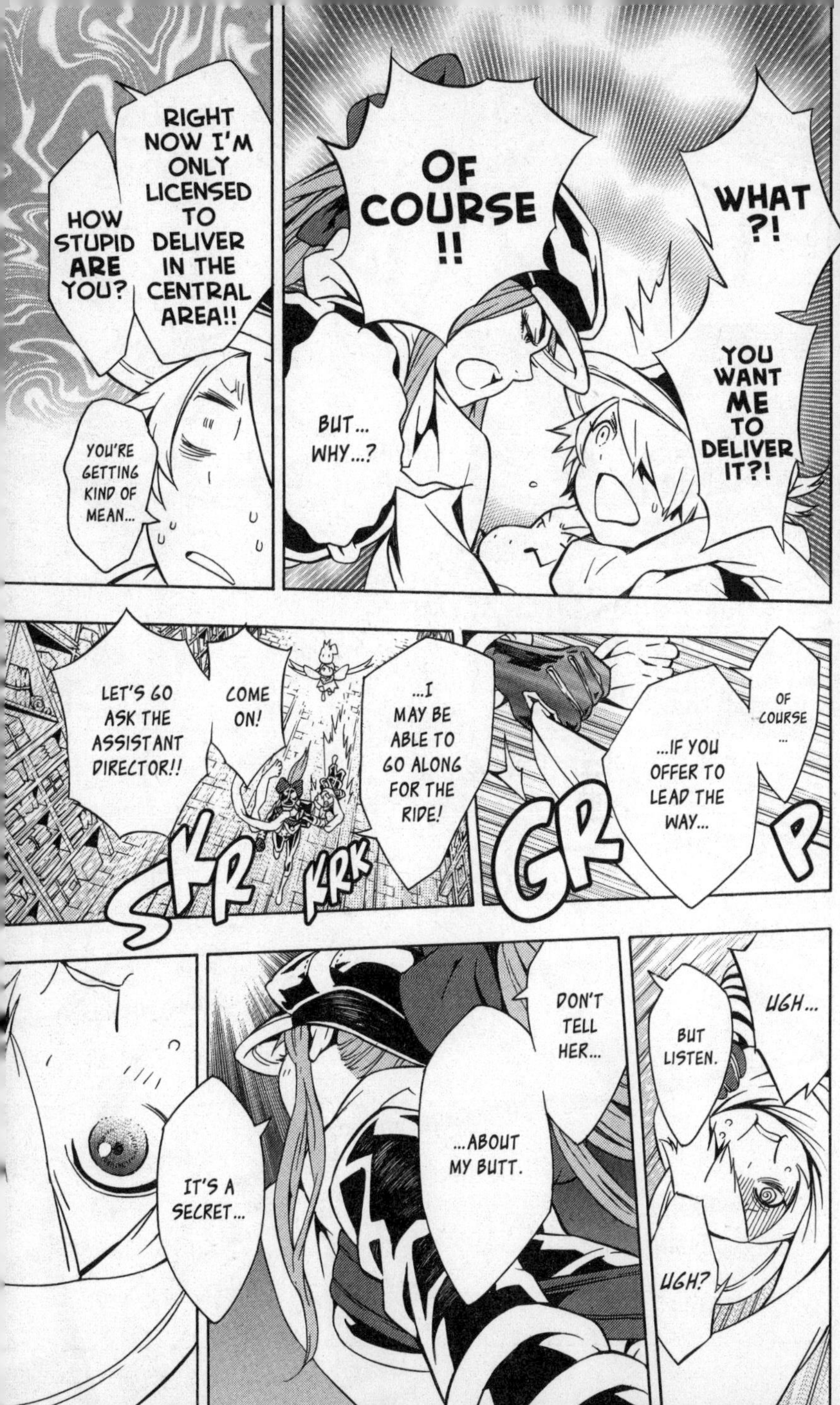
WHAT?!
YOU WANT ME TO DELIVER IT?!
OF COURSE!!
BUT... WHY...?
RIGHT NOW I'M ONLY LICENSED TO DELIVER IN THE CENTRAL AREA!!
HOW STUPID ARE YOU?
YOU'RE GETTING KIND OF MEAN...
OF COURSE...
...IF YOU OFFER TO LEAD THE WAY...
GR
P
...I MAY BE ABLE TO GO ALONG FOR THE RIDE!
COME ON!
LET'S GO ASK THE ASSISTANT DIRECTOR!!
SKR
KRK
UGH...
BUT LISTEN.
UGH?
DON'T TELL HER...
...ABOUT MY BUTT.
IT'S A SECRET...

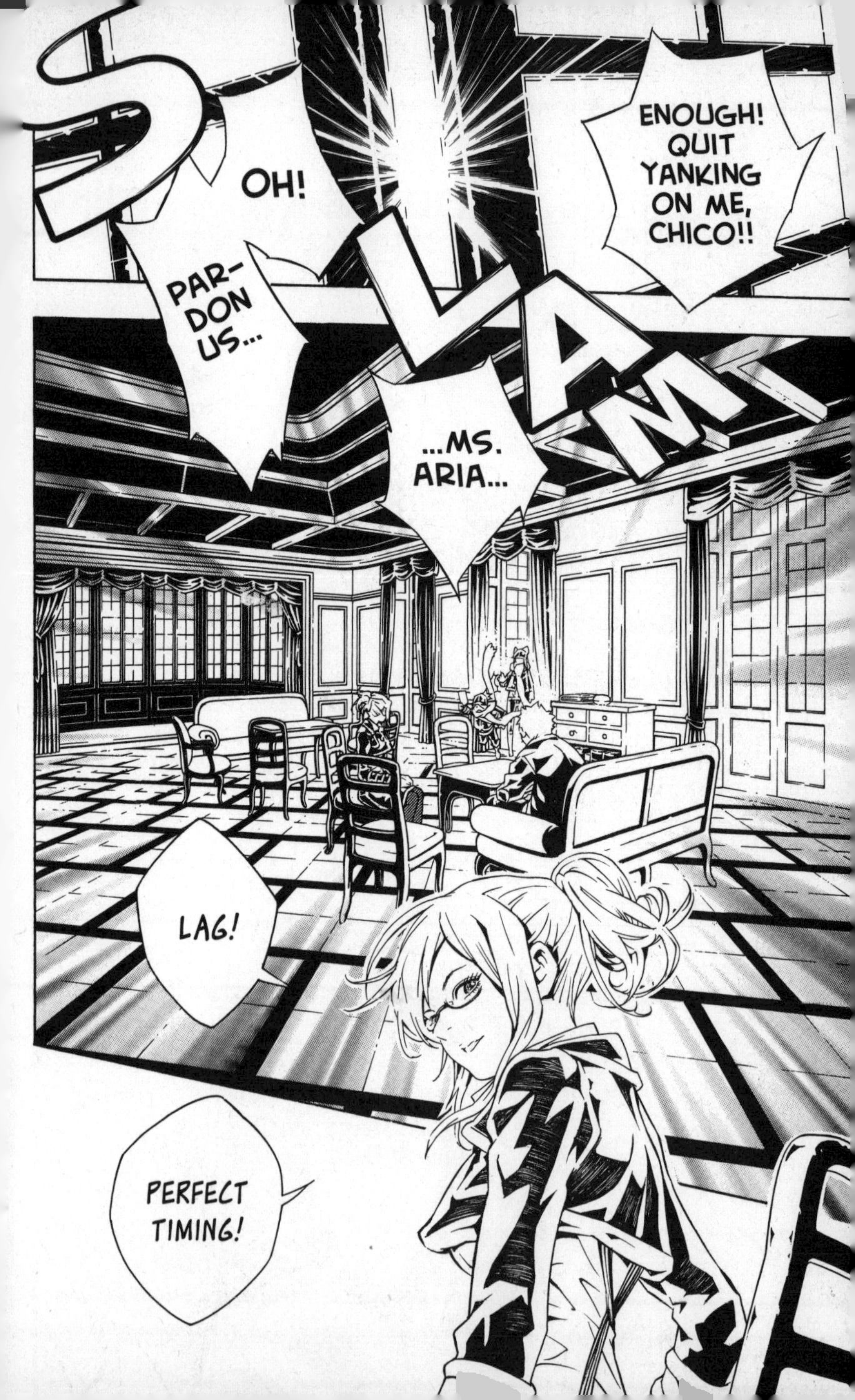
ENOUGH! QUIT YANKING ON ME, CHICO!!
SLAM
OH!
PAR-DON US...
...MS. ARIA...
LAG!
PERFECT TIMING!

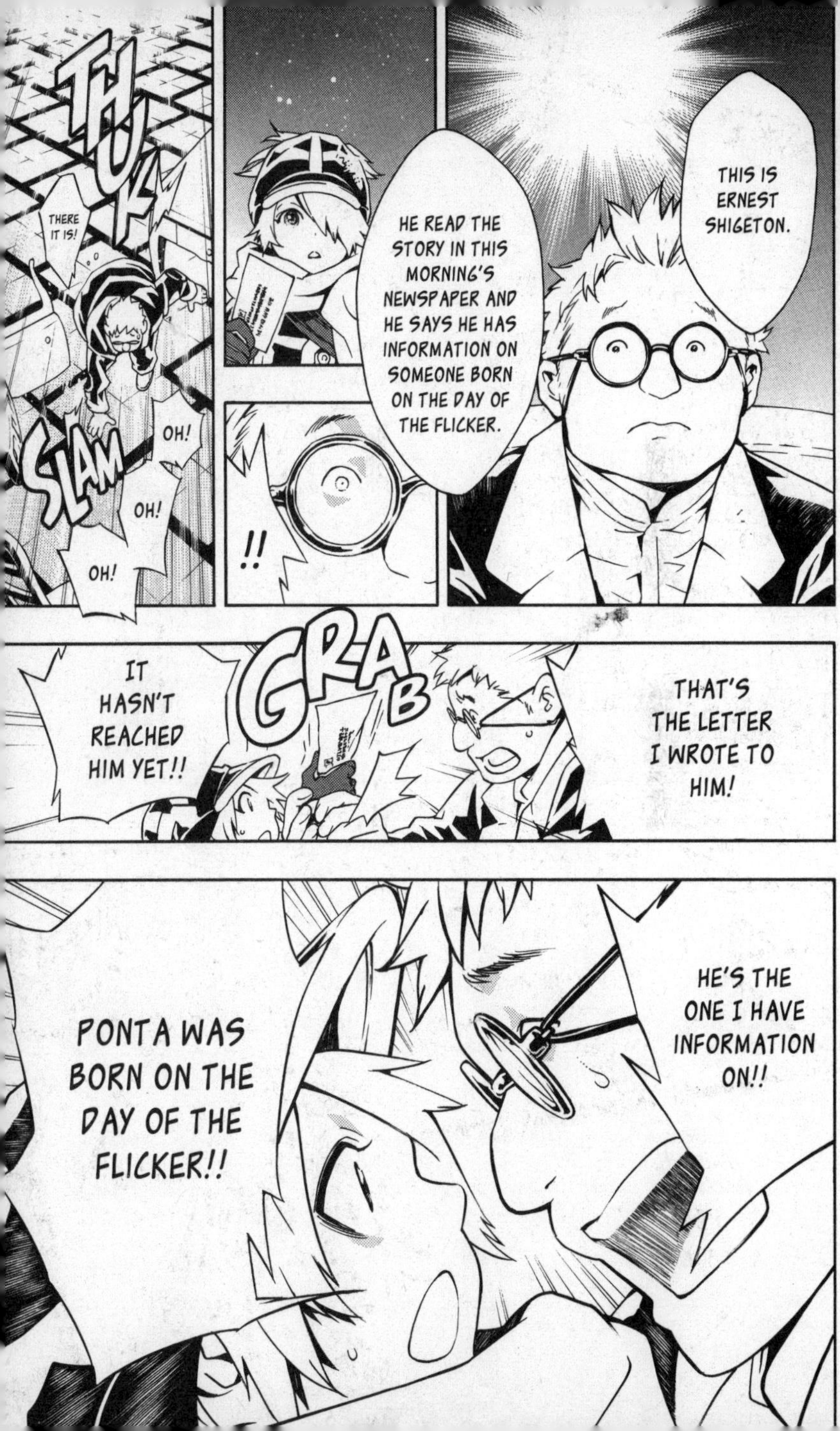
THIS IS ERNEST SHIGETON.
HE READ THE STORY IN THIS MORNING'S NEWSPAPER AND HE SAYS HE HAS INFORMATION ON SOMEONE BORN ON THE DAY OF THE FLICKER.
!!
THUK
THERE IT IS!
SLAM
OH!
OH!
OH!
THAT'S THE LETTER I WROTE TO HIM!
GRAB
IT HASN'T REACHED HIM YET!!
HE'S THE ONE I HAVE INFORMATION ON!!
PONTA WAS BORN ON THE DAY OF THE FLICKER!!

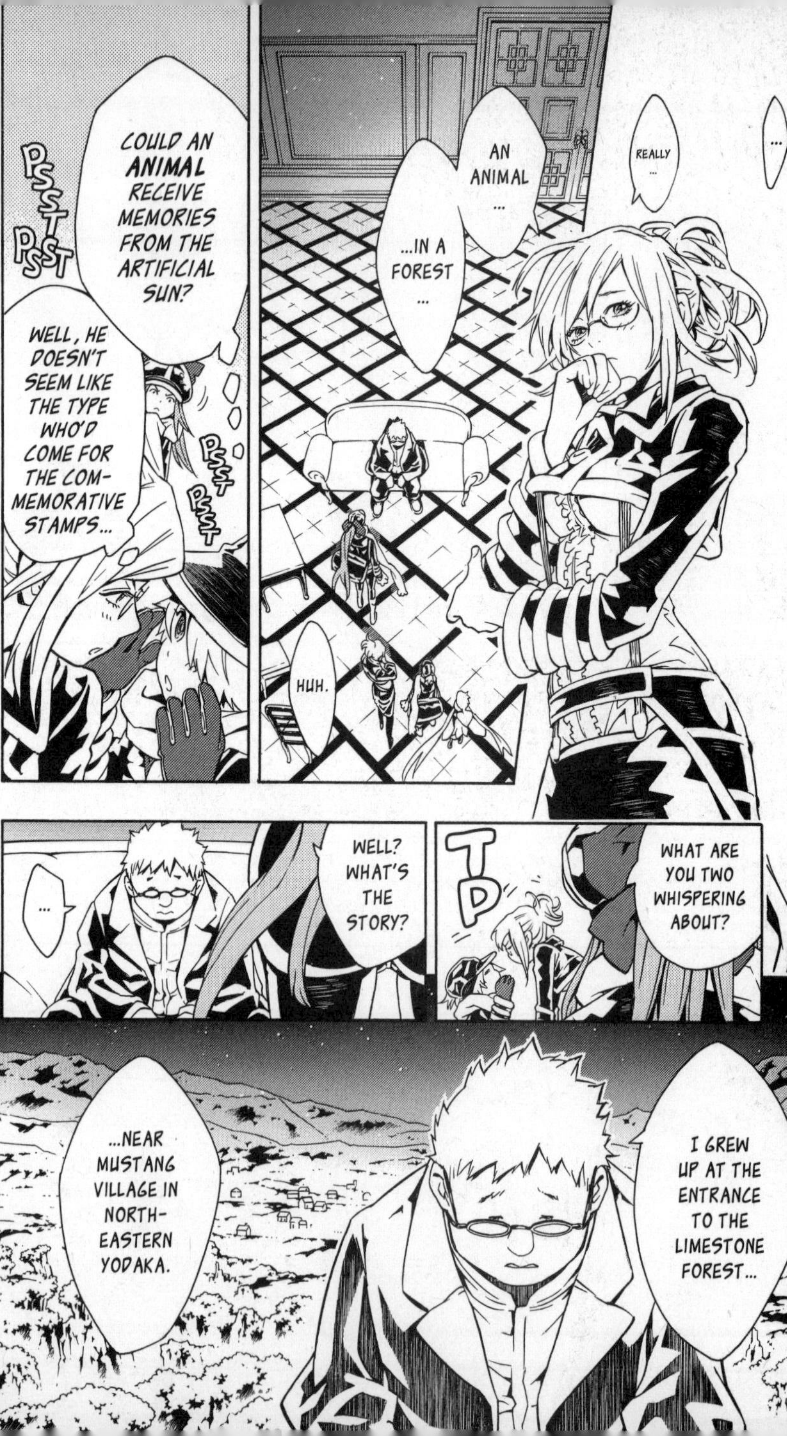
...
REALLY ...
AN ANIMAL ...
...IN A FOREST ...
HUH.
COULD AN ANIMAL RECEIVE MEMORIES FROM THE ARTIFICIAL SUN?
PSST PSST
WELL, HE DOESN'T SEEM LIKE THE TYPE WHO'D COME FOR THE COM-MEMORATIVE STAMPS...
PSST PSST
TP
WHAT ARE YOU TWO WHISPERING ABOUT?
WELL? WHAT'S THE STORY?
...
I GREW UP AT THE ENTRANCE TO THE LIMESTONE FOREST...
...NEAR MUSTANG VILLAGE IN NORTH-EASTERN YODAKA.

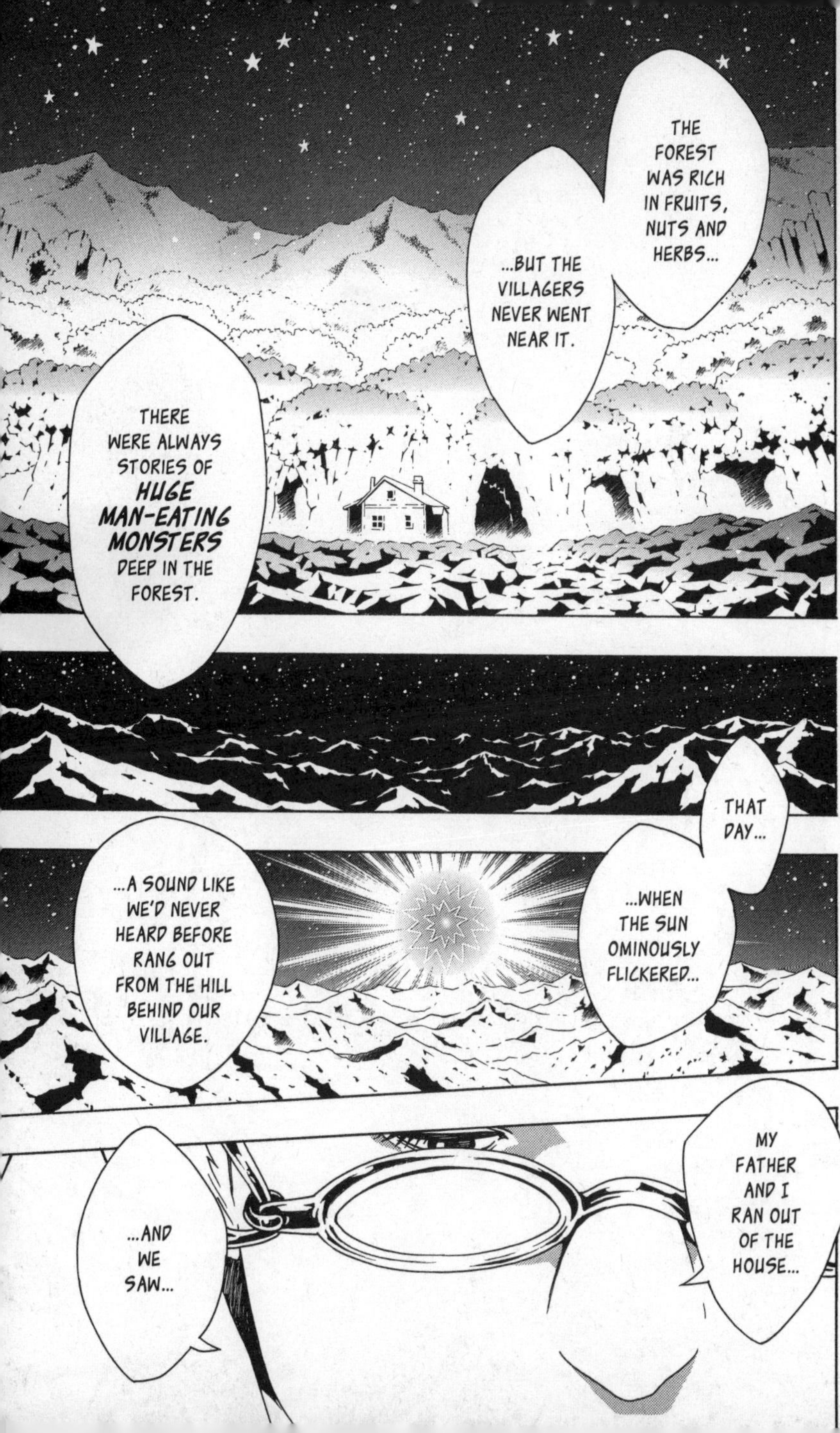
THE FOREST WAS RICH IN FRUITS, NUTS AND HERBS...
...BUT THE VILLAGERS NEVER WENT NEAR IT.
THERE WERE ALWAYS STORIES OF HUGE MAN-EATING MONSTERS DEEP IN THE FOREST.
THAT DAY...
...WHEN THE SUN OMINOUSLY FLICKERED...
...A SOUND LIKE WE'D NEVER HEARD BEFORE RANG OUT FROM THE HILL BEHIND OUR VILLAGE.
MY FATHER AND I RAN OUT OF THE HOUSE...
...AND WE SAW...

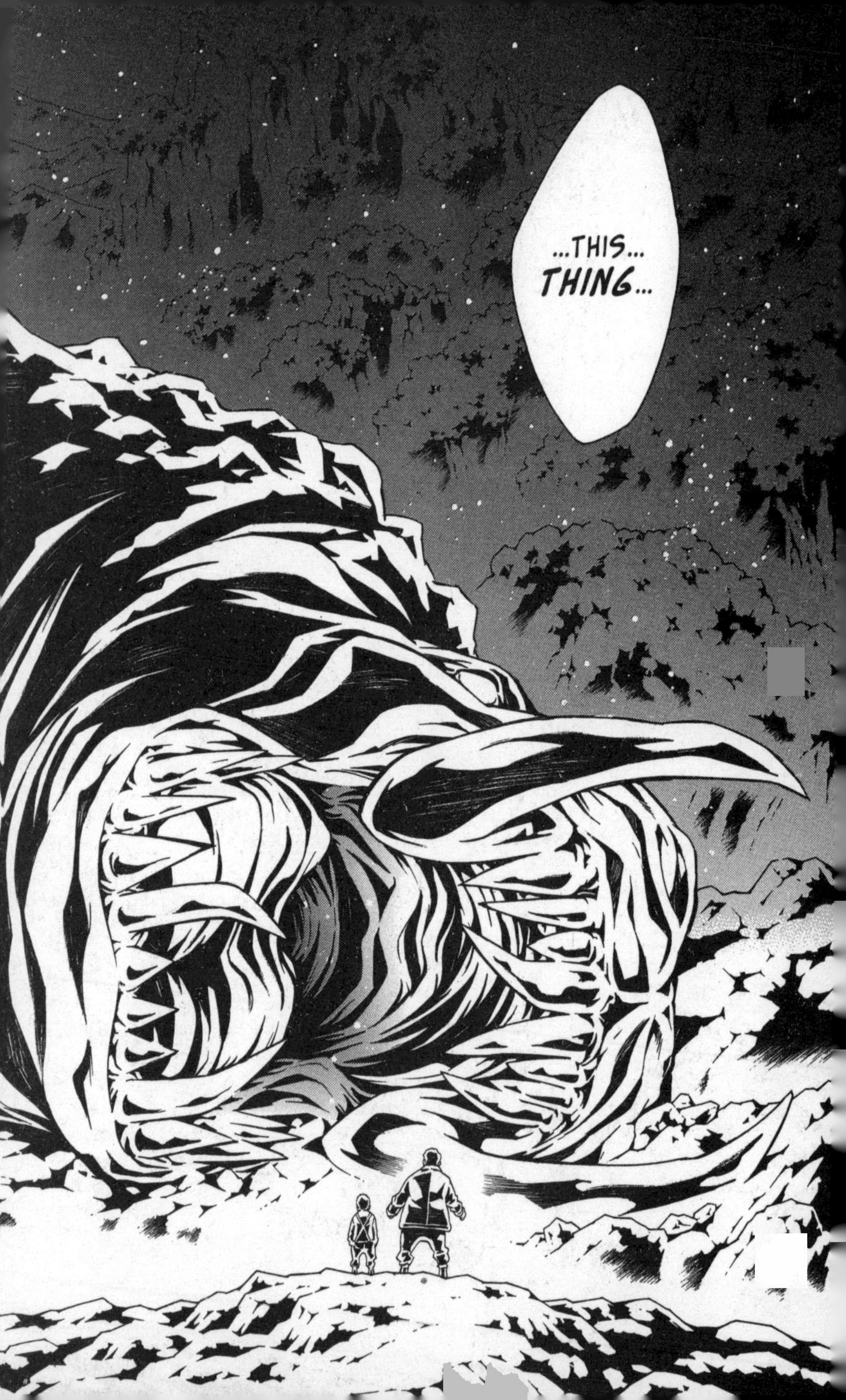
...THIS... THING...

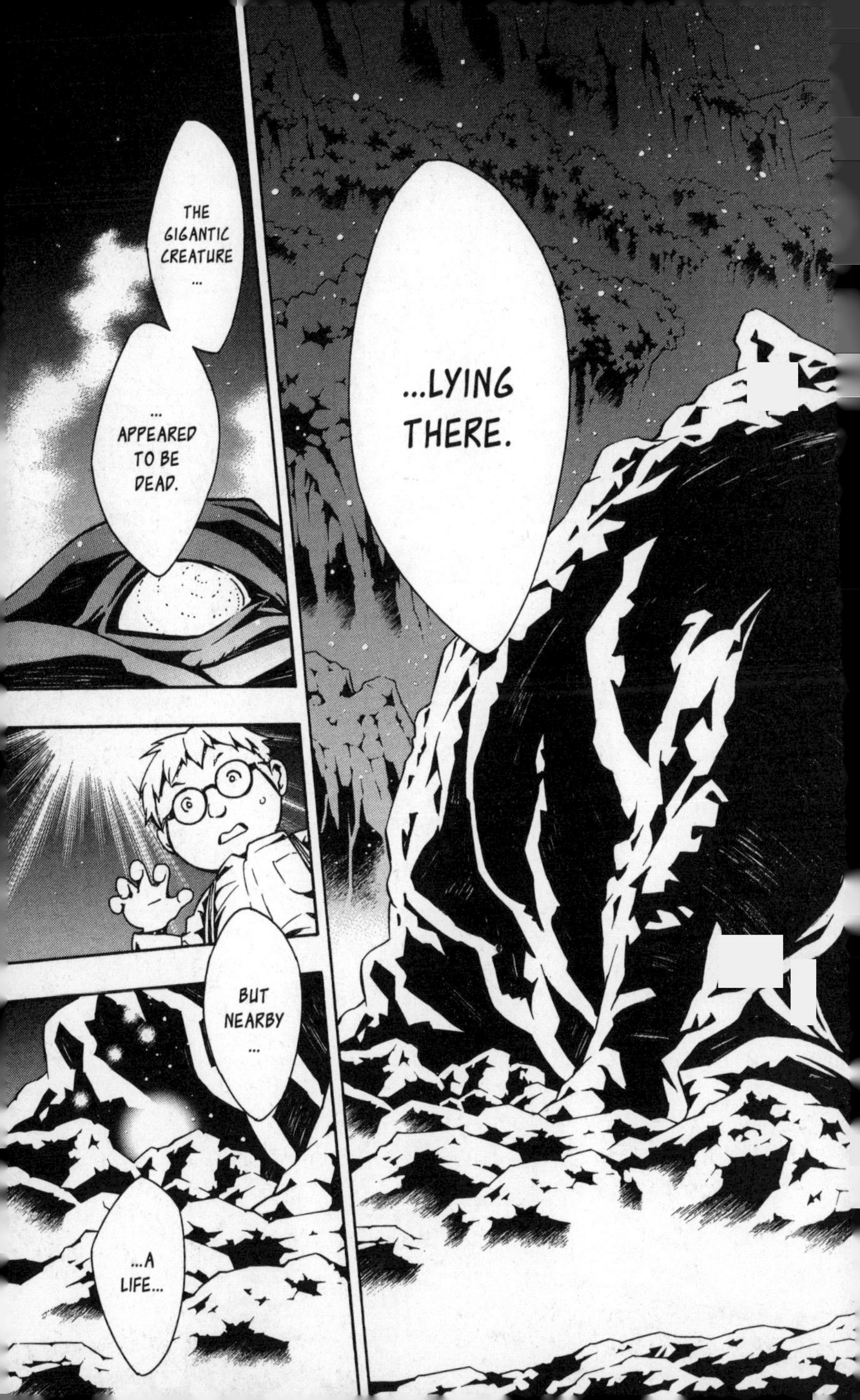
...LYING THERE.
THE GIGANTIC CREATURE ...
... APPEARED TO BE DEAD.
BUT NEARBY ...
...A LIFE...

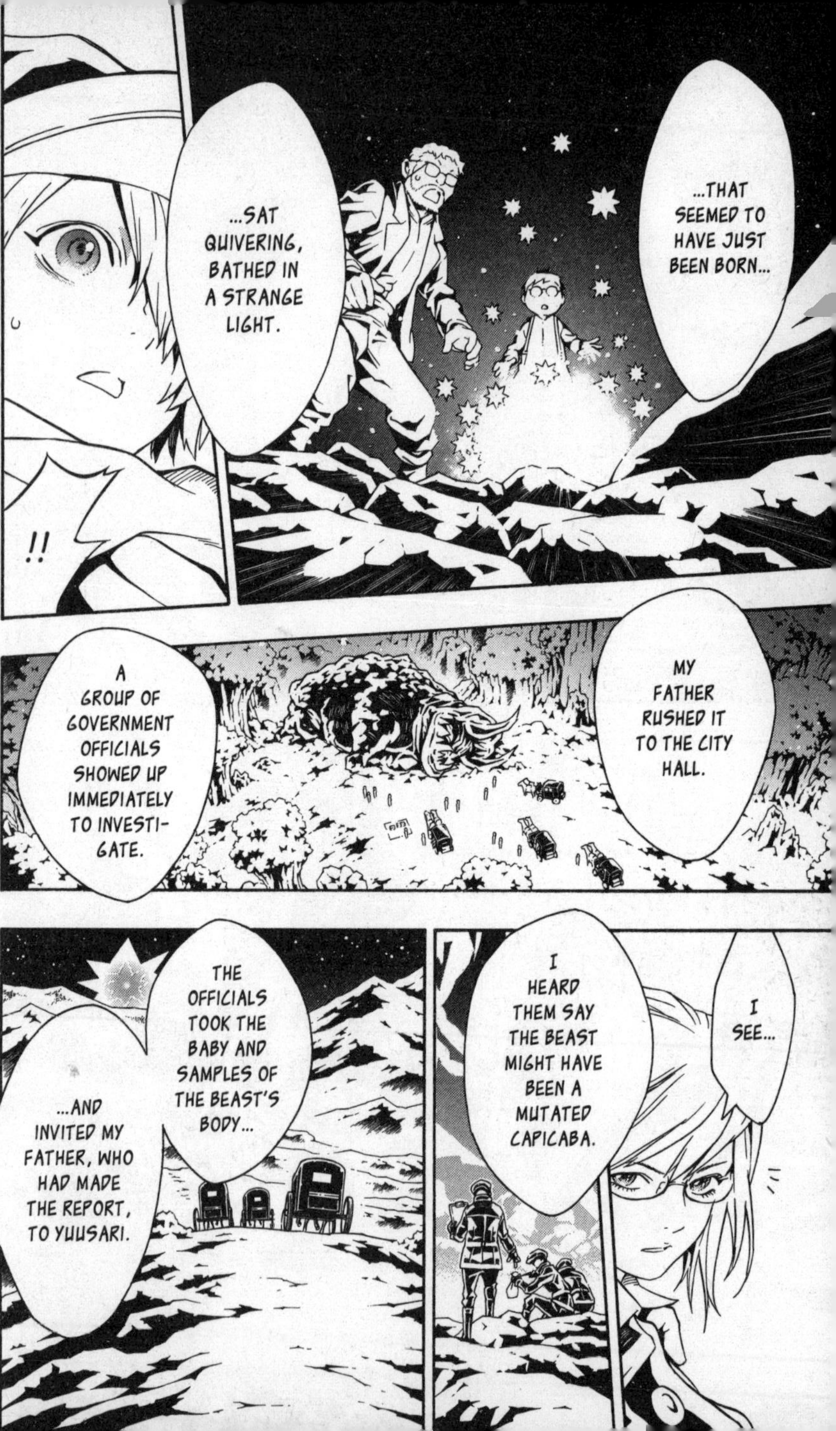
...THAT SEEMED TO HAVE JUST BEEN BORN...
...SAT QUIVERING, BATHED IN A STRANGE LIGHT.
!!
MY FATHER RUSHED IT TO THE CITY HALL.
A GROUP OF GOVERNMENT OFFICIALS SHOWED UP IMMEDIATELY TO INVESTI- GATE.
I SEE...
I HEARD THEM SAY THE BEAST MIGHT HAVE BEEN A MUTATED CAPICABA.
THE OFFICIALS TOOK THE BABY AND SAMPLES OF THE BEAST'S BODY...
...AND INVITED MY FATHER, WHO HAD MADE THE REPORT, TO YUUSARI.

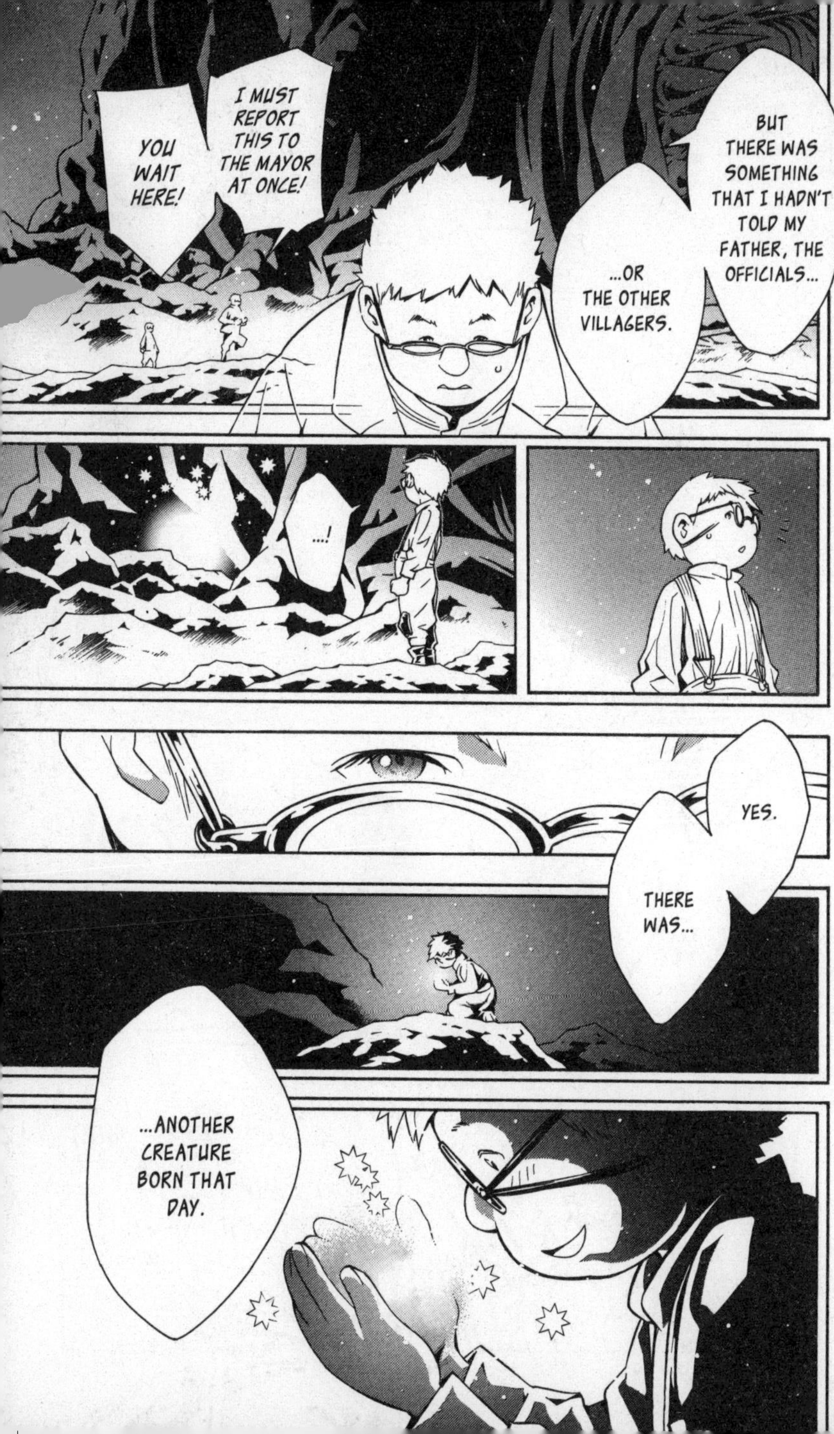

BUT THERE WAS SOMETHING THAT I HADN'T TOLD MY FATHER, THE OFFICIALS...
...OR THE OTHER VILLAGERS.
I MUST REPORT THIS TO THE MAYOR AT ONCE!
YOU WAIT HERE!
...!
YES.
THERE WAS...
...ANOTHER CREATURE BORN THAT DAY.

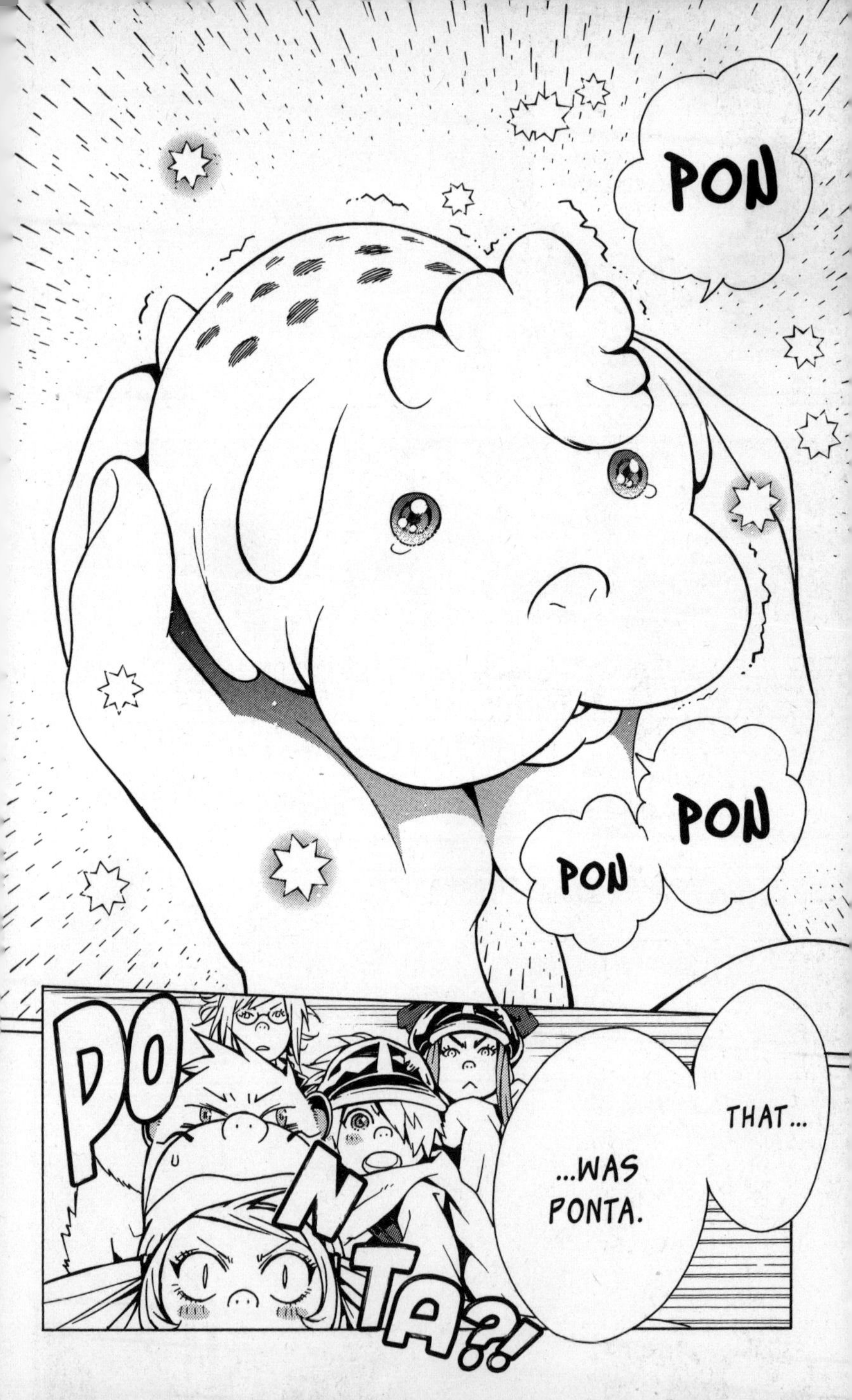
PON
PON
PON
THAT...
...WAS PONTA.
PONTA?!

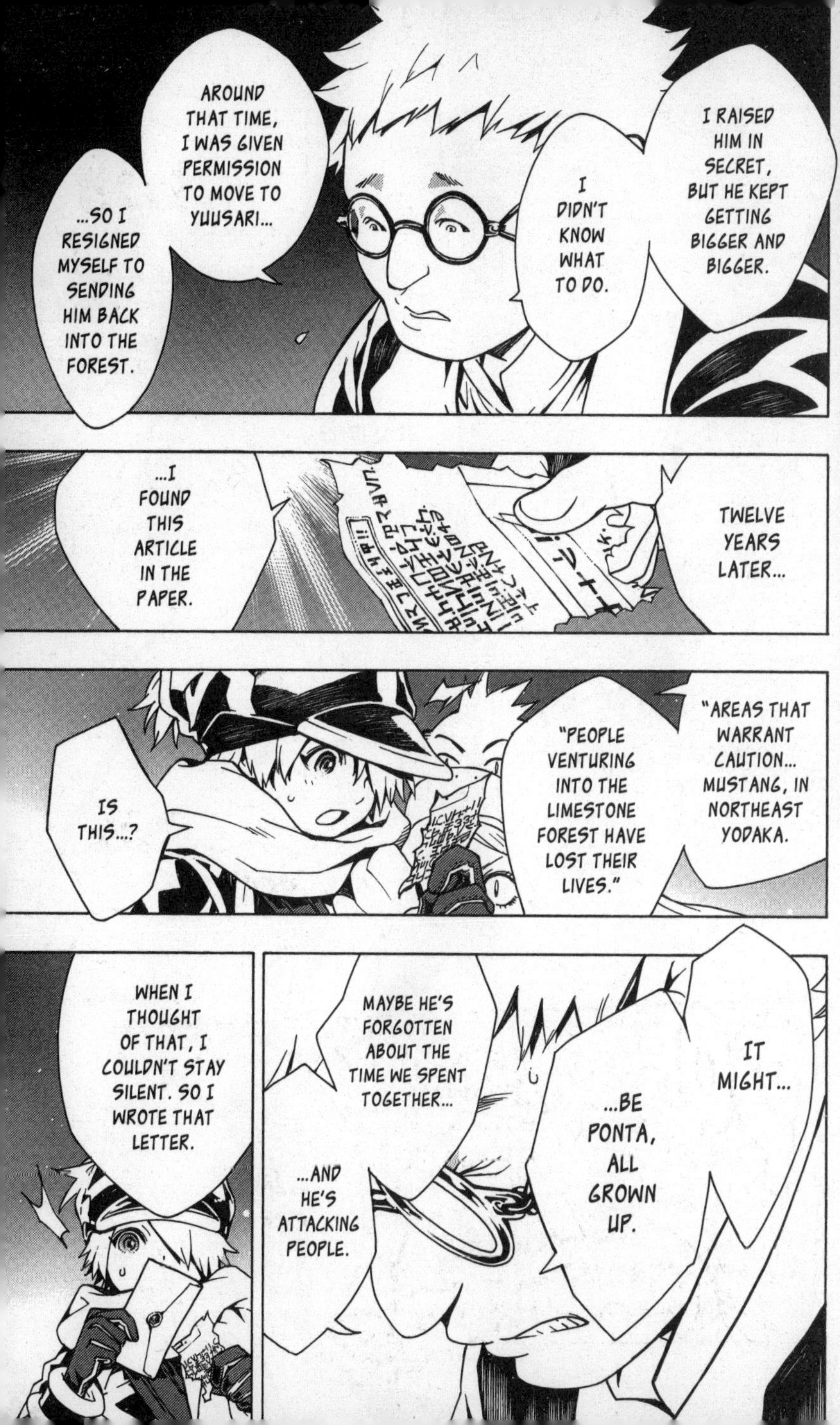
I RAISED HIM IN SECRET, BUT HE KEPT GETTING BIGGER AND BIGGER.
I DIDN'T KNOW WHAT TO DO.
AROUND THAT TIME, I WAS GIVEN PERMISSION TO MOVE TO YUUSARI...
...SO I RESIGNED MYSELF TO SENDING HIM BACK INTO THE FOREST.
TWELVE YEARS LATER...
...I FOUND THIS ARTICLE IN THE PAPER.
"AREAS THAT WARRANT CAUTION... MUSTANG, IN NORTHEAST YODAKA.
"PEOPLE VENTURING INTO THE LIMESTONE FOREST HAVE LOST THEIR LIVES."
IS THIS...?
IT MIGHT...
...BE PONTA, ALL GROWN UP.
MAYBE HE'S FORGOTTEN ABOUT THE TIME WE SPENT TOGETHER...
...AND HE'S ATTACKING PEOPLE.
WHEN I THOUGHT OF THAT, I COULDN'T STAY SILENT. SO I WROTE THAT LETTER.

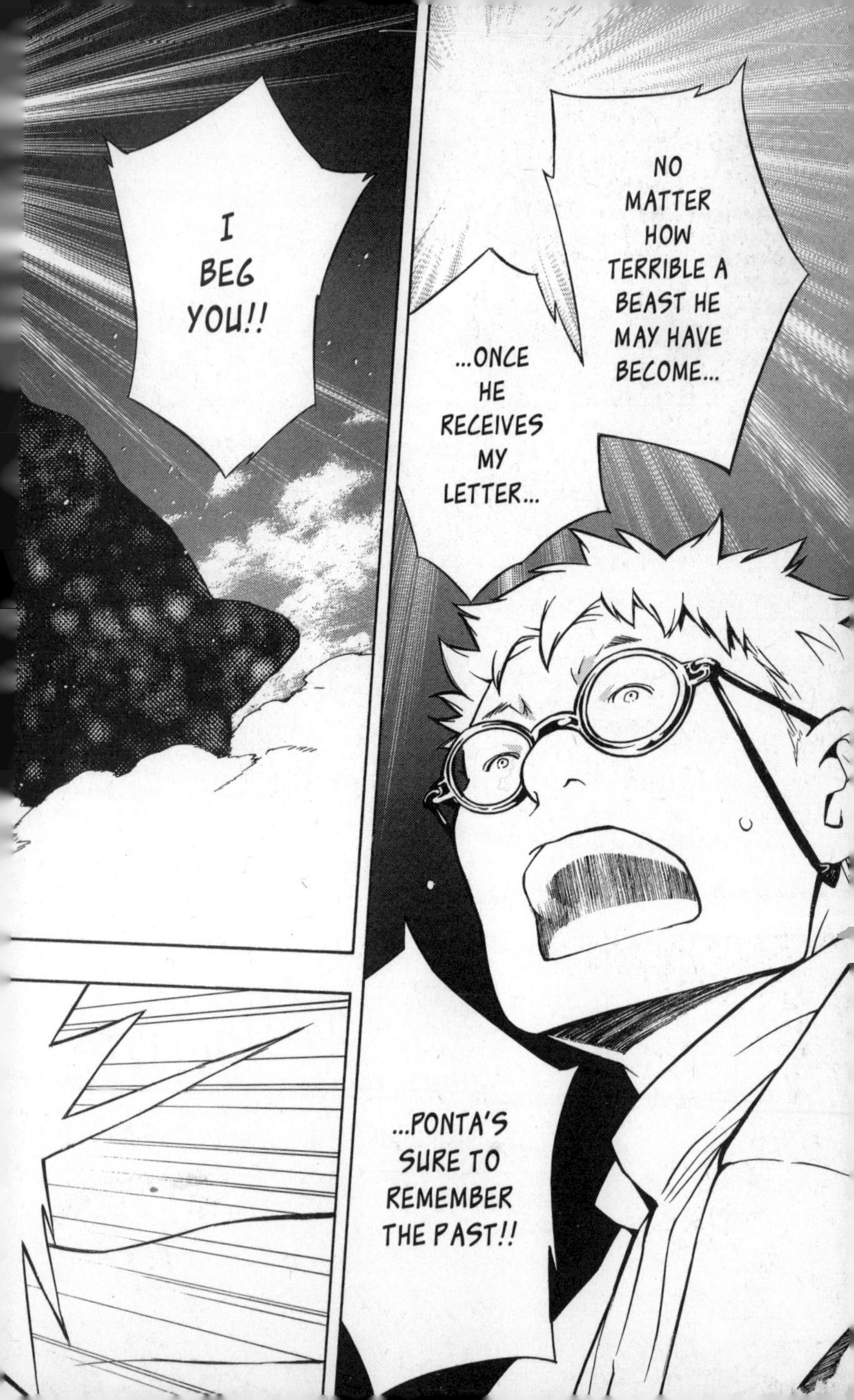
NO MATTER HOW TERRIBLE A BEAST HE MAY HAVE BECOME...
...ONCE HE RECEIVES MY LETTER...
...PONTA'S SURE TO REMEMBER THE PAST!!
I BEG YOU!!

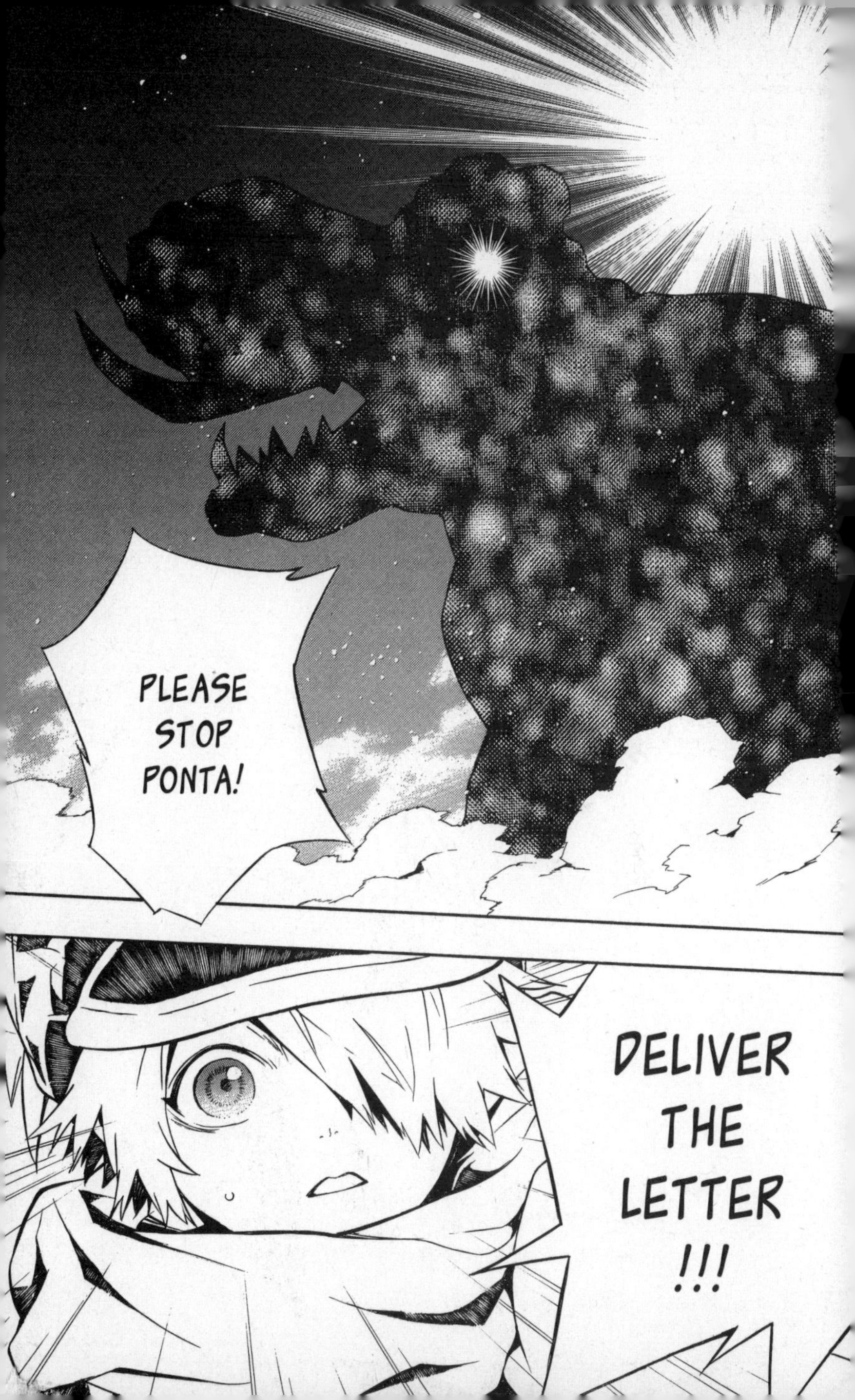
PLEASE STOP PONTA!
DELIVER THE LETTER !!!

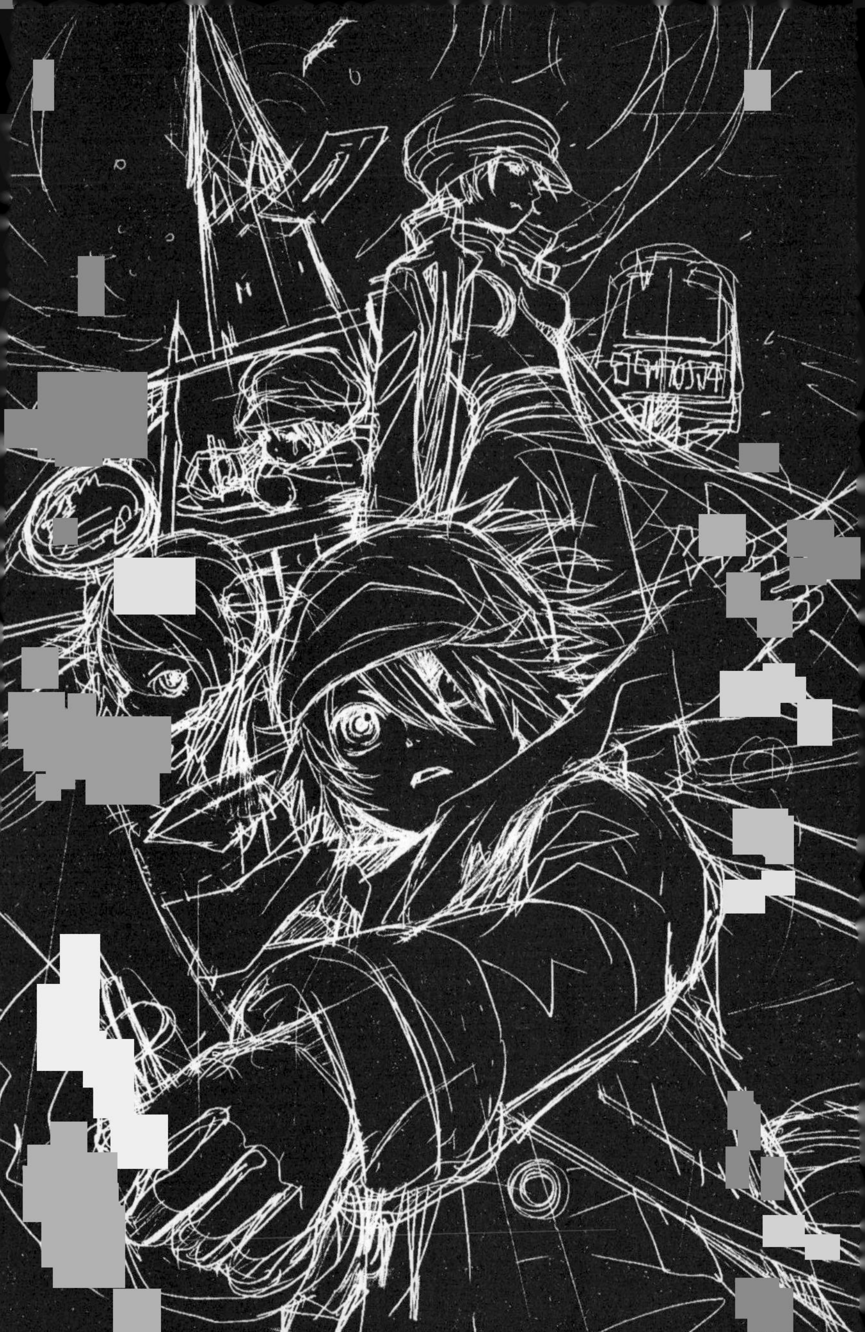

Rough draft of the cover for a drama CD.

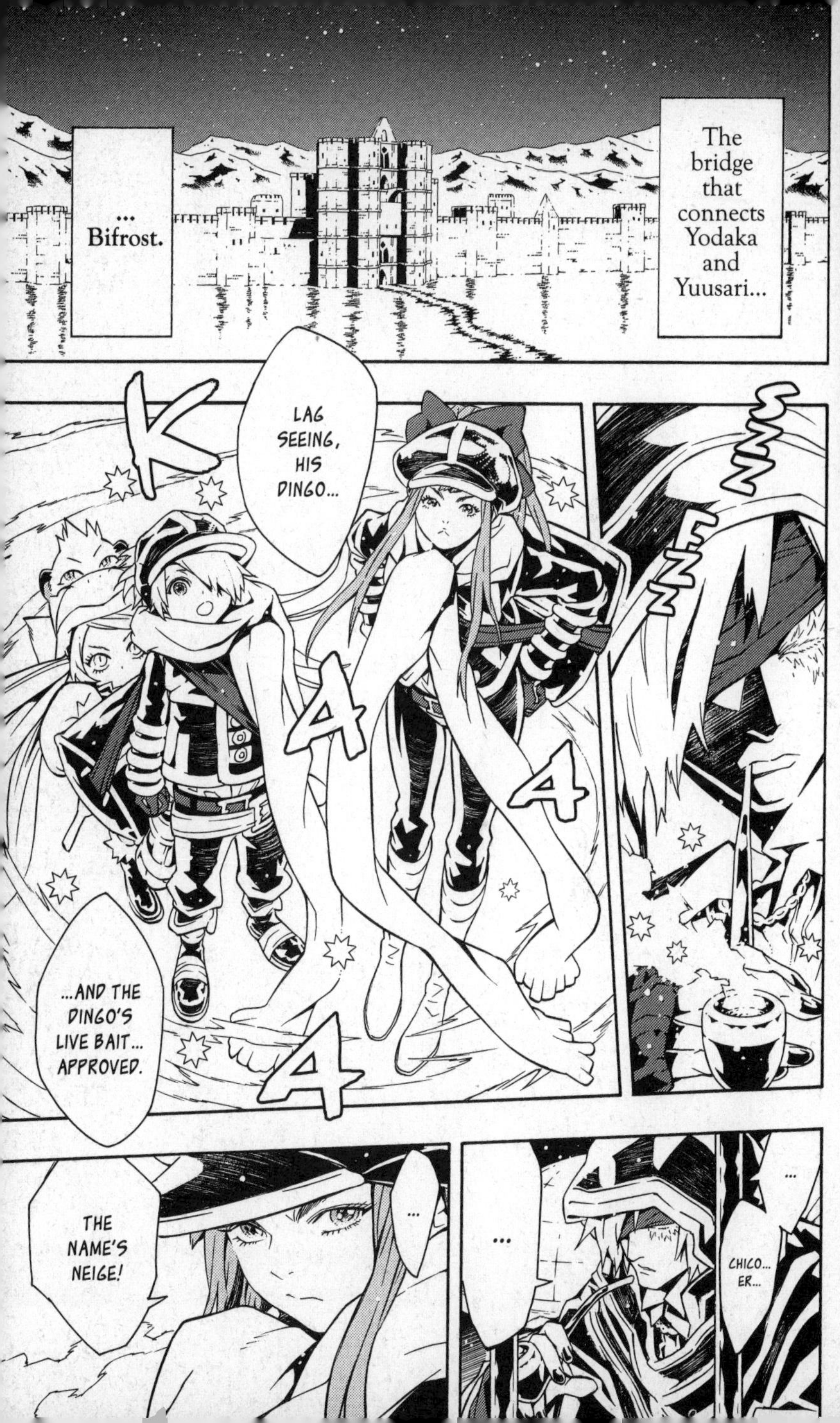
The bridge that connects Yodaka and Yuusari...
... Bifrost.
SWN
FZZ
K
LAG SEEING, HIS DINGO...
4
4
4
...AND THE DINGO'S LIVE BAIT... APPROVED.
...
CHICO... ER...
...
...
THE NAME'S NEIGE!

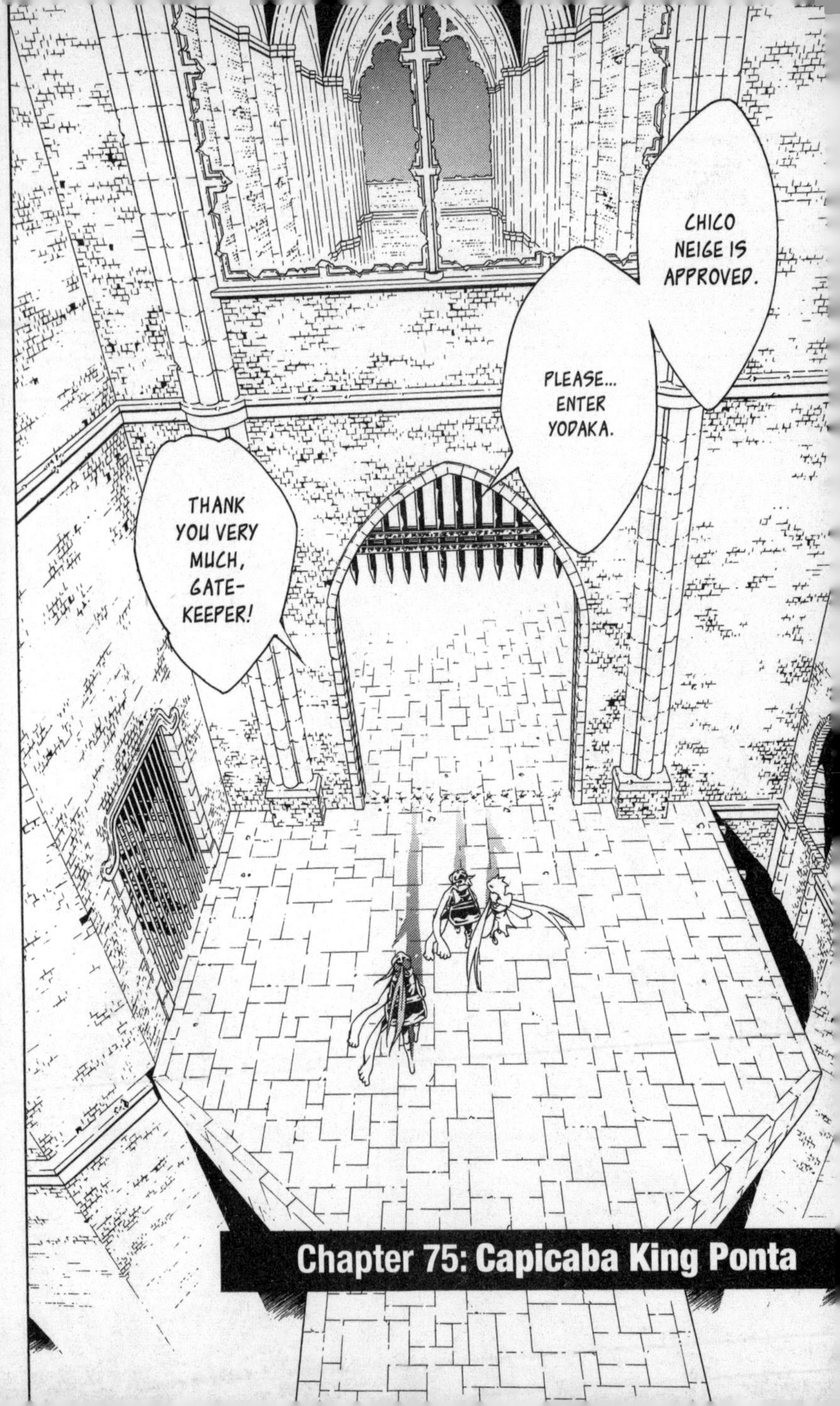
CHICO NEIGE IS APPROVED.
PLEASE... ENTER YODAKA.
THANK YOU VERY MUCH, GATE-KEEPER!

Chapter 75: Capicaba King Ponta

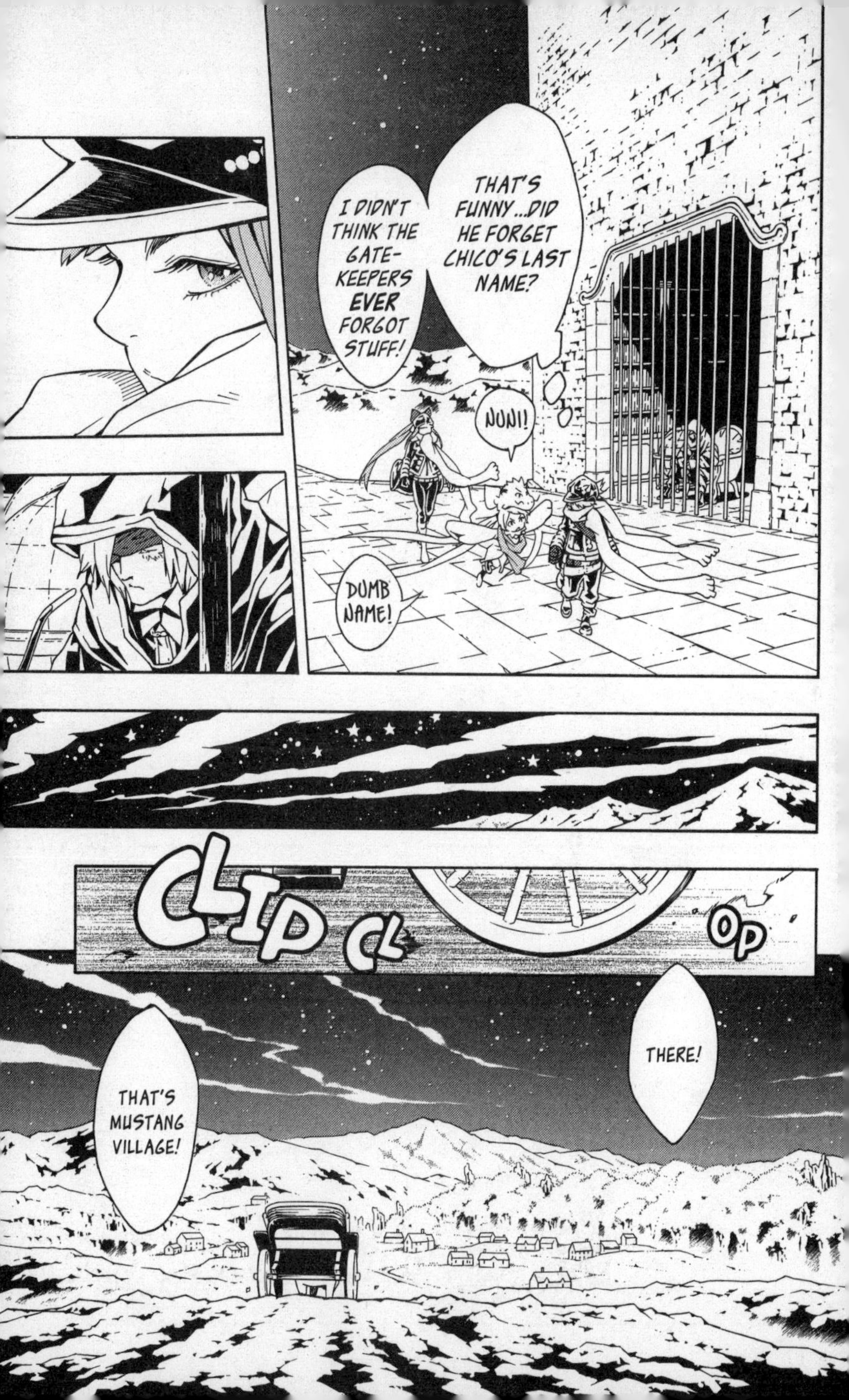
THAT'S FUNNY...DID HE FORGET CHICO'S LAST NAME?
I DIDN'T THINK THE GATE-KEEPERS EVER FORGOT STUFF!
NUNI!
DUMB NAME!
CLIP CLOP
THERE!
THAT'S MUSTANG VILLAGE!

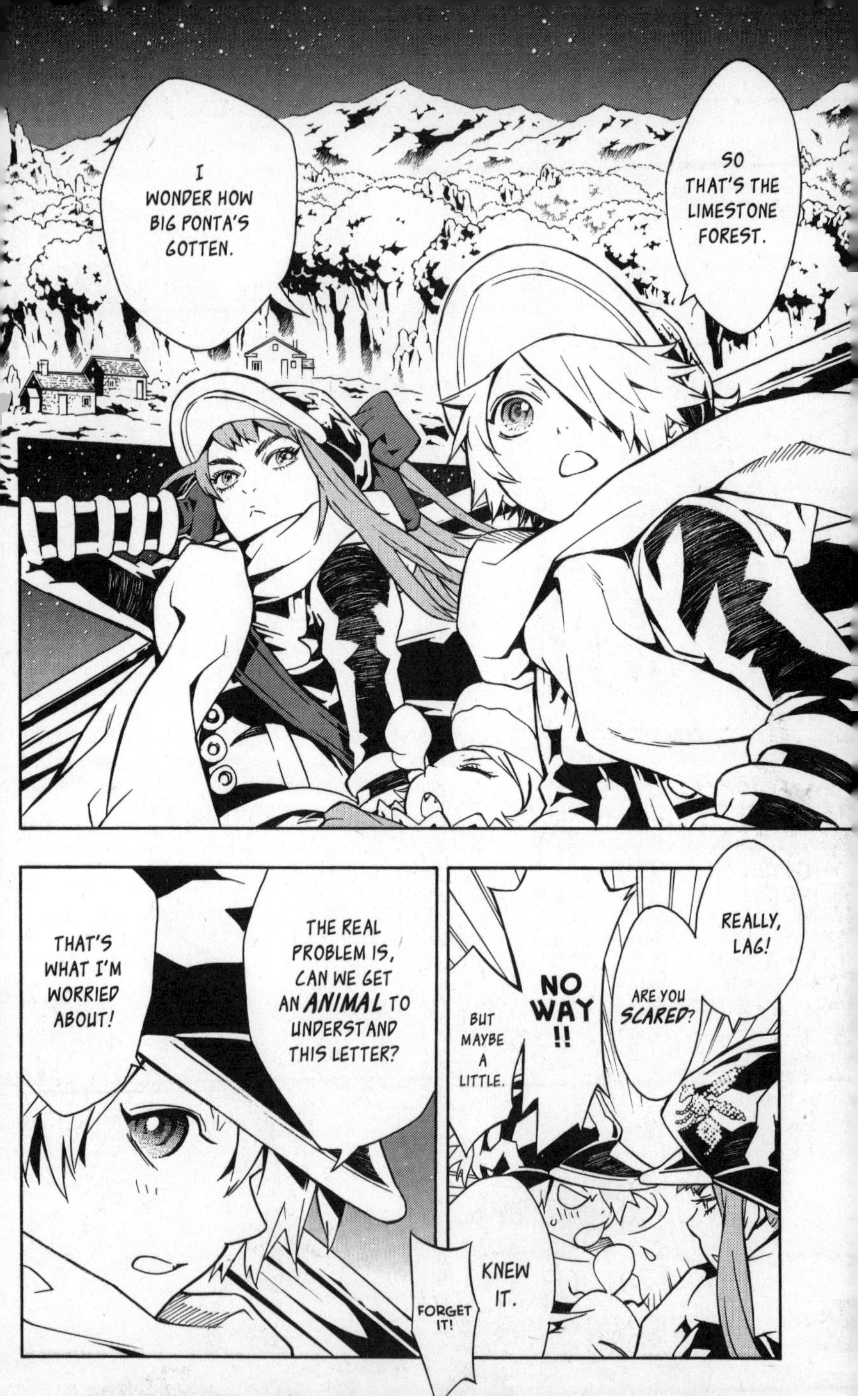

SO THAT'S THE LIMESTONE FOREST.
I WONDER HOW BIG PONTA'S GOTTEN.
REALLY, LAG!
ARE YOU SCARED?
NO WAY!!
BUT MAYBE A LITTLE.
KNEW IT.
FORGET IT!
THE REAL PROBLEM IS, CAN WE GET AN ANIMAL TO UNDERSTAND THIS LETTER?
THAT'S WHAT I'M WORRIED ABOUT!

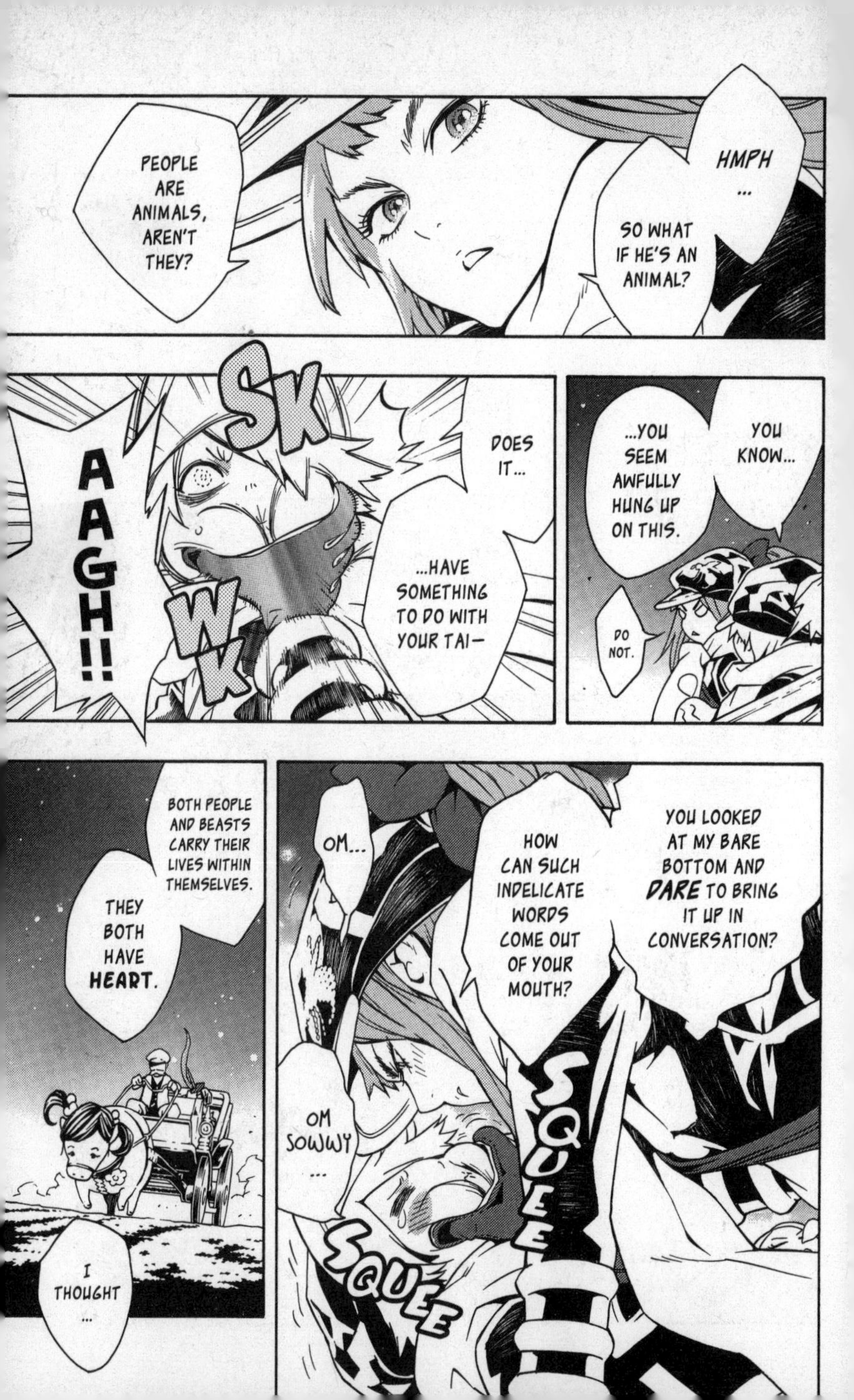
HMPH ...
SO WHAT IF HE'S AN ANIMAL?
PEOPLE ARE ANIMALS, AREN'T THEY?
YOU KNOW...
...YOU SEEM AWFULLY HUNG UP ON THIS.
DO NOT.
DOES IT...
...HAVE SOMETHING TO DO WITH YOUR TAI—
SK
AAGH!!
WK
YOU LOOKED AT MY BARE BOTTOM AND **DARE** TO BRING IT UP IN CONVERSATION?
HOW CAN SUCH INDELICATE WORDS COME OUT OF YOUR MOUTH?
OM...
SQUEE
OM SOWWY ...
SQUEE
BOTH PEOPLE AND BEASTS CARRY THEIR LIVES WITHIN THEMSELVES.
THEY BOTH HAVE **HEART**.
I THOUGHT ...

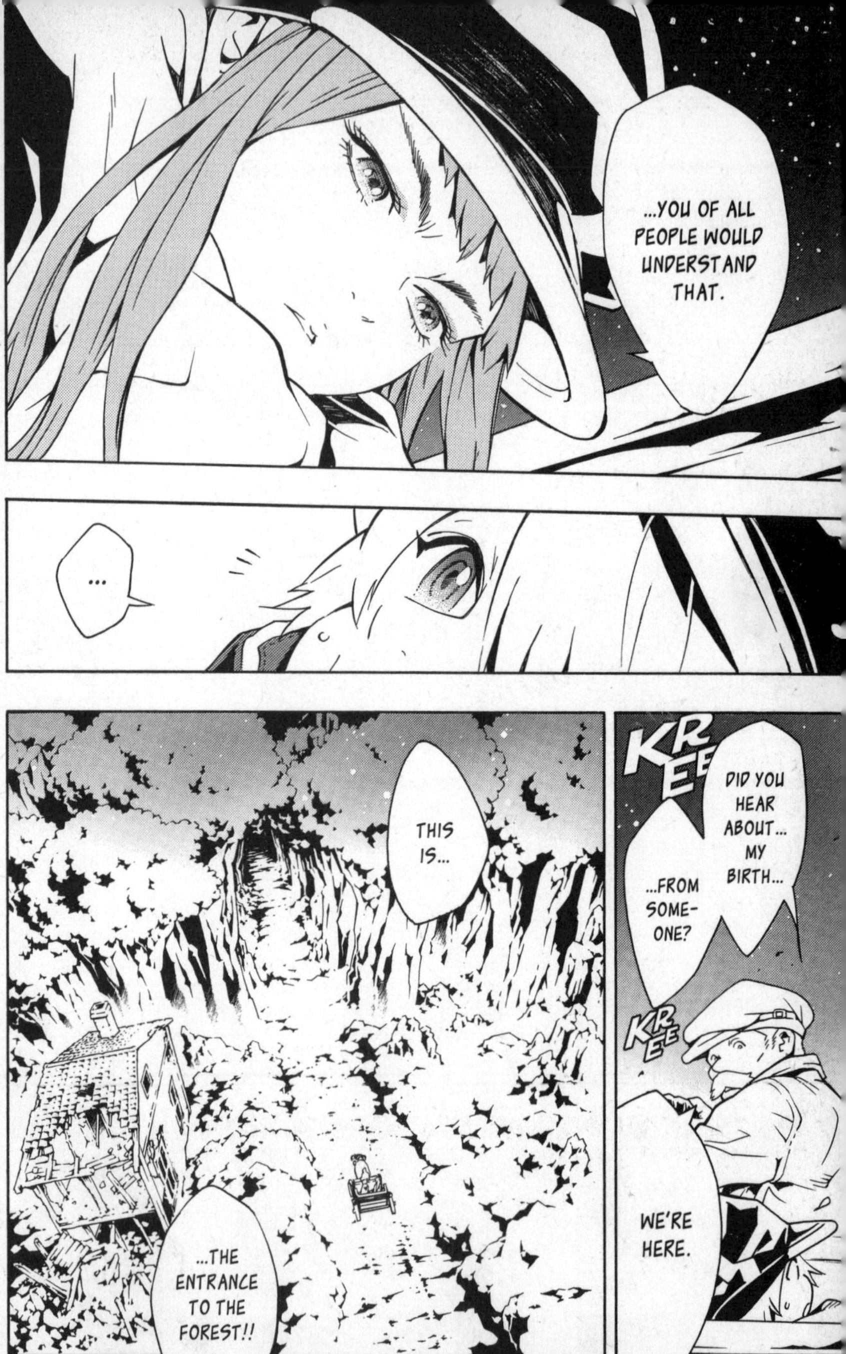
...YOU OF ALL PEOPLE WOULD UNDERSTAND THAT.
...
KREE
DID YOU HEAR ABOUT... MY BIRTH...
...FROM SOMEONE?
KREE
WE'RE HERE.
THIS IS...
...THE ENTRANCE TO THE FOREST!!

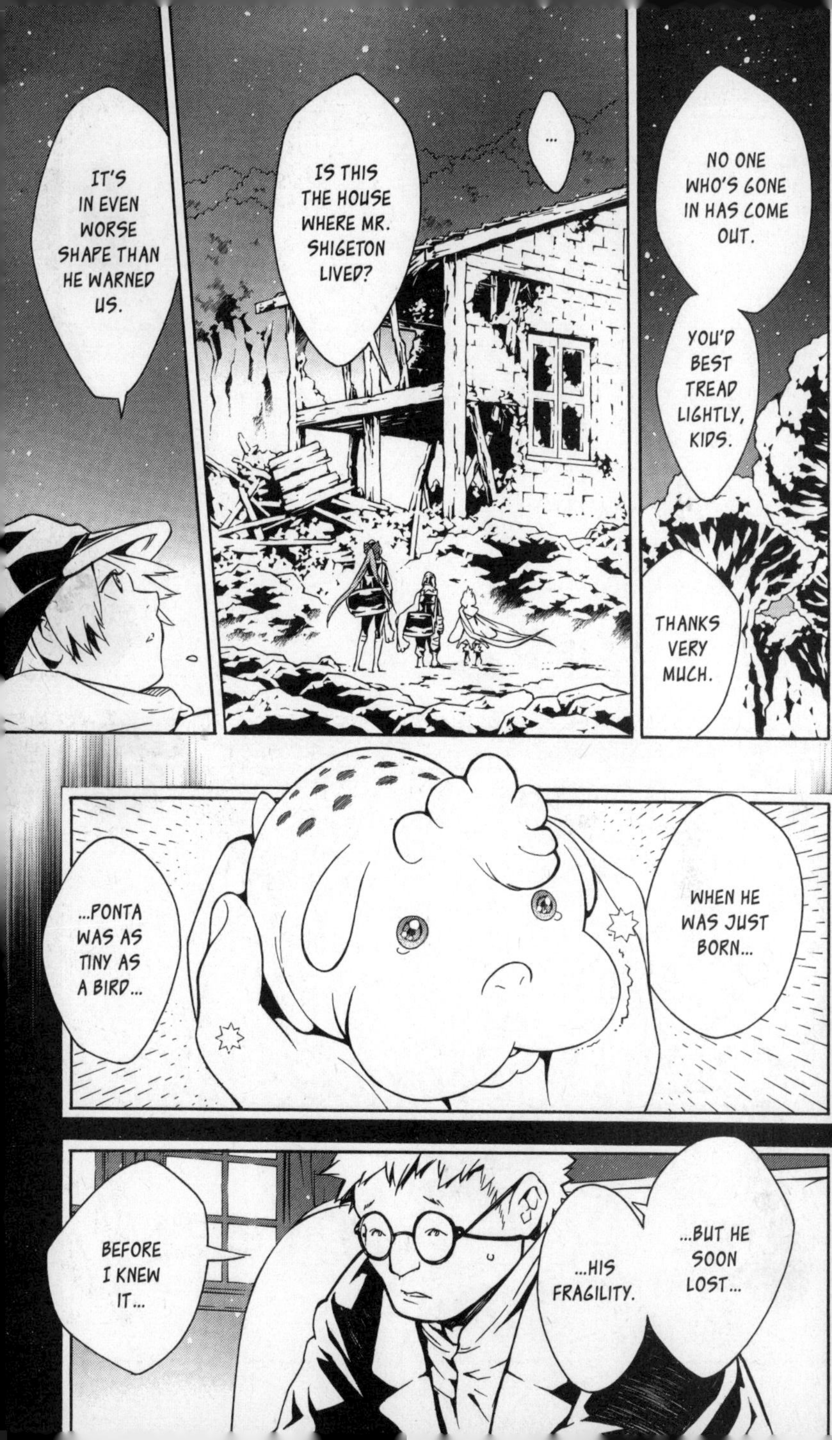
NO ONE WHO'S GONE IN HAS COME OUT.
YOU'D BEST TREAD LIGHTLY, KIDS.
THANKS VERY MUCH.
...
IS THIS THE HOUSE WHERE MR. SHIGETON LIVED?
IT'S IN EVEN WORSE SHAPE THAN HE WARNED US.
WHEN HE WAS JUST BORN...
...PONTA WAS AS TINY AS A BIRD...
...BUT HE SOON LOST...
...HIS FRAGILITY.
BEFORE I KNEW IT...

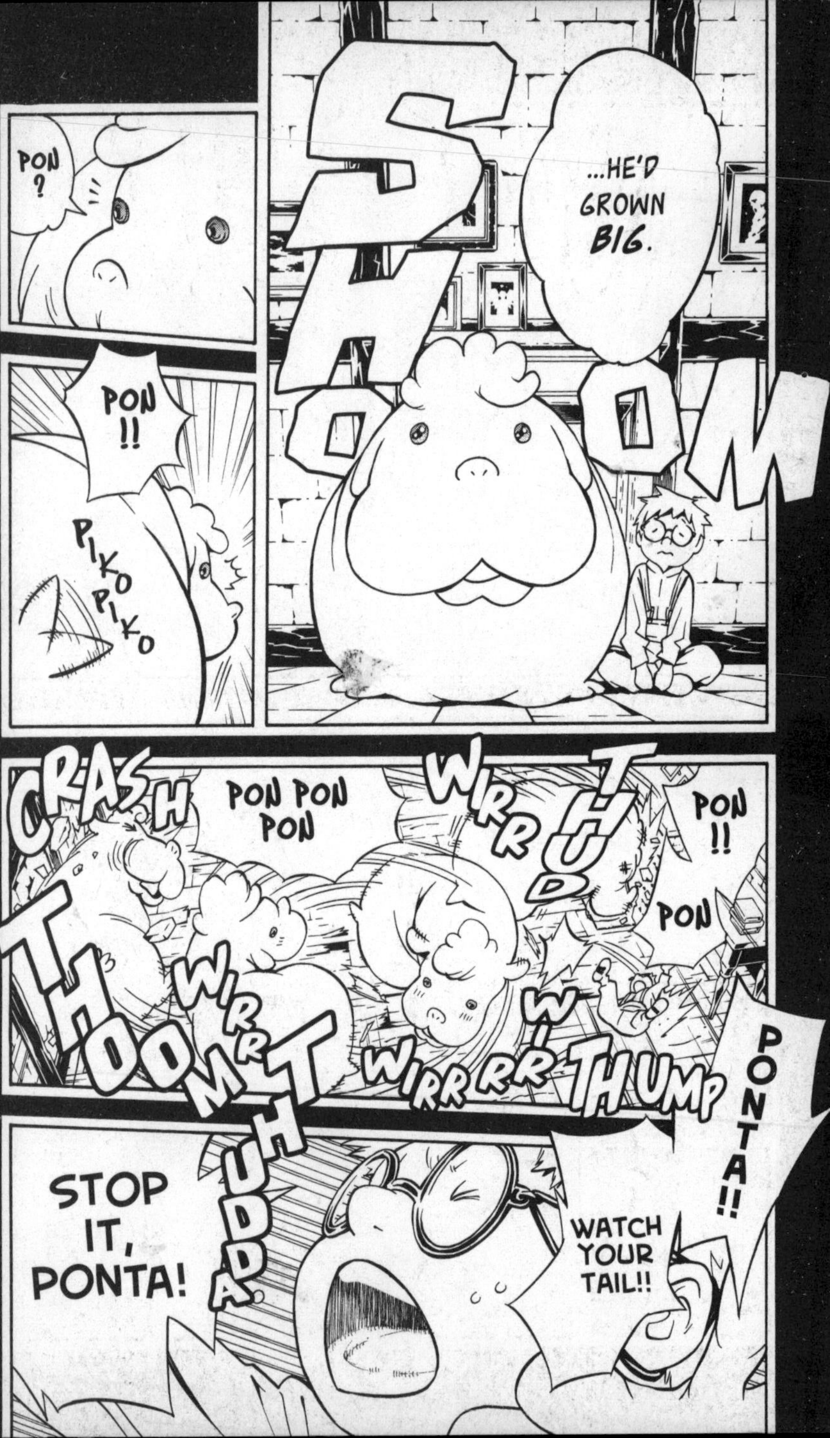
...HE'D GROWN BIG.
ZOOM
PON ?
PON !!
PIKO PIKO
PON !!
PON
THUD
WIRR
PON PON PON
CRASH
WIRR WIRR RR
THUMP
WIRR
THOOM
PONTA!!
WATCH YOUR TAIL!!
HUDDA.
STOP IT, PONTA!

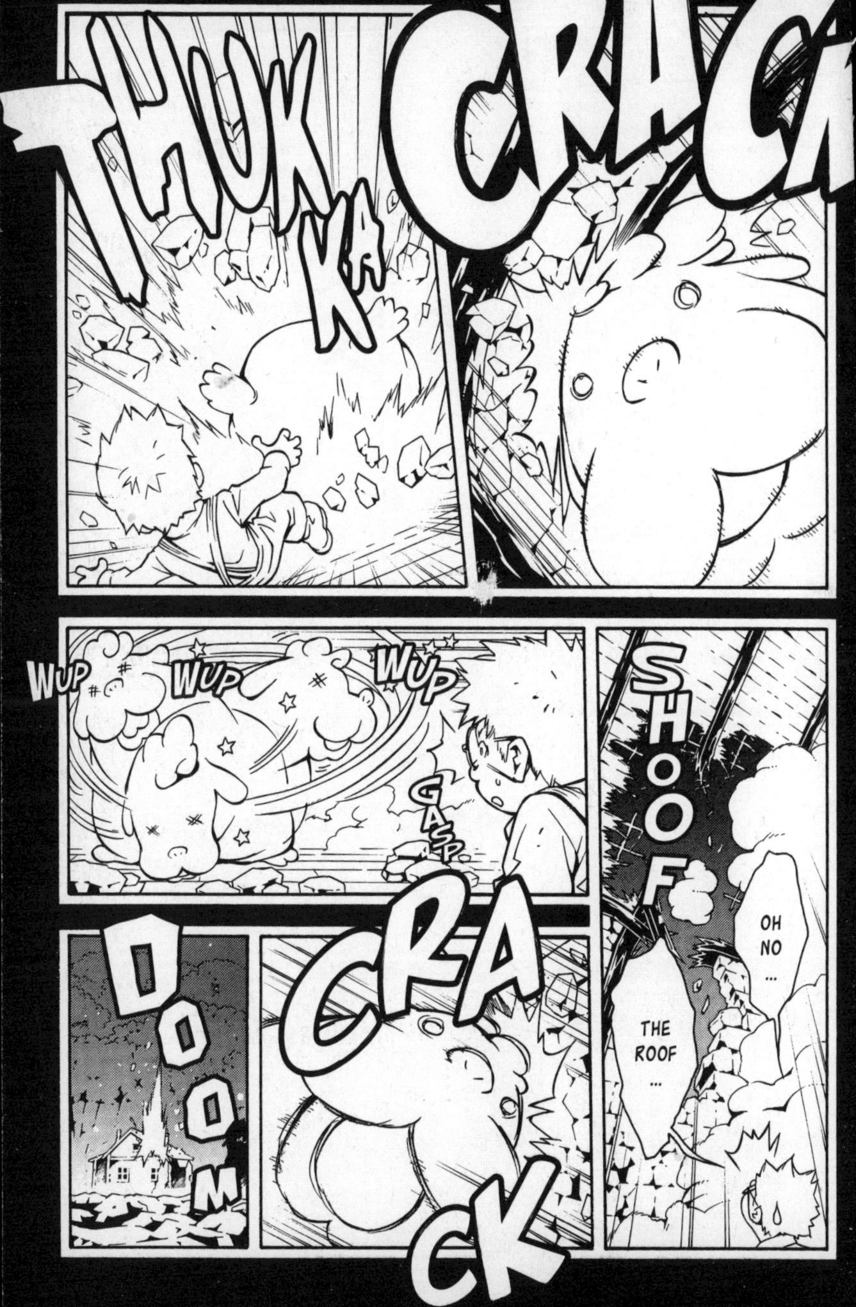
THUK
KA
CRAC
SHOOF
OH NO ...
THE ROOF ...
WUP
WUP
WUP
GASP
CRACK
DOOOM

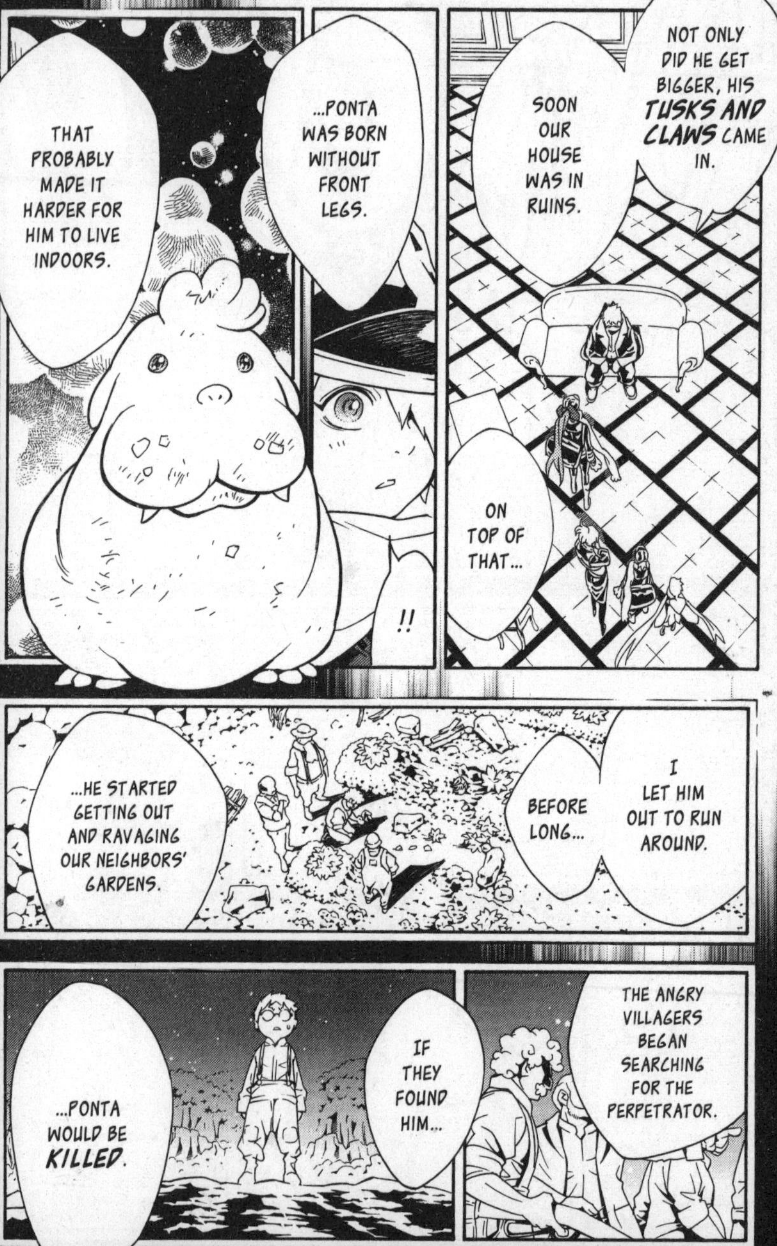

NOT ONLY DID HE GET BIGGER, HIS **TUSKS AND CLAWS** CAME IN.
SOON OUR HOUSE WAS IN RUINS.
ON TOP OF THAT...
...PONTA WAS BORN WITHOUT FRONT LEGS.
!!
THAT PROBABLY MADE IT HARDER FOR HIM TO LIVE INDOORS.
I LET HIM OUT TO RUN AROUND.
BEFORE LONG...
...HE STARTED GETTING OUT AND RAVAGING OUR NEIGHBORS' GARDENS.
THE ANGRY VILLAGERS BEGAN SEARCHING FOR THE PERPETRATOR.
IF THEY FOUND HIM...
...PONTA WOULD BE **KILLED**.

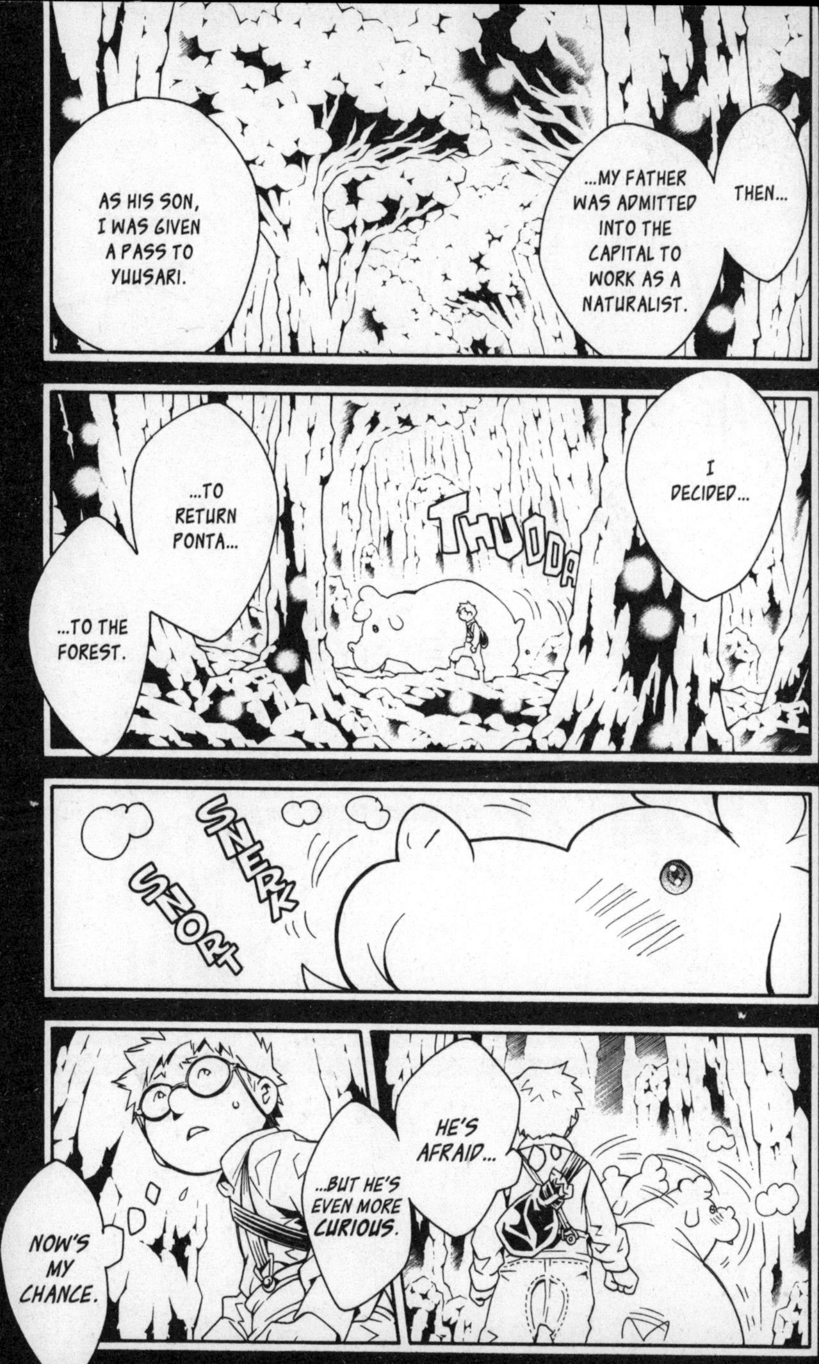
THEN...
...MY FATHER WAS ADMITTED INTO THE CAPITAL TO WORK AS A NATURALIST.
AS HIS SON, I WAS GIVEN A PASS TO YUUSARI.
I DECIDED...
THUDDA
...TO RETURN PONTA...
...TO THE FOREST.
SNERK
SNORT
HE'S AFRAID...
...BUT HE'S EVEN MORE CURIOUS.
NOW'S MY CHANCE.

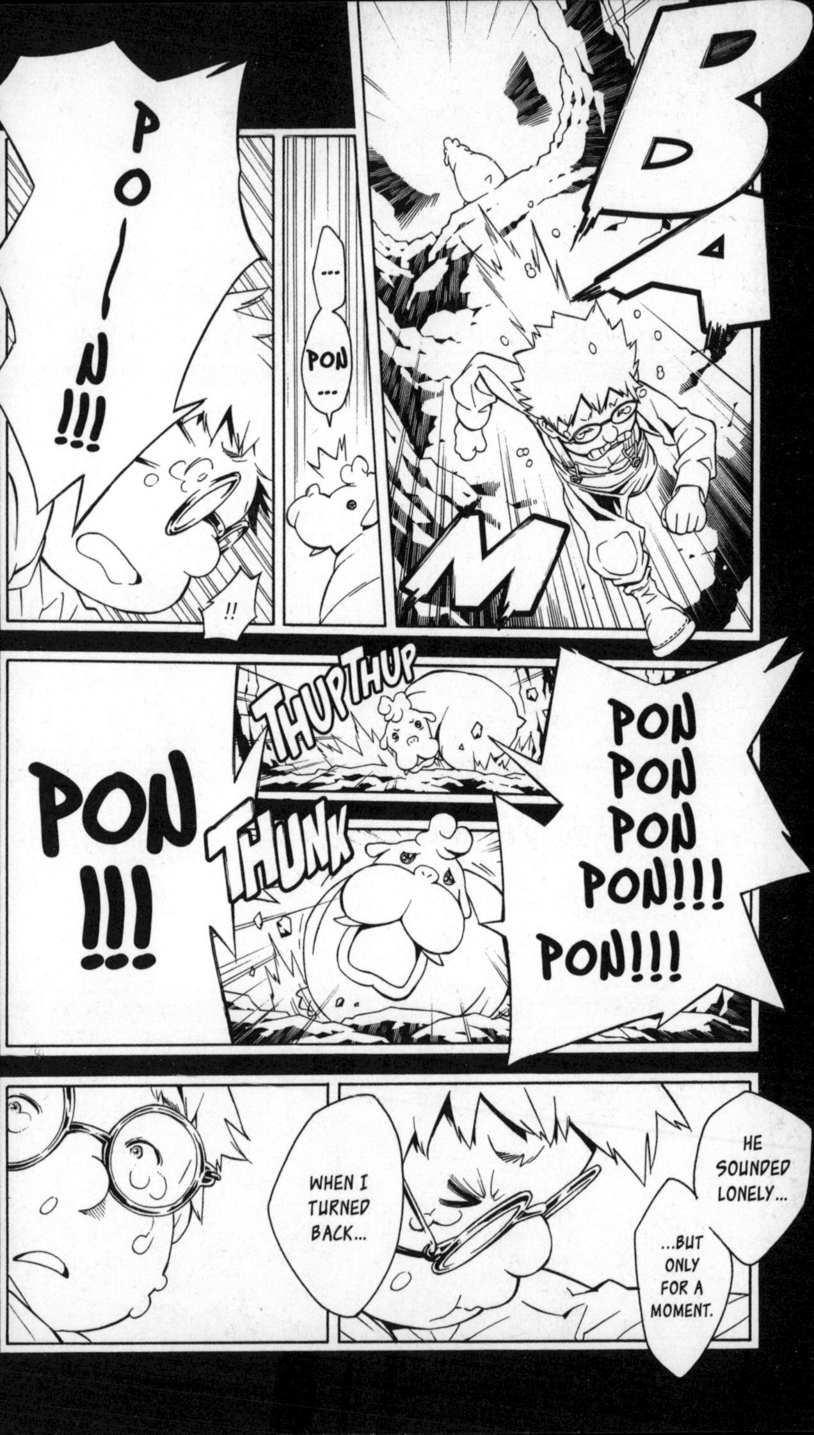
B
D
A
M
...
PON
...
PO-I-N!!!
!!
PON
PON
PON
PON!!!
PON!!!
THUPTHUP
THUNK
PON!!!
HE SOUNDED LONELY...
...BUT ONLY FOR A MOMENT.
WHEN I TURNED BACK...

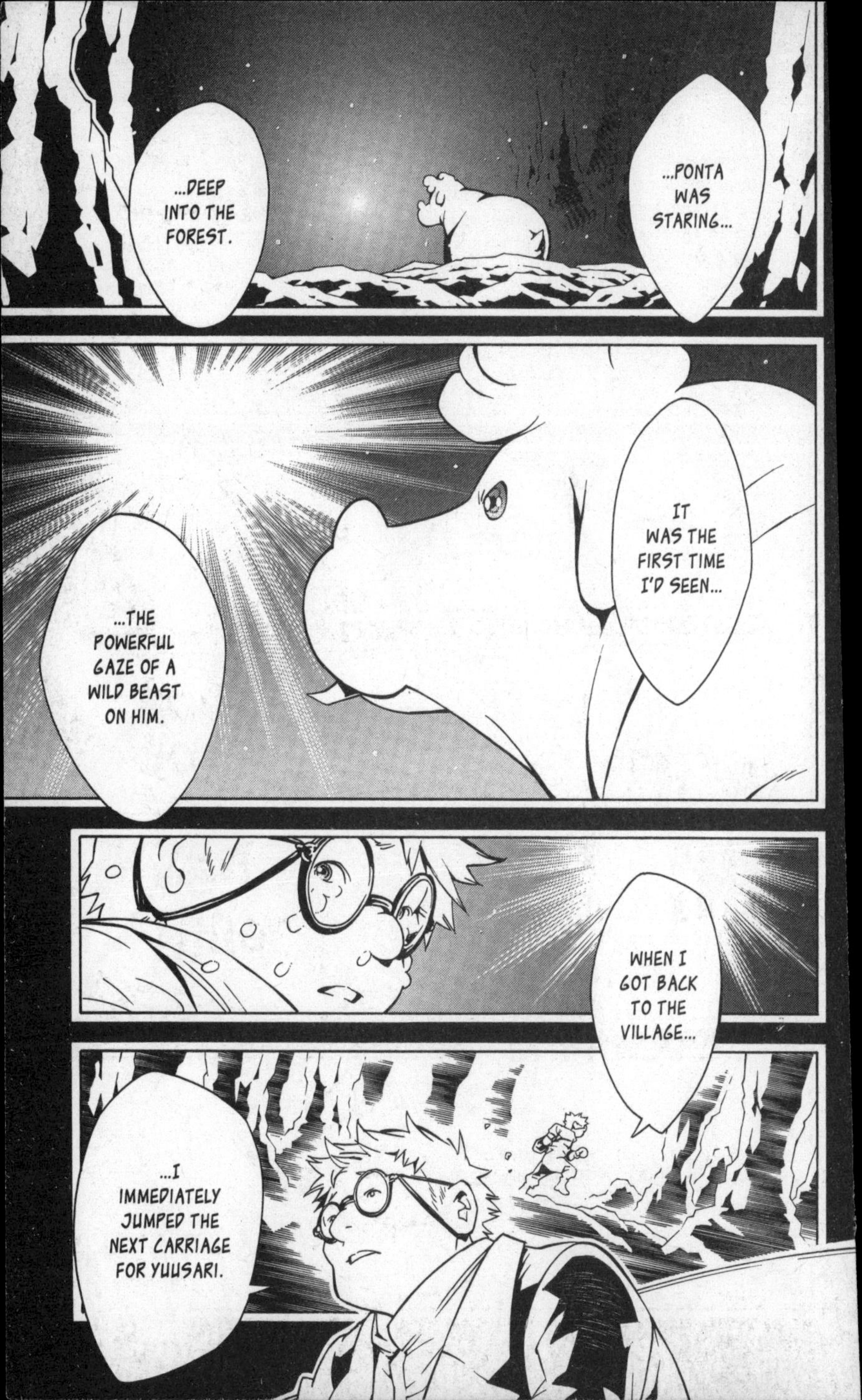
...PONTA WAS STARING...
...DEEP INTO THE FOREST.
IT WAS THE FIRST TIME I'D SEEN...
...THE POWERFUL GAZE OF A WILD BEAST ON HIM.
WHEN I GOT BACK TO THE VILLAGE...
...I IMMEDIATELY JUMPED THE NEXT CARRIAGE FOR YUUSARI.

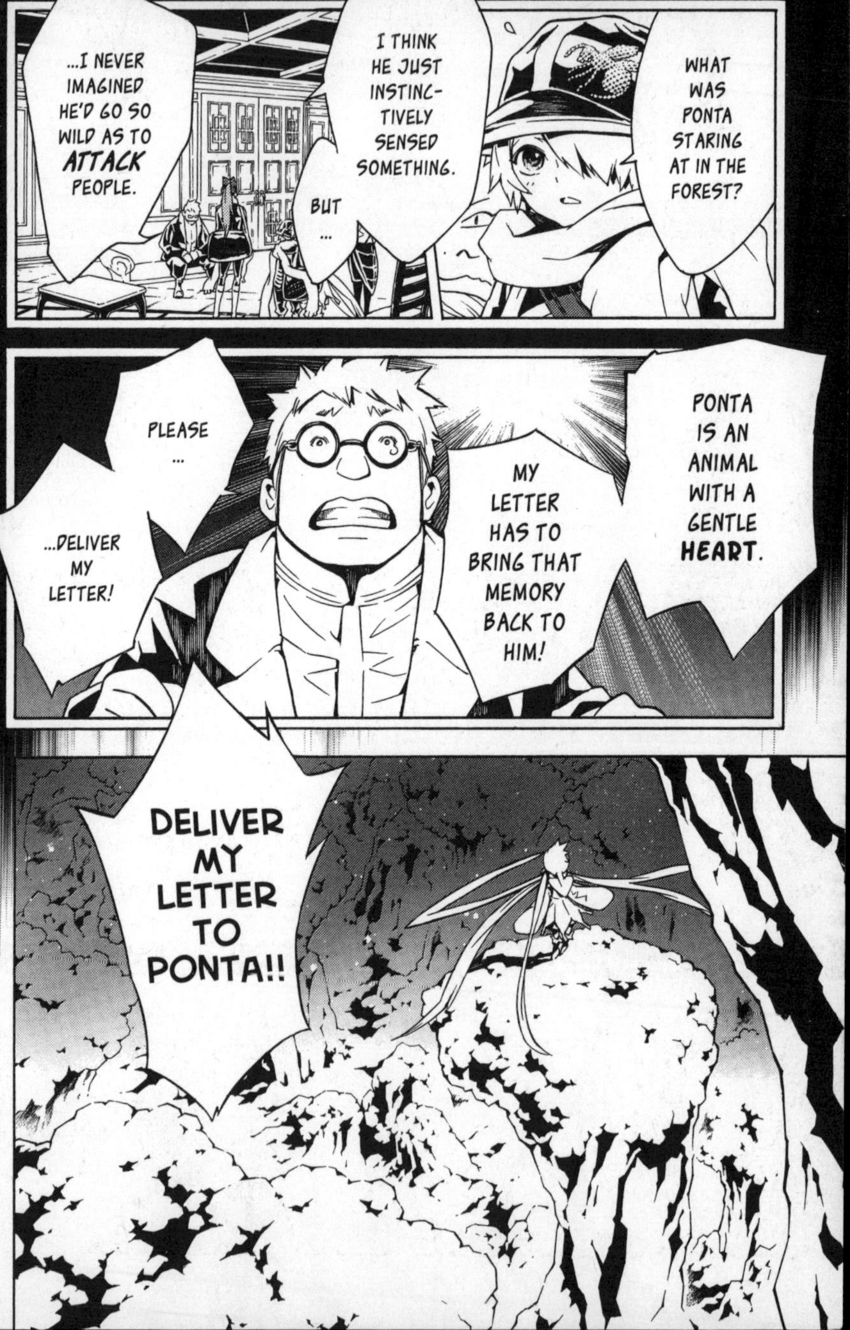
WHAT WAS PONTA STARING AT IN THE FOREST?
I THINK HE JUST INSTINCTIVELY SENSED SOMETHING.
BUT ...
...I NEVER IMAGINED HE'D GO SO WILD AS TO ATTACK PEOPLE.
PONTA IS AN ANIMAL WITH A GENTLE HEART.
MY LETTER HAS TO BRING THAT MEMORY BACK TO HIM!
PLEASE ...
...DELIVER MY LETTER!
DELIVER MY LETTER TO PONTA!!

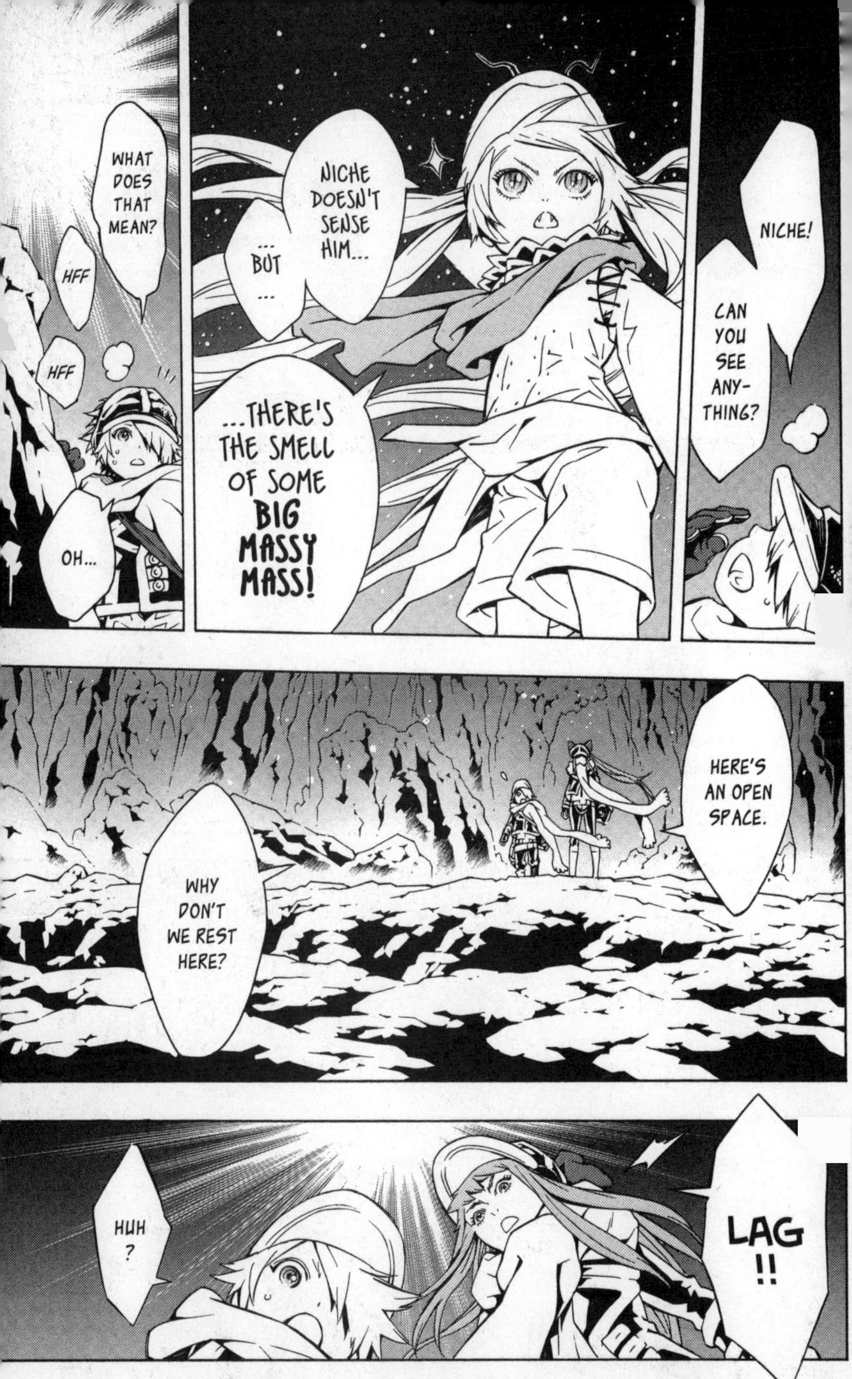
NICHE!
CAN YOU SEE ANYTHING?
NICHE DOESN'T SENSE HIM...
...BUT...
...THERE'S THE SMELL OF SOME **BIG MASSY MASS!**
WHAT DOES THAT MEAN?
HFF
HFF
OH...
HERE'S AN OPEN SPACE.
WHY DON'T WE REST HERE?
LAG!!
HUH?

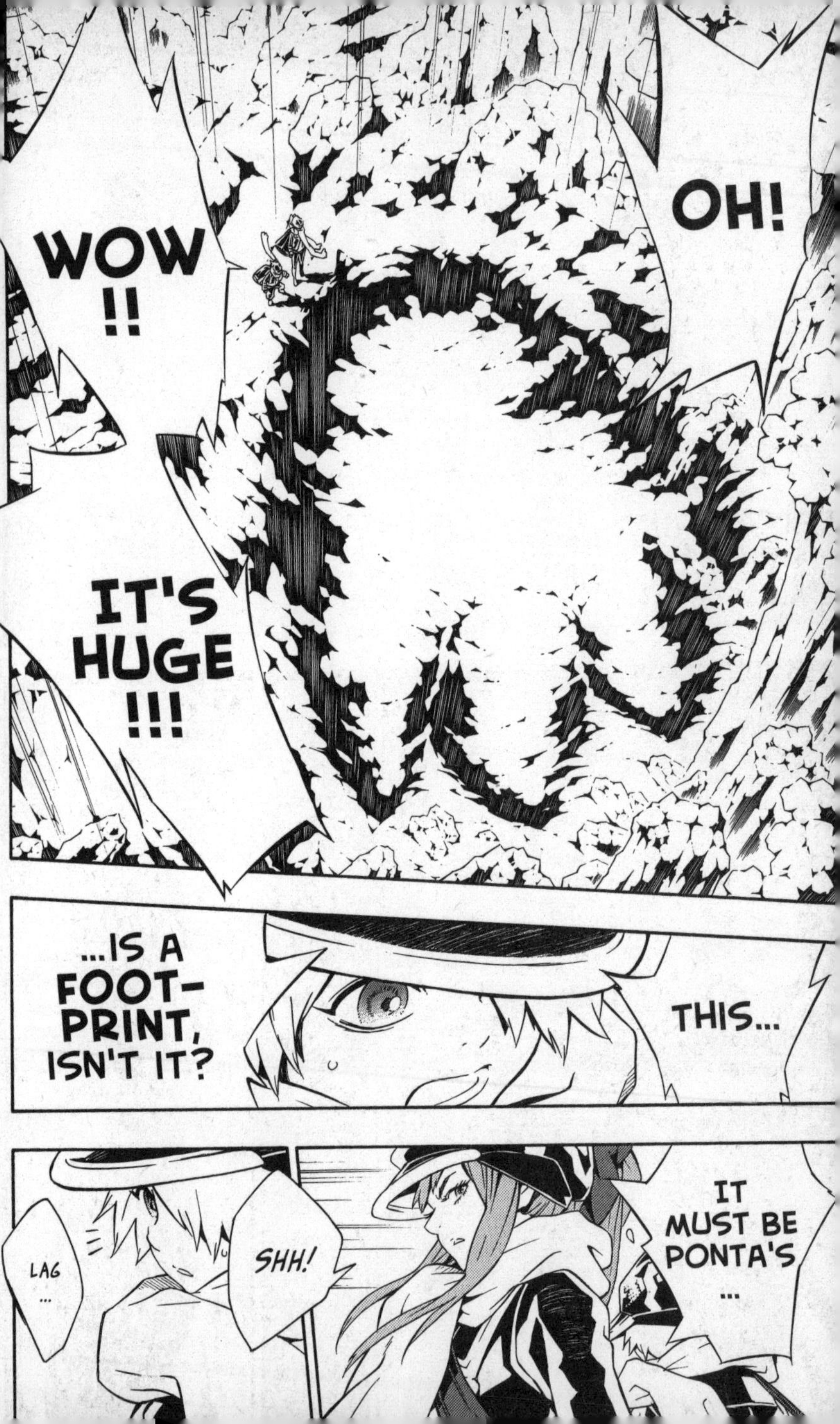
OH!
WOW!!
IT'S HUGE!!!
THIS...
...IS A FOOT-PRINT, ISN'T IT?
IT MUST BE PONTA'S...
SHH!
LAG...

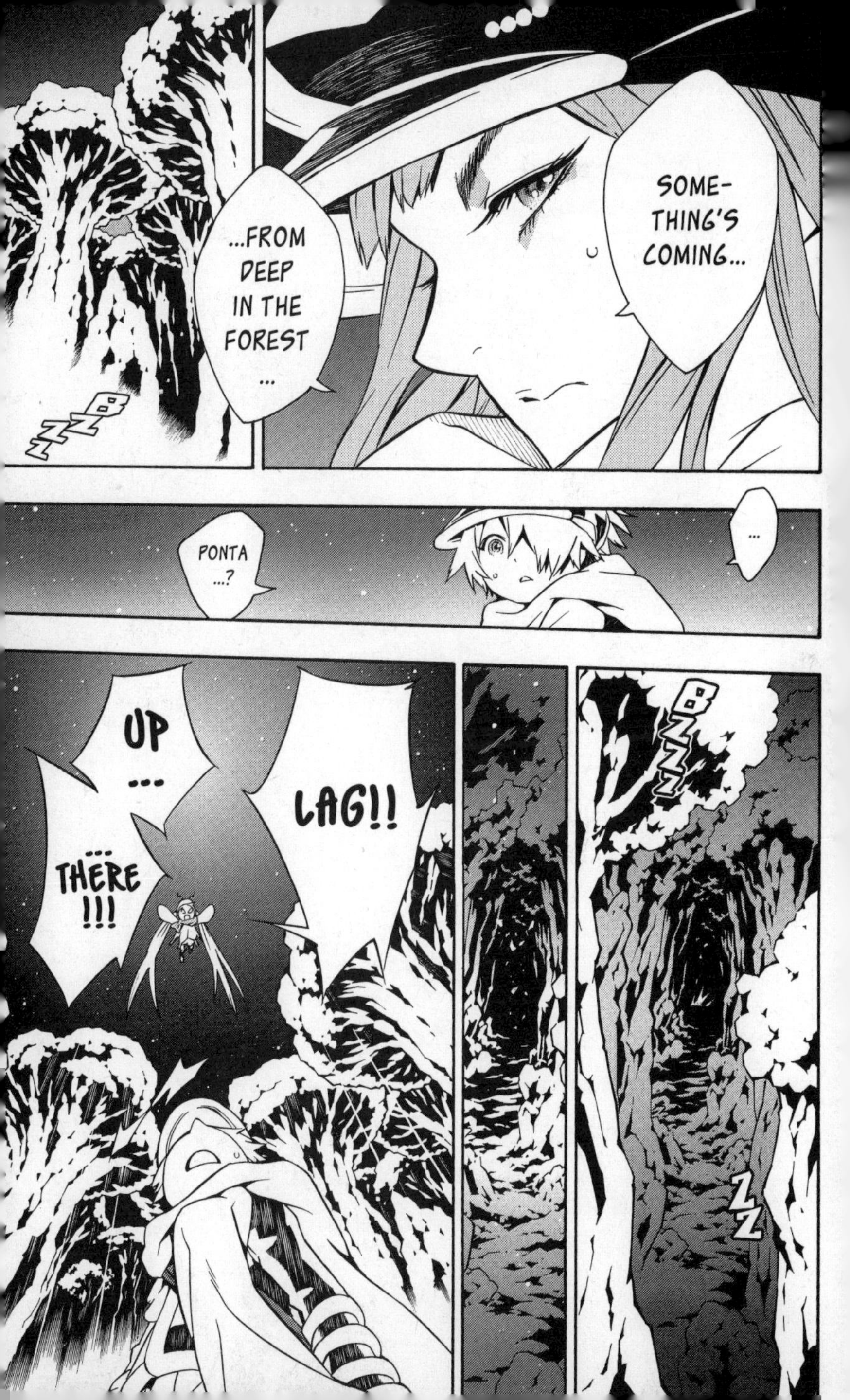
SOME-THING'S COMING...
...FROM DEEP IN THE FOREST ...
BZZZ
...
PONTA ...?
BZZZ
ZZ
LAG!!
UP ... ... THERE!!!

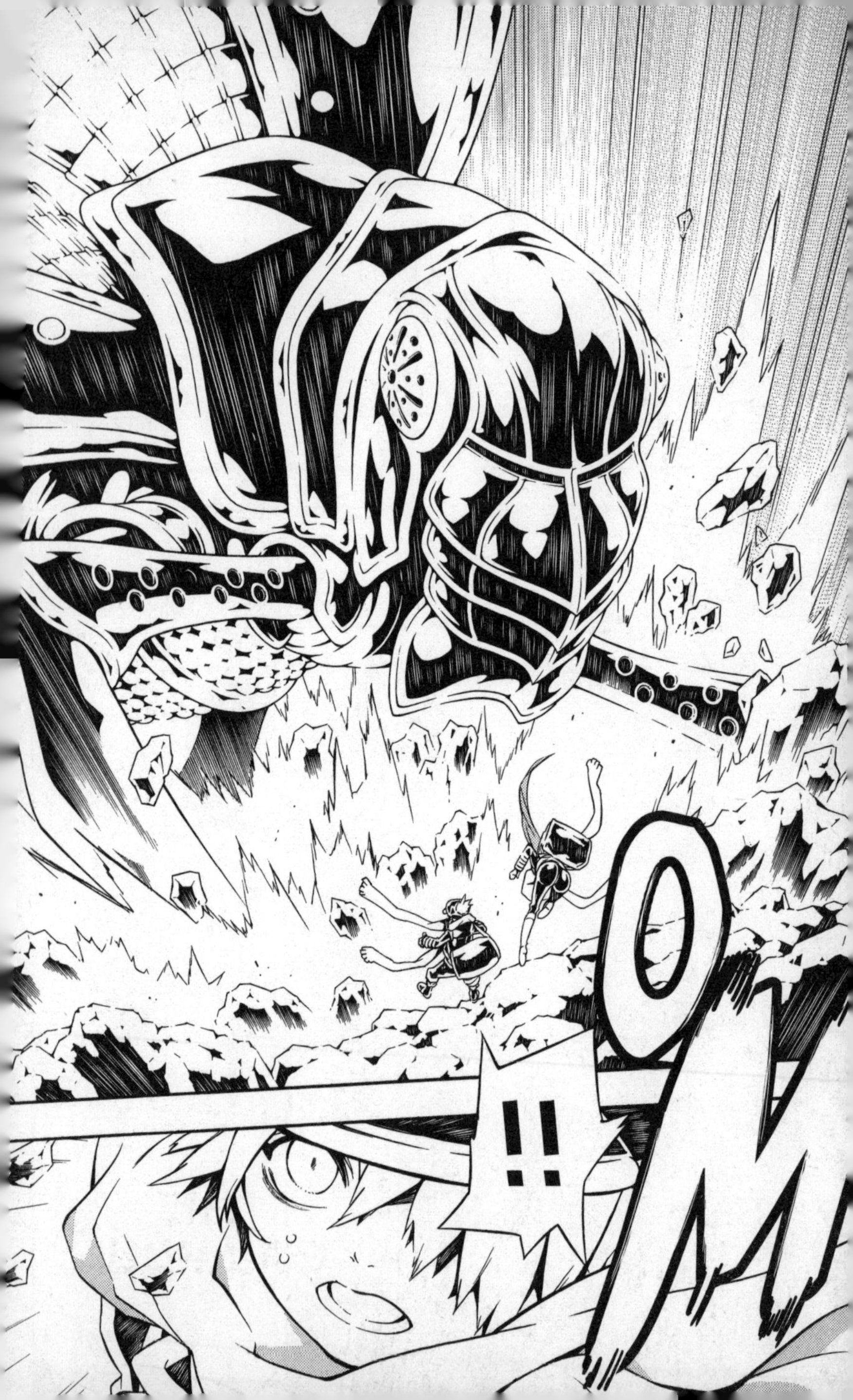
!!

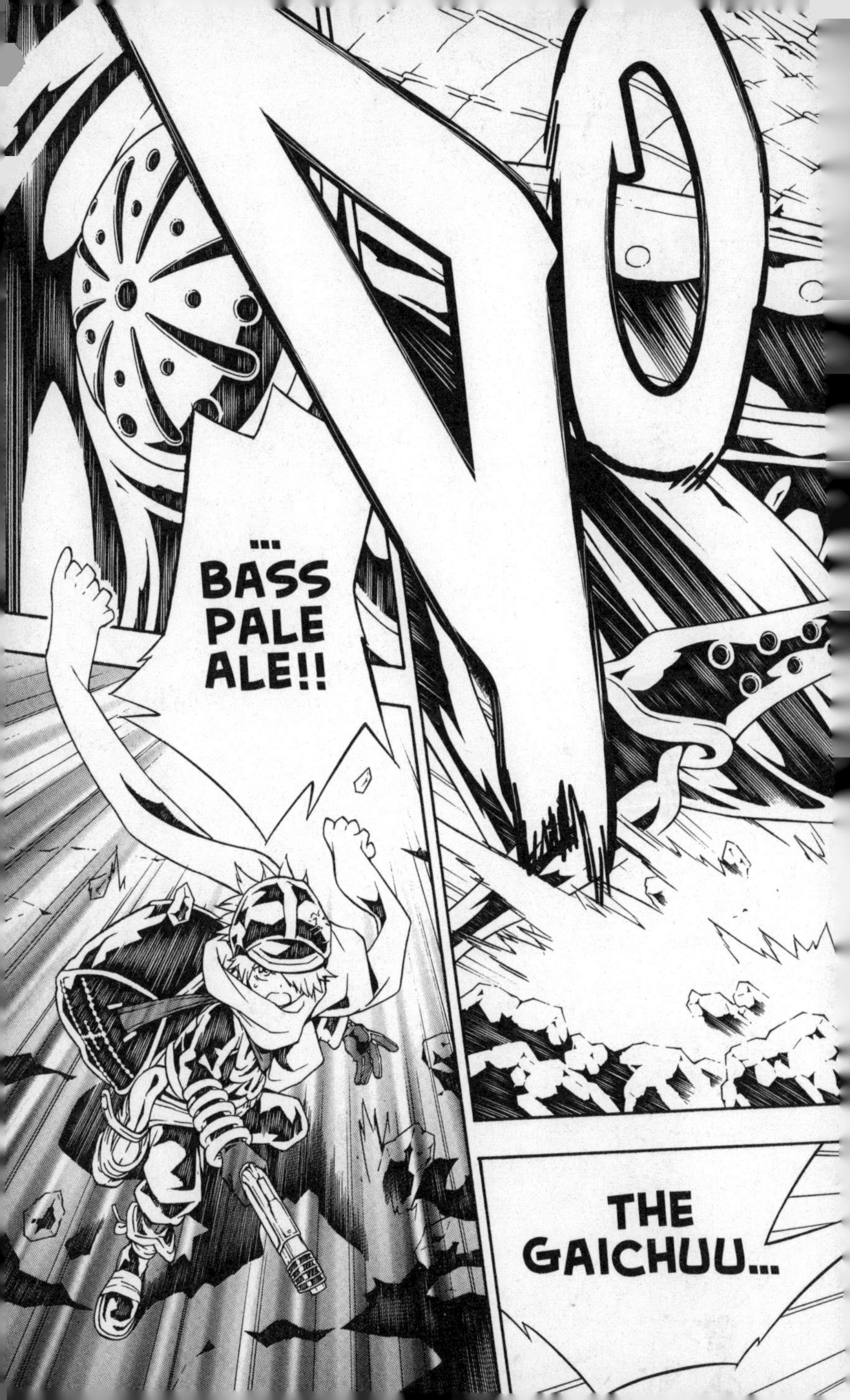
...BASS PALE ALE!!
THE GAICHUU...

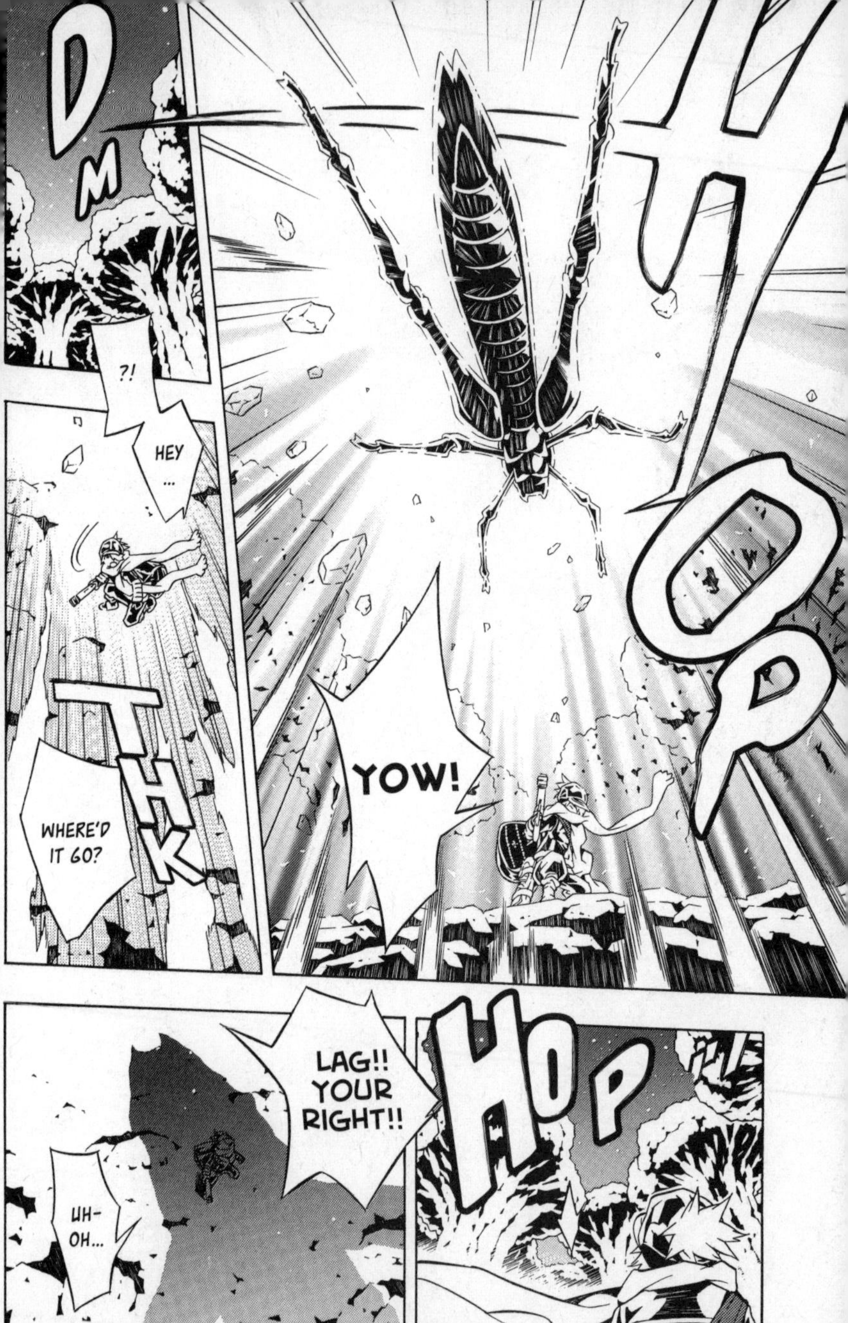
YOW!
DM
?!
HEY ...
THK
WHERE'D IT GO?
HOP
LAG!! YOUR RIGHT!!
UH-OH...

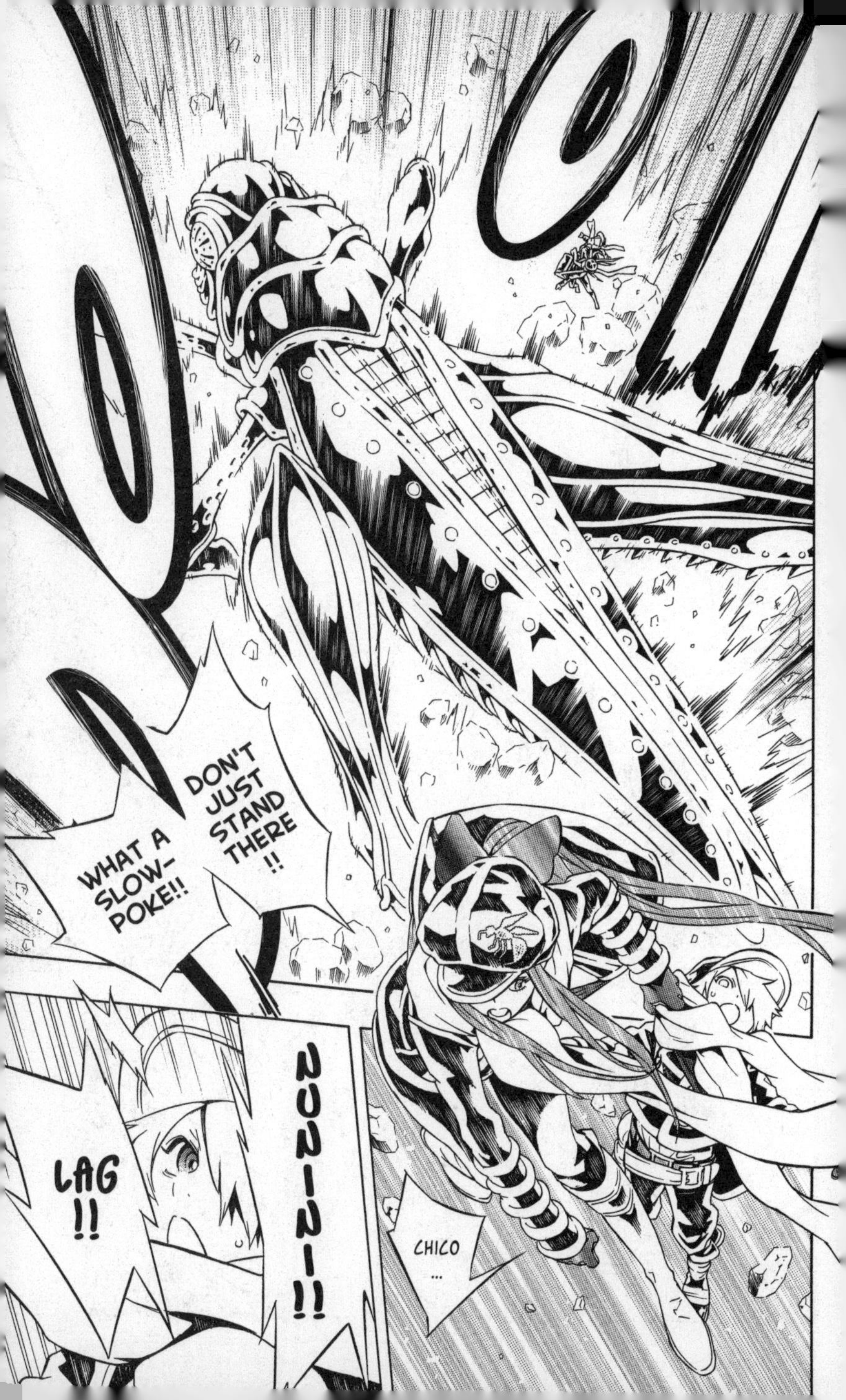
DON'T JUST STAND THERE!!
WHAT A SLOW-POKE!!
CHICO...
NUNINI!!
LAG!!

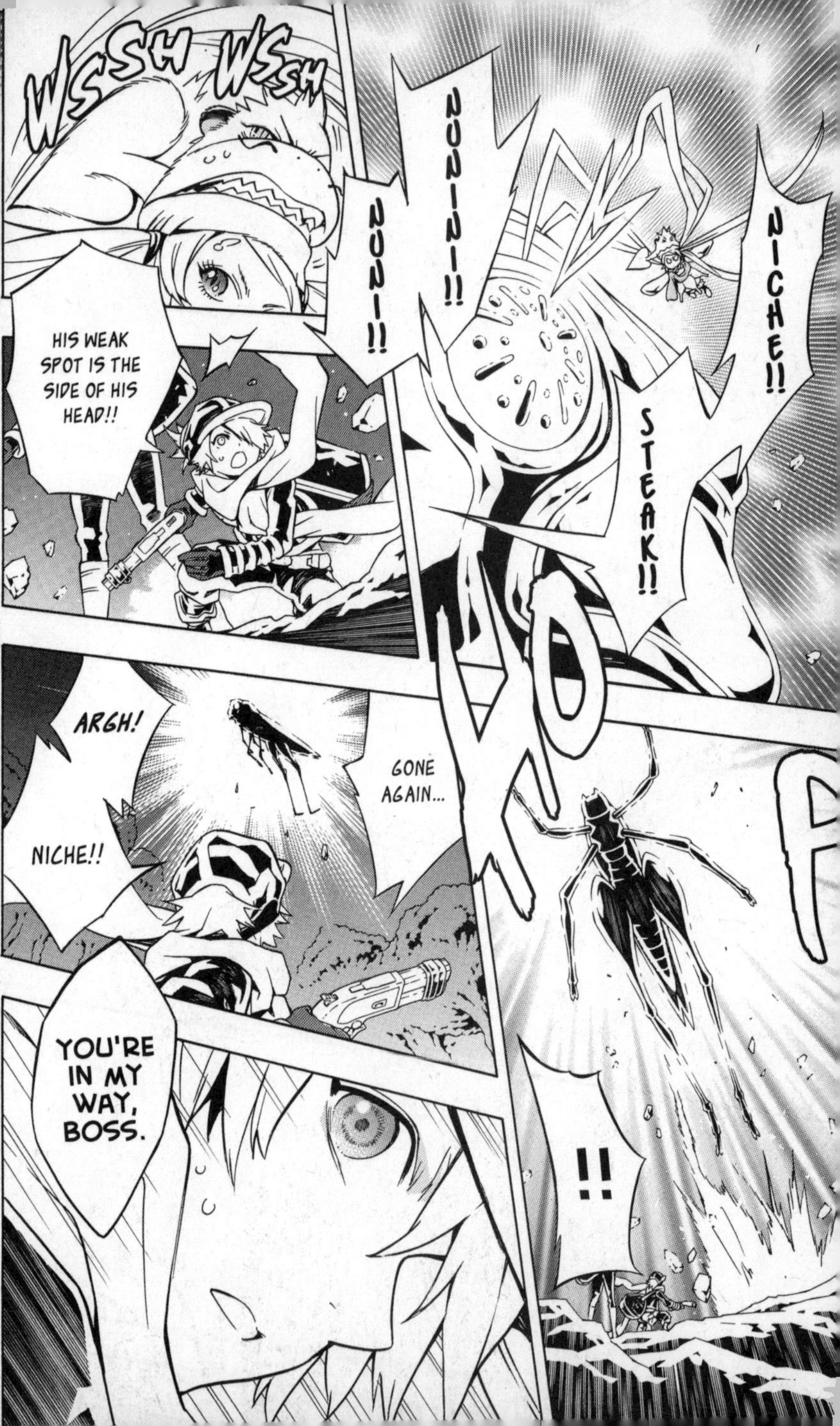
NICHE!!
STEAK!!
NUNINI!!
NUNI!!
WSSH WSSH
HIS WEAK SPOT IS THE SIDE OF HIS HEAD!!
!!
GONE AGAIN...
ARGH!
NICHE!!
YOU'RE IN MY WAY, BOSS.

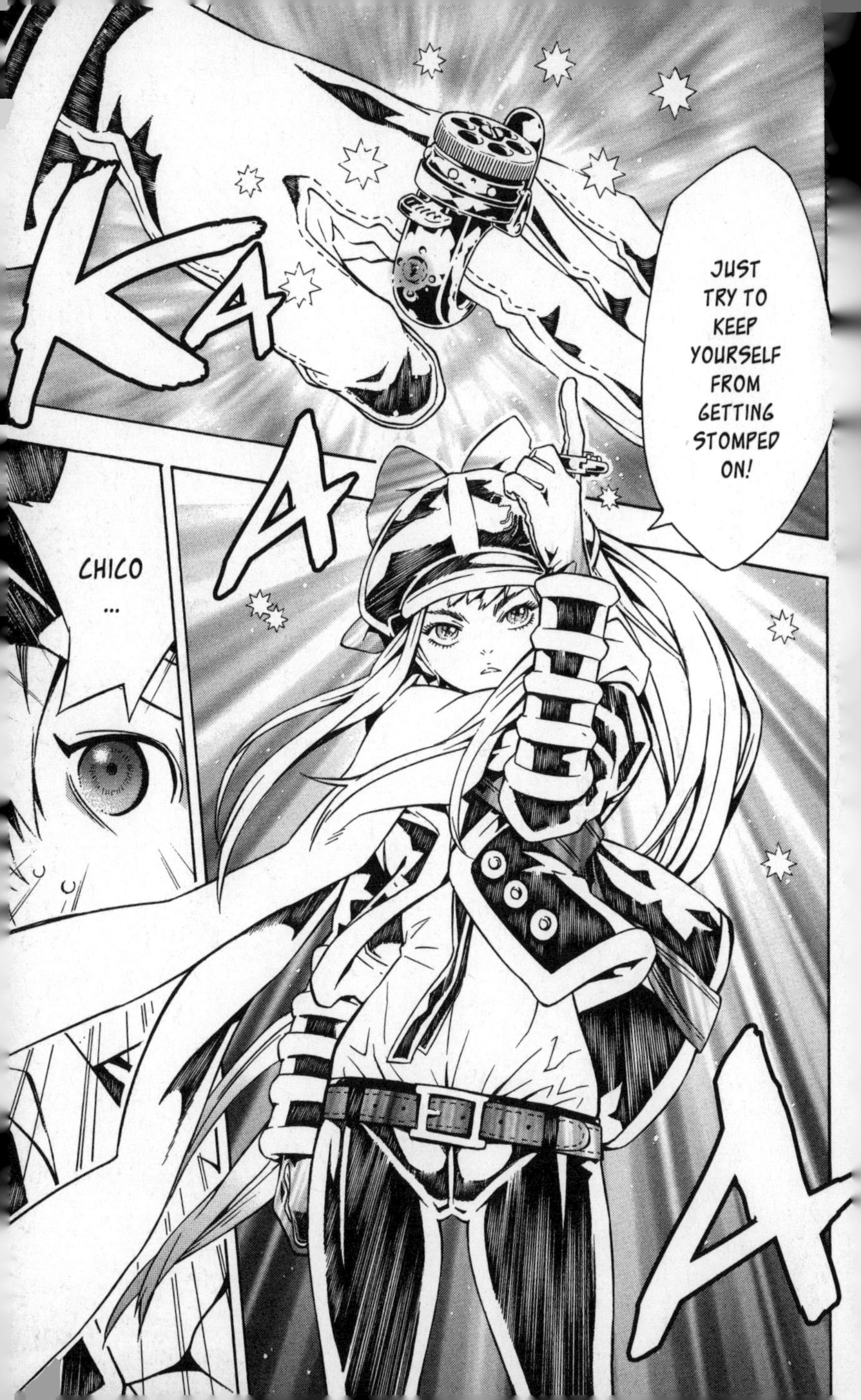
JUST TRY TO KEEP YOURSELF FROM GETTING STOMPED ON!
KA A A
CHICO ...

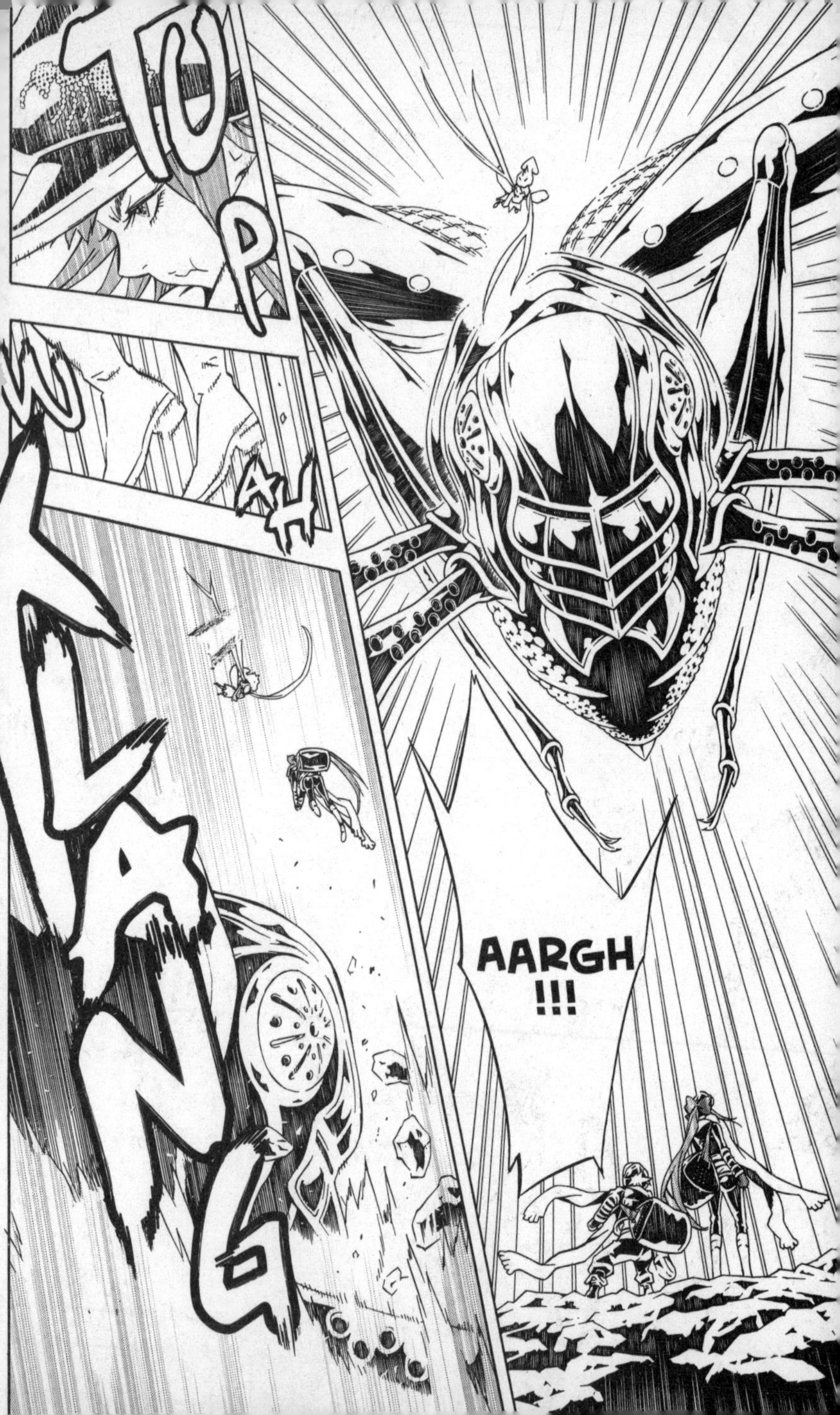
AARGH
!!!
TUP
AH

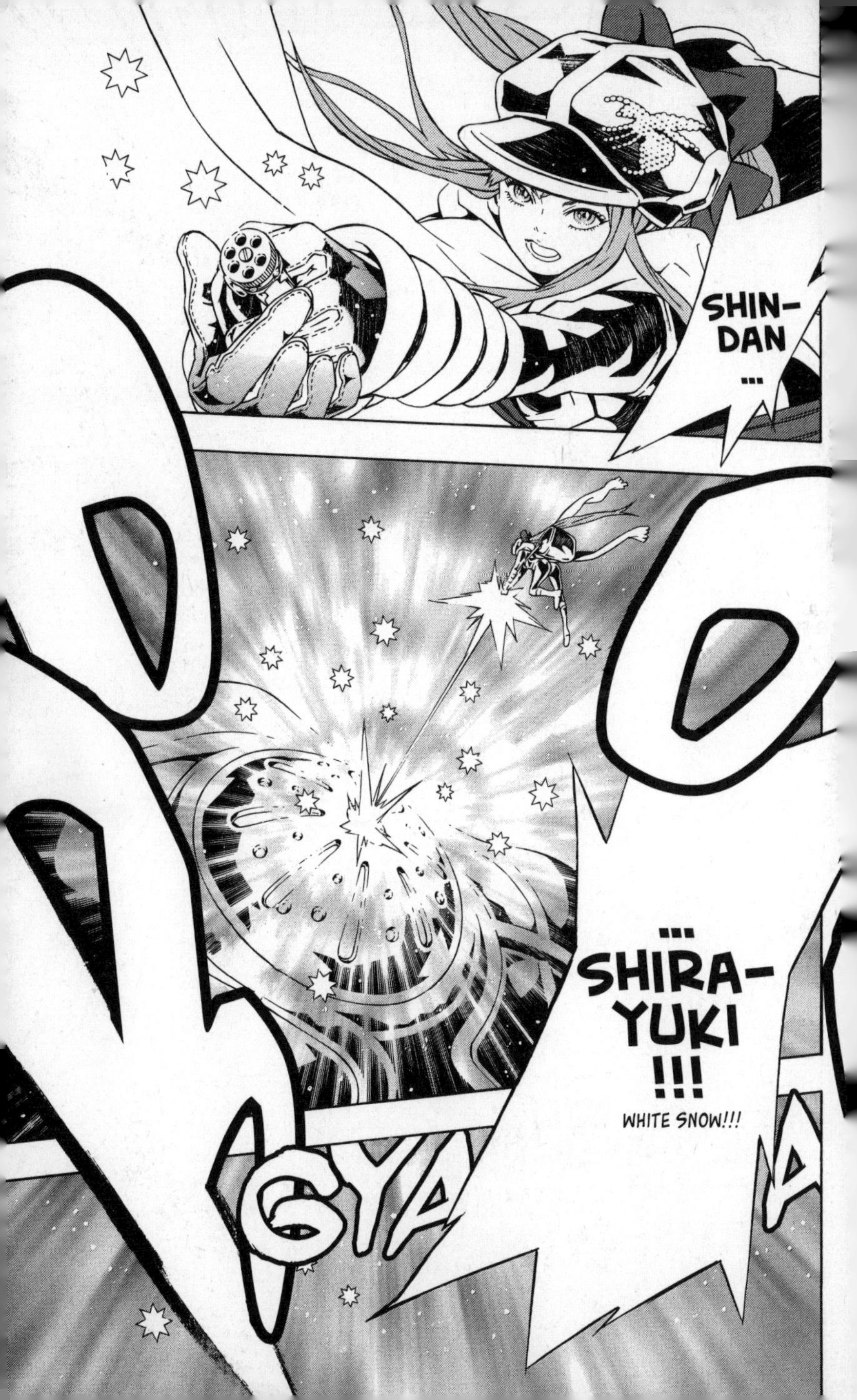
SHIN-DAN ...
... SHIRA-YUKI !!!
WHITE SNOW!!!
GYA A

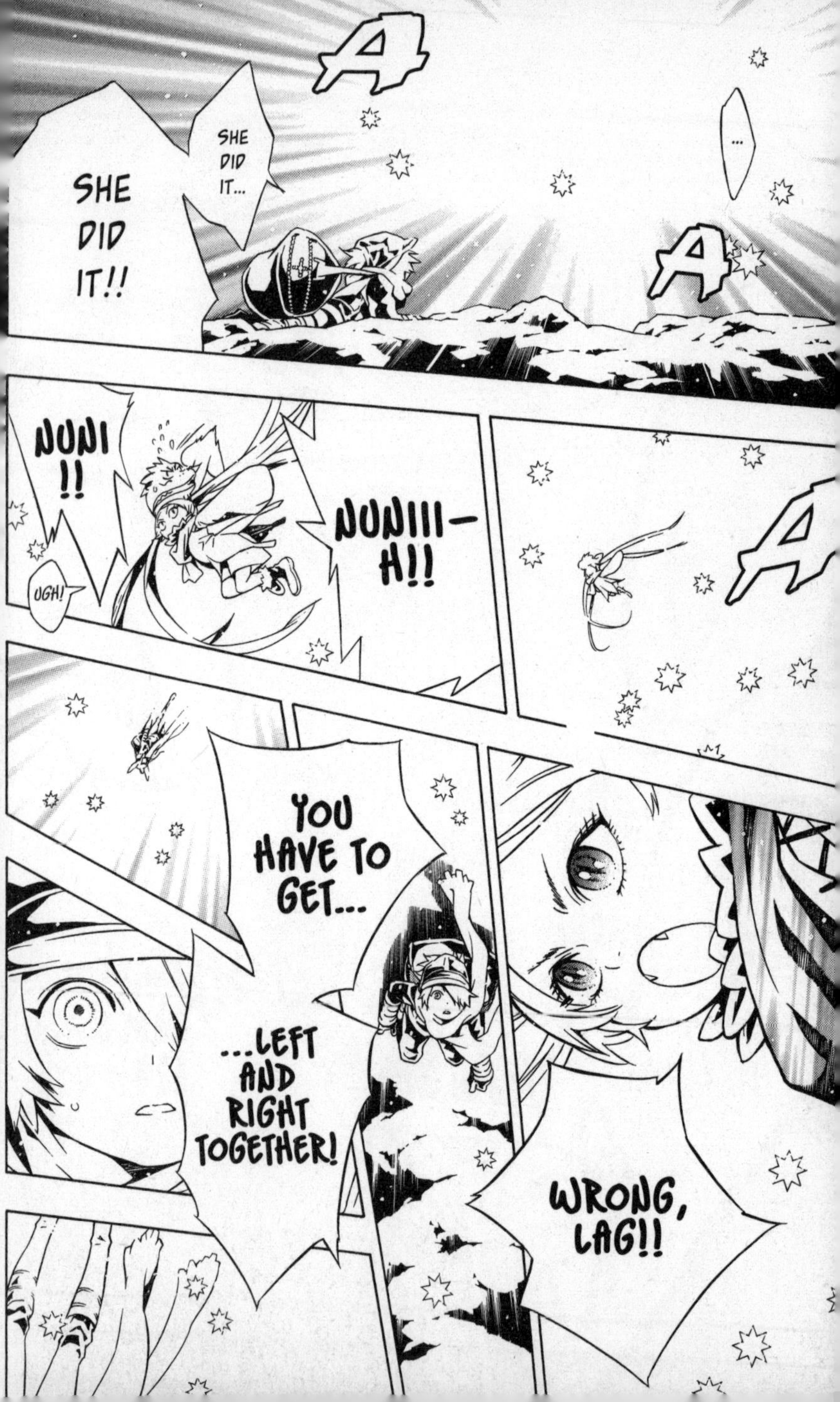
A
...
A
SHE DID IT...
SHE DID IT!!
A
NUNIII-H!!
NUNI!!
UGH!
YOU HAVE TO GET...
...LEFT AND RIGHT TOGETHER!
WRONG, LAG!!

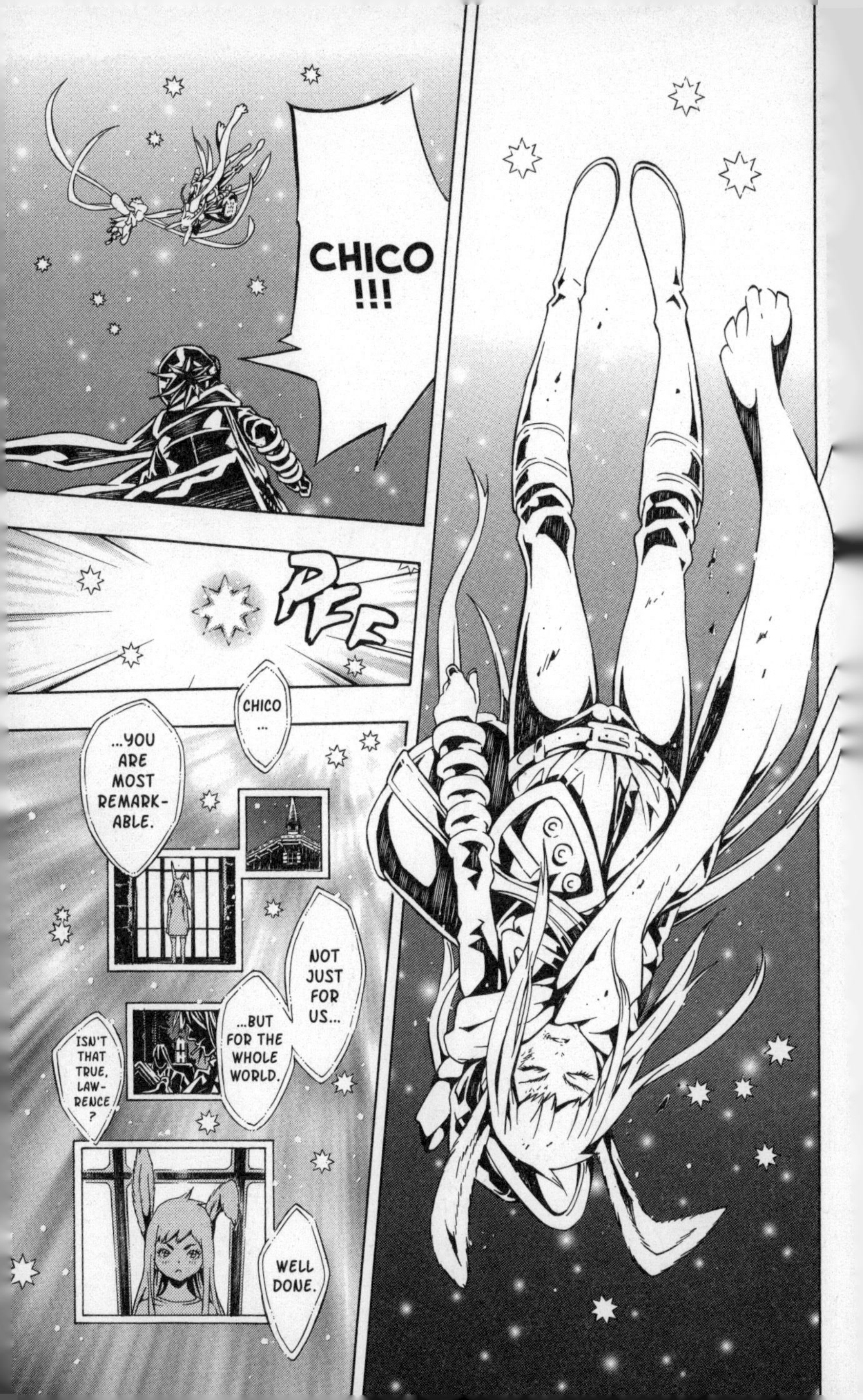
CHICO !!!
PFF
CHICO ...
...YOU ARE MOST REMARK-ABLE.
NOT JUST FOR US...
...BUT FOR THE WHOLE WORLD.
ISN'T THAT TRUE, LAW-RENCE ?
WELL DONE.

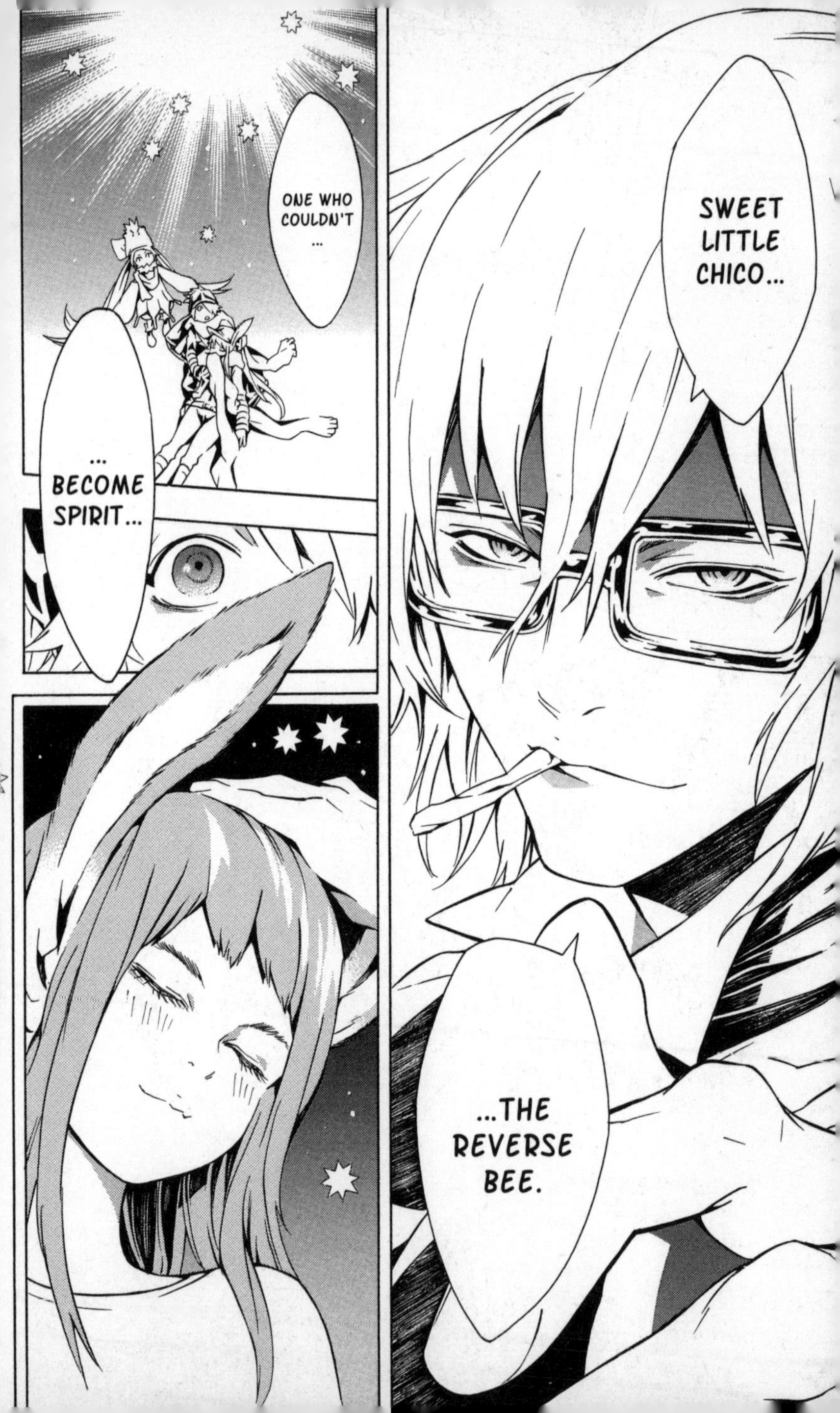
SWEET LITTLE CHICO...
...THE REVERSE BEE.
ONE WHO COULDN'T ...
... BECOME SPIRIT...

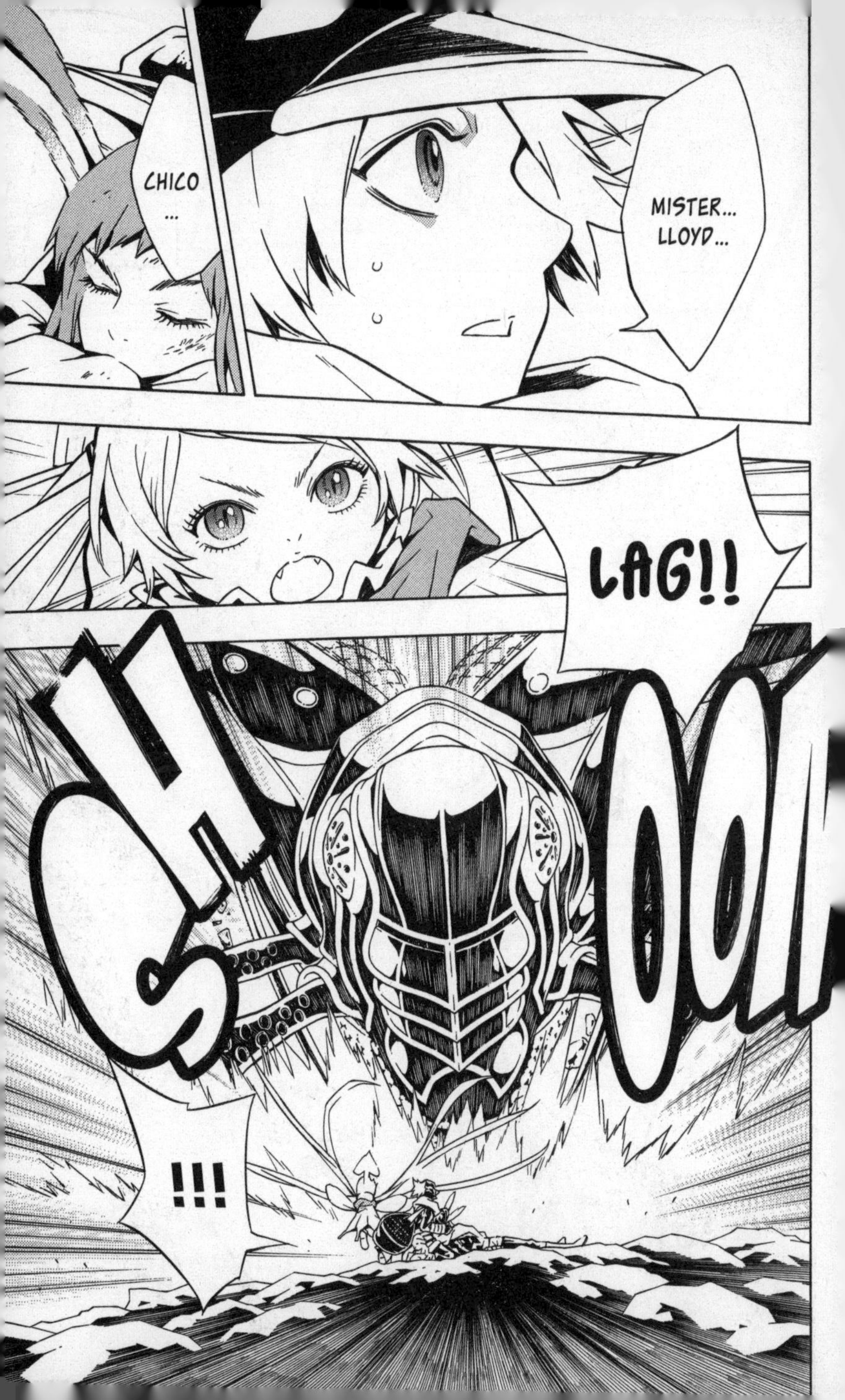
MISTER... LLOYD...
CHICO ...
LAG!!
SHOO
!!!

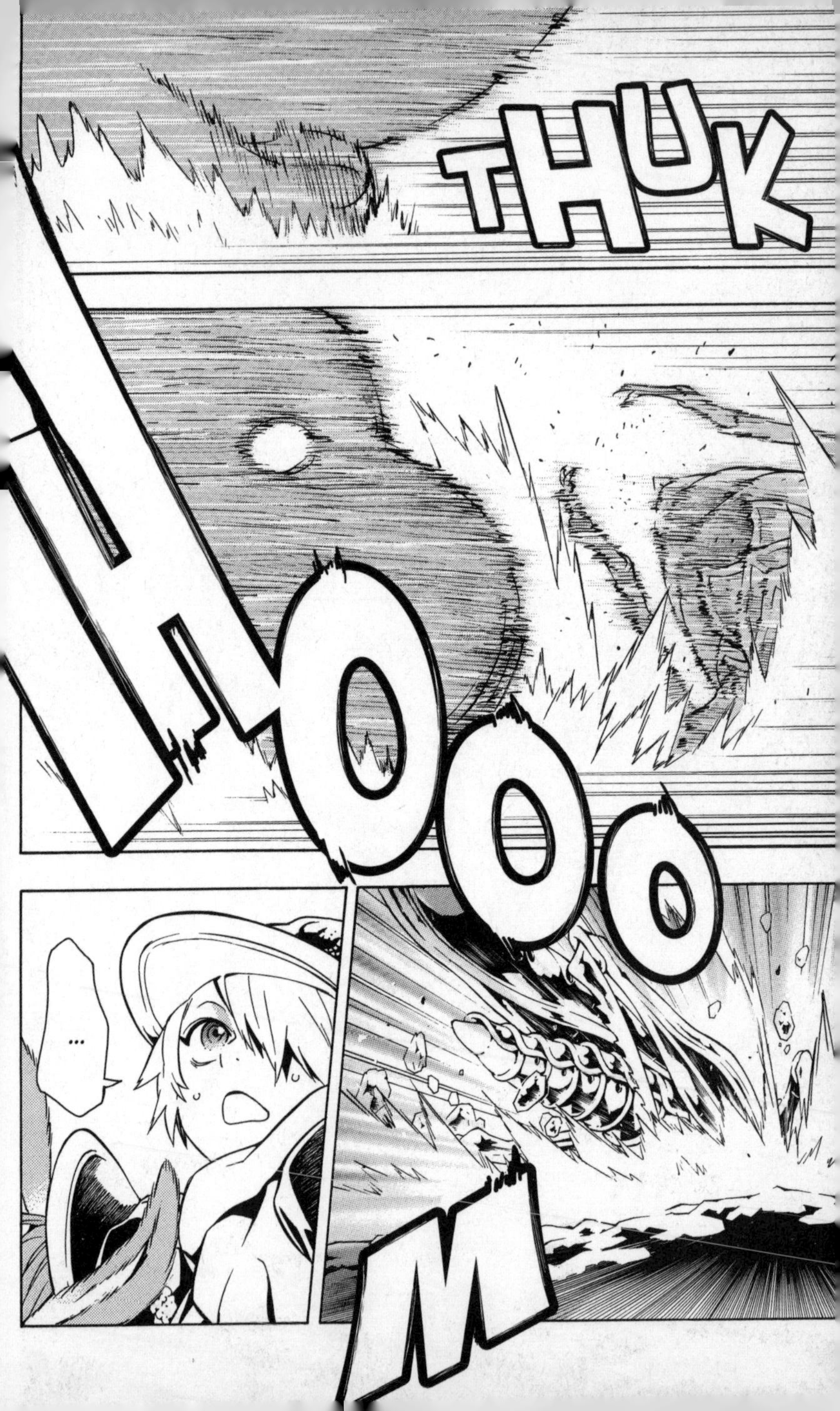
THUK
FOOOOM
...

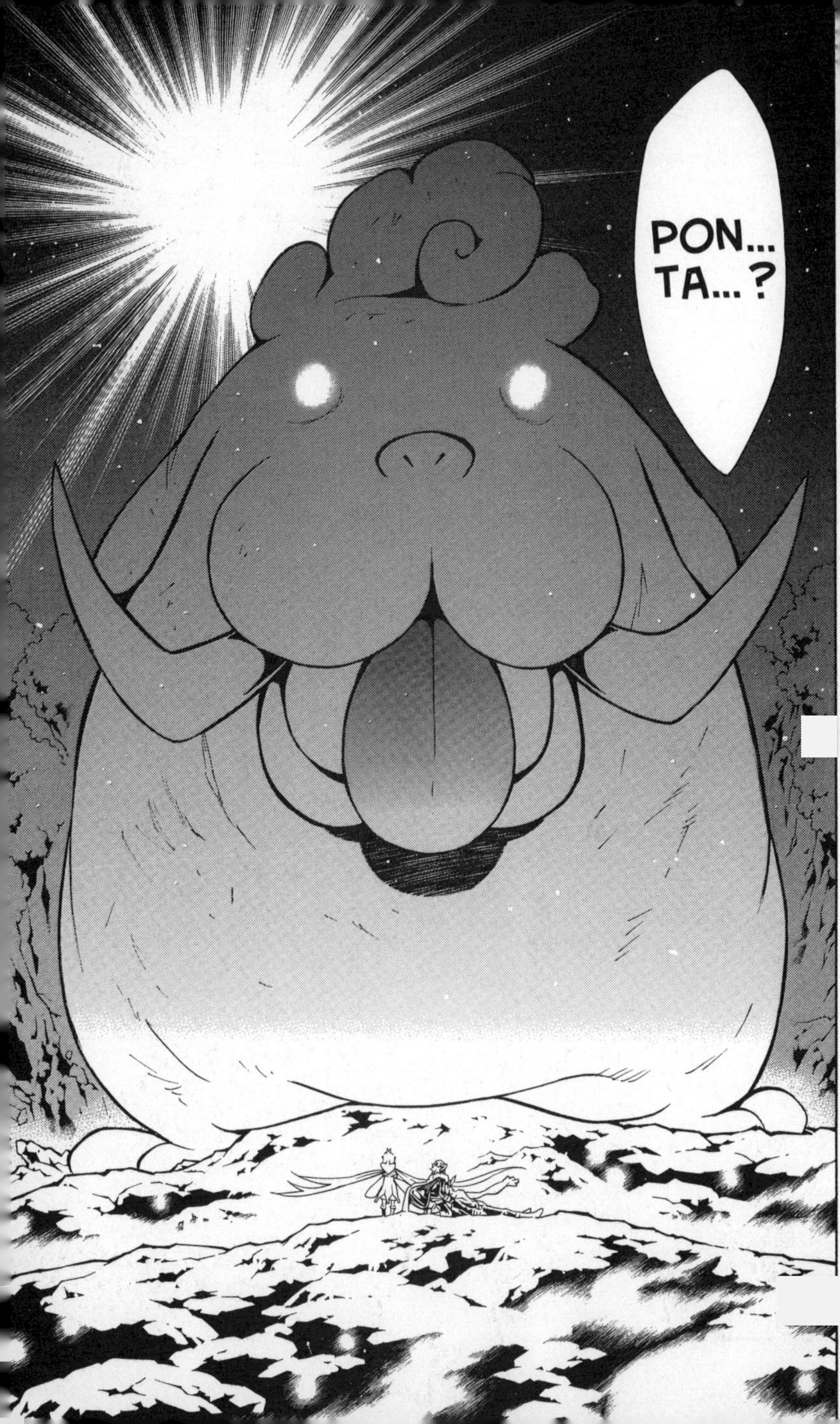
PON... TA...?

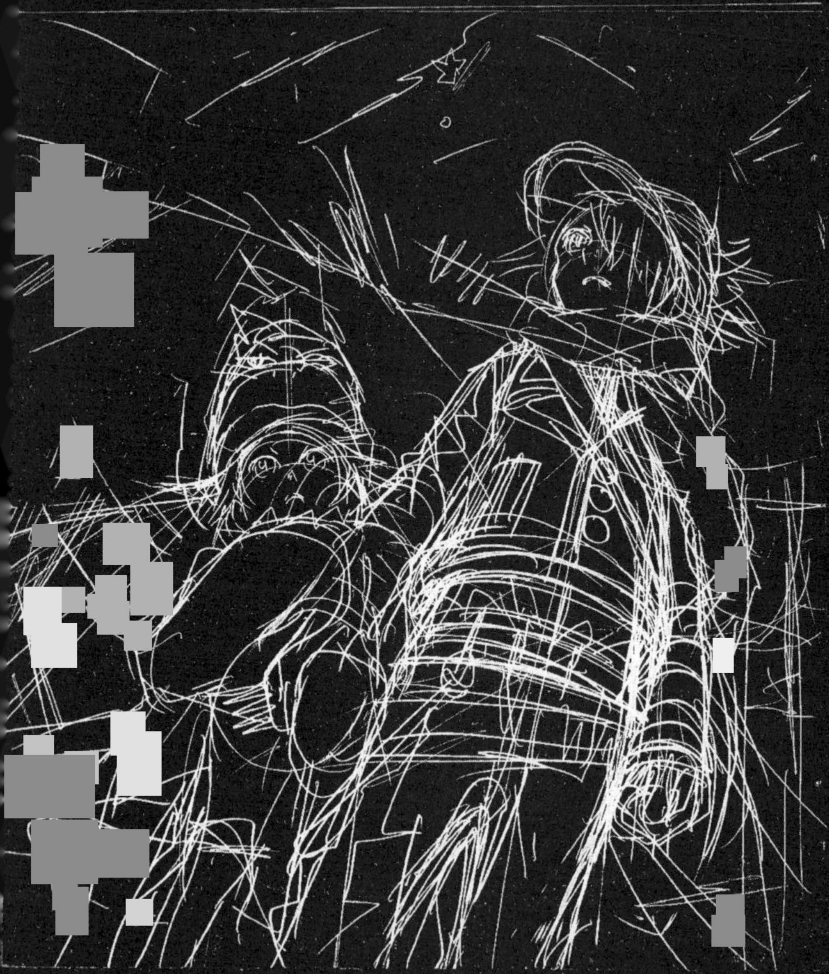

Rough draft of art for the 2nd anime DVD box set.

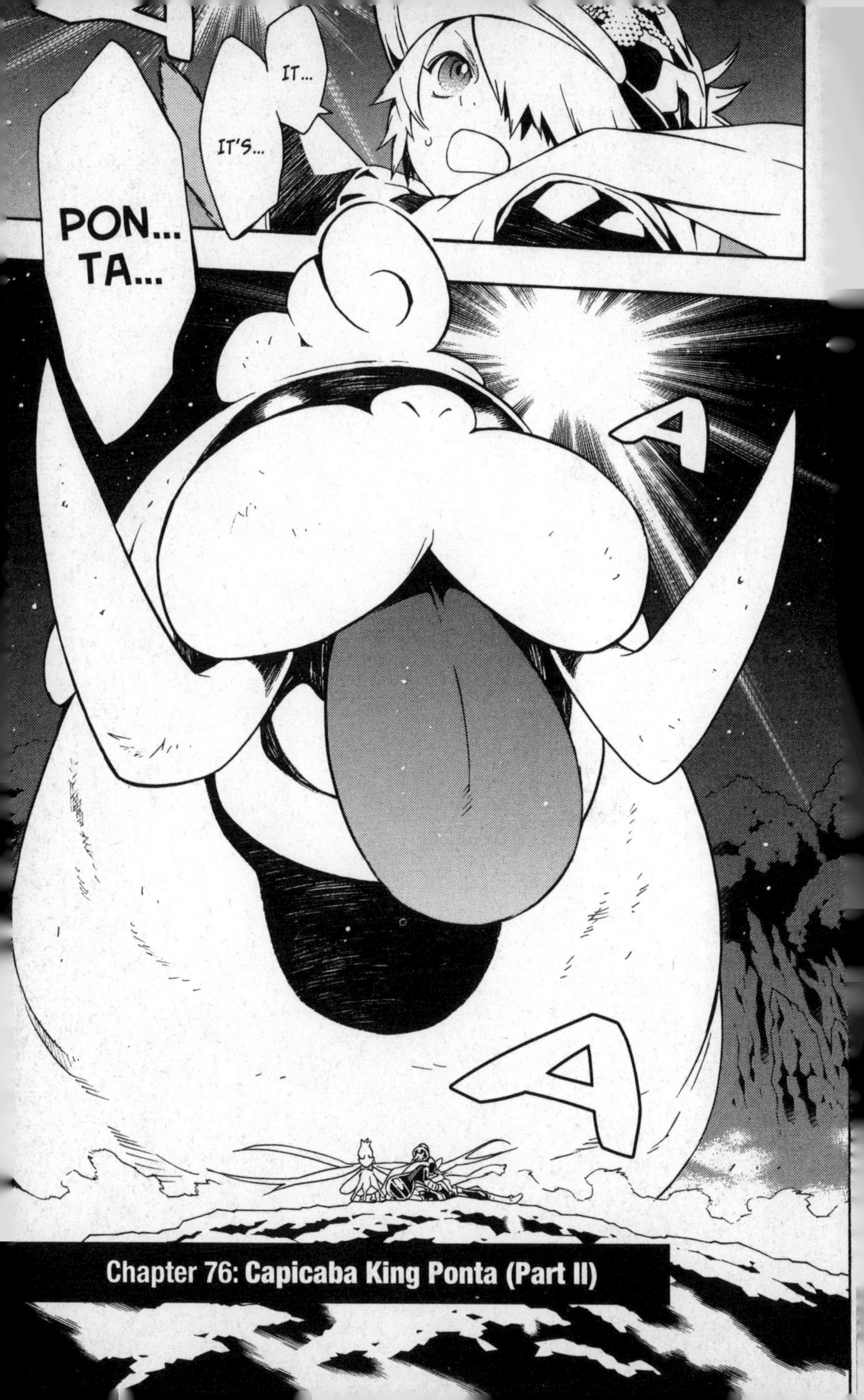
A
IT...
IT'S...
PON... TA...
A
A

Chapter 76: Capicaba King Ponta (Part II)

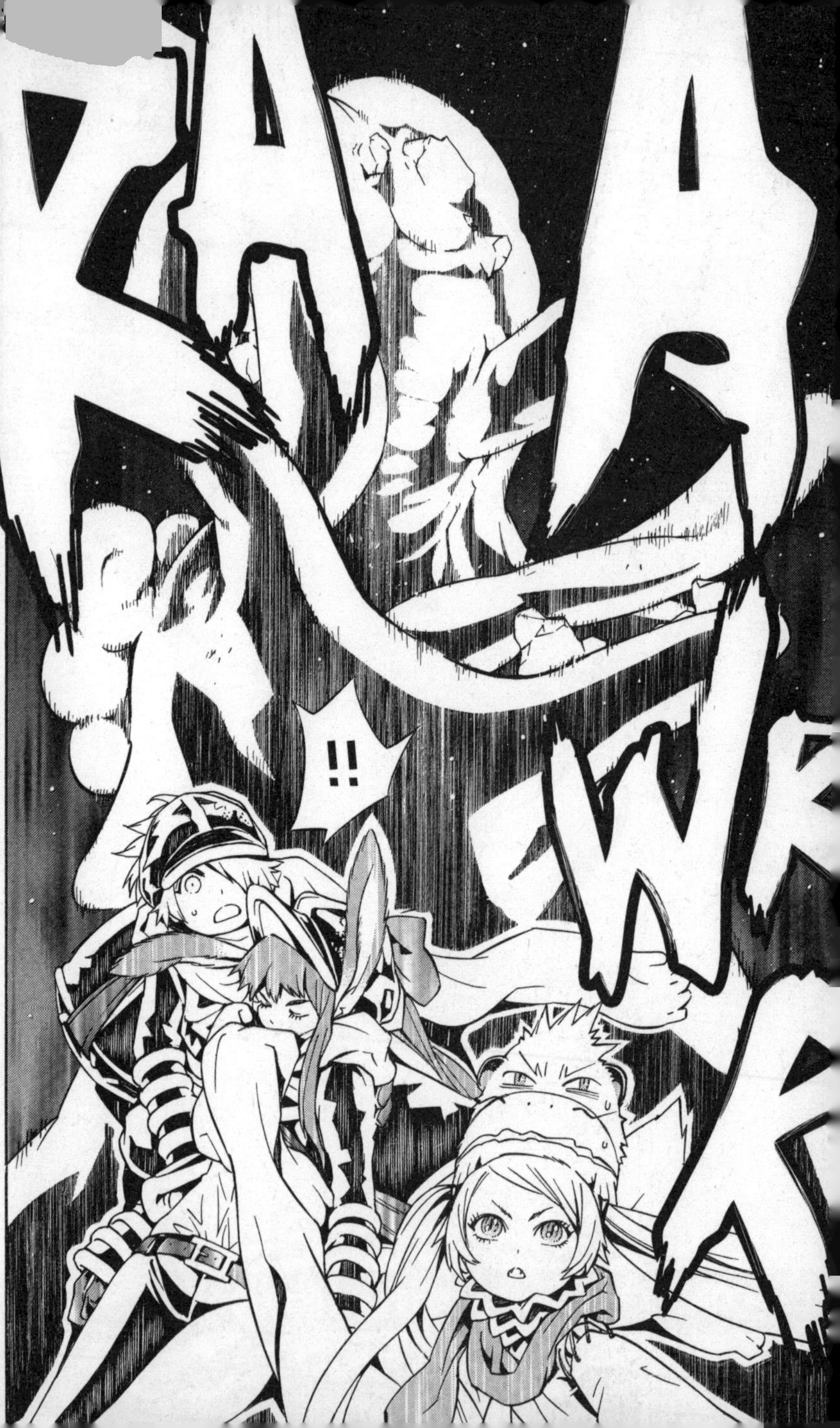
!!

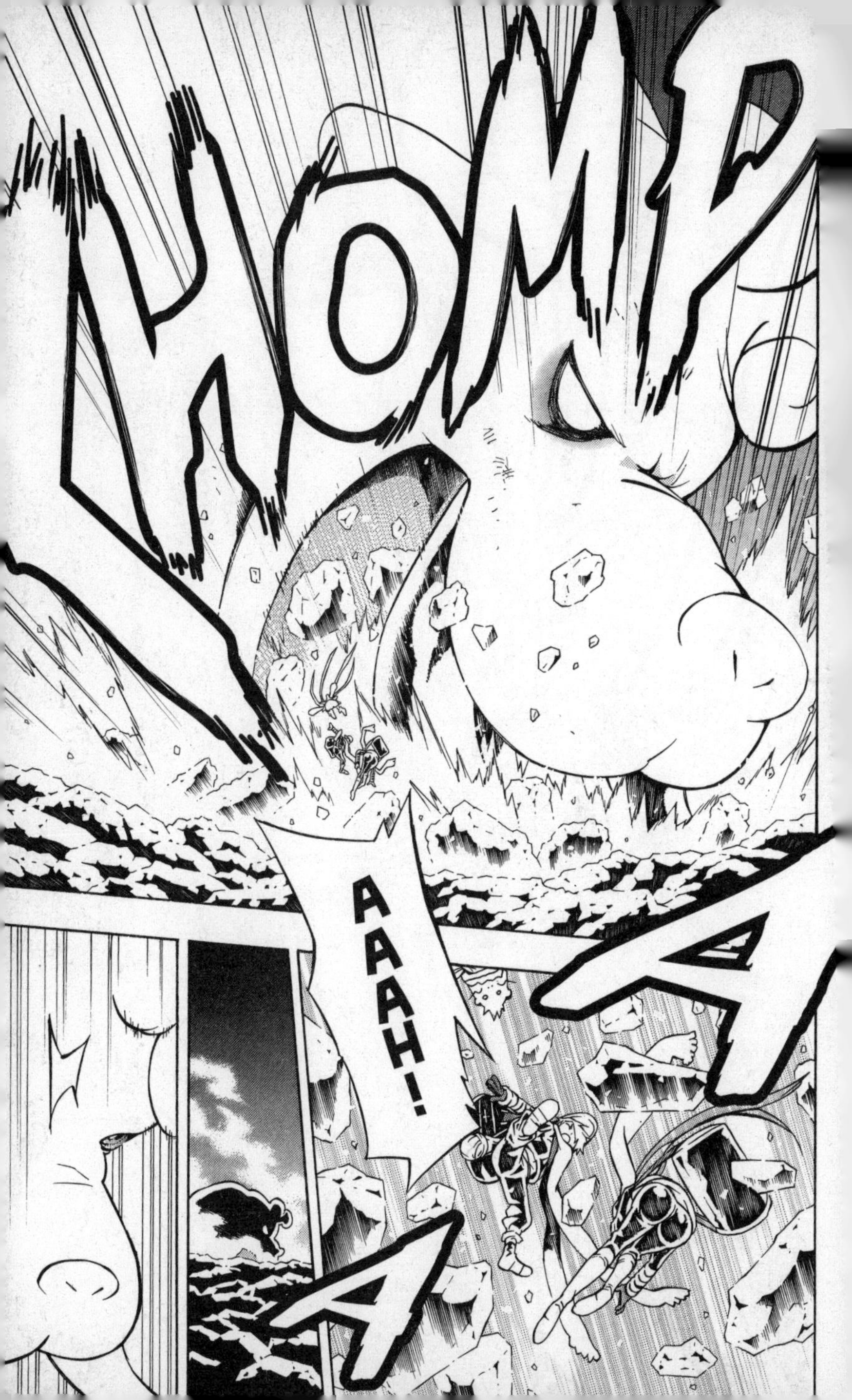
CHOMP
AAAH!
A
A

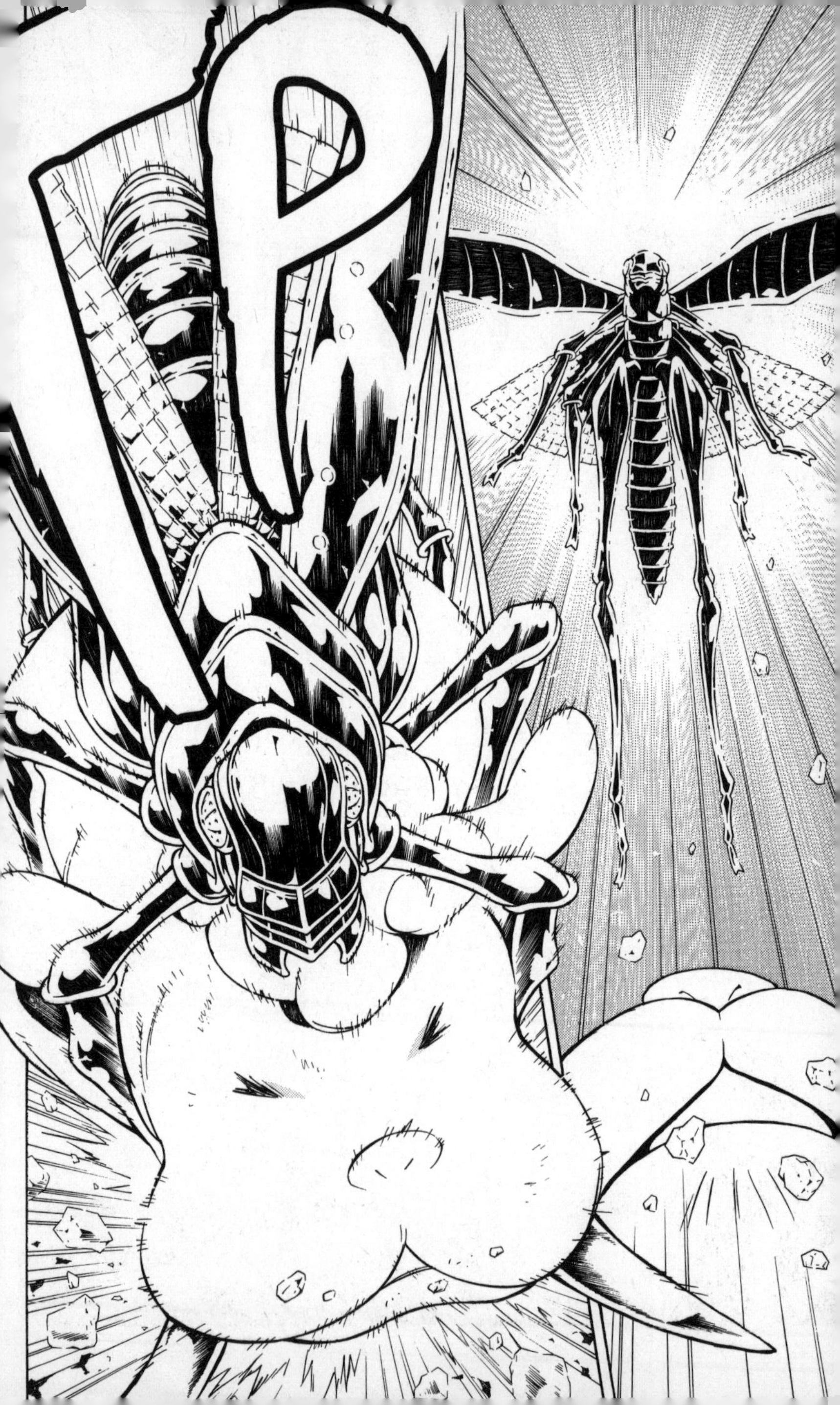

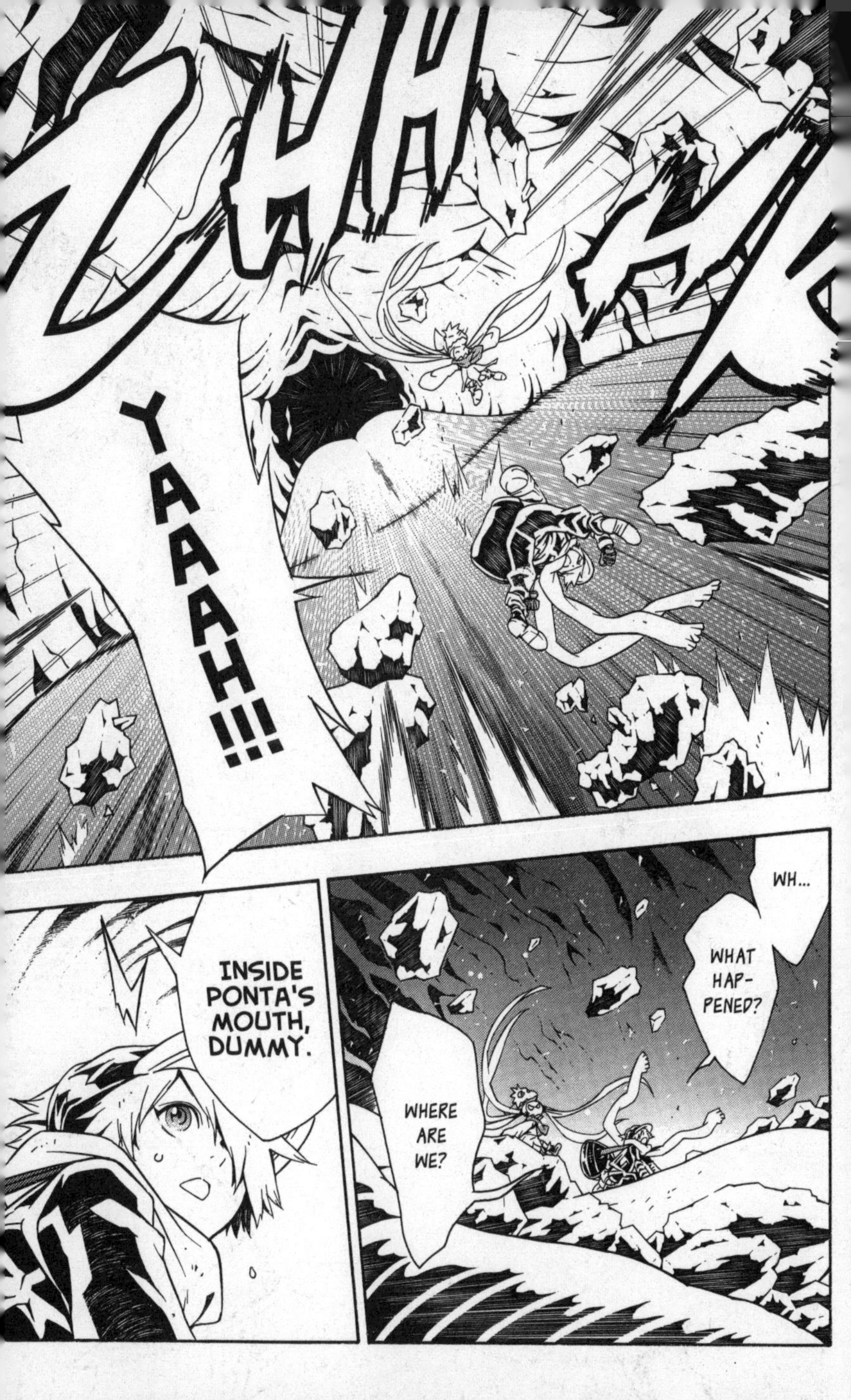
YAAAAH!!!
WH...
WHAT HAP-PENED?
WHERE ARE WE?
INSIDE PONTA'S MOUTH, DUMMY.

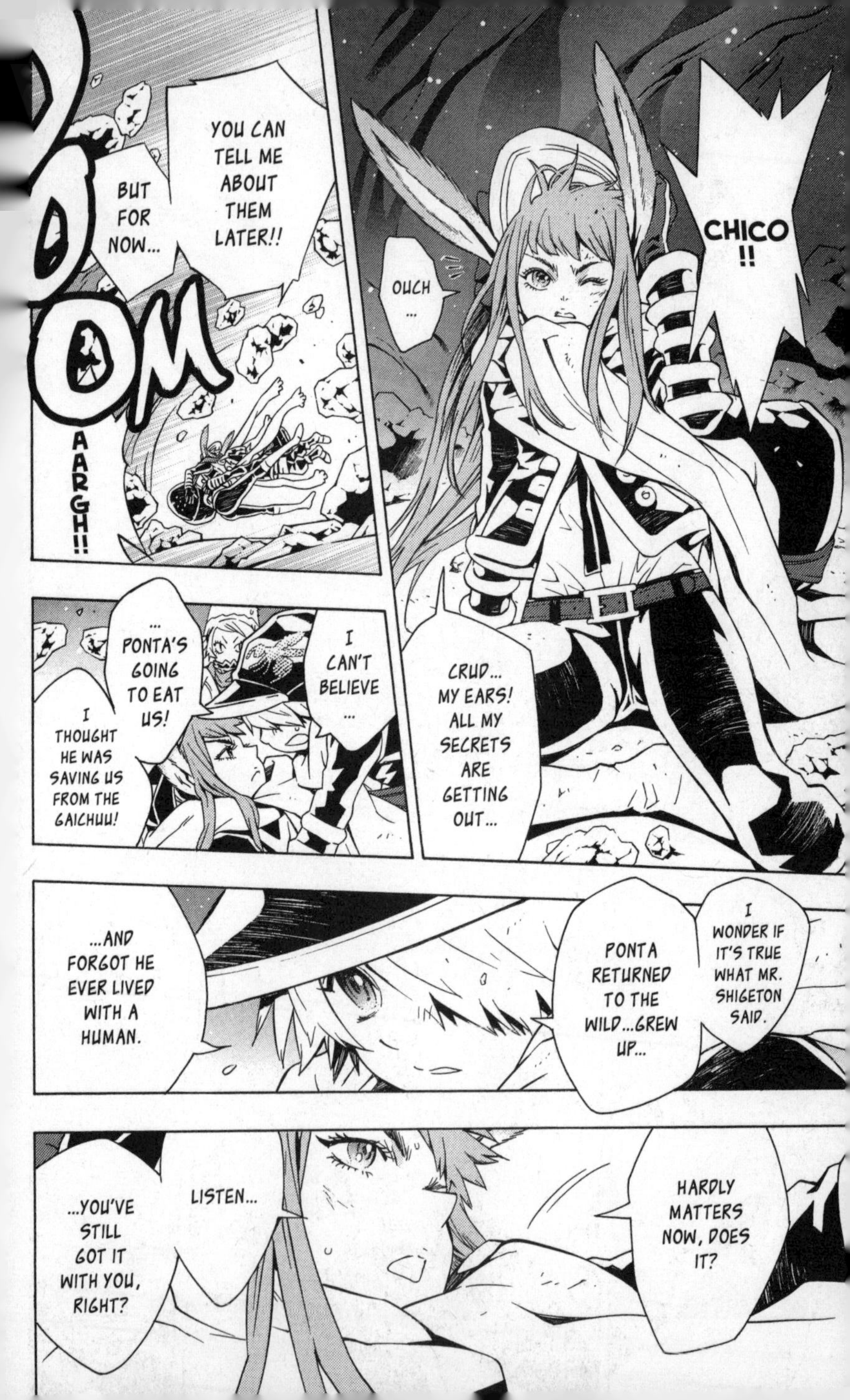
CHICO!!
OUCH...
CRUD... MY EARS! ALL MY SECRETS ARE GETTING OUT...
YOU CAN TELL ME ABOUT THEM LATER!!
BUT FOR NOW...
OM
AARGH!!
I CAN'T BELIEVE...
...PONTA'S GOING TO EAT US!
I THOUGHT HE WAS SAVING US FROM THE GAICHUU!
I WONDER IF IT'S TRUE WHAT MR. SHIGETON SAID.
PONTA RETURNED TO THE WILD...GREW UP...
...AND FORGOT HE EVER LIVED WITH A HUMAN.
HARDLY MATTERS NOW, DOES IT?
LISTEN...
...YOU'VE STILL GOT IT WITH YOU, RIGHT?

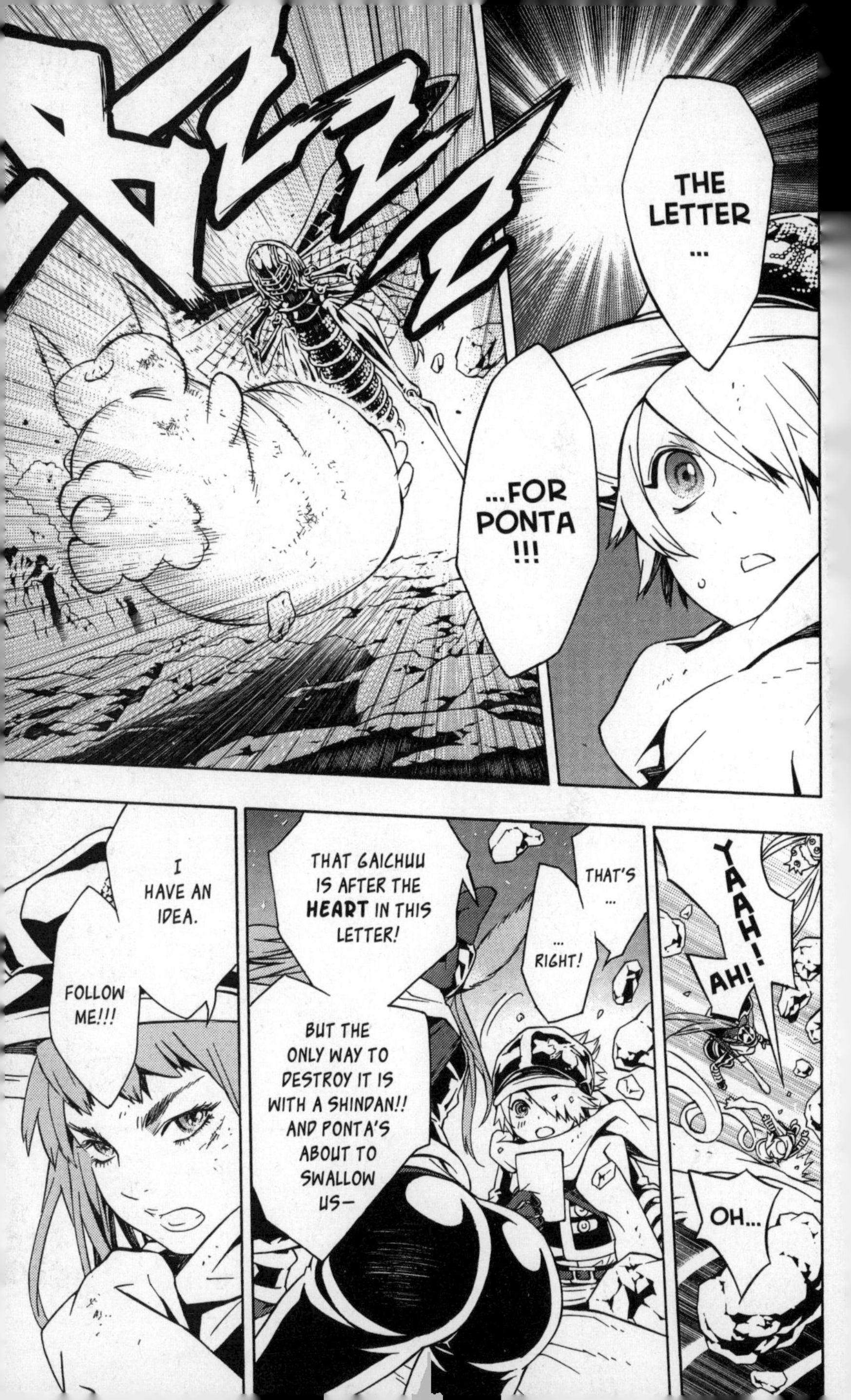
THE LETTER ...
...FOR PONTA !!!
YAAAH!
AH!
OH...
THAT GAICHUU IS AFTER THE HEART IN THIS LETTER!
BUT THE ONLY WAY TO DESTROY IT IS WITH A SHINDAN!! AND PONTA'S ABOUT TO SWALLOW US—
THAT'S ...
... RIGHT!
I HAVE AN IDEA.
FOLLOW ME!!!

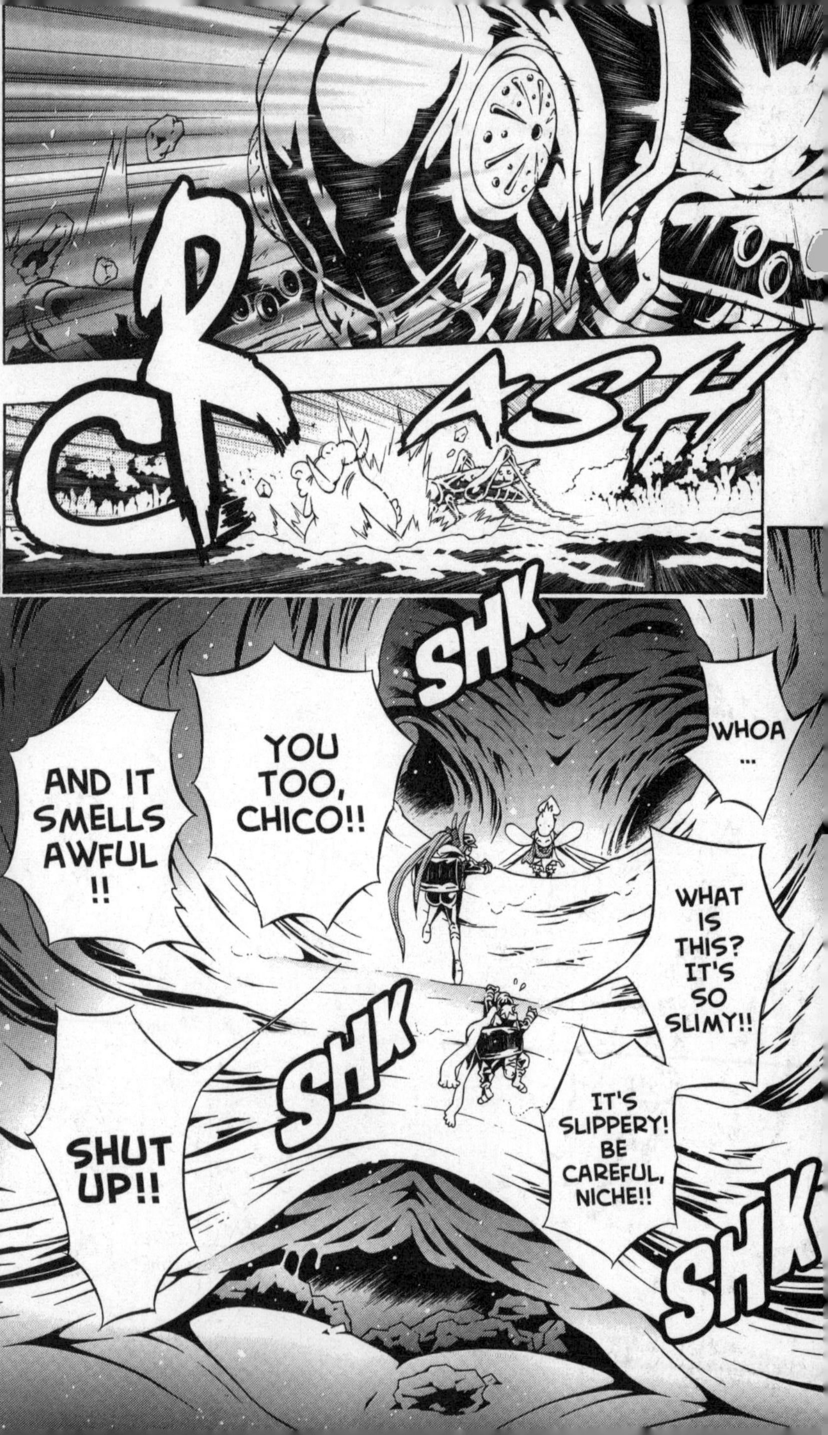
CRASH
SHK
WHOA...
YOU TOO, CHICO!!
AND IT SMELLS AWFUL!!
WHAT IS THIS? IT'S SO SLIMY!!
IT'S SLIPPERY! BE CAREFUL, NICHE!!
SHK
SHUT UP!!
SHK

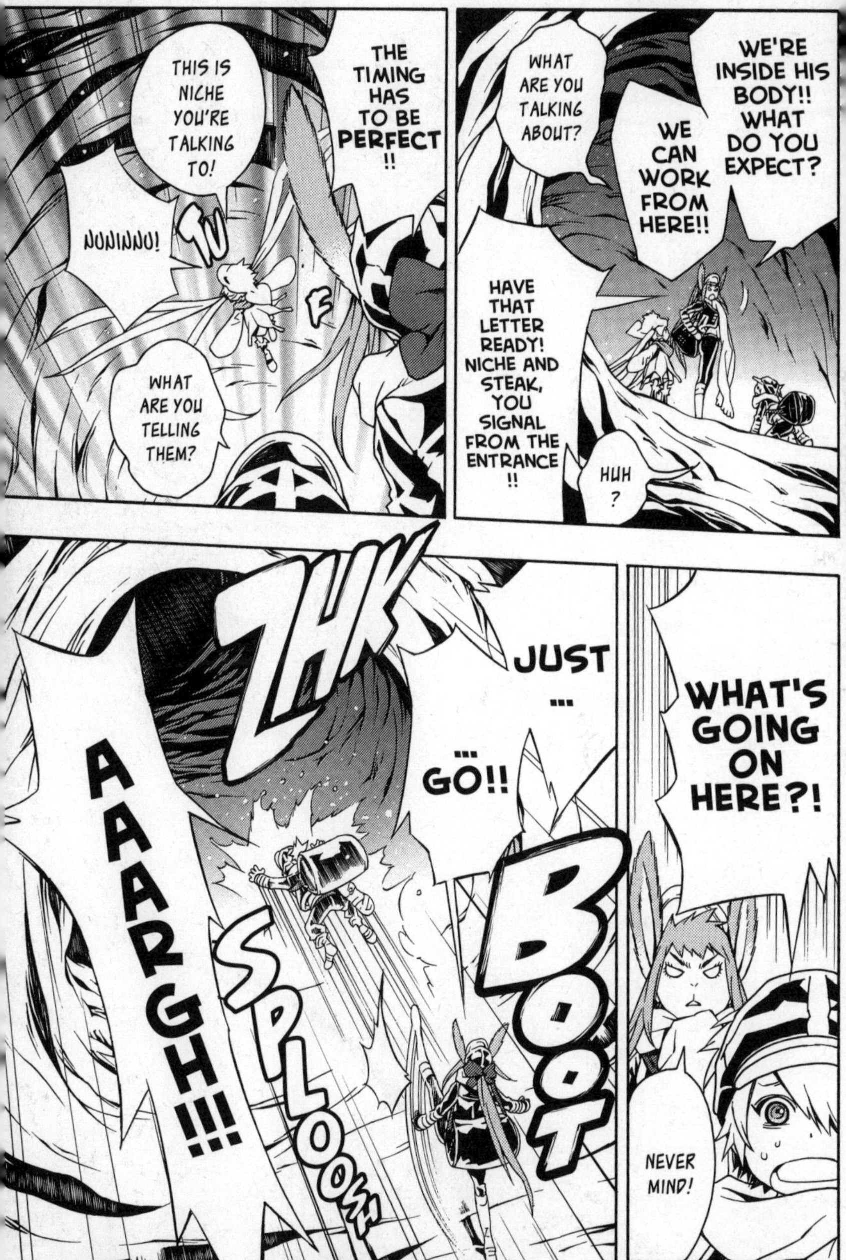
WE'RE INSIDE HIS BODY!! WHAT DO YOU EXPECT?
WE CAN WORK FROM HERE!!
WHAT ARE YOU TALKING ABOUT?
HAVE THAT LETTER READY! NICHE AND STEAK, YOU SIGNAL FROM THE ENTRANCE!!
HUH?
THE TIMING HAS TO BE PERFECT!!
THIS IS NICHE YOU'RE TALKING TO!
TU
NUNINNU!
F
WHAT ARE YOU TELLING THEM?
WHAT'S GOING ON HERE?!
NEVER MIND!
ZHK
JUST...
...GÖ!!
BOOT
AAARGH!!!
SPLOOOSH

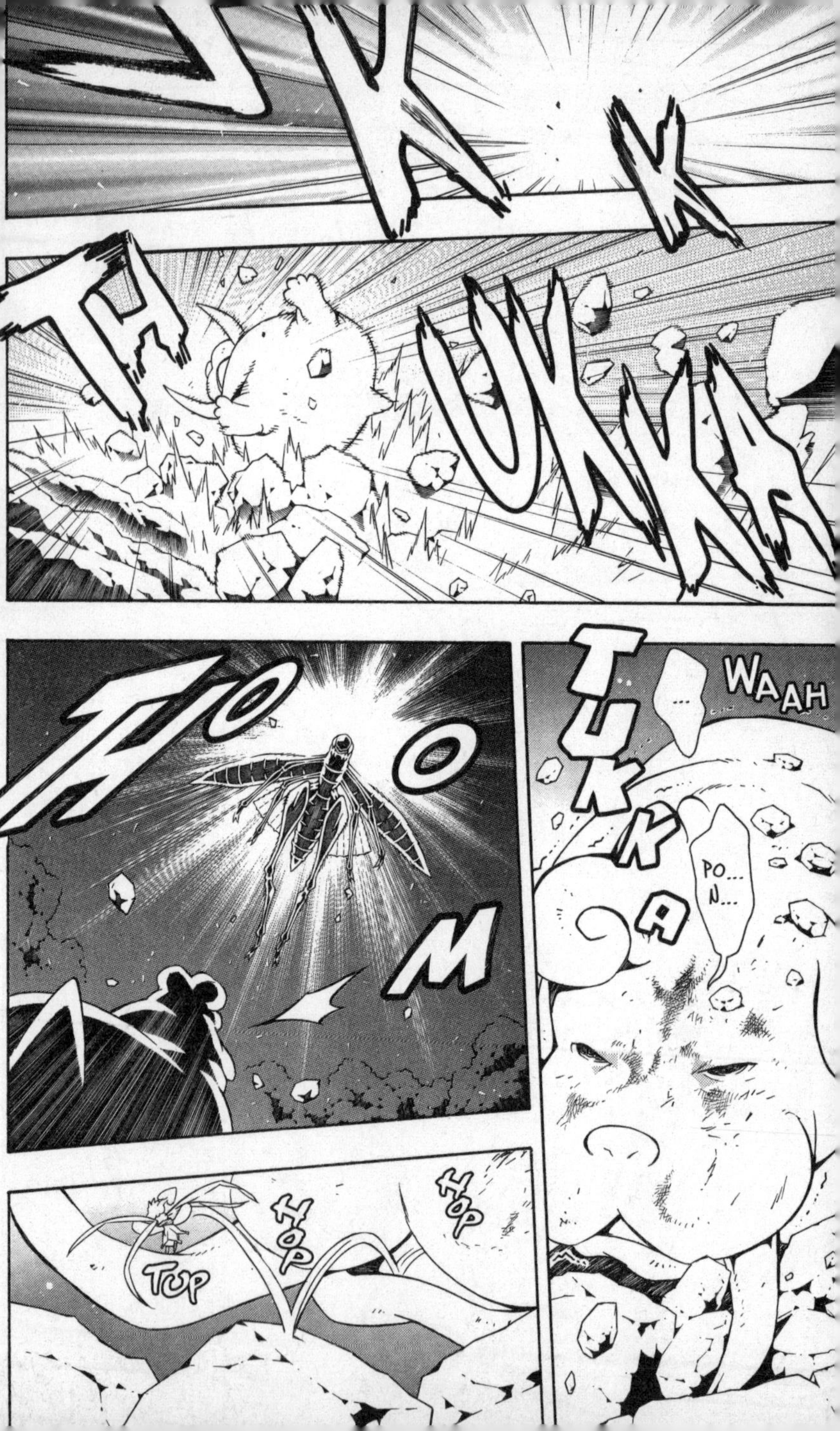
ZAKK
THUNKA
TUKKA
WAAH
...
PO... N...
THOOOM
TUP
HOP
HOP

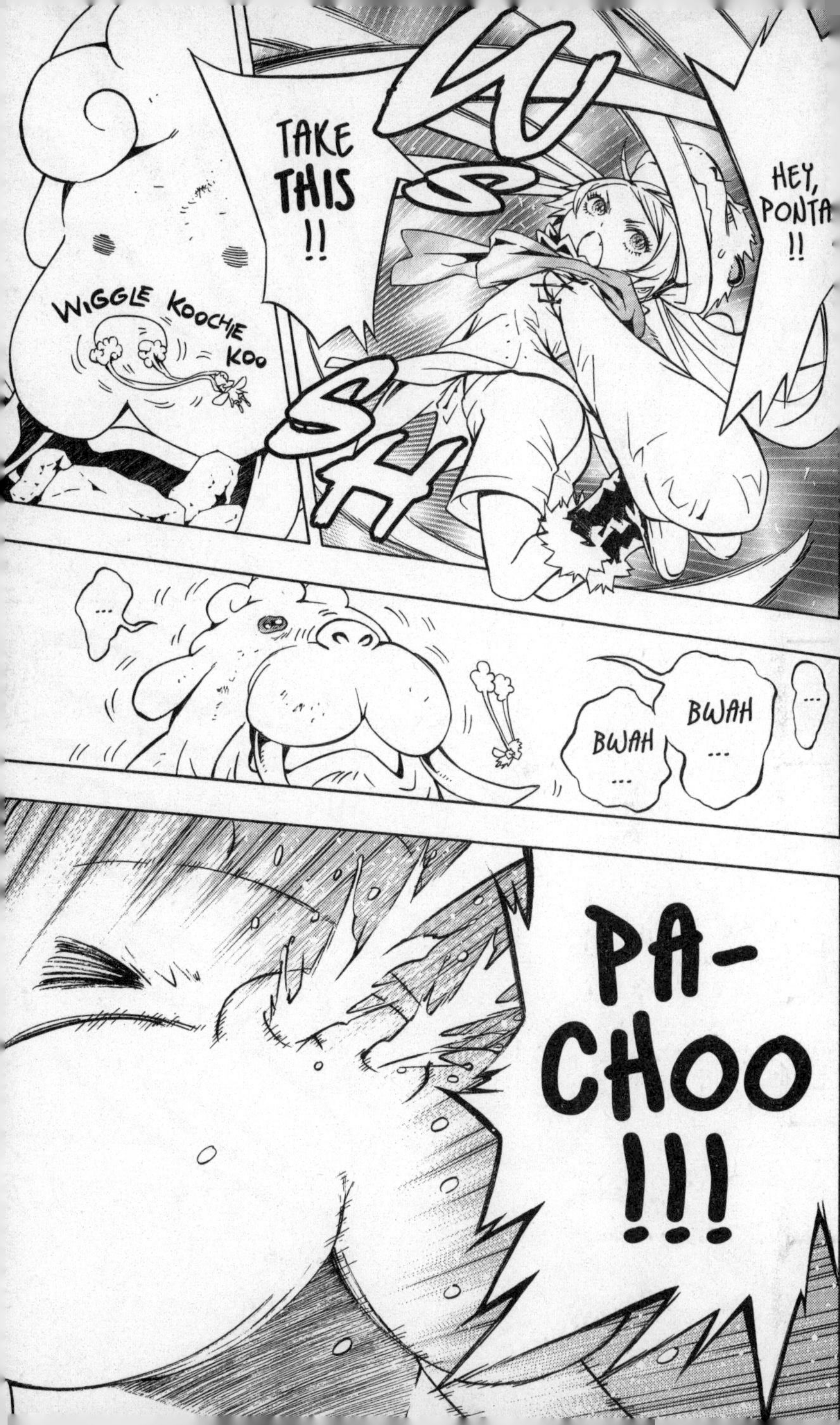
HEY, PONTA!!
TAKE THIS!!
WIGGLE KOOCHIE KOO
...
BWAH ...
BWAH ...
...
PA-CHOO!!!

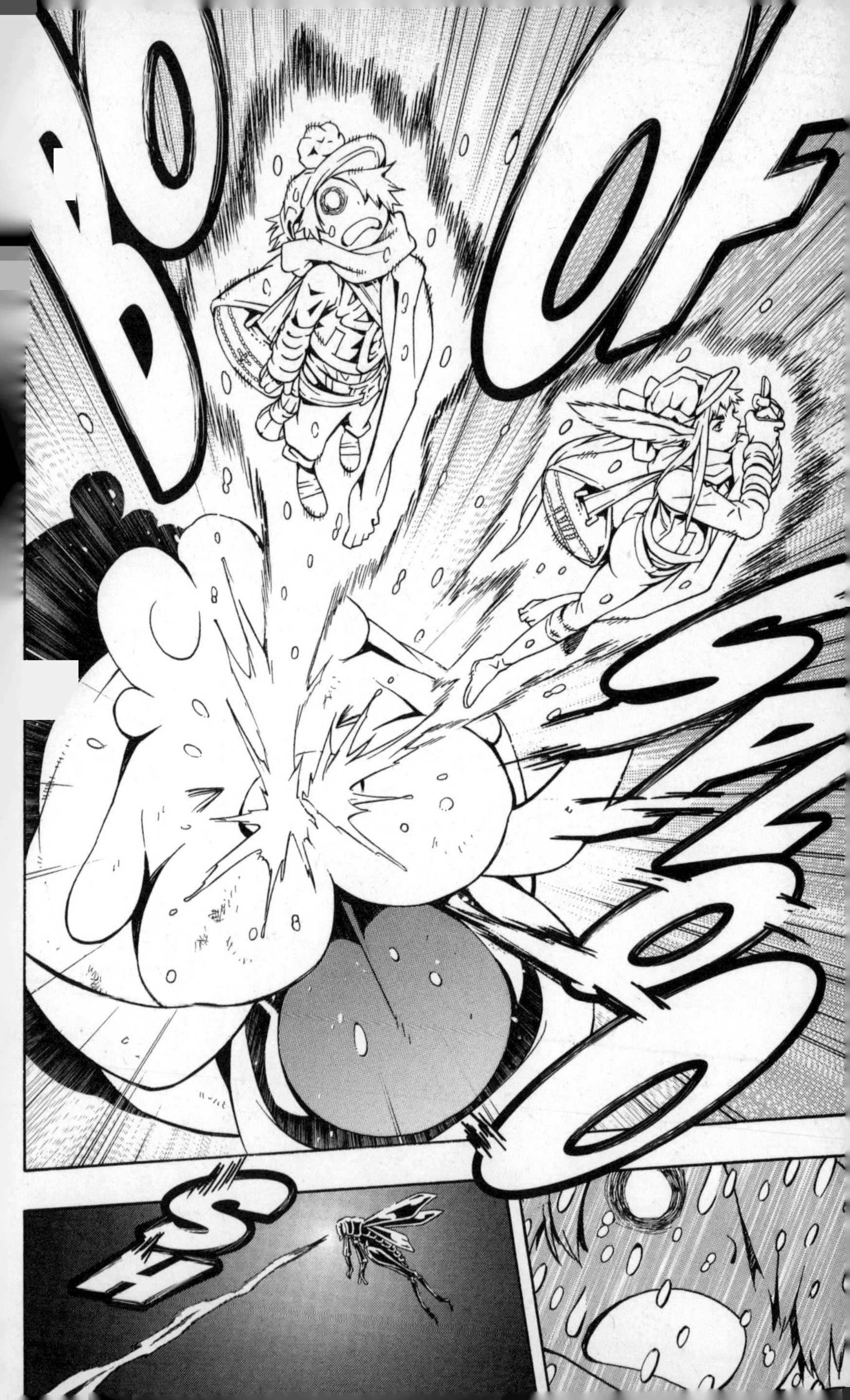

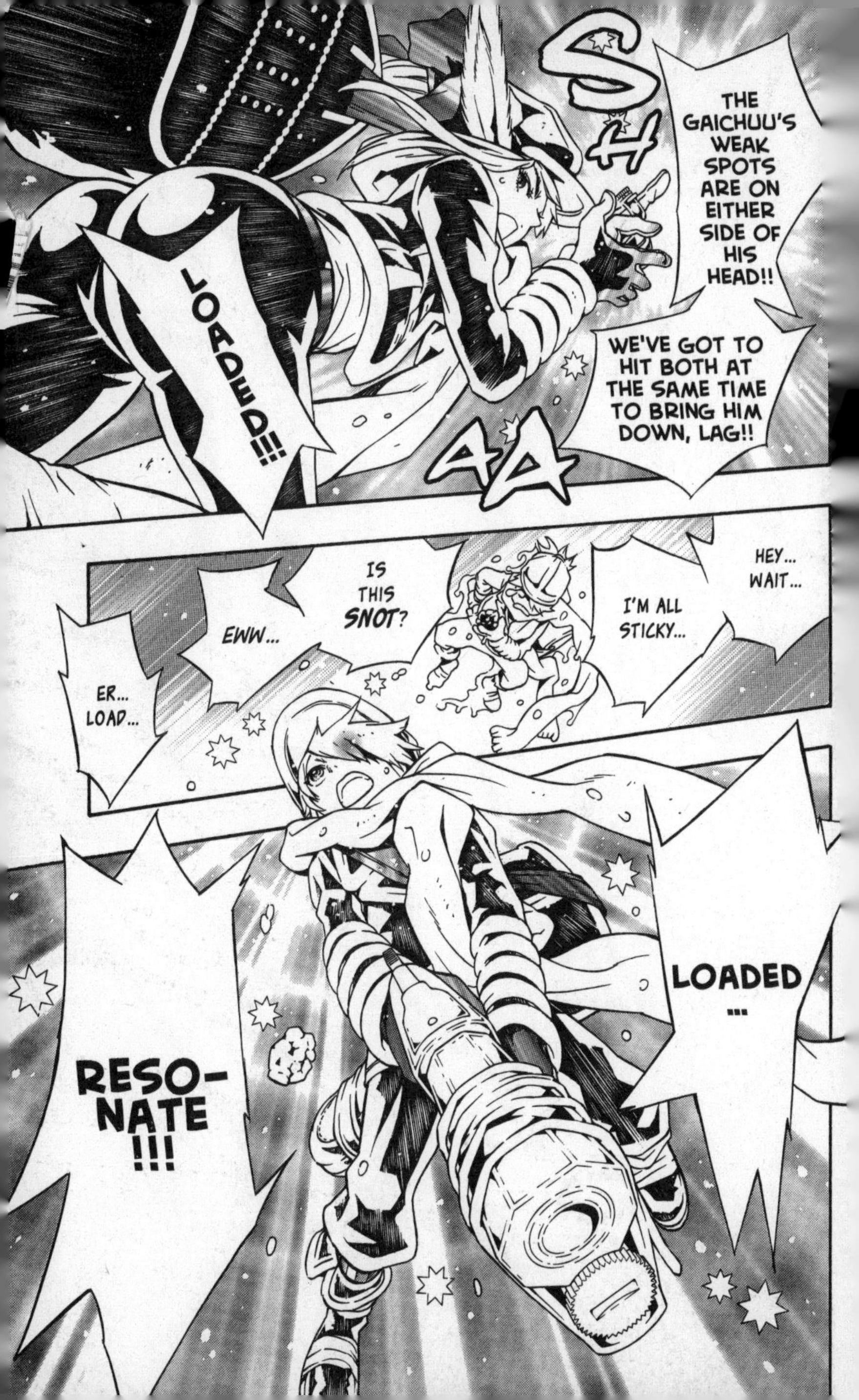
SHAA
THE GAICHUU'S WEAK SPOTS ARE ON EITHER SIDE OF HIS HEAD!!
WE'VE GOT TO HIT BOTH AT THE SAME TIME TO BRING HIM DOWN, LAG!!
LOADED!!!
HEY... WAIT...
I'M ALL STICKY...
IS THIS SNOT?
EWW...
ER... LOAD...
LOADED...
RESO-NATE!!!

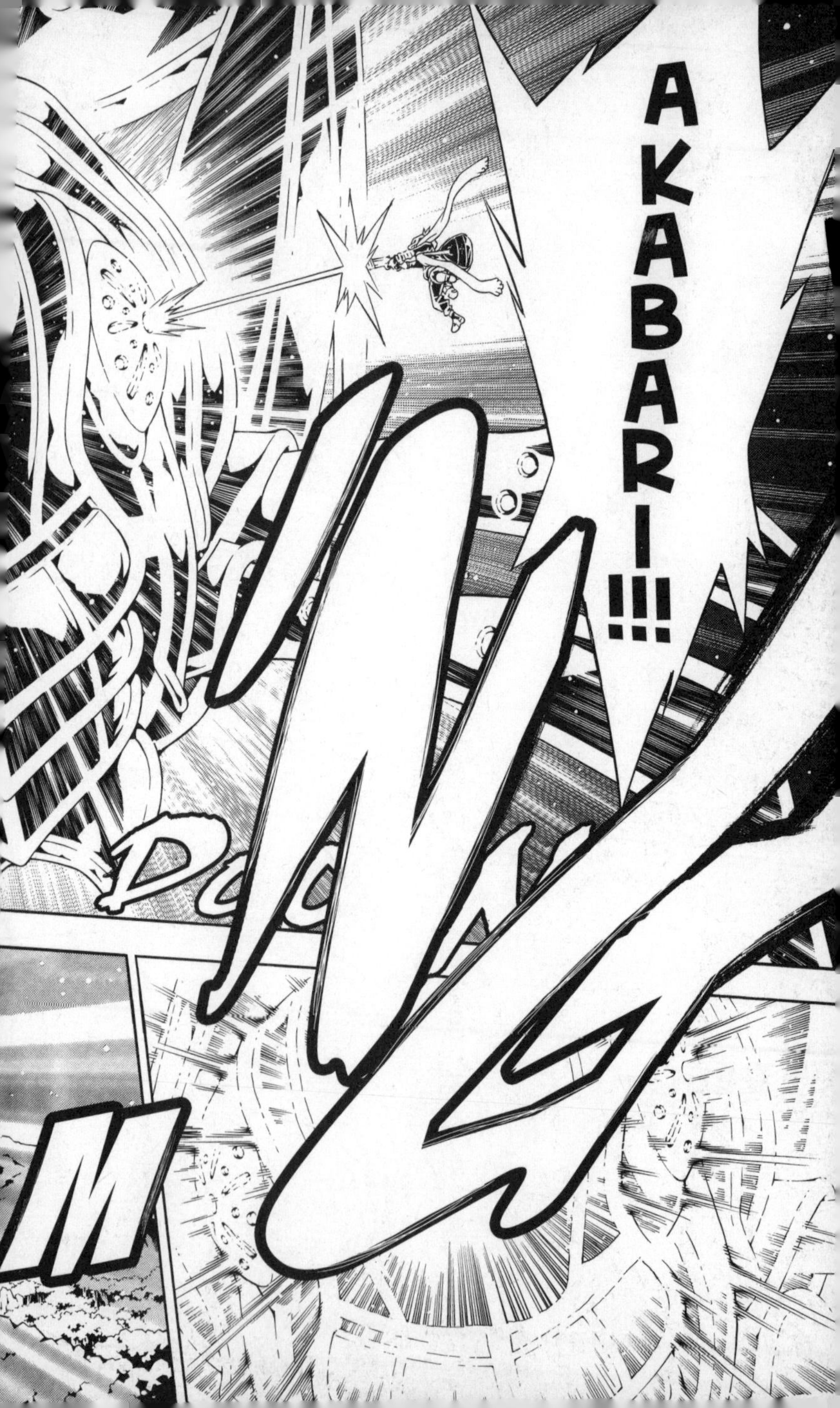
AKABARI!!!

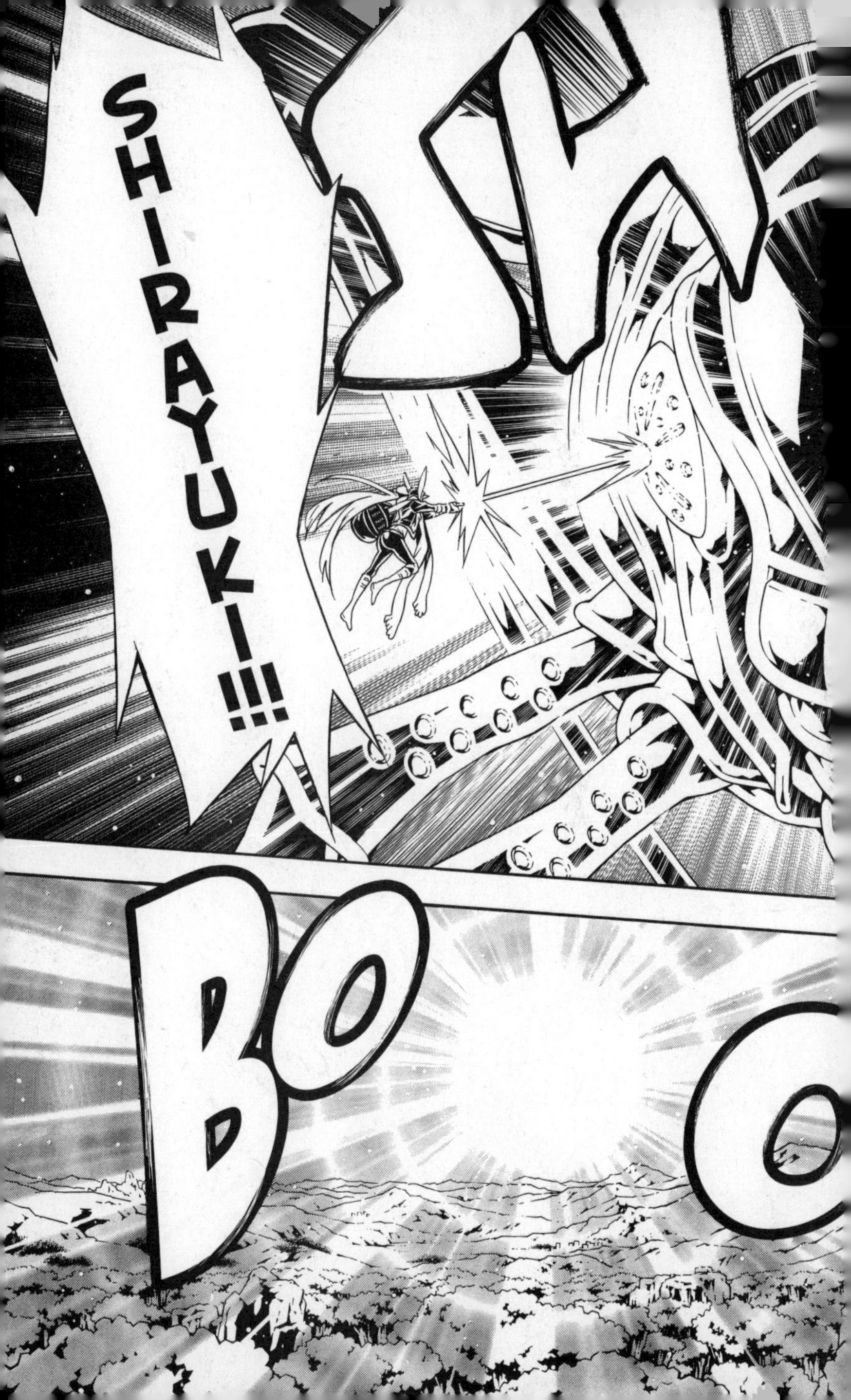
SHIRAYUKI!!!
BOO

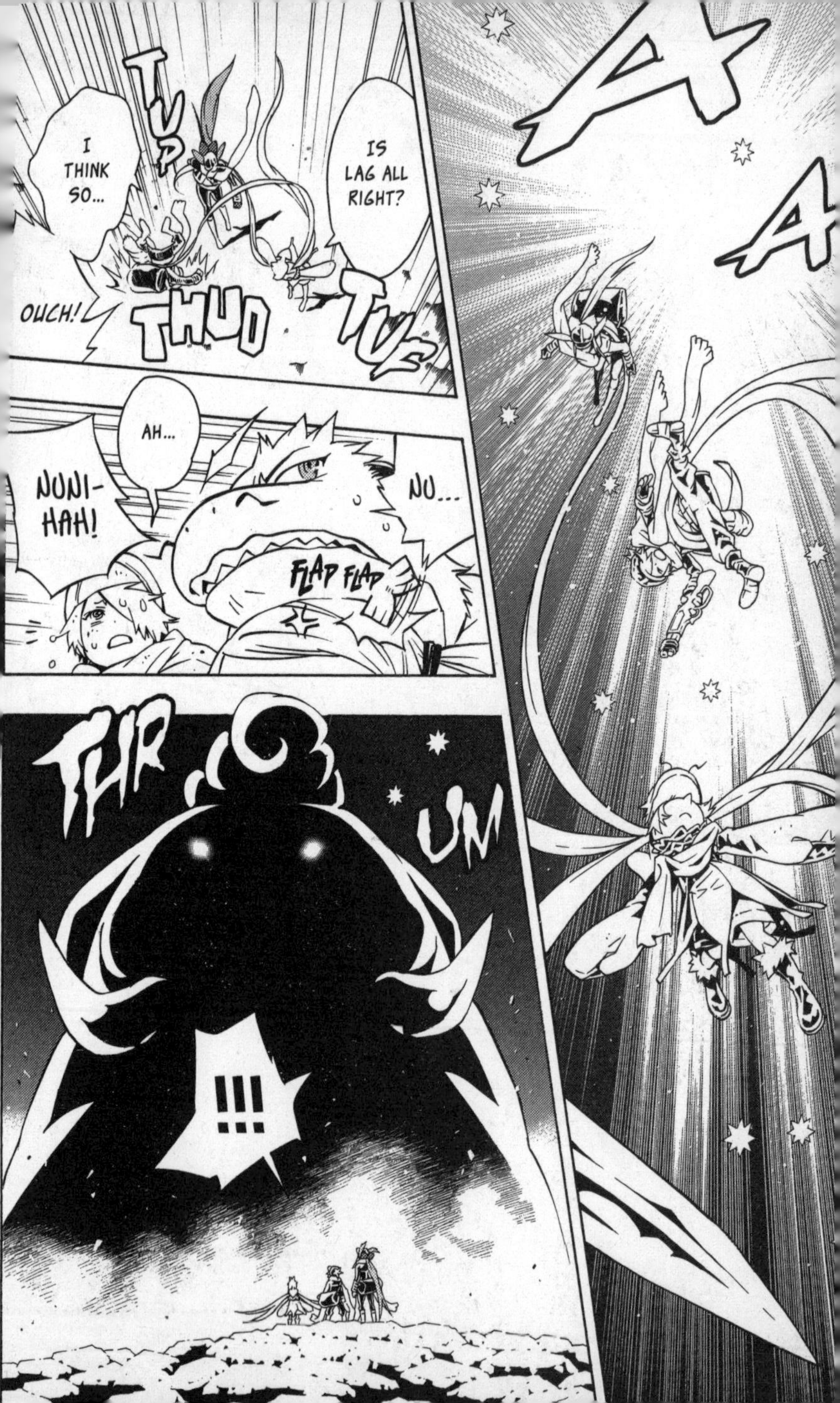
AA
IS LAG ALL RIGHT?
TUP
I THINK SO...
TUP
THUD
OUCH!
NU...
AH...
NUNI-HAH!
FLAP FLAP
THRUM
!!!

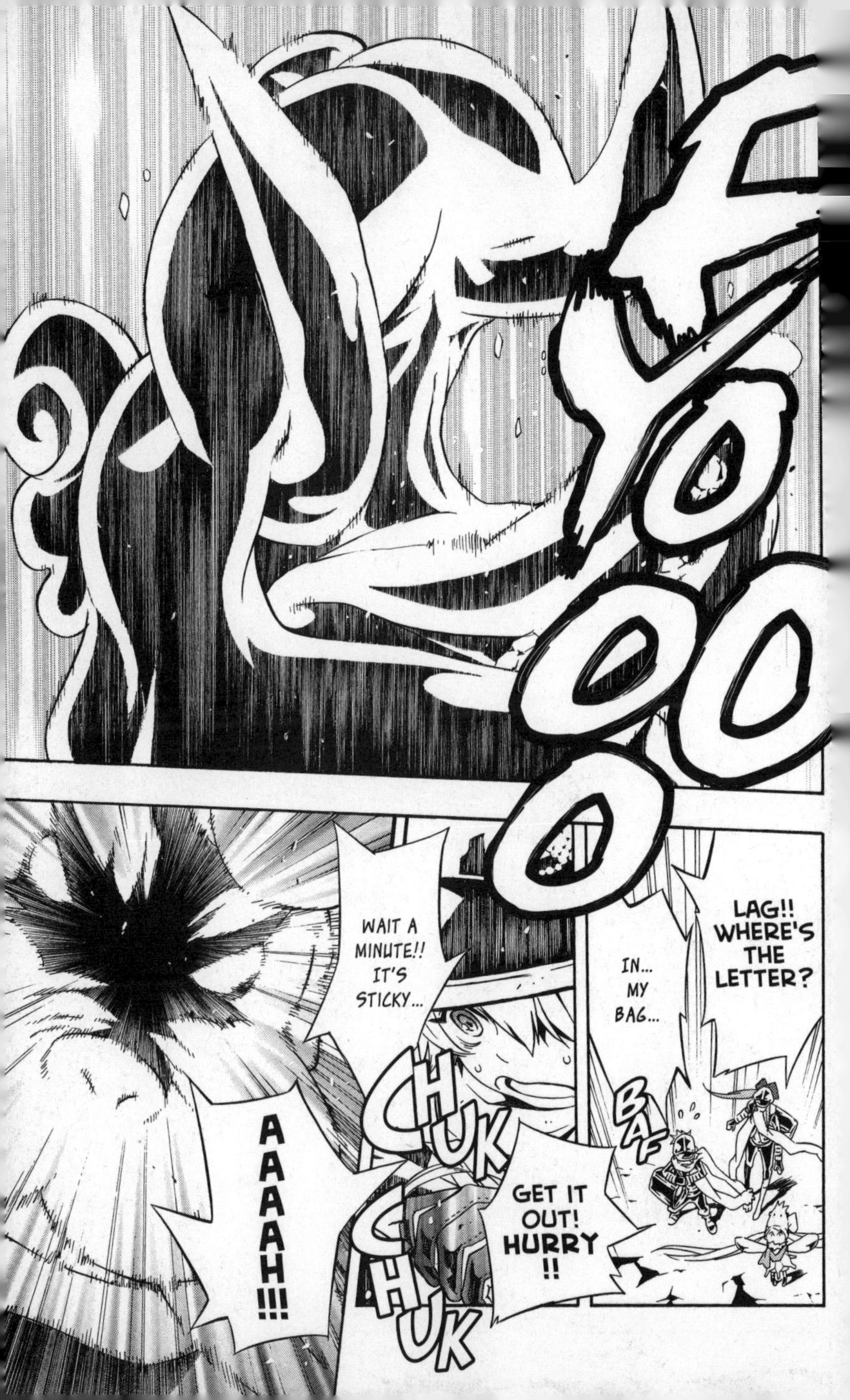
LAG!! WHERE'S THE LETTER?
IN... MY BAG...
BAF
WAIT A MINUTE!! IT'S STICKY...
GET IT OUT! HURRY!!
CHUK CHUK CHUK
AAAAAH!!!

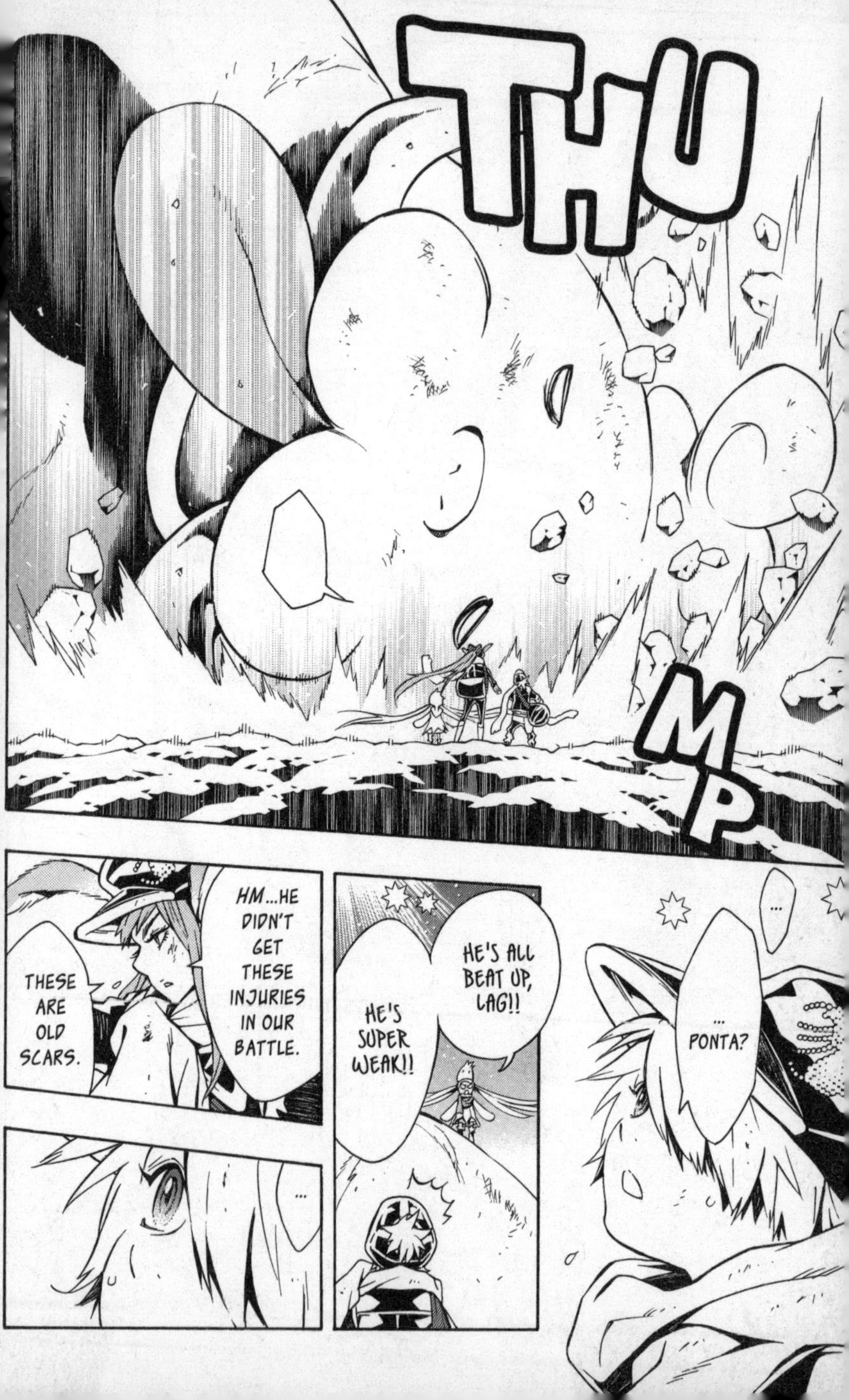
THUMP
...
... PONTA?
HE'S ALL BEAT UP, LAG!!
HE'S SUPER WEAK!!
HM...HE DIDN'T GET THESE INJURIES IN OUR BATTLE.
THESE ARE OLD SCARS.
...

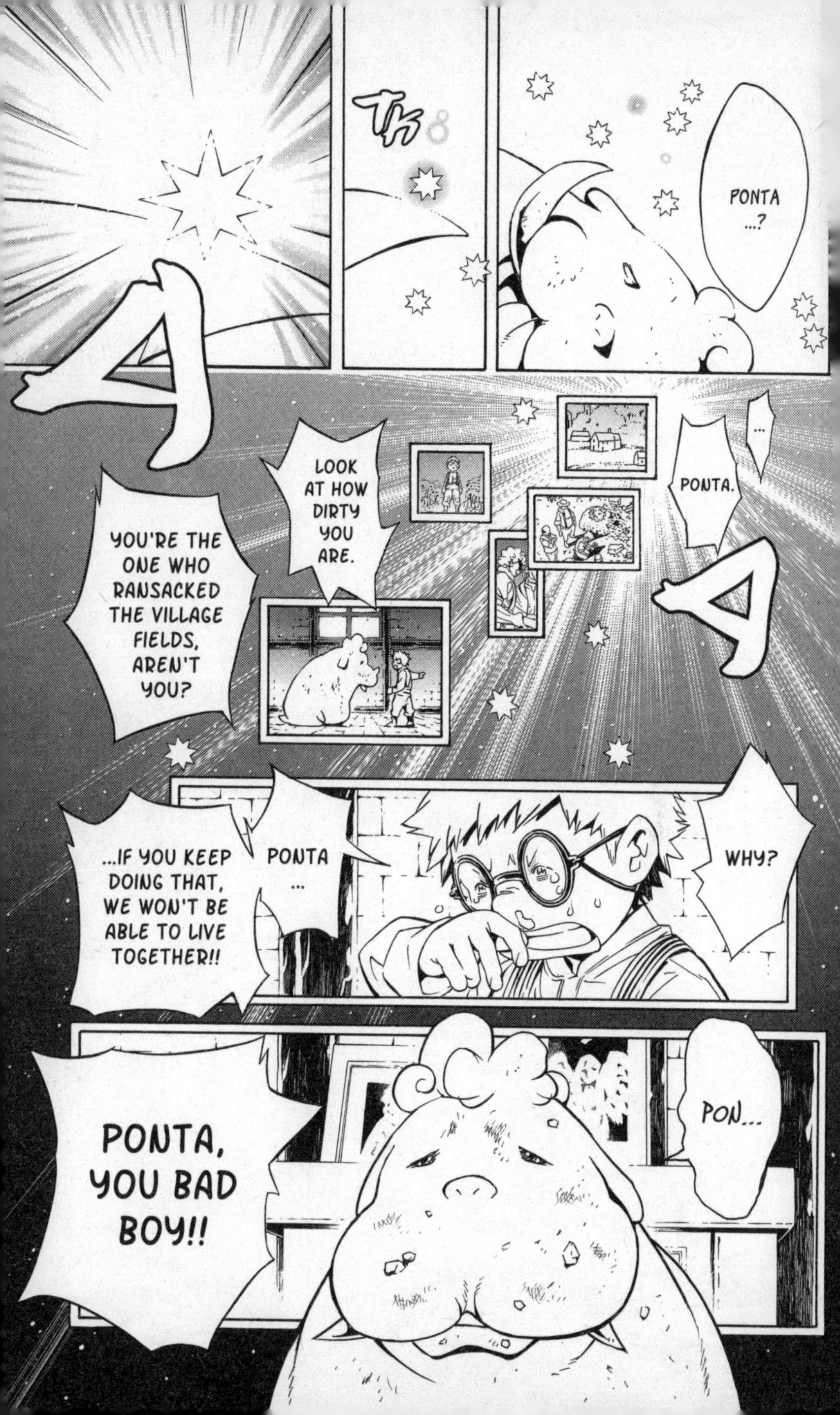
PONTA ...?
...
PONTA.
LOOK AT HOW DIRTY YOU ARE.
YOU'RE THE ONE WHO RANSACKED THE VILLAGE FIELDS, AREN'T YOU?
WHY?
PONTA ...
...IF YOU KEEP DOING THAT, WE WON'T BE ABLE TO LIVE TOGETHER!!
PON...
PONTA, YOU BAD BOY!!

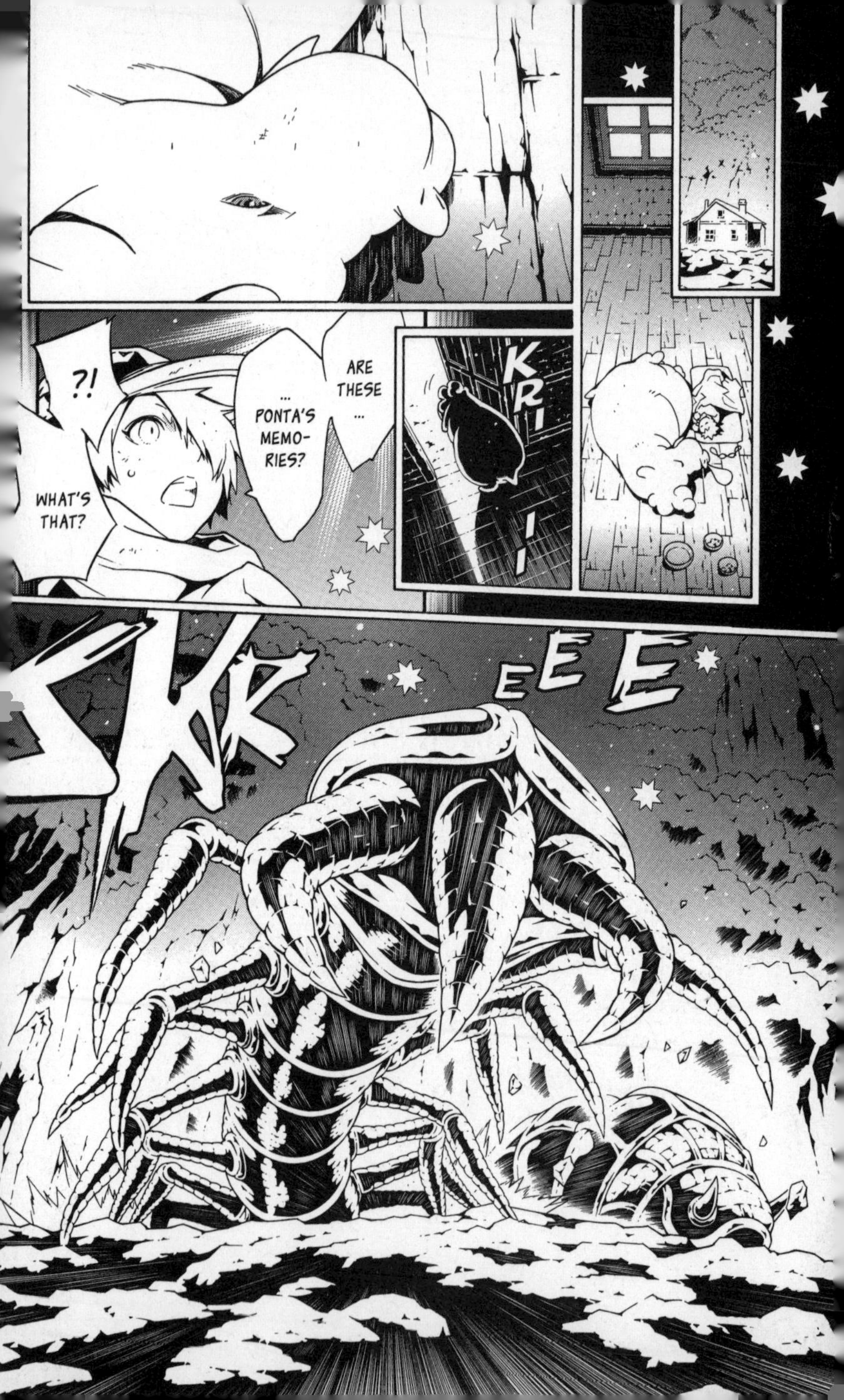
KRI
!!
ARE THESE ...
... PONTA'S MEMORIES?
?!
WHAT'S THAT?
KR
EEE

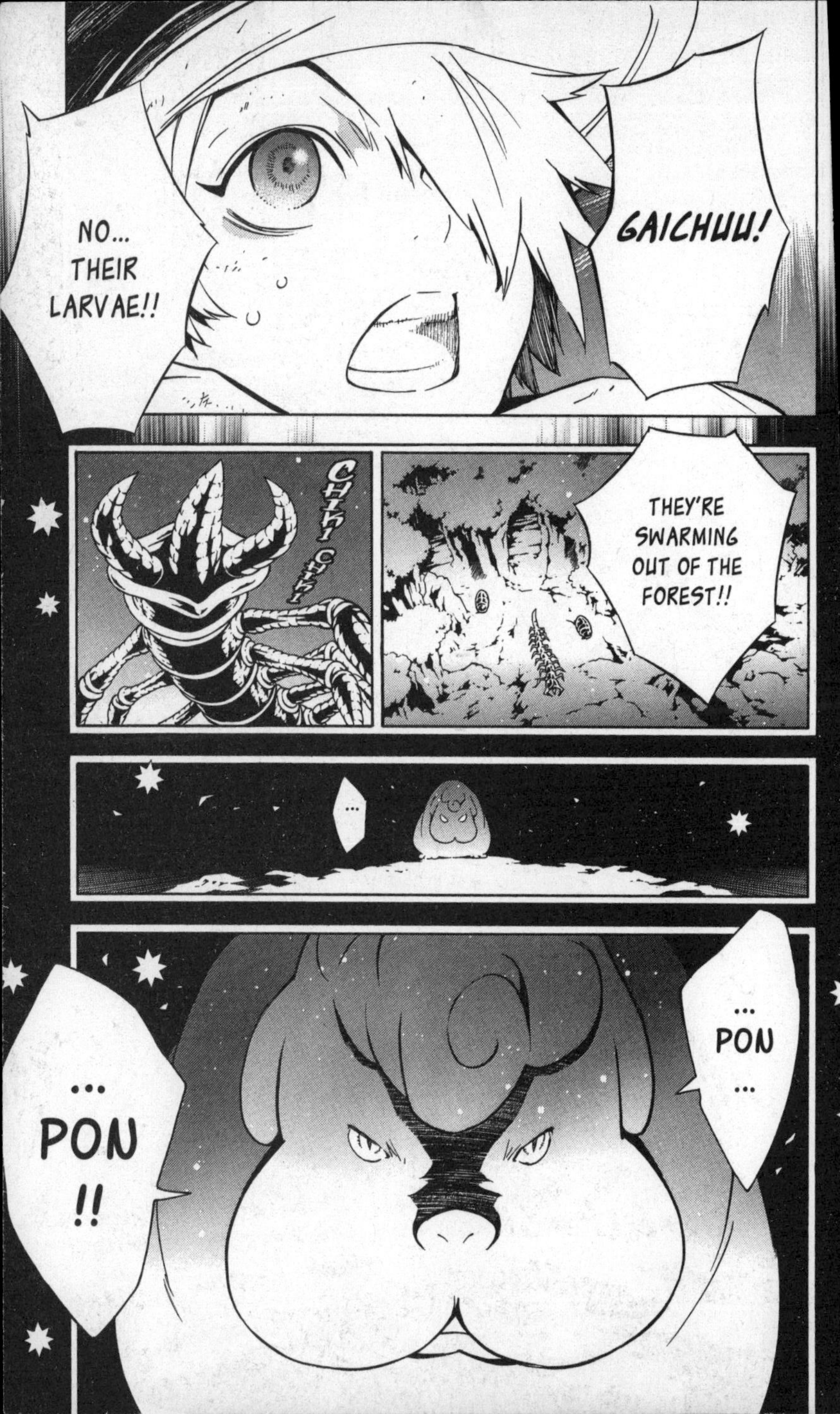
GAICHUU!
NO... THEIR LARVAE!!
THEY'RE SWARMING OUT OF THE FOREST!!
CHIKI CHIKI
...
... PON ...
... PON !!

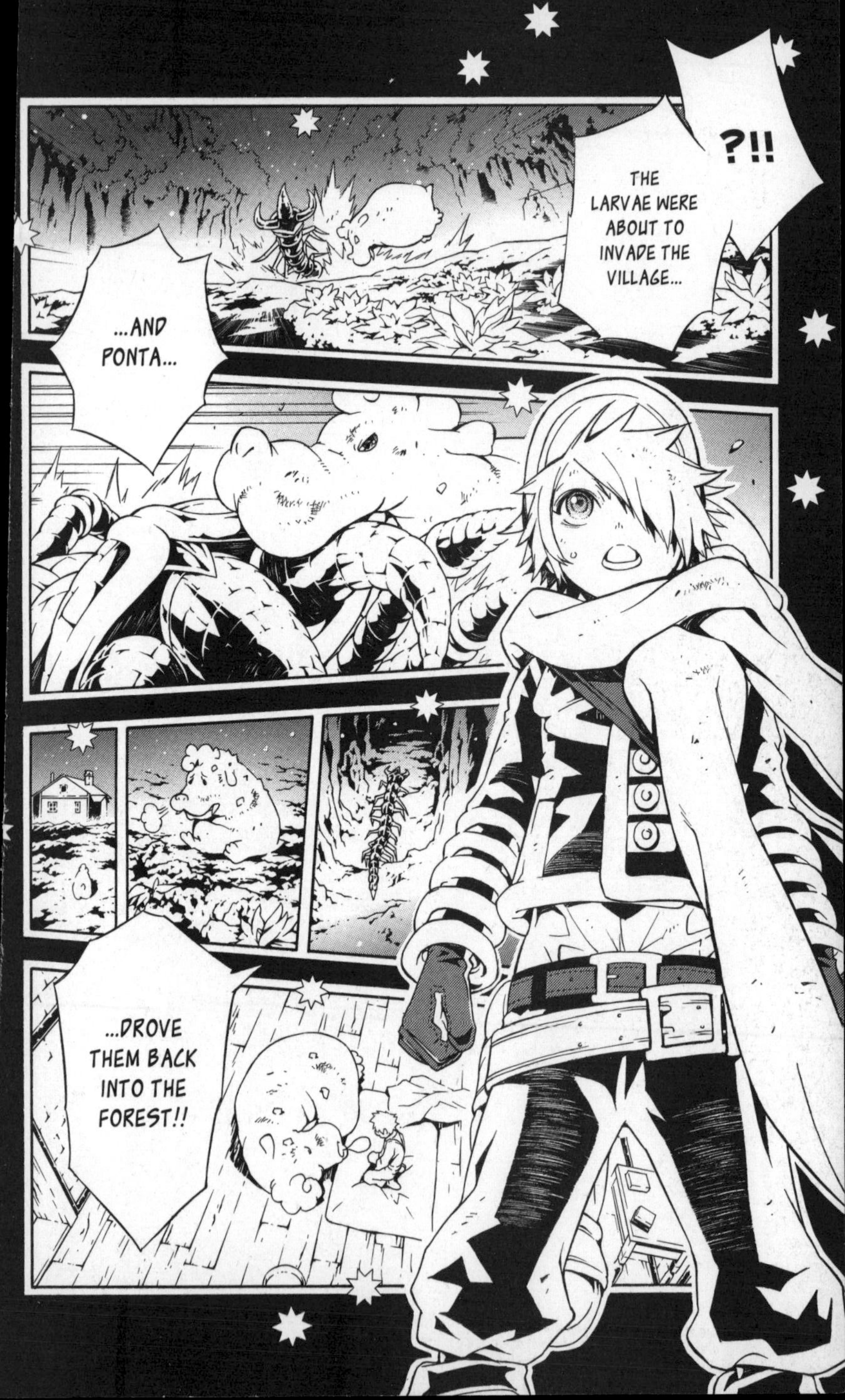
?!!
THE LARVAE WERE ABOUT TO INVADE THE VILLAGE...
...AND PONTA...
...DROVE THEM BACK INTO THE FOREST!!

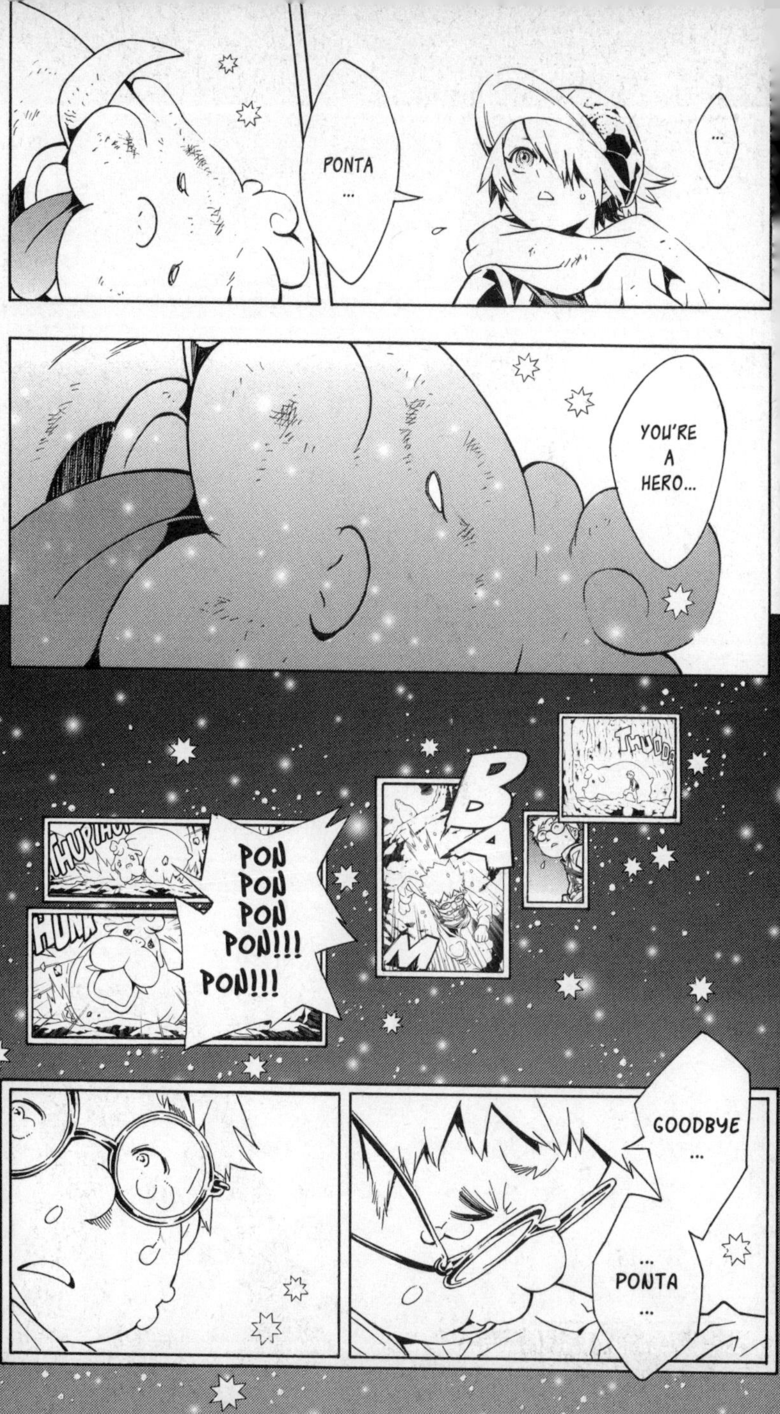
...
PONTA ...
YOU'RE A HERO...
THUDDA
BAM
PON PON PON PON!!! PON!!!
GOODBYE ...
... PONTA ...

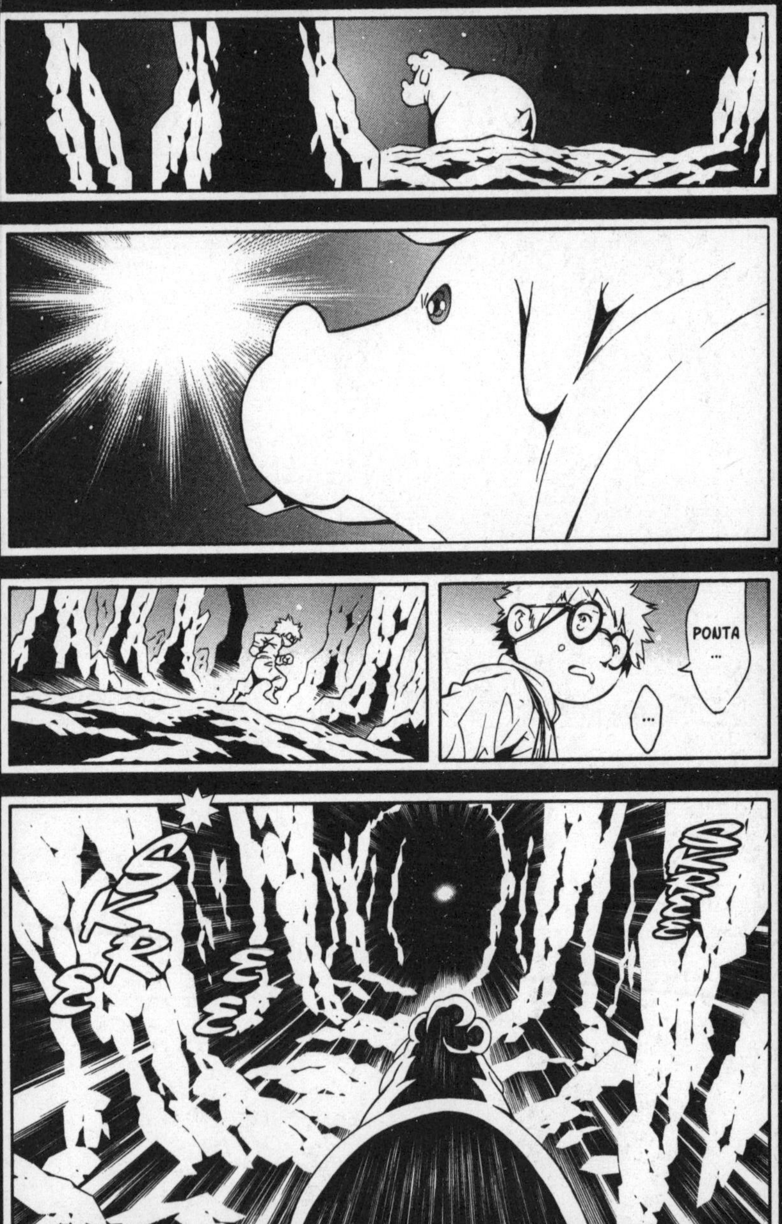
PONTA ...
...
SKREEEEE

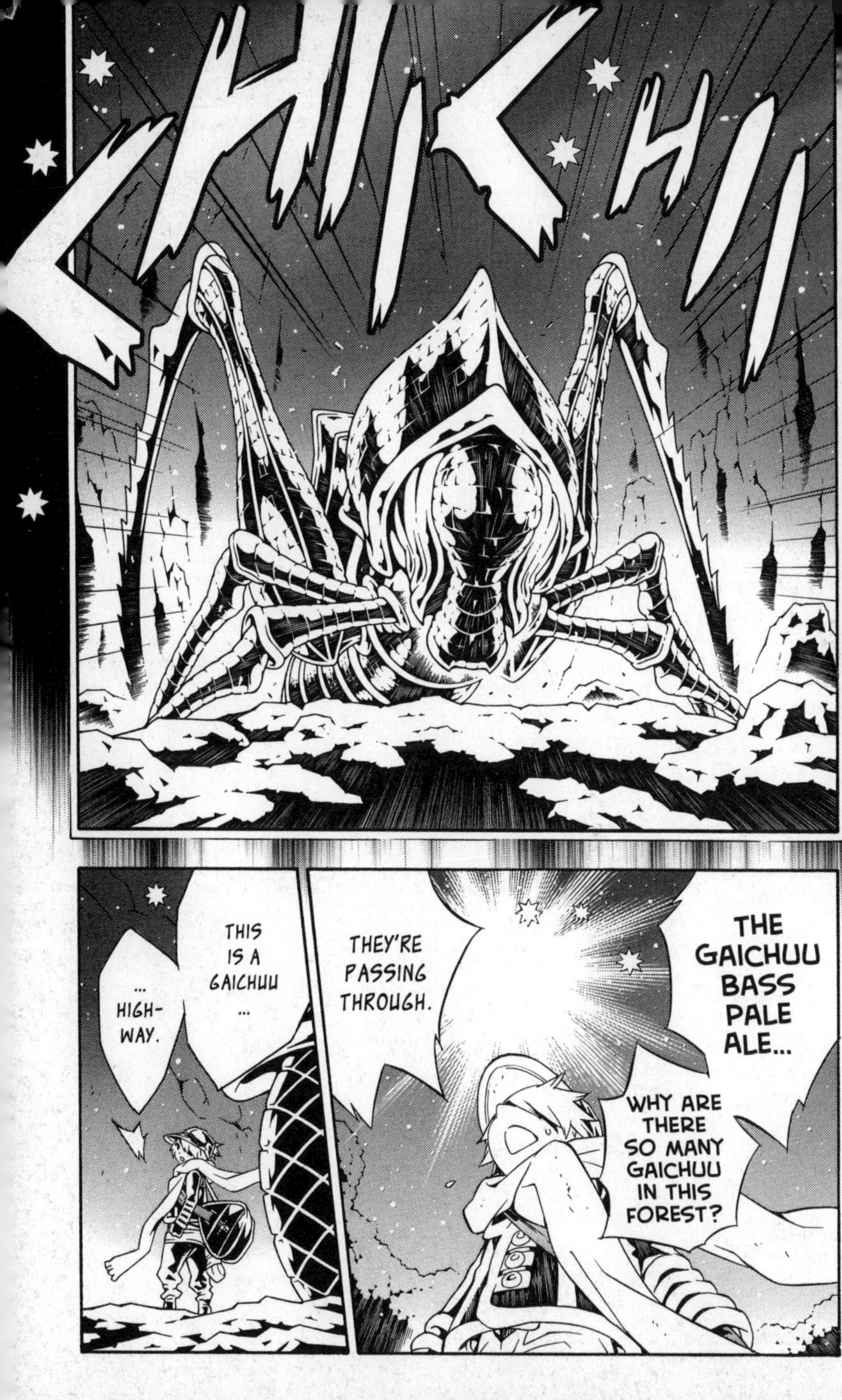
THE GAICHUU BASS PALE ALE...
WHY ARE THERE SO MANY GAICHUU IN THIS FOREST?
THEY'RE PASSING THROUGH.
THIS IS A GAICHUU ...
... HIGH-WAY.

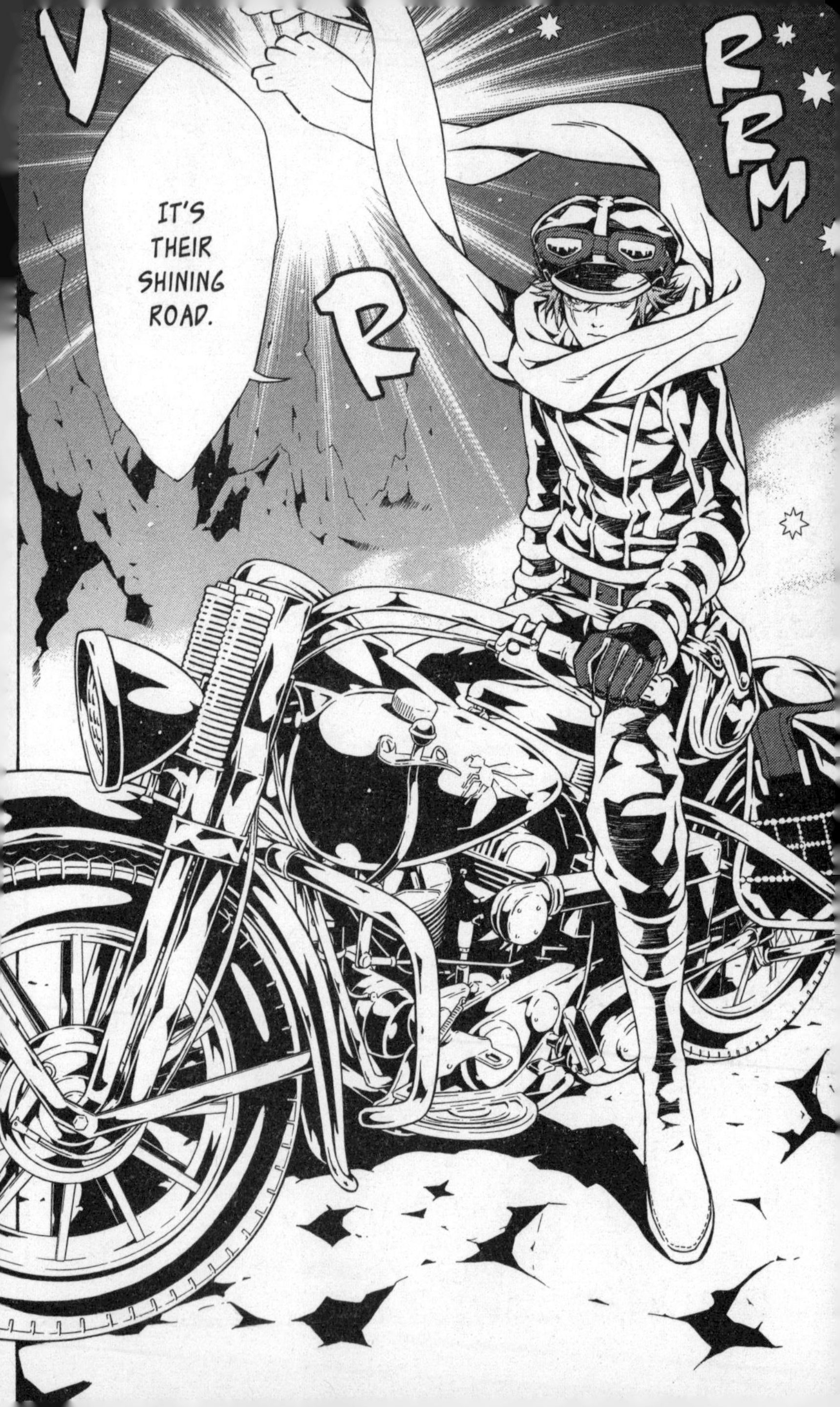
V R RRM
IT'S THEIR SHINING ROAD.

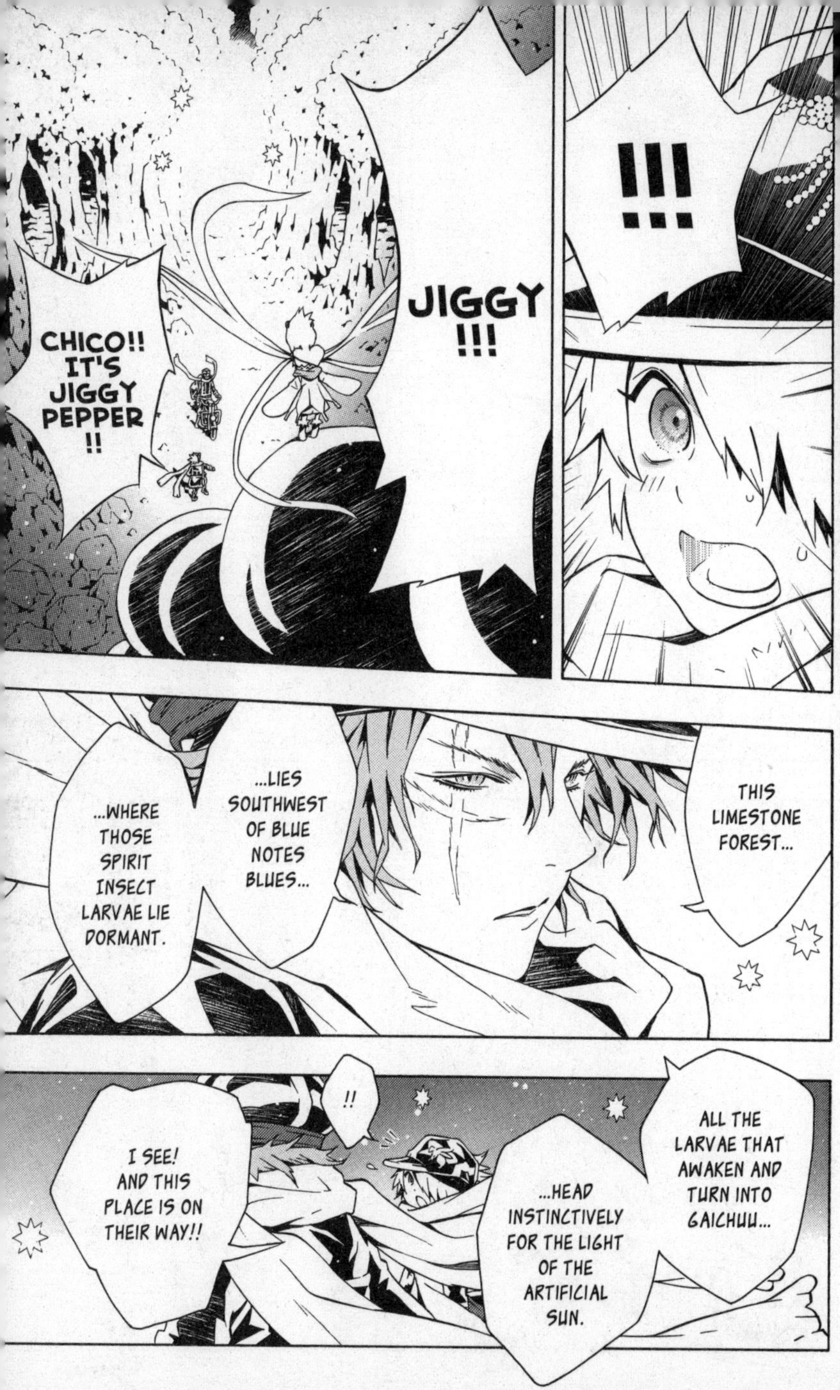
!!!
JIGGY !!!
CHICO!! IT'S JIGGY PEPPER !!
THIS LIMESTONE FOREST...
...LIES SOUTHWEST OF BLUE NOTES BLUES...
...WHERE THOSE SPIRIT INSECT LARVAE LIE DORMANT.
ALL THE LARVAE THAT AWAKEN AND TURN INTO GAICHUU...
...HEAD INSTINCTIVELY FOR THE LIGHT OF THE ARTIFICIAL SUN.
!!
I SEE! AND THIS PLACE IS ON THEIR WAY!!

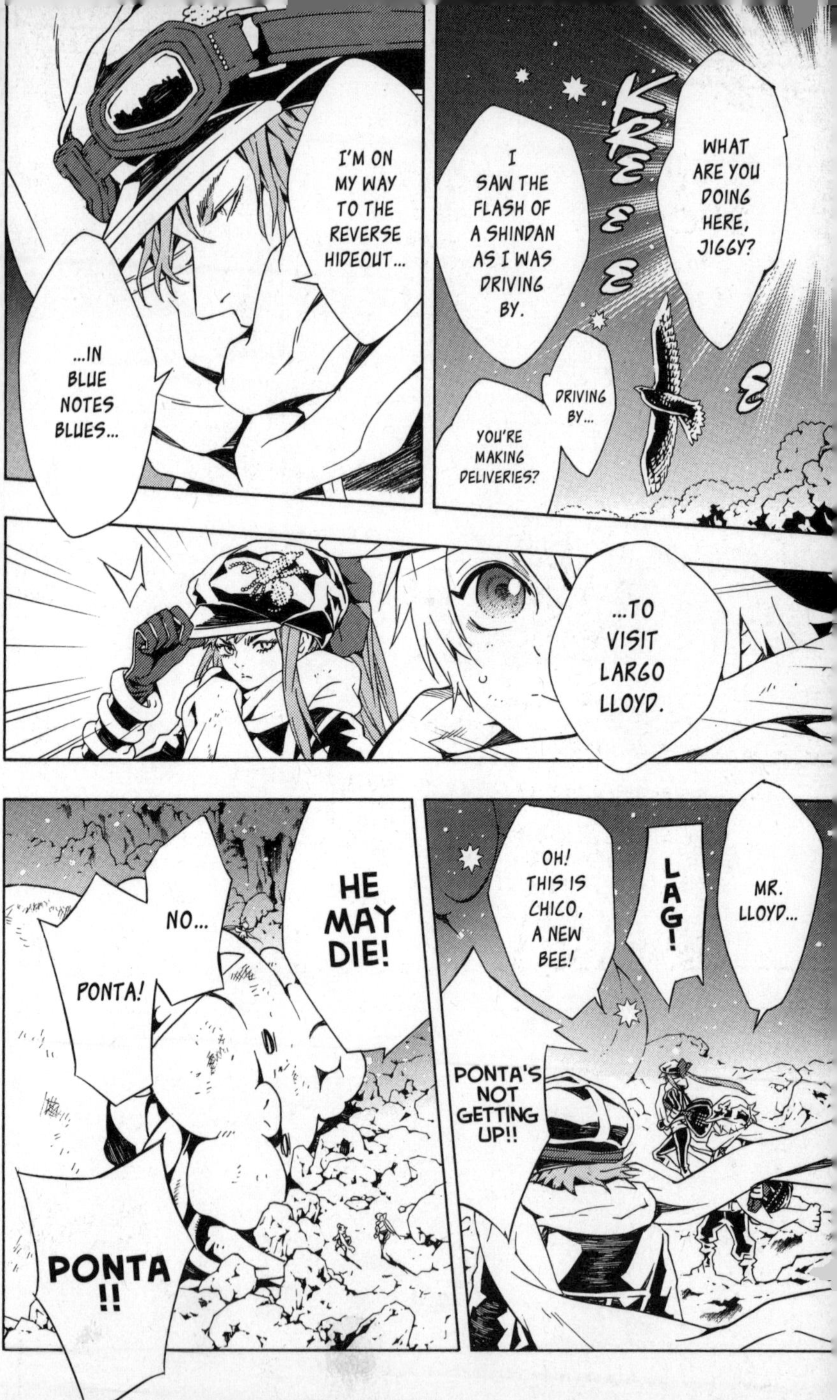
WHAT ARE YOU DOING HERE, JIGGY?
KREEEE
I SAW THE FLASH OF A SHINDAN AS I WAS DRIVING BY.
DRIVING BY...
YOU'RE MAKING DELIVERIES?
I'M ON MY WAY TO THE REVERSE HIDEOUT...
...IN BLUE NOTES BLUES...
...TO VISIT LARGO LLOYD.
MR. LLOYD...
LAG!
OH! THIS IS CHICO, A NEW BEE!
PONTA'S NOT GETTING UP!!
HE MAY DIE!
NO...
PONTA!
PONTA !!

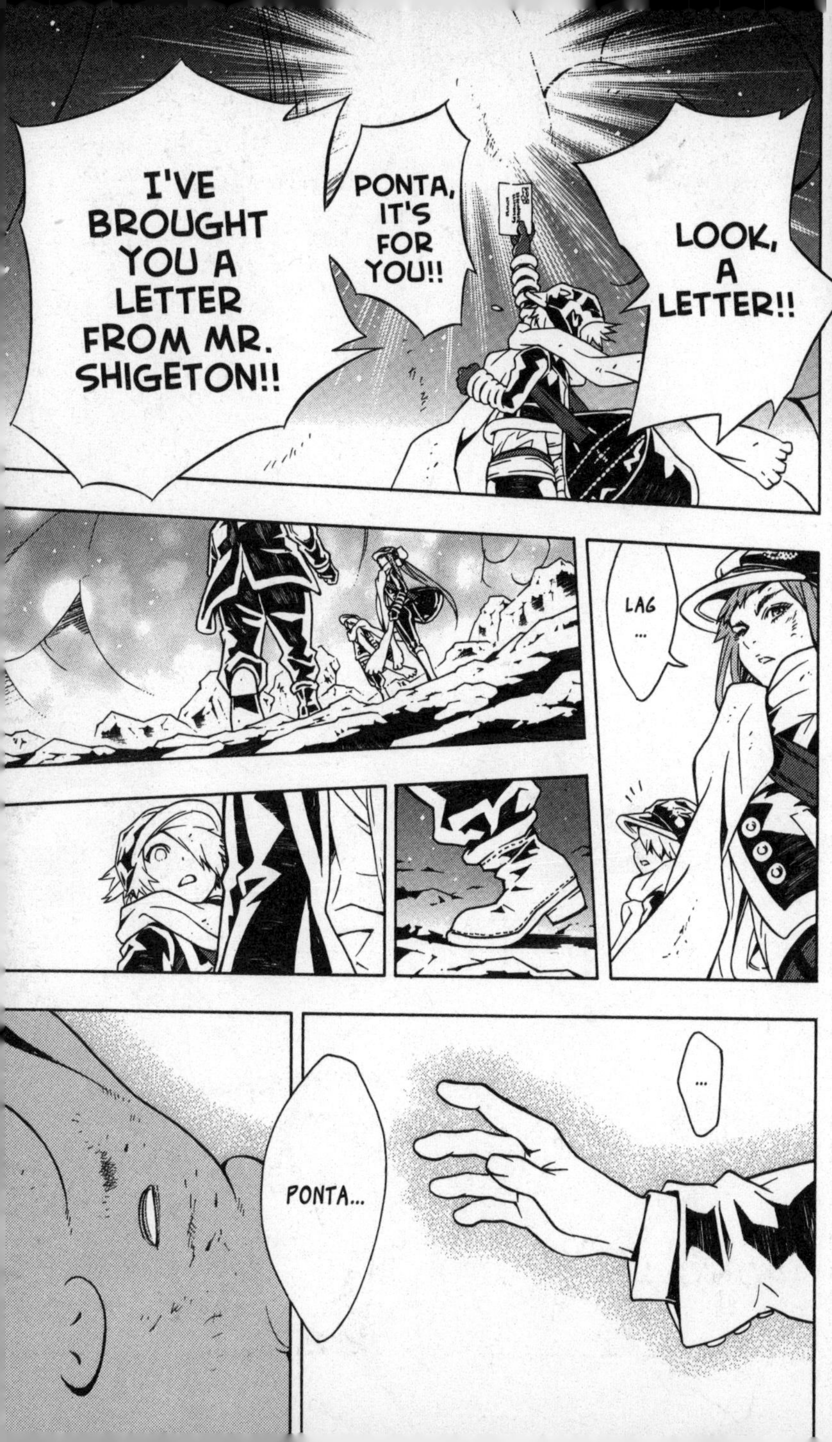
LOOK, A LETTER!!
PONTA, IT'S FOR YOU!!
I'VE BROUGHT YOU A LETTER FROM MR. SHIGETON!!
LAG ...
...
PONTA...

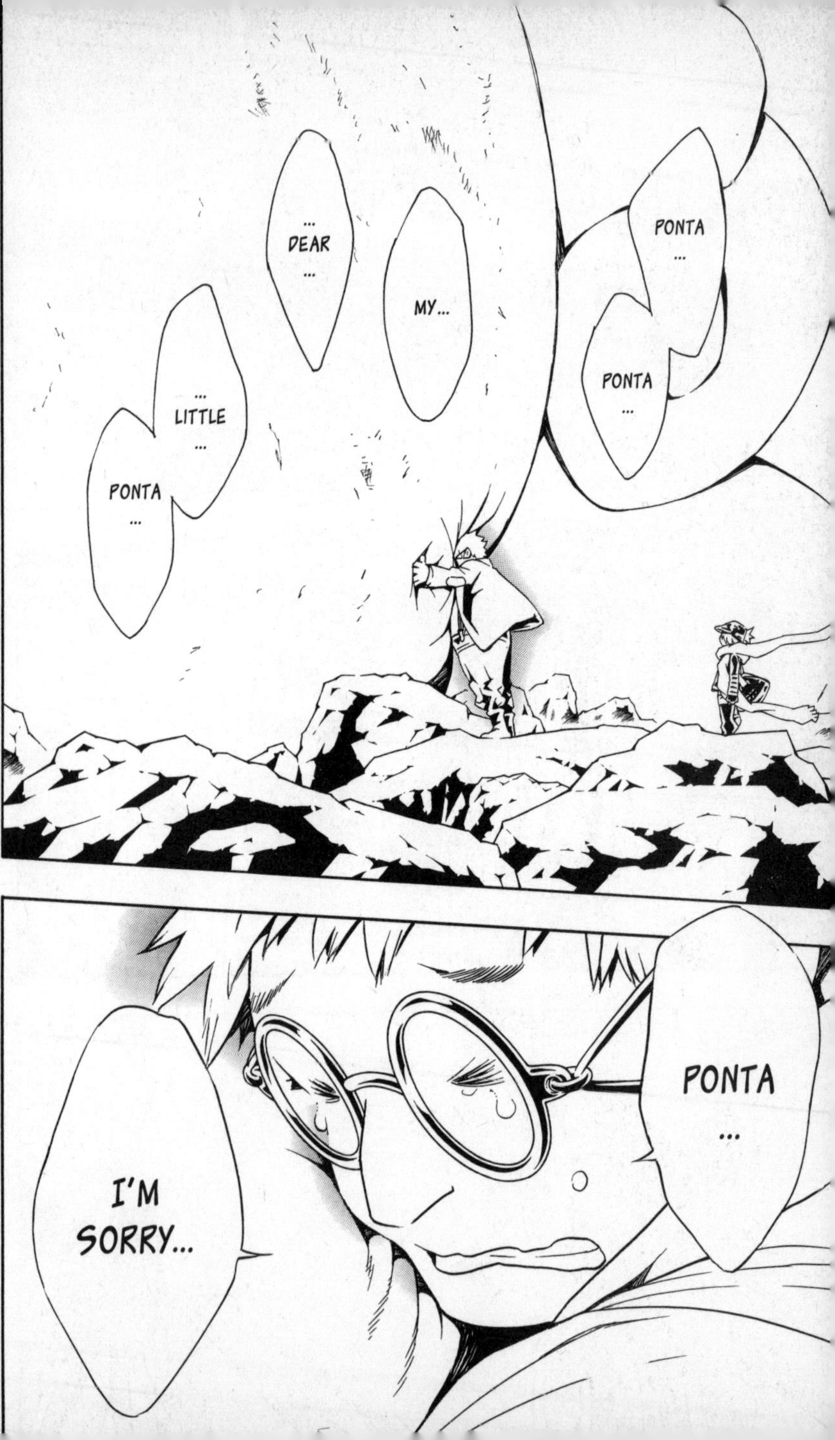
PONTA ...
PONTA ...
MY...
... DEAR ...
... LITTLE ...
PONTA ...
PONTA ...
I'M SORRY...

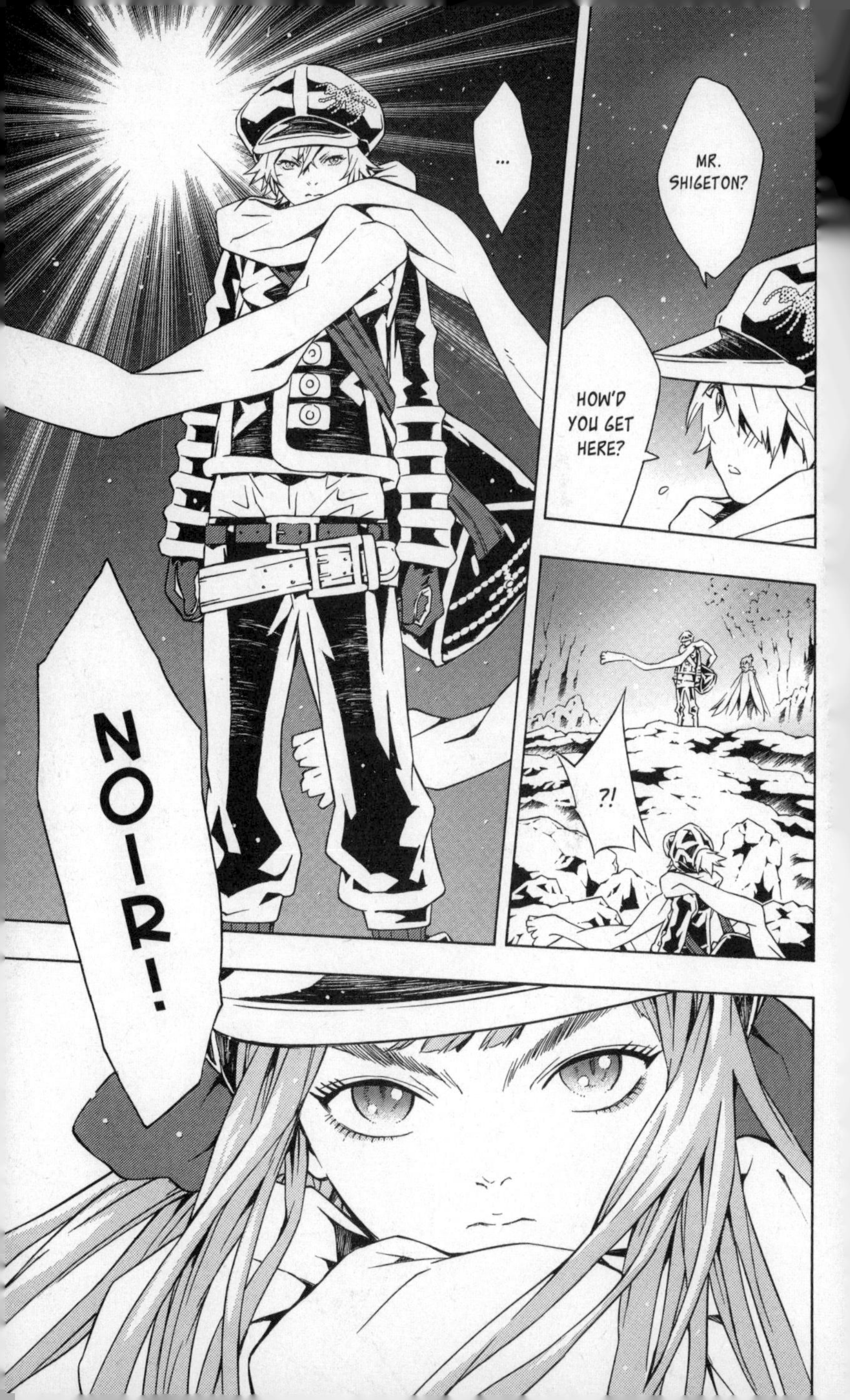
MR. SHIGETON?
HOW'D YOU GET HERE?
?!
...
NOIR!

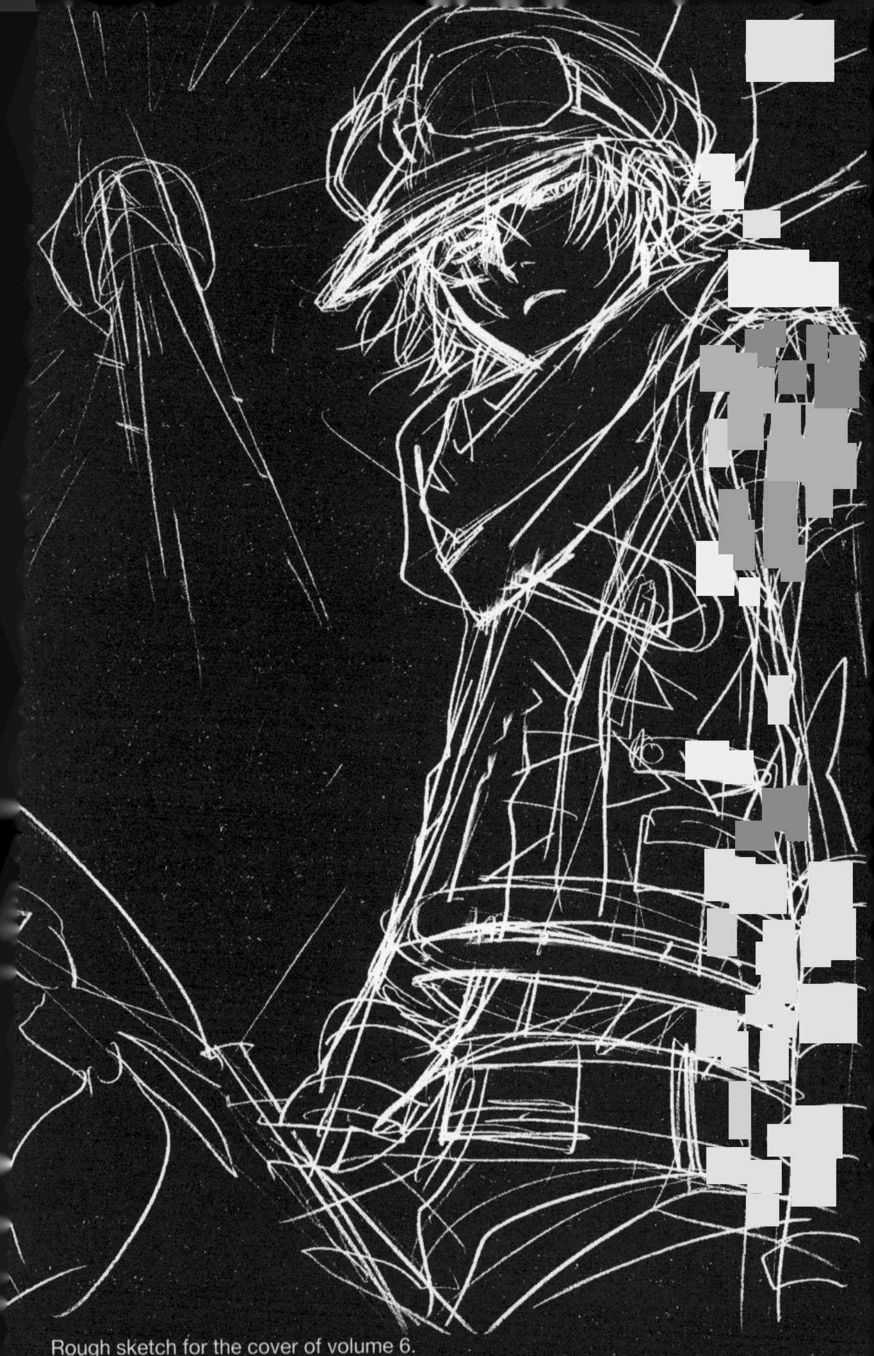

Rough sketch for the cover of volume 6.

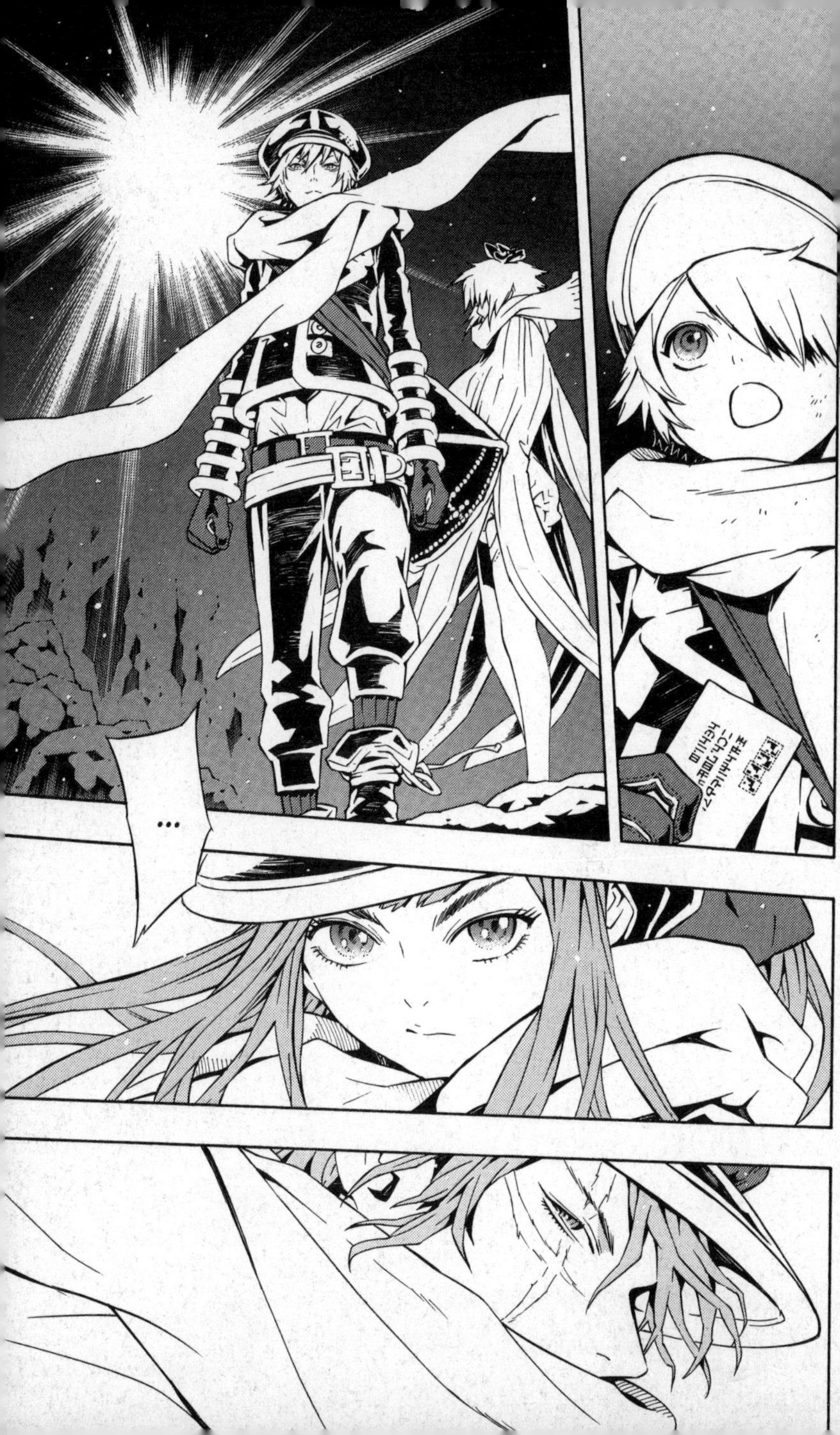
...

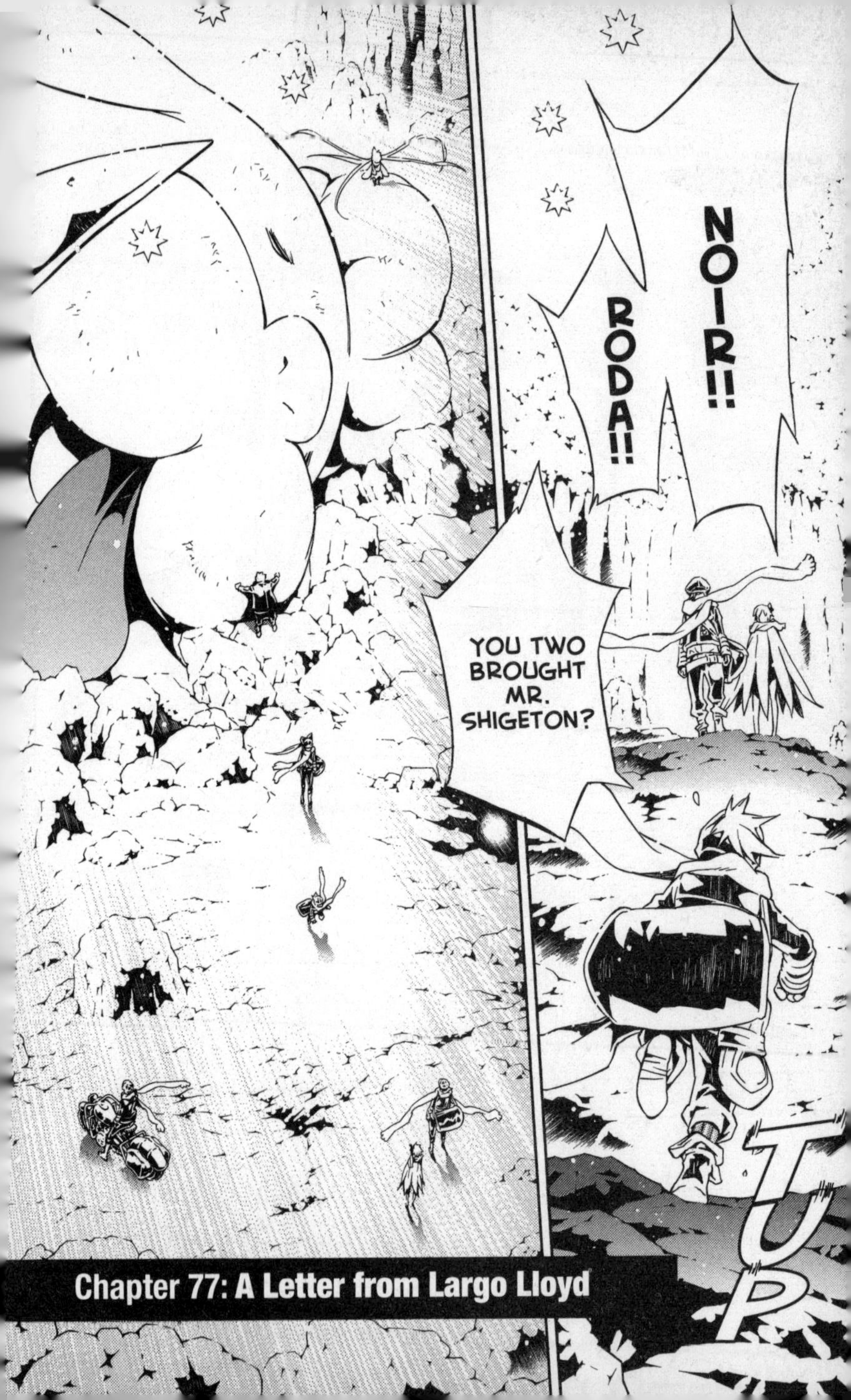
NOIR!!
RODA!!
YOU TWO BROUGHT MR. SHIGETON?
TUP

Chapter 77: A Letter from Largo Lloyd

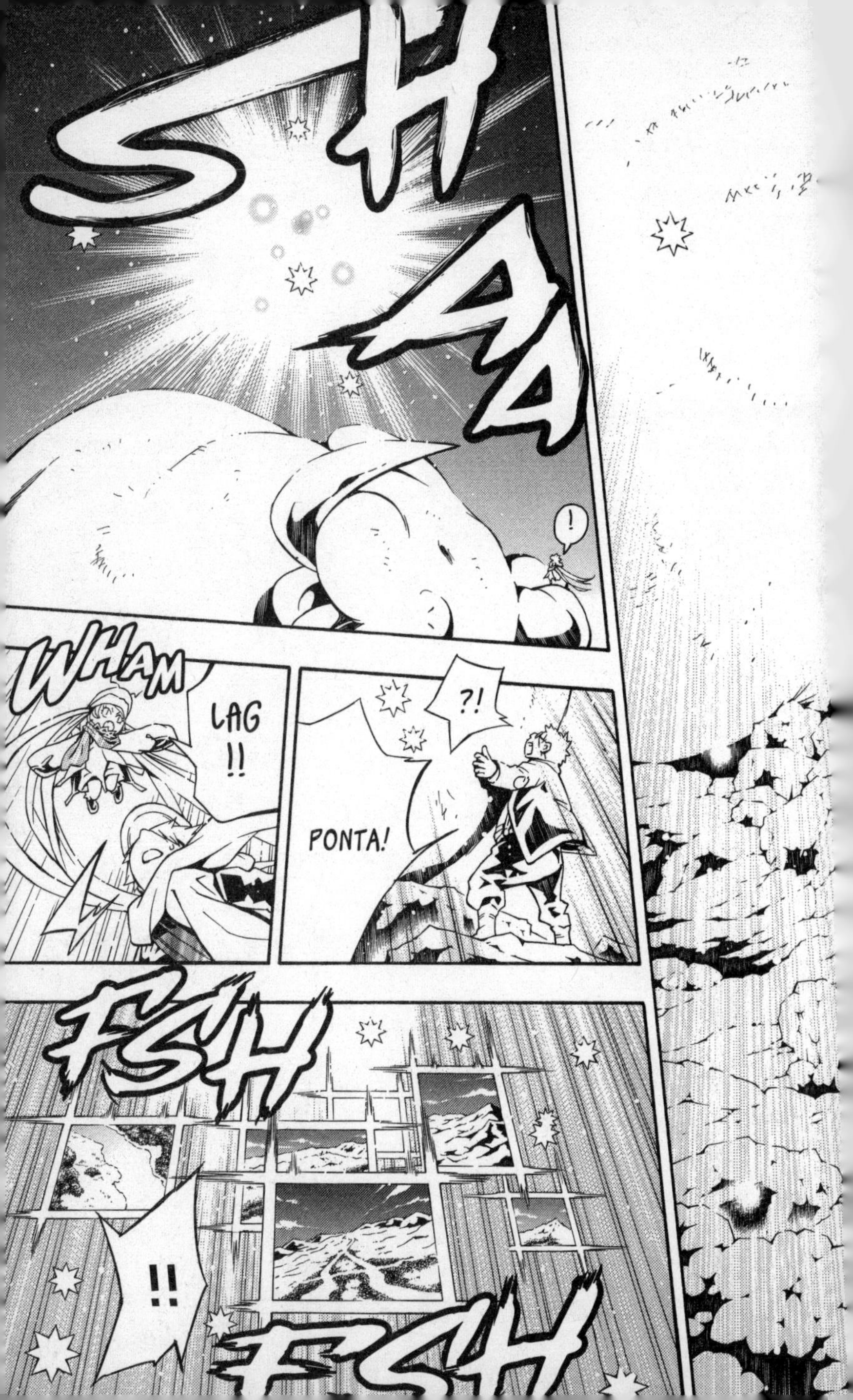
SHAA
!
?!
PONTA!
WHAM
LAG !!
FSH
!!
FSH

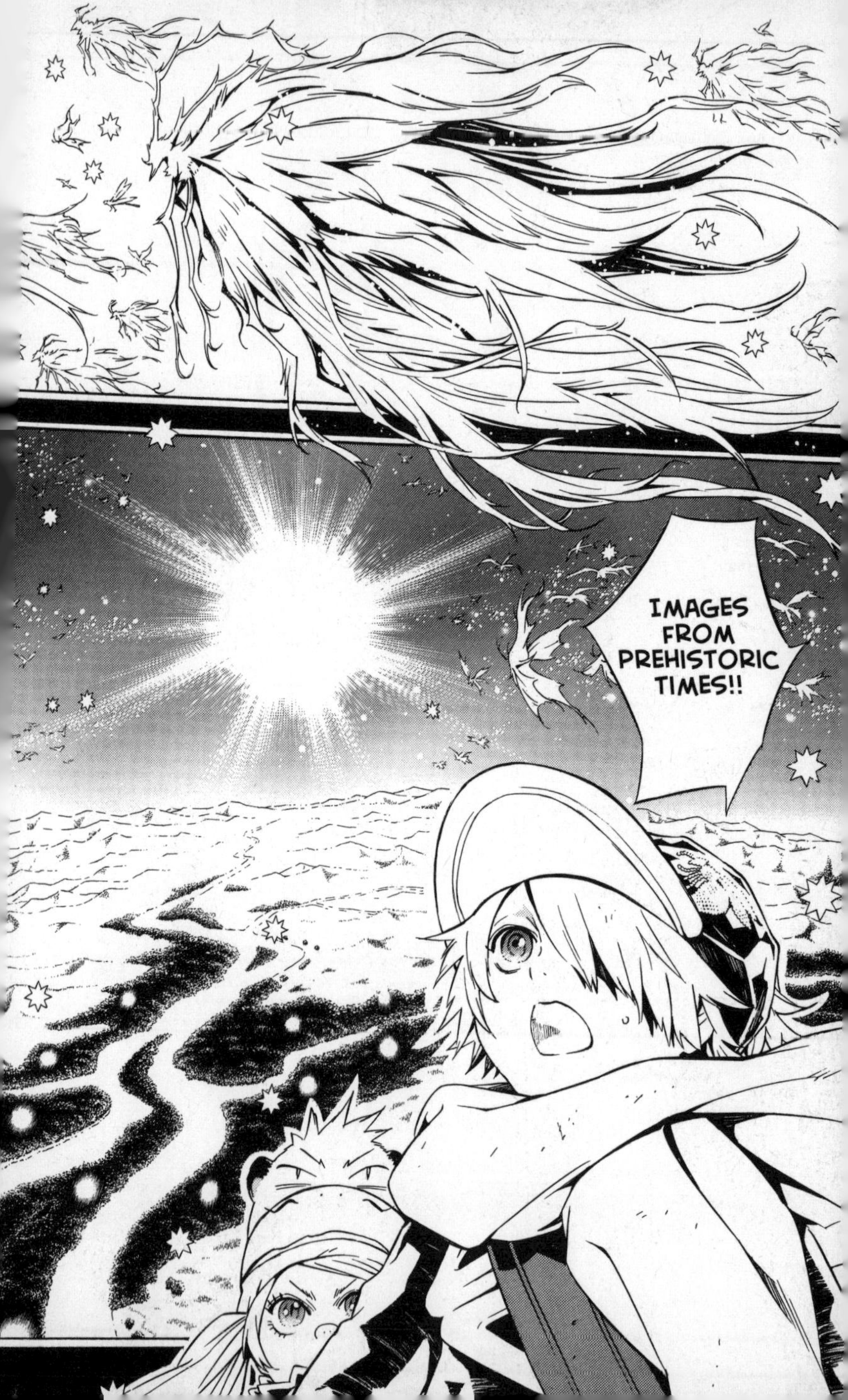
IMAGES FROM PREHISTORIC TIMES!!

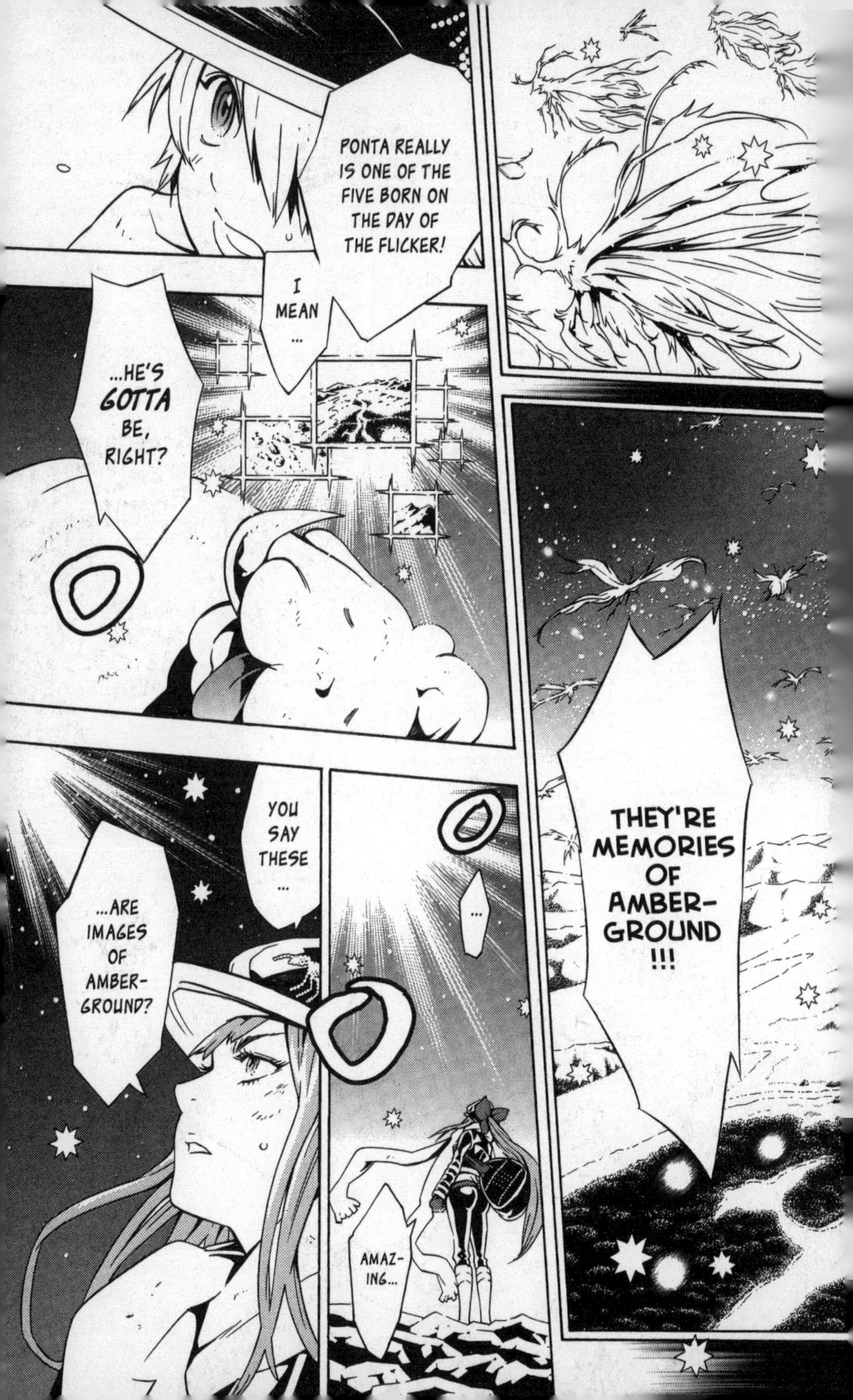
PONTA REALLY IS ONE OF THE FIVE BORN ON THE DAY OF THE FLICKER!
I MEAN ...
...HE'S GOTTA BE, RIGHT?
THEY'RE MEMORIES OF AMBER-GROUND!!!
...
AMAZ-ING...
YOU SAY THESE ...
...ARE IMAGES OF AMBER-GROUND?

IS THAT A FLOCK OF SPIRIT INSECTS...

...FLYING AROUND THE SUN?

...

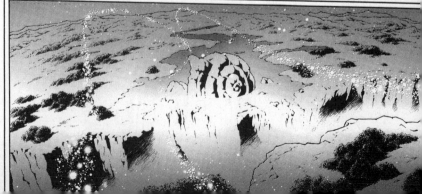

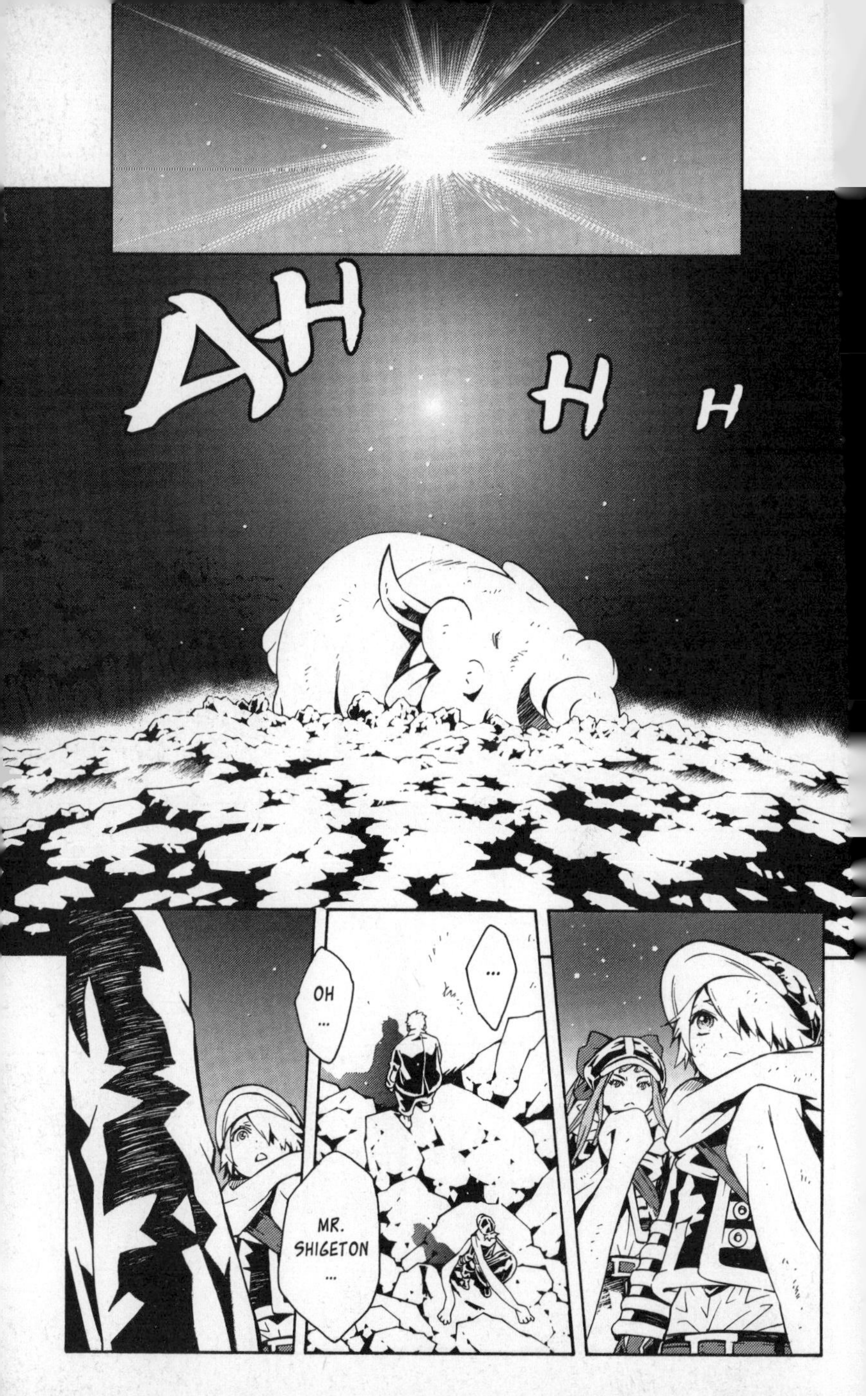
AH H H
...
OH ...
MR. SHIGETON ...

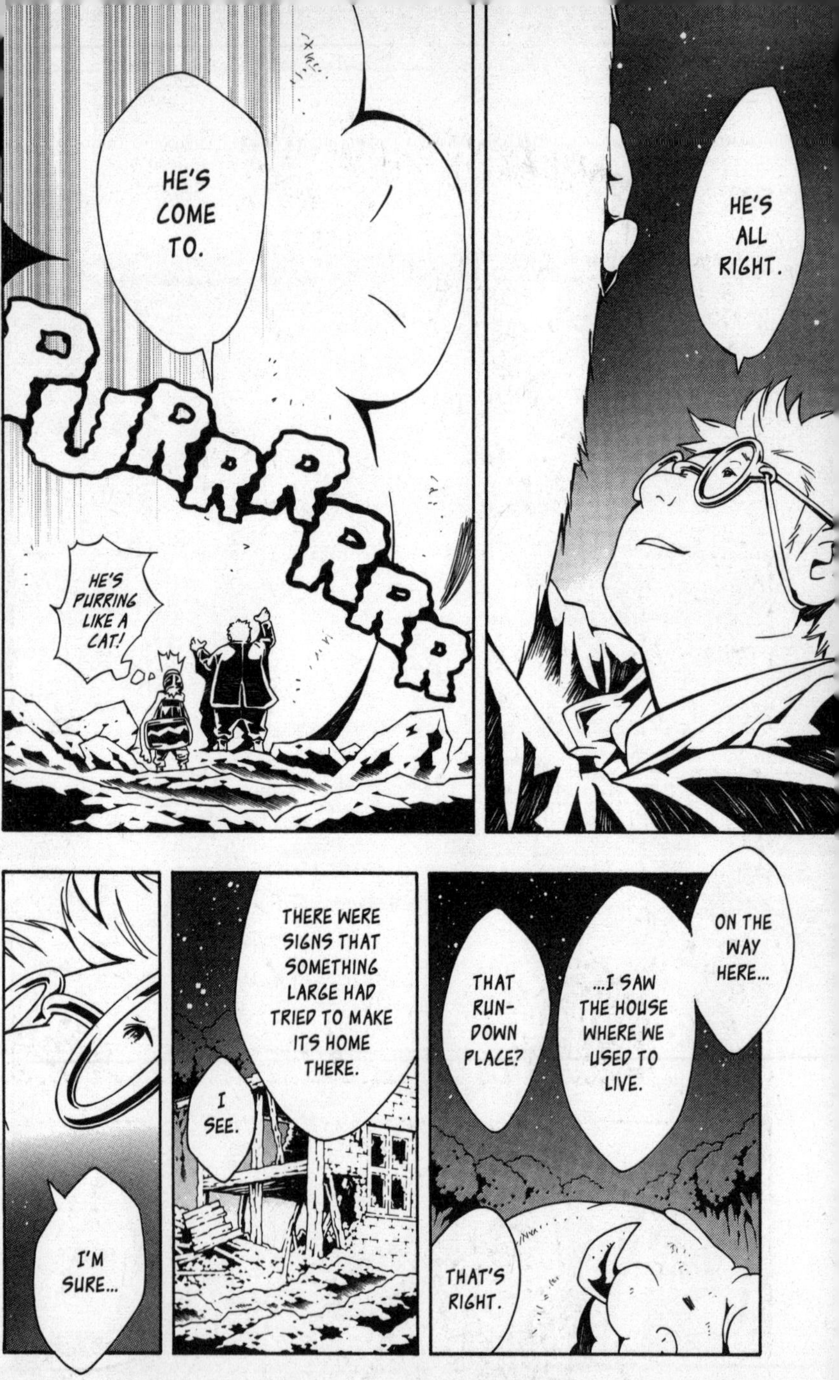
HE'S ALL RIGHT.
HE'S COME TO.
PURRRRRR
HE'S PURRING LIKE A CAT!
ON THE WAY HERE...
...I SAW THE HOUSE WHERE WE USED TO LIVE.
THAT RUN-DOWN PLACE?
THAT'S RIGHT.
THERE WERE SIGNS THAT SOMETHING LARGE HAD TRIED TO MAKE ITS HOME THERE.
I SEE.
I'M SURE...

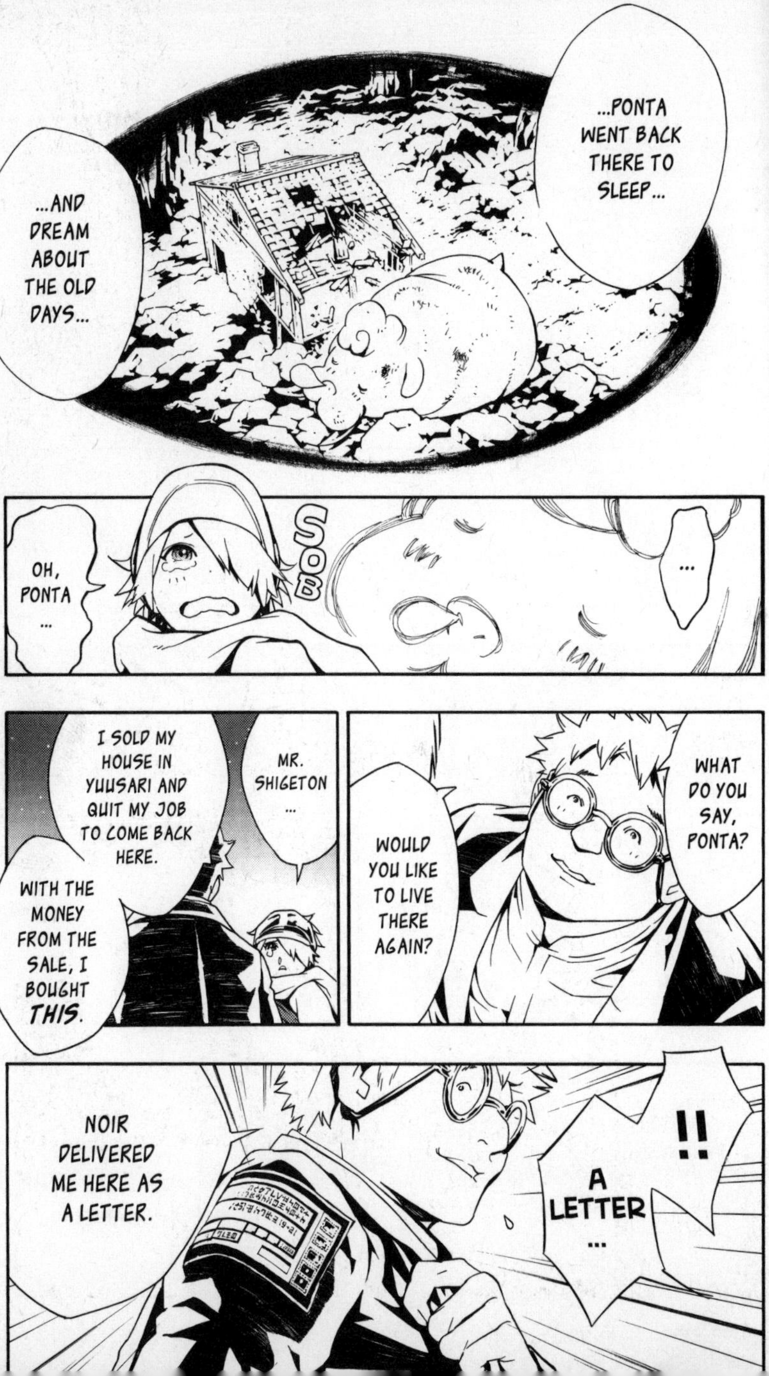
...PONTA WENT BACK THERE TO SLEEP...
...AND DREAM ABOUT THE OLD DAYS...
...
SOB
OH, PONTA ...
WHAT DO YOU SAY, PONTA?
WOULD YOU LIKE TO LIVE THERE AGAIN?
MR. SHIGETON ...
I SOLD MY HOUSE IN YUUSARI AND QUIT MY JOB TO COME BACK HERE.
WITH THE MONEY FROM THE SALE, I BOUGHT *THIS*.
!!
A LETTER ...
NOIR DELIVERED ME HERE AS A LETTER.

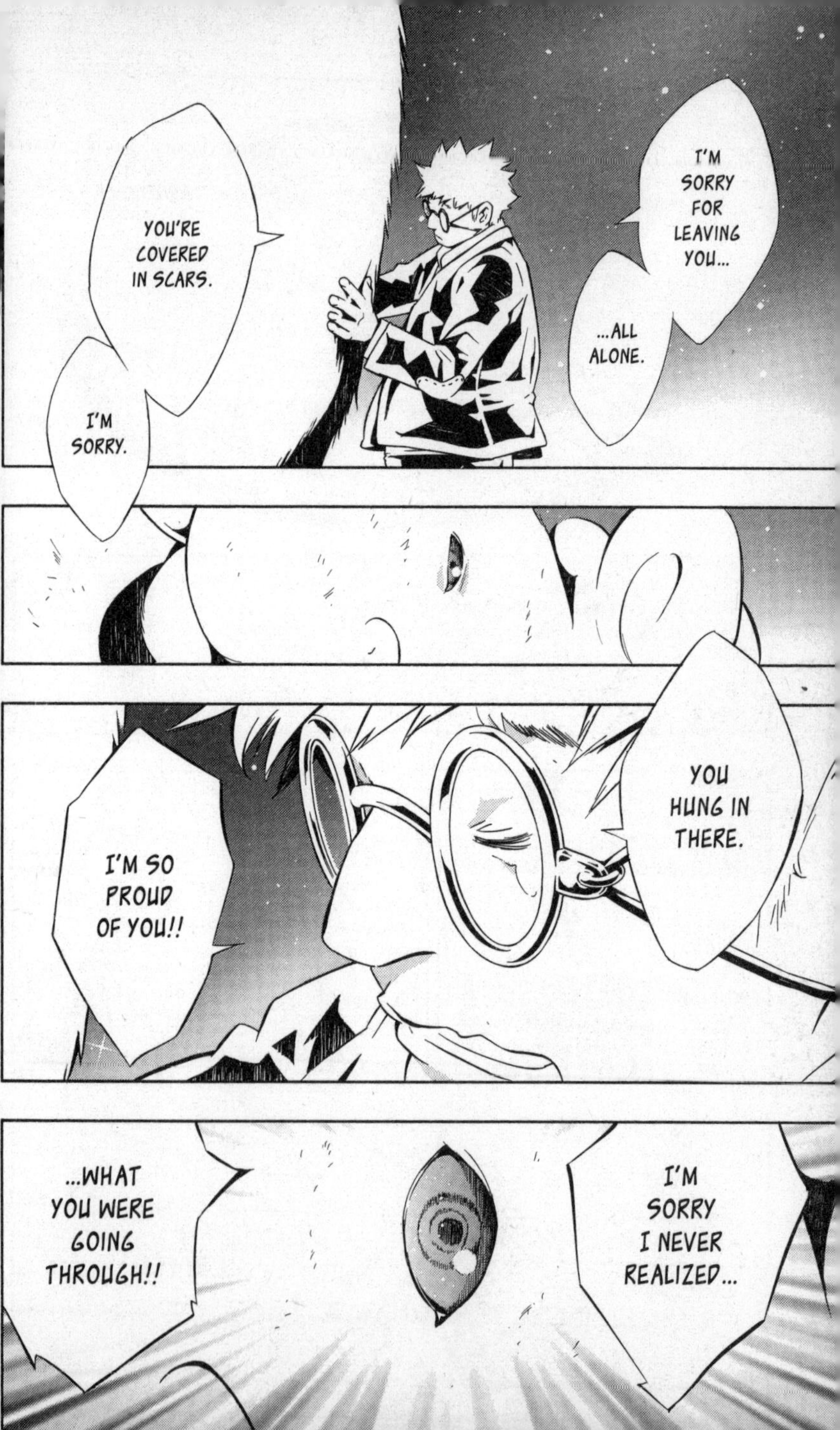
I'M SORRY FOR LEAVING YOU...
...ALL ALONE.
YOU'RE COVERED IN SCARS.
I'M SORRY.
YOU HUNG IN THERE.
I'M SO PROUD OF YOU!!
I'M SORRY I NEVER REALIZED...
...WHAT YOU WERE GOING THROUGH!!

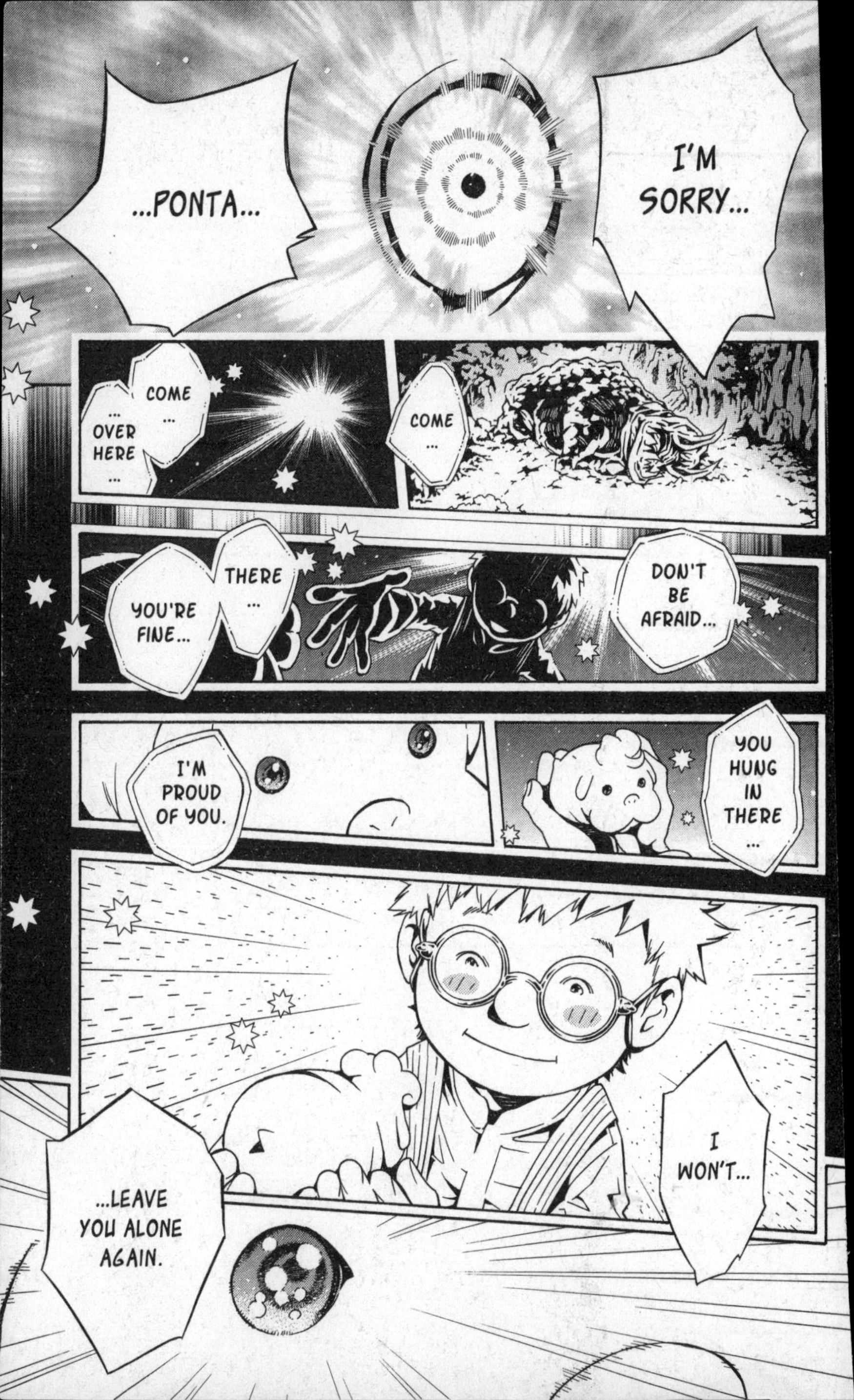
I'M SORRY...
...PONTA...
COME ...
COME ...
... OVER HERE ...
DON'T BE AFRAID...
THERE ...
YOU'RE FINE...
YOU HUNG IN THERE ...
I'M PROUD OF YOU.
I WON'T...
...LEAVE YOU ALONE AGAIN.

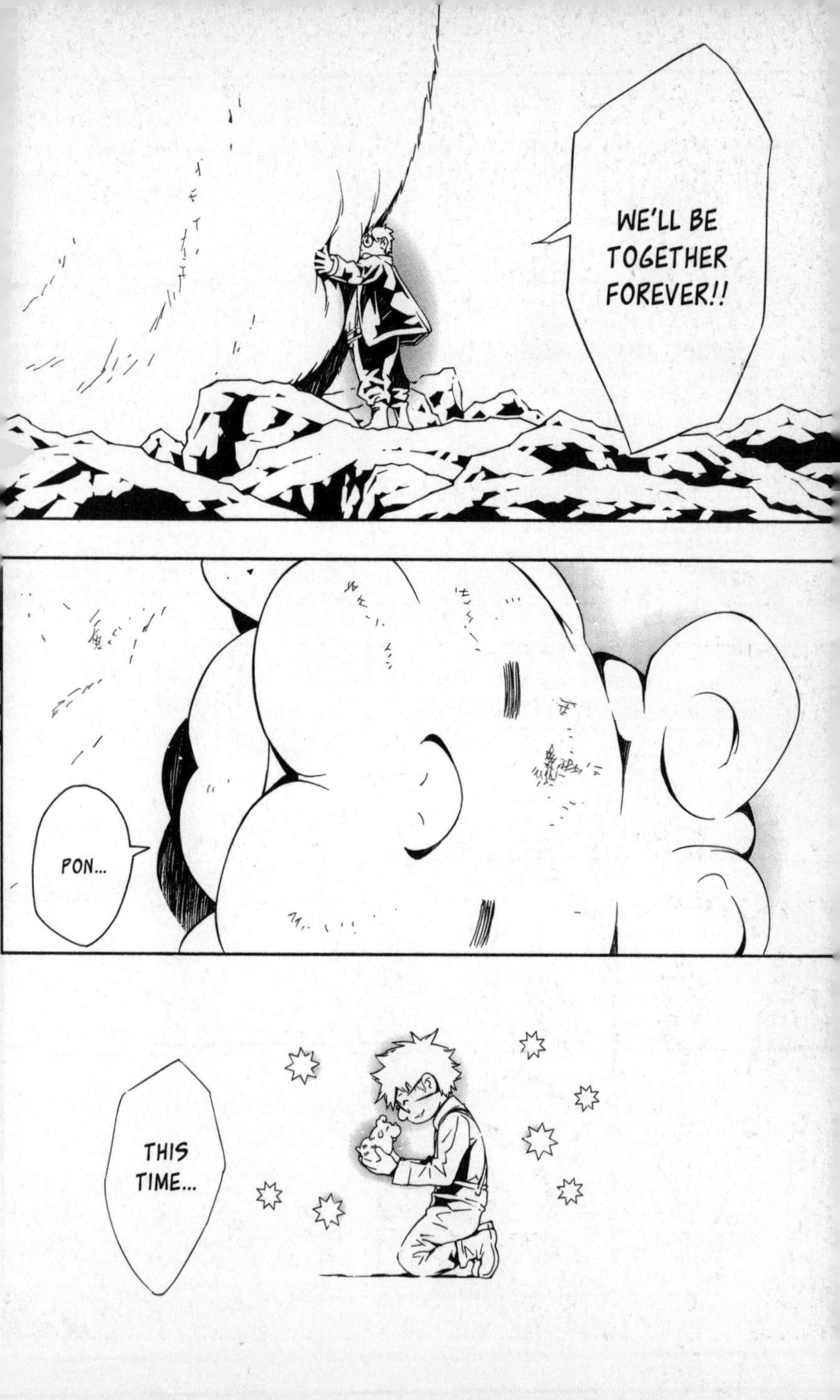
WE'LL BE TOGETHER FOREVER!!
PON...
THIS TIME...

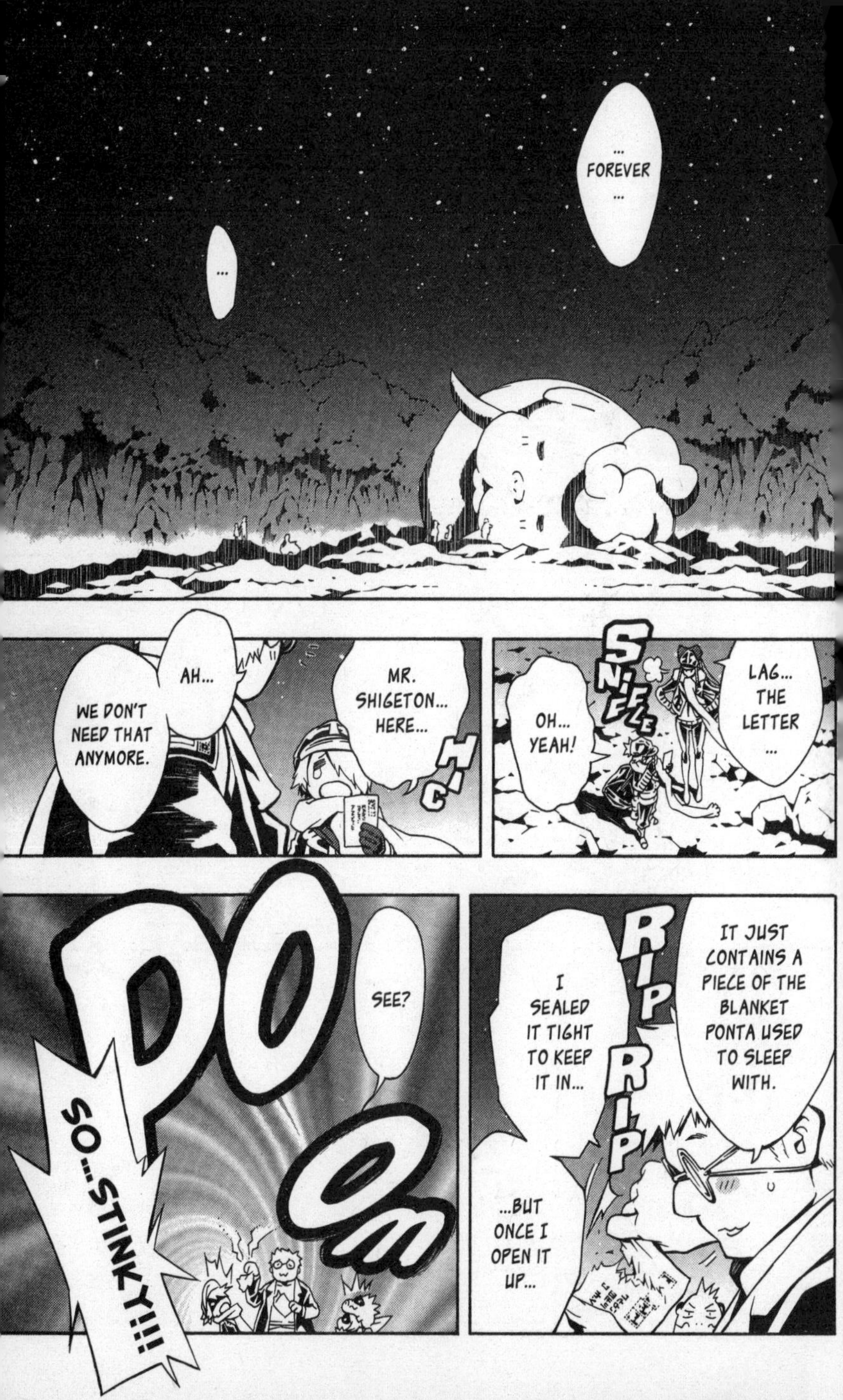

... FOREVER ...
...
LAG... THE LETTER ...
SNIFFLE
OH... YEAH!
MR. SHIGETON... HERE...
HIC
AH...
WE DON'T NEED THAT ANYMORE.
IT JUST CONTAINS A PIECE OF THE BLANKET PONTA USED TO SLEEP WITH.
RIP RIP
I SEALED IT TIGHT TO KEEP IT IN...
...BUT ONCE I OPEN IT UP...
SEE?
DOOOM
SO...STINKY!!!

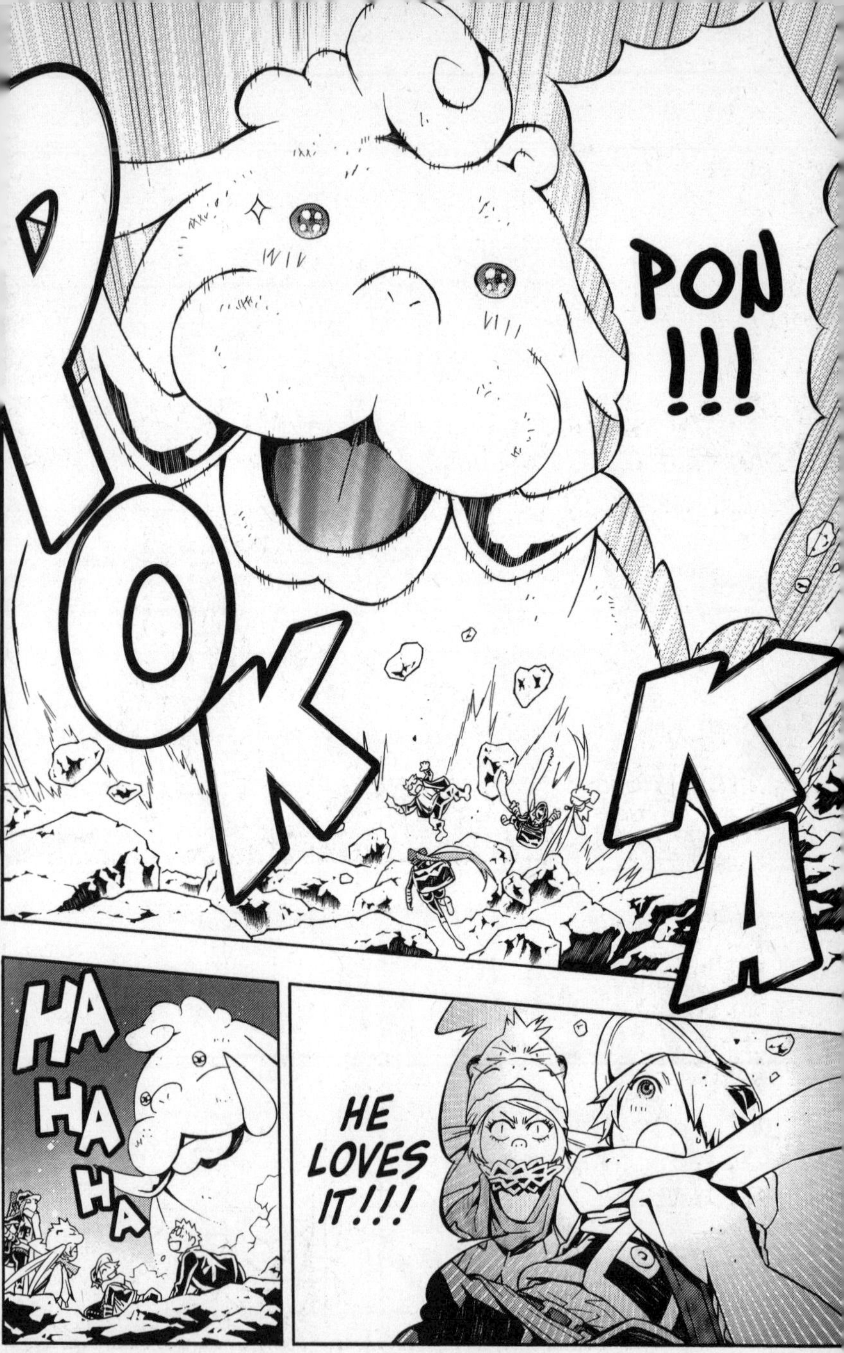
PON!!!
DOKKA
HE LOVES IT!!!
HA HA HA HA

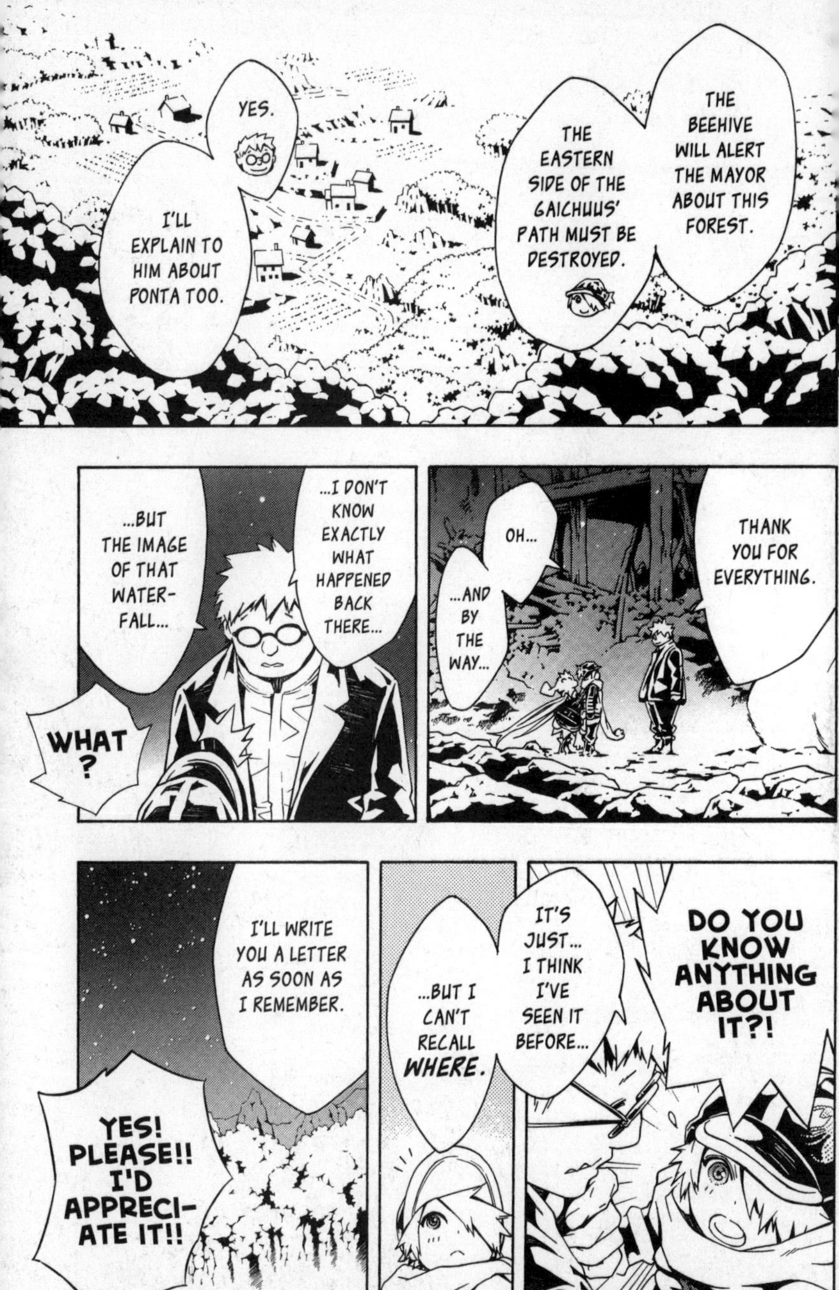
THE BEEHIVE WILL ALERT THE MAYOR ABOUT THIS FOREST.
THE EASTERN SIDE OF THE GAICHUUS' PATH MUST BE DESTROYED.
YES.
I'LL EXPLAIN TO HIM ABOUT PONTA TOO.
THANK YOU FOR EVERYTHING.
OH...
...AND BY THE WAY...
...I DON'T KNOW EXACTLY WHAT HAPPENED BACK THERE...
...BUT THE IMAGE OF THAT WATER-FALL...
WHAT?
DO YOU KNOW ANYTHING ABOUT IT?!
IT'S JUST... I THINK I'VE SEEN IT BEFORE...
...BUT I CAN'T RECALL WHERE.
I'LL WRITE YOU A LETTER AS SOON AS I REMEMBER.
YES! PLEASE!! I'D APPRECIATE IT!!

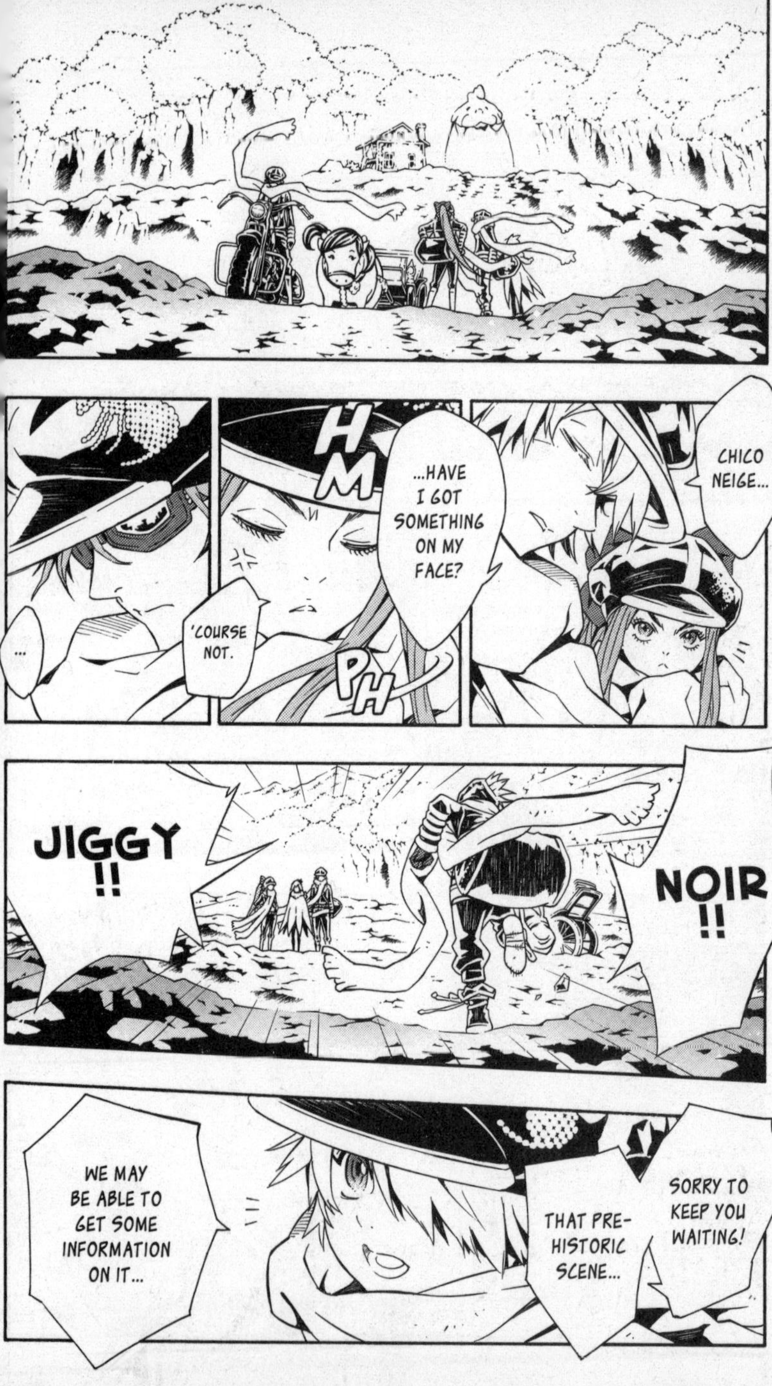
CHICO NEIGE...
...HAVE I GOT SOMETHING ON MY FACE?
HM
'COURSE NOT.
PH
...
NOIR!!
JIGGY!!
SORRY TO KEEP YOU WAITING!
THAT PRE-HISTORIC SCENE...
WE MAY BE ABLE TO GET SOME INFORMATION ON IT...

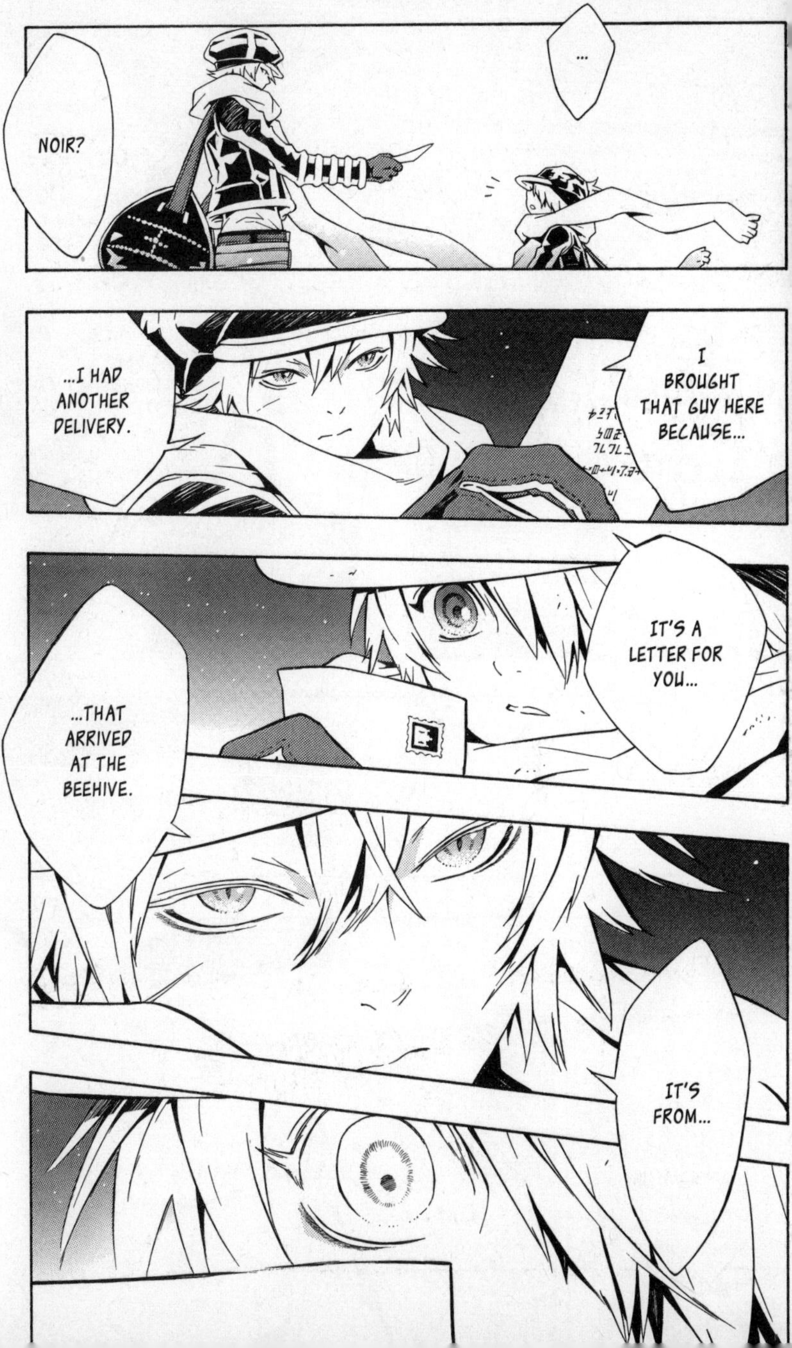
...
NOIR?
I BROUGHT THAT GUY HERE BECAUSE...
...I HAD ANOTHER DELIVERY.
IT'S A LETTER FOR YOU...
...THAT ARRIVED AT THE BEEHIVE.
IT'S FROM...

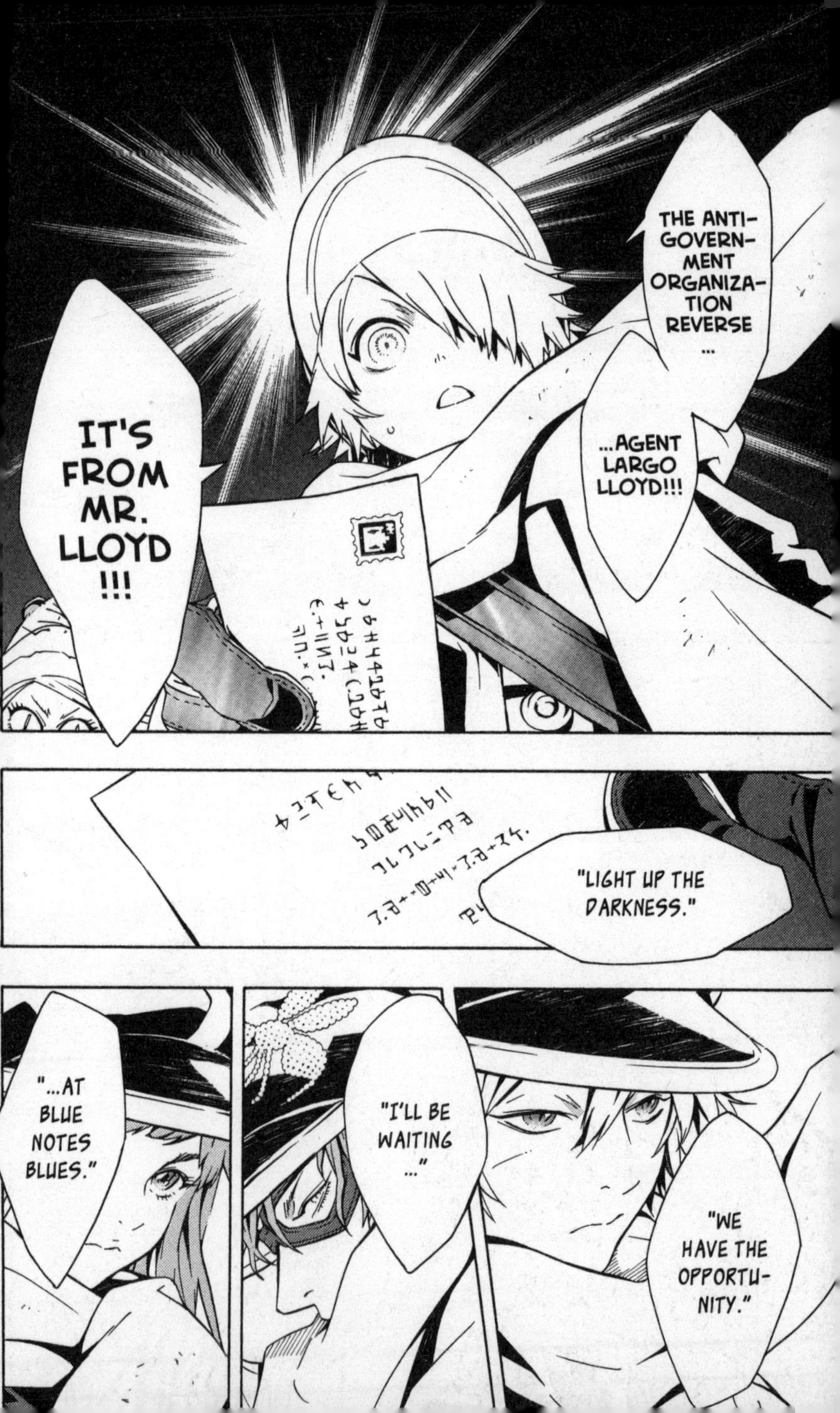
THE ANTI-GOVERNMENT ORGANIZATION REVERSE ...
...AGENT LARGO LLOYD!!!
IT'S FROM MR. LLOYD!!!
"LIGHT UP THE DARKNESS."
"WE HAVE THE OPPORTUNITY."
"I'LL BE WAITING ..."
"...AT BLUE NOTES BLUES."

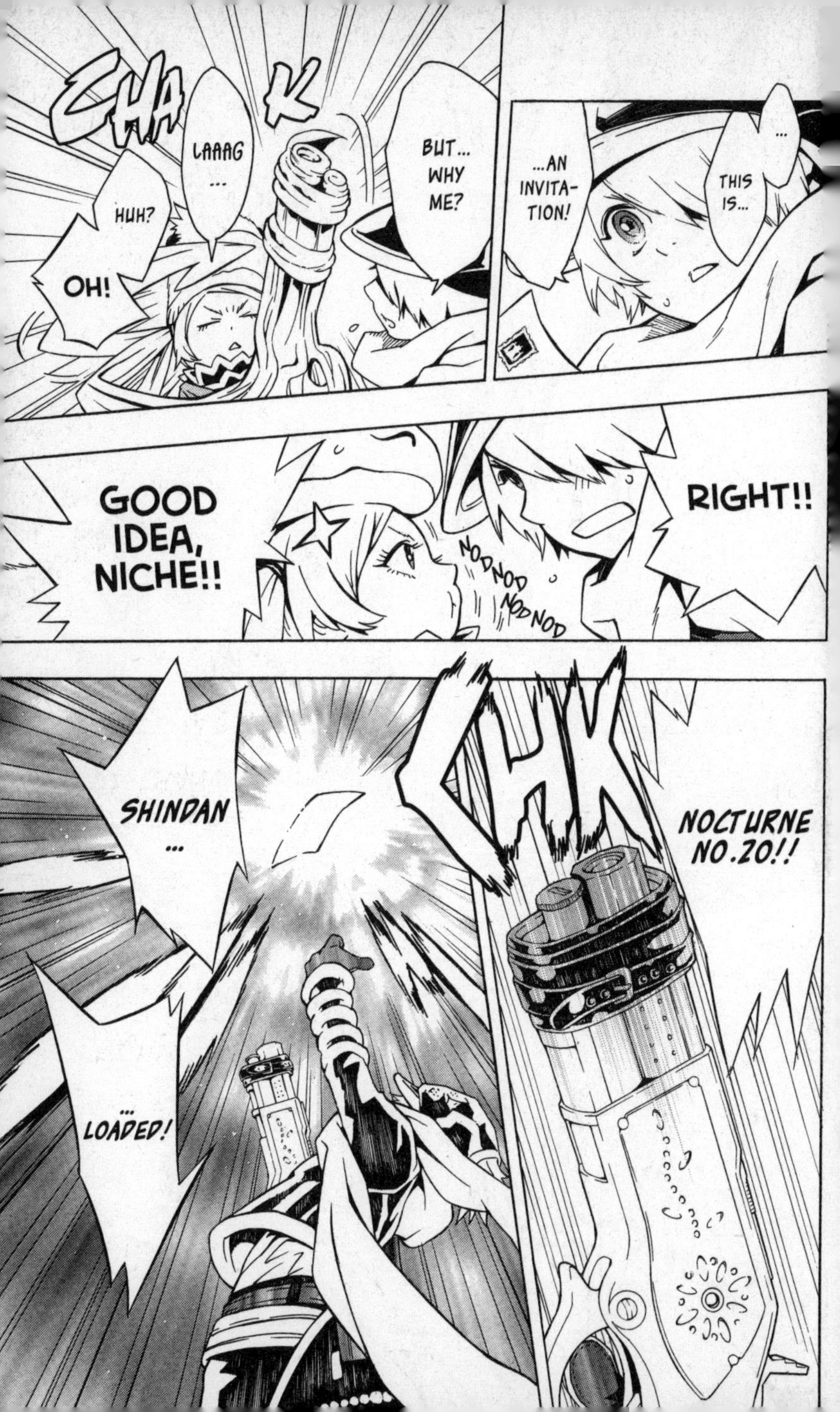
...
THIS IS...
...AN INVITATION!
BUT... WHY ME?
CHA K
LAAAG...
HUH?
OH!
RIGHT!!
NOD NOD NOD NOD
GOOD IDEA, NICHE!!
NOCTURNE NO.20!!
CHK
SHINDAN...
...LOADED!

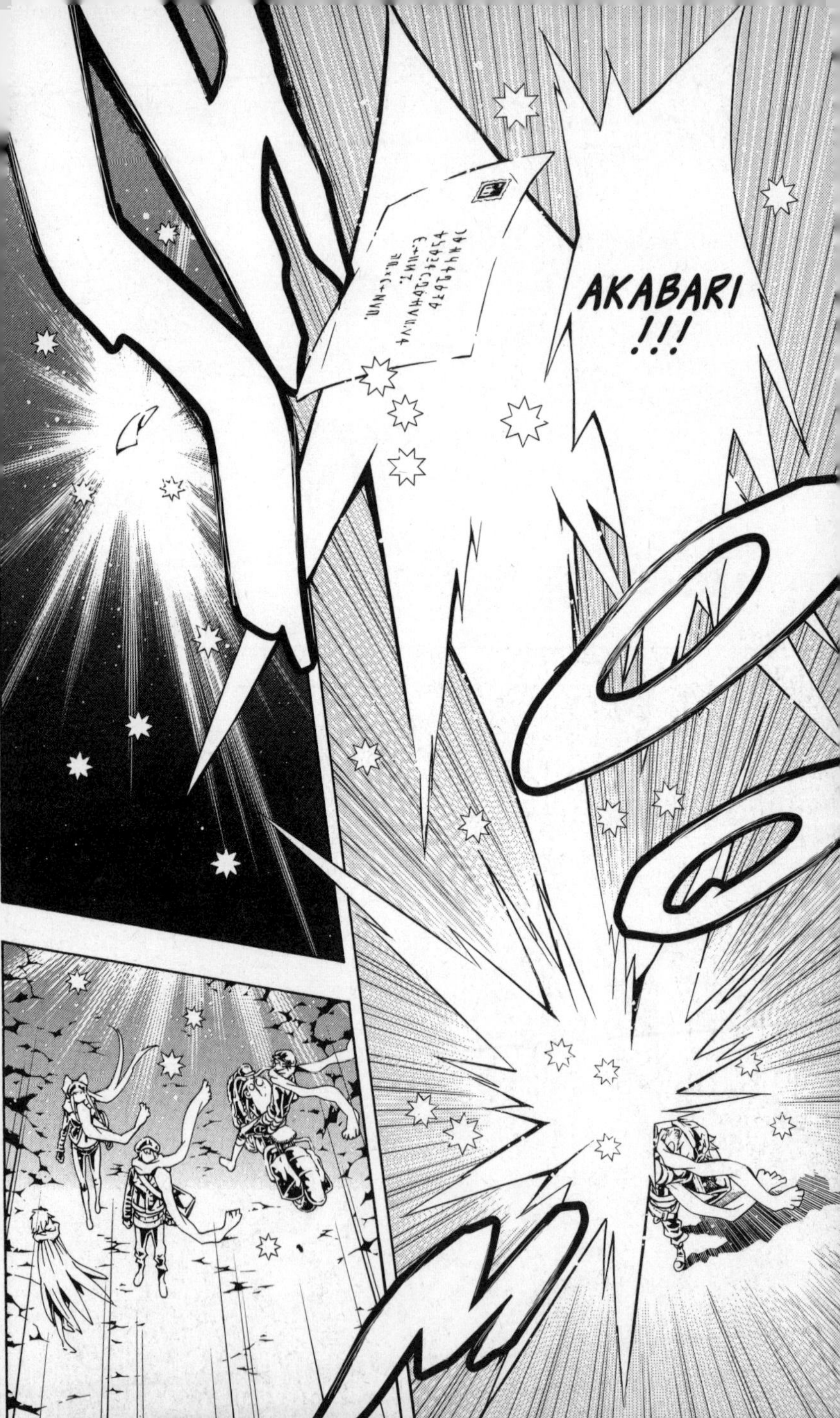
AKABARI !!!

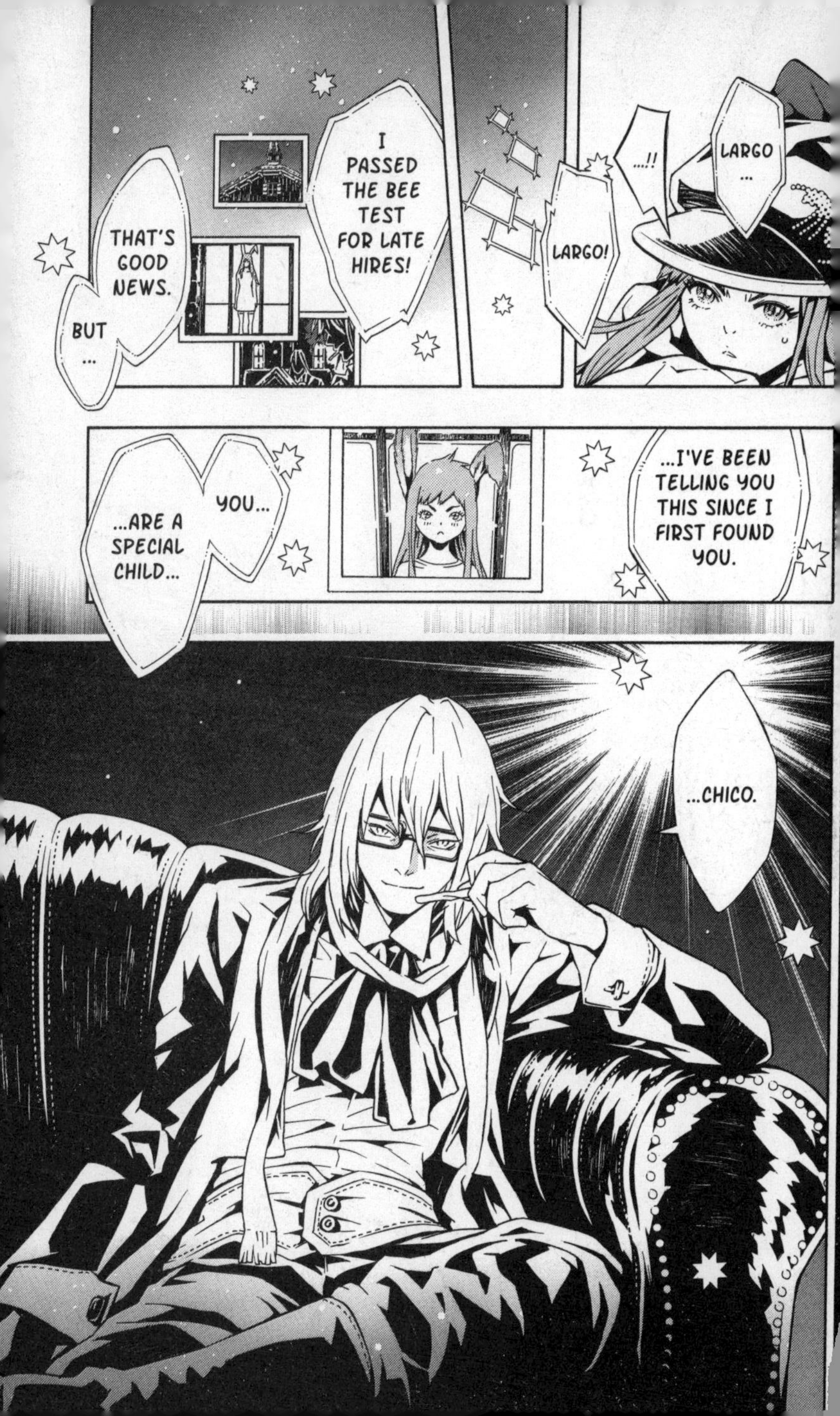
LARGO ...
...!!
LARGO!
I PASSED THE BEE TEST FOR LATE HIRES!
THAT'S GOOD NEWS.
BUT ...
...I'VE BEEN TELLING YOU THIS SINCE I FIRST FOUND YOU.
YOU...
...ARE A SPECIAL CHILD...
...CHICO.

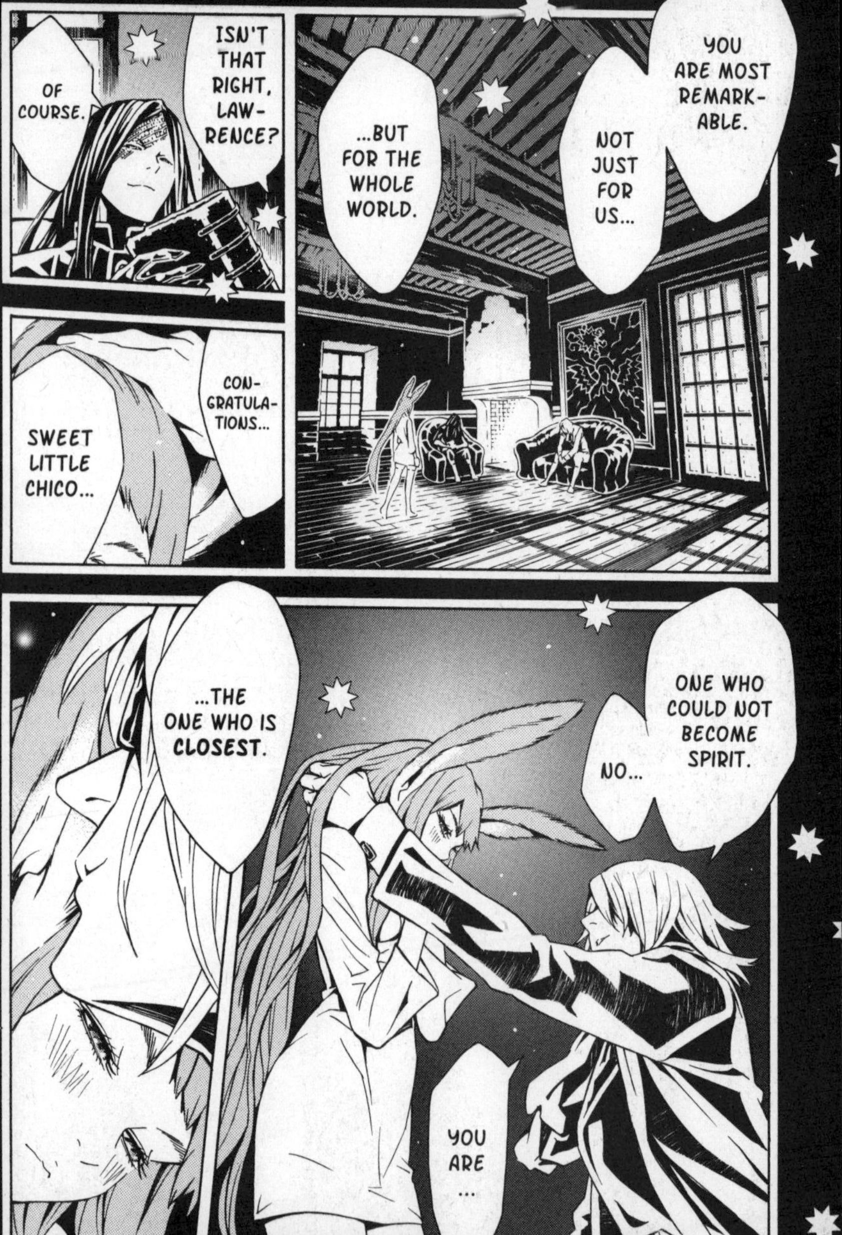
YOU ARE MOST REMARKABLE.
NOT JUST FOR US...
...BUT FOR THE WHOLE WORLD.
ISN'T THAT RIGHT, LAWRENCE?
OF COURSE.
CONGRATULATIONS...
SWEET LITTLE CHICO...
ONE WHO COULD NOT BECOME SPIRIT.
NO...
...THE ONE WHO IS **CLOSEST**.
YOU ARE ...

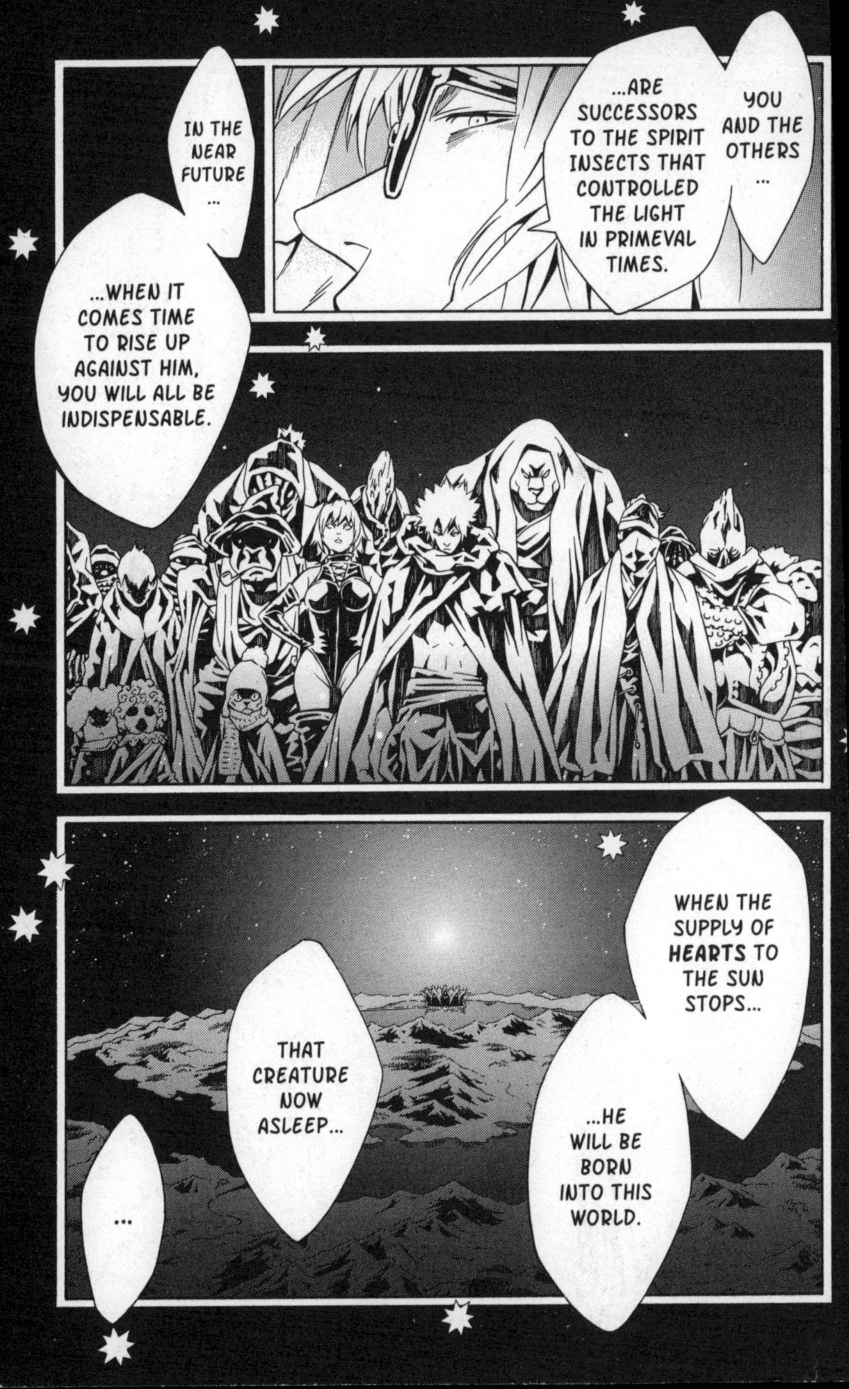
YOU AND THE OTHERS...
...ARE SUCCESSORS TO THE SPIRIT INSECTS THAT CONTROLLED THE LIGHT IN PRIMEVAL TIMES.
IN THE NEAR FUTURE...
...WHEN IT COMES TIME TO RISE UP AGAINST HIM, YOU WILL ALL BE INDISPENSABLE.
WHEN THE SUPPLY OF HEARTS TO THE SUN STOPS...
...HE WILL BE BORN INTO THIS WORLD.
THAT CREATURE NOW ASLEEP...
...

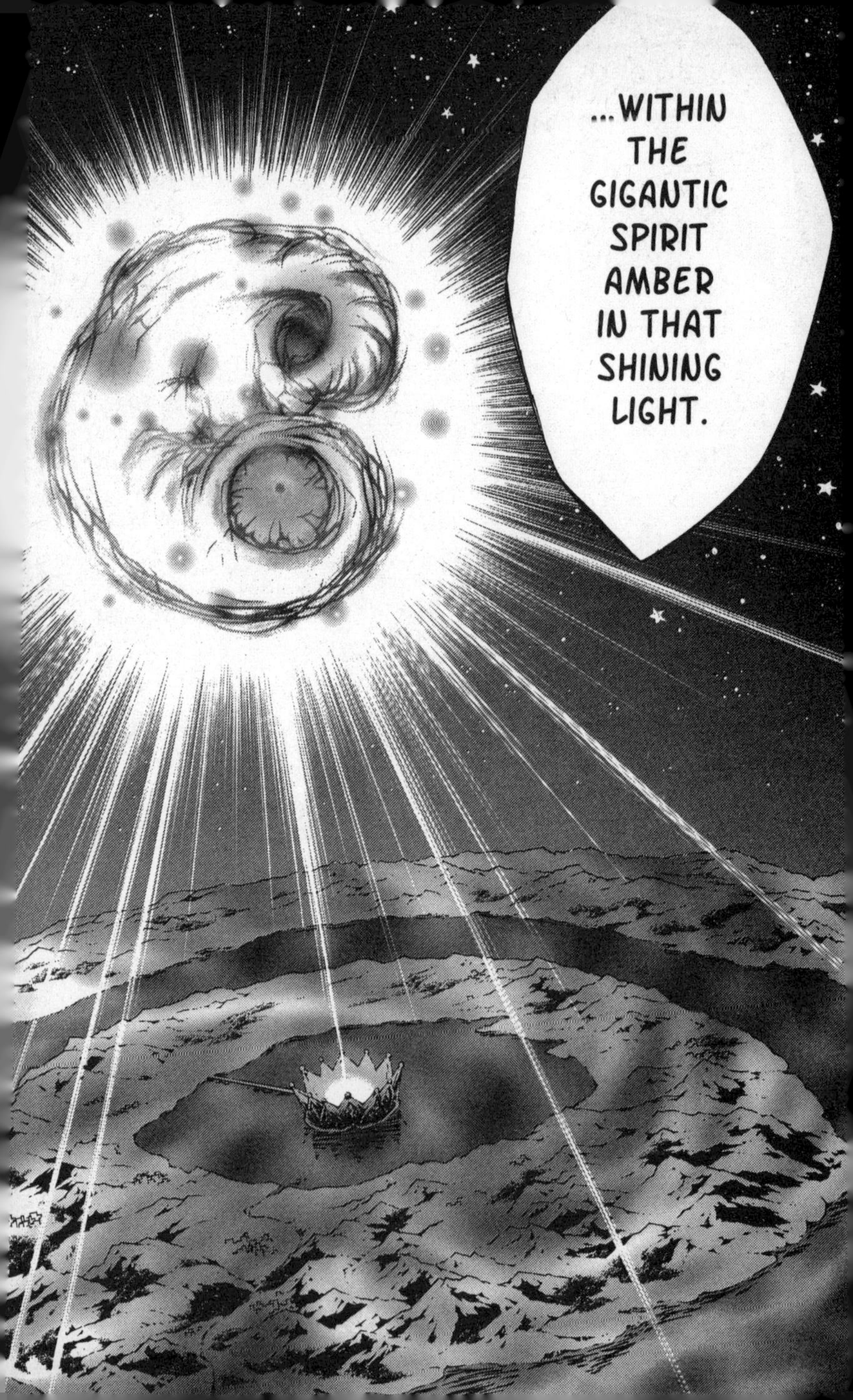
...WITHIN THE GIGANTIC SPIRIT AMBER IN THAT SHINING LIGHT.

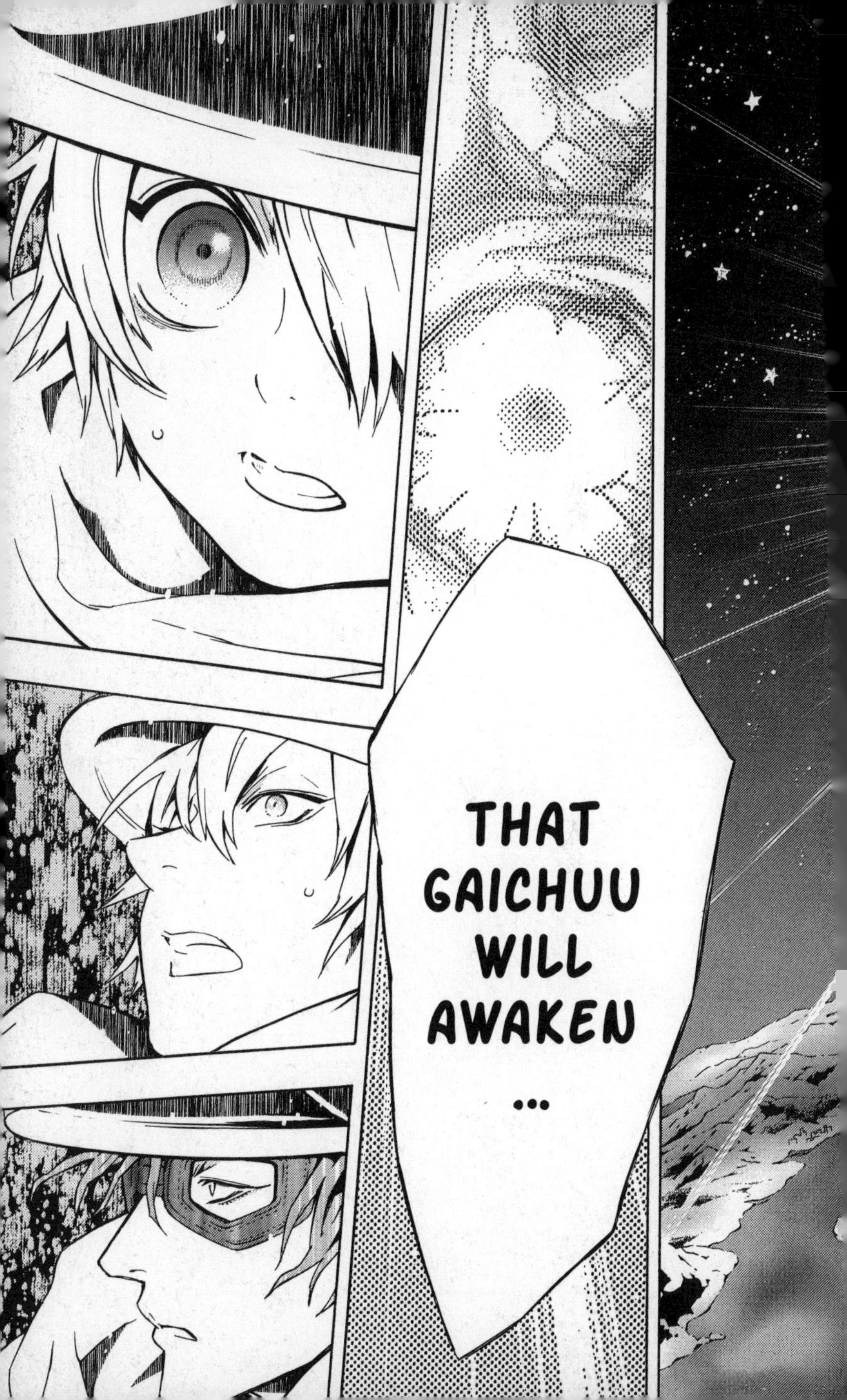
THAT GAICHUU WILL AWAKEN ...

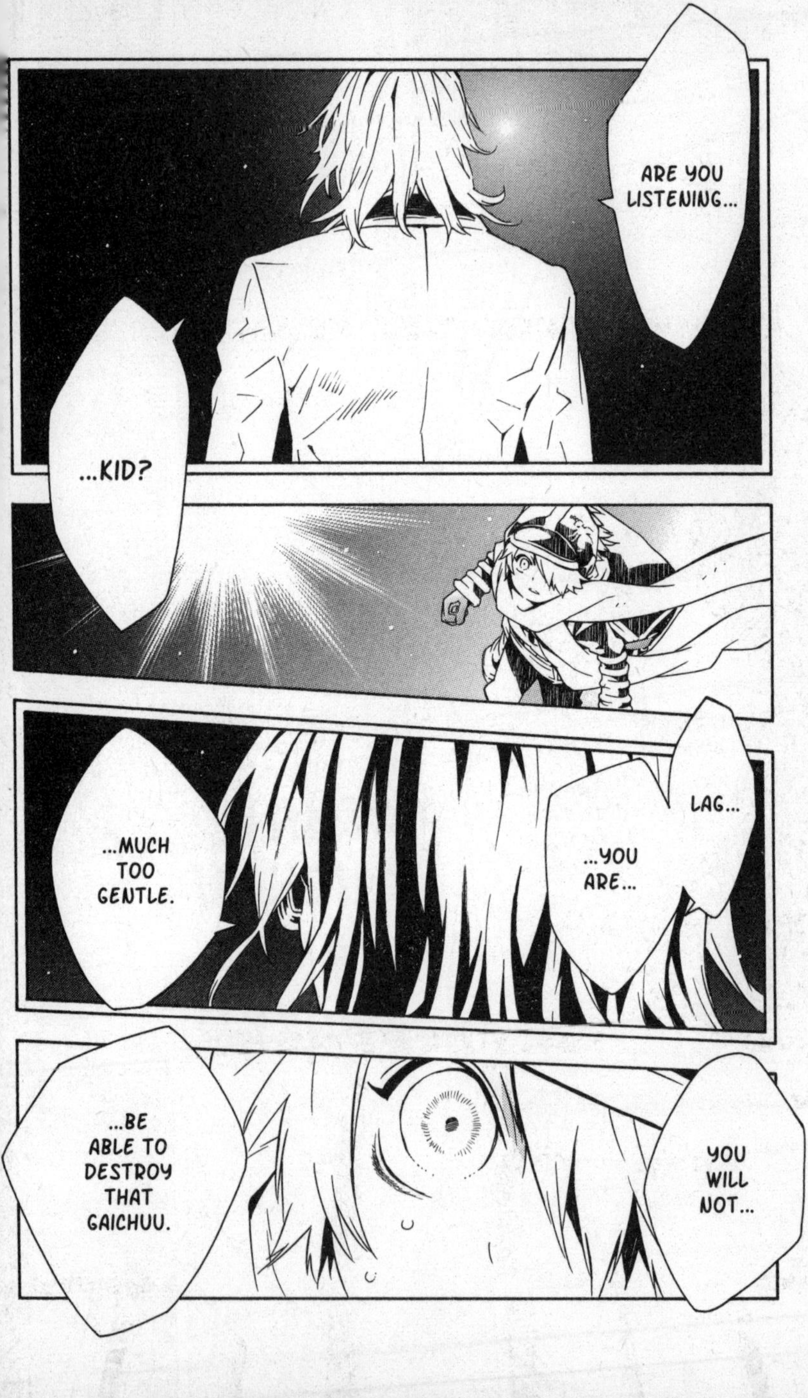
ARE YOU LISTENING...
...KID?
LAG...
...YOU ARE...
...MUCH TOO GENTLE.
YOU WILL NOT...
...BE ABLE TO DESTROY THAT GAICHUU.

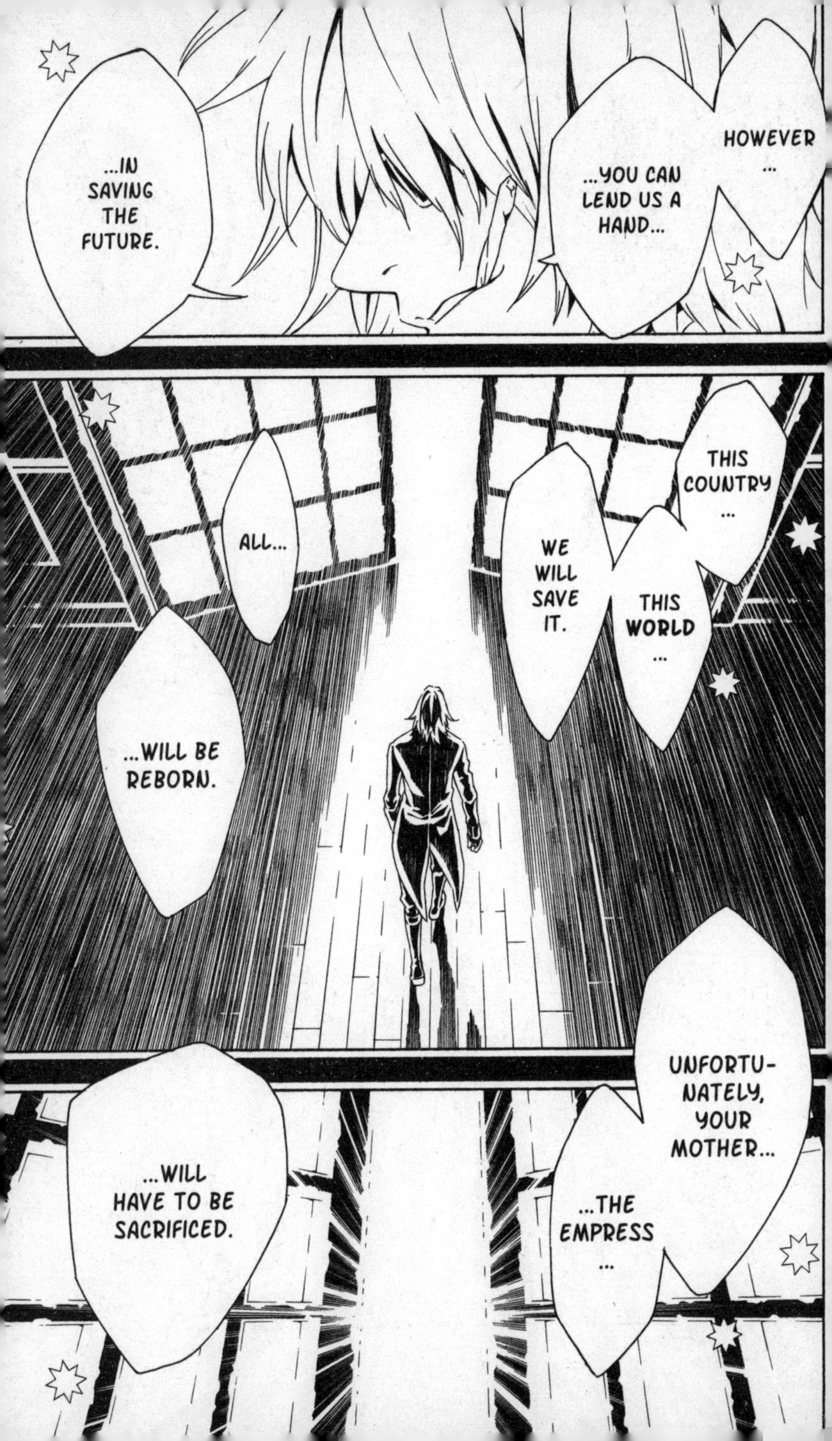
HOWEVER...
...YOU CAN LEND US A HAND...
...IN SAVING THE FUTURE.
THIS COUNTRY...
THIS WORLD...
WE WILL SAVE IT.
ALL...
...WILL BE REBORN.
UNFORTU-NATELY, YOUR MOTHER...
...THE EMPRESS...
...WILL HAVE TO BE SACRIFICED.

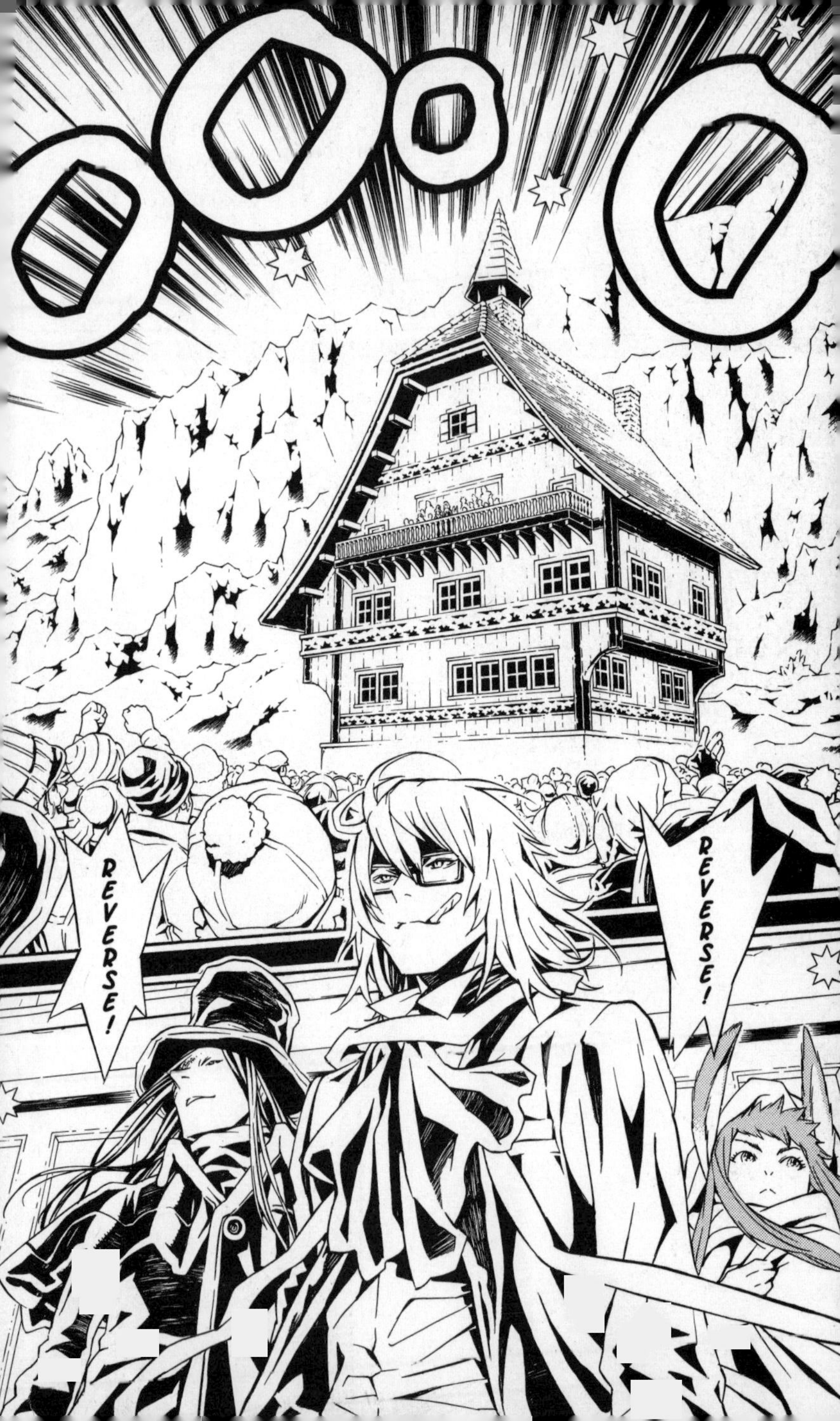
REVERSE!
REVERSE!

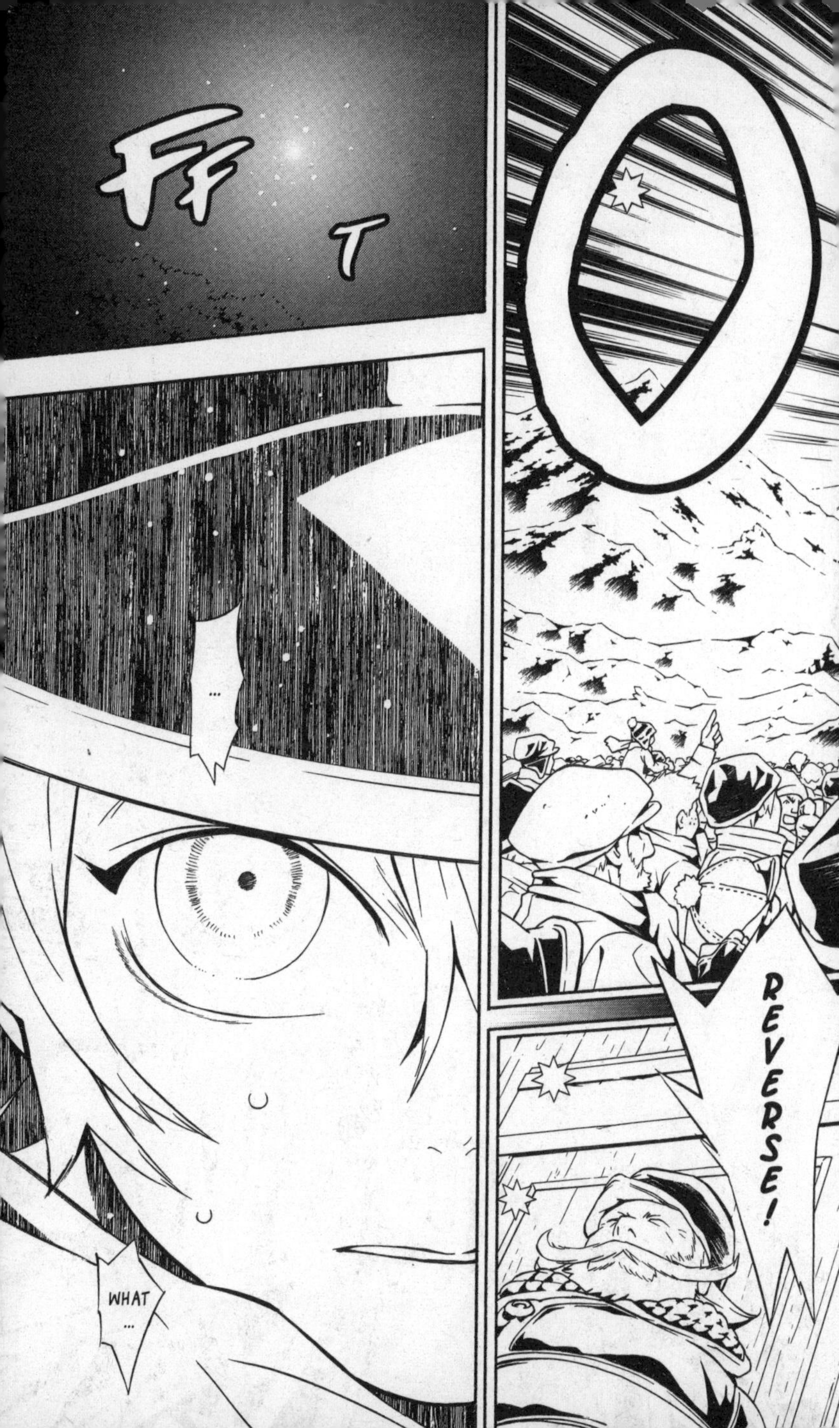
REVERSE!
FFT
...
WHAT ...

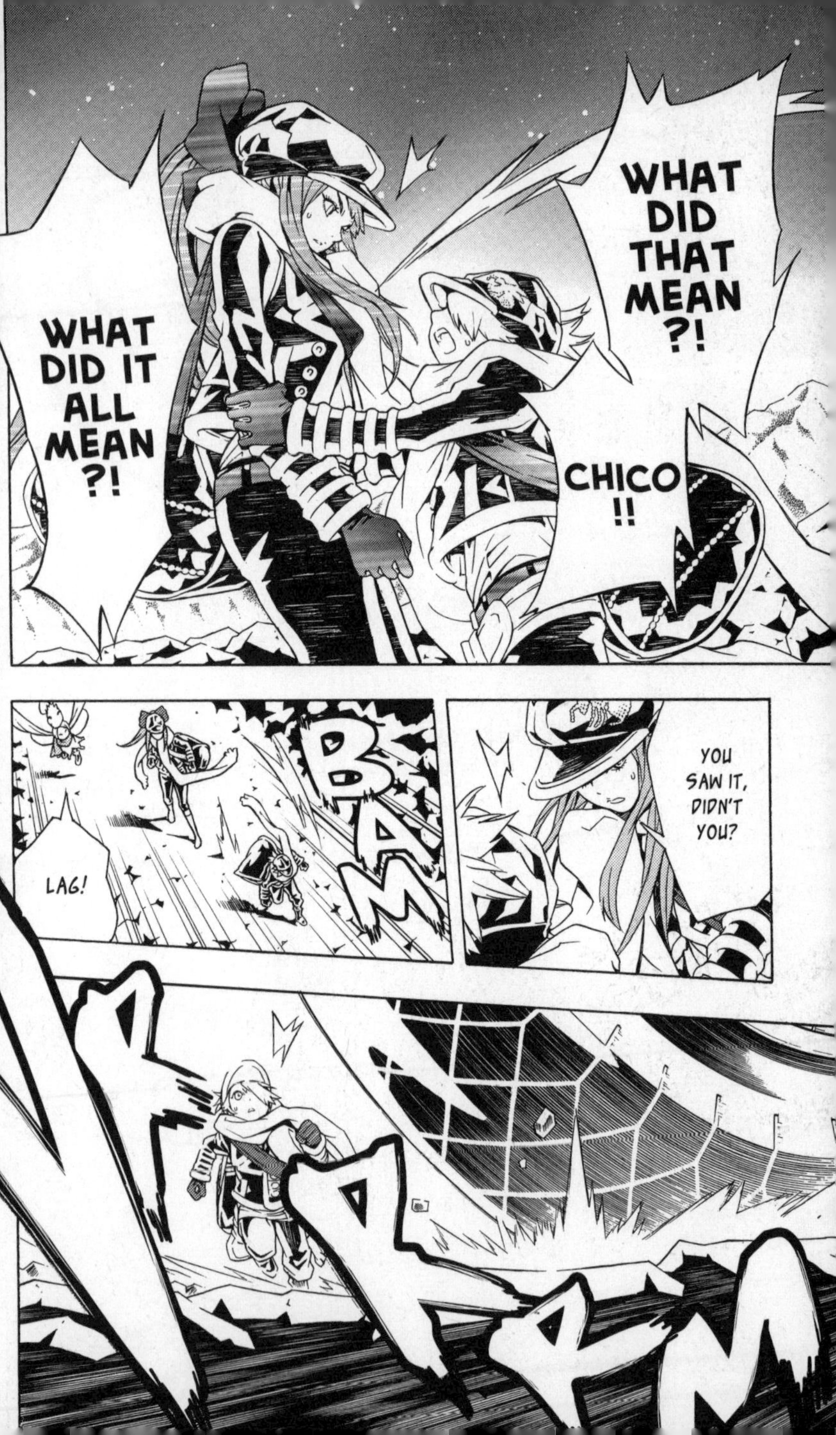
WHAT DID THAT MEAN ?!
CHICO !!
WHAT DID IT ALL MEAN ?!
YOU SAW IT, DIDN'T YOU?
BAM
LAG!

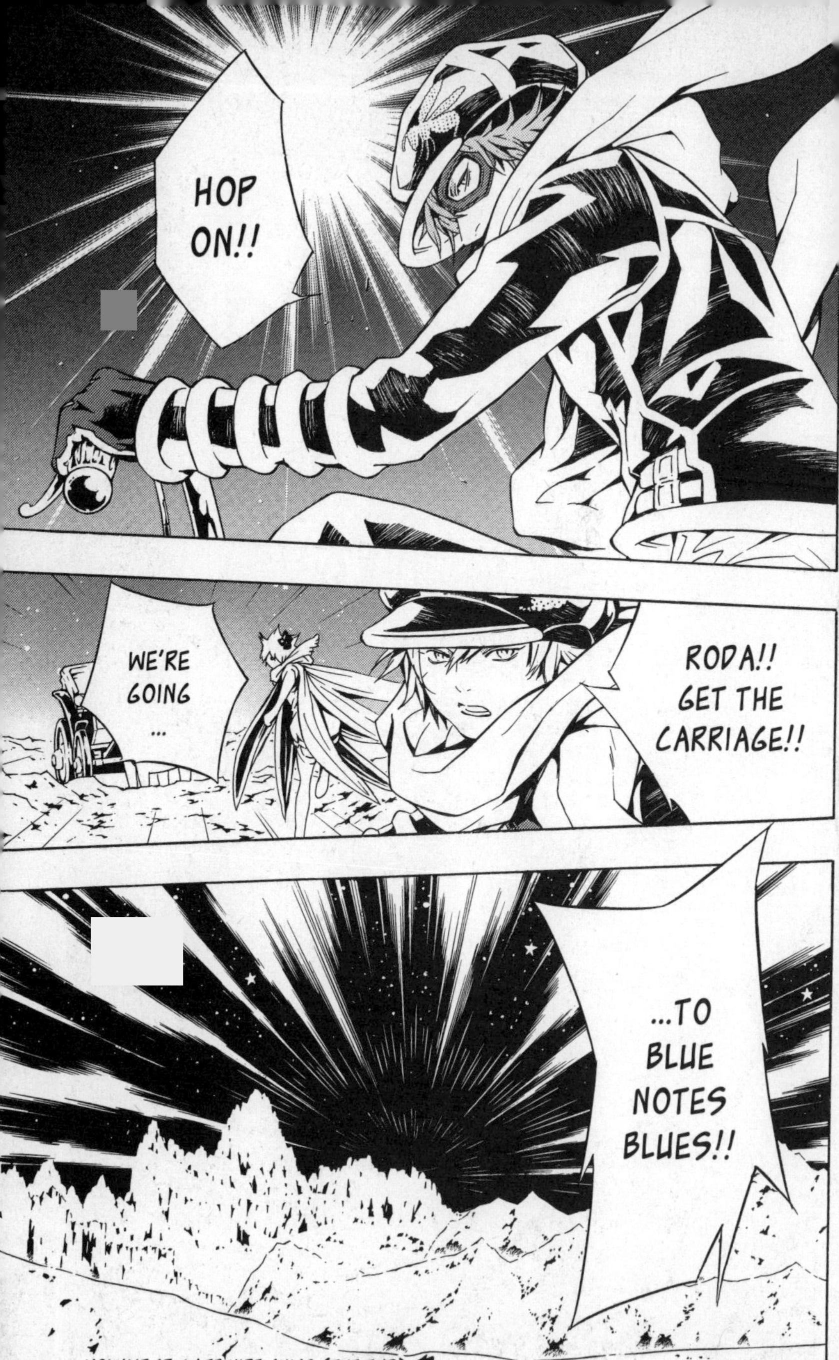
HOP ON!!
RODA!! GET THE CARRIAGE!!
WE'RE GOING ...
...TO BLUE NOTES BLUES!!
VOLUME 17: LATE HIRE CHICO (THE END)

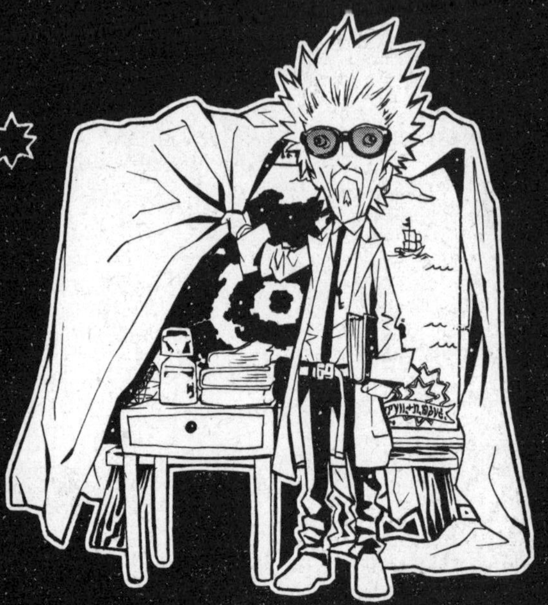

Dr. Thunderland's Reference Desk

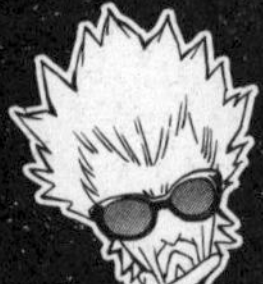

In thc last volume you found me drowning my sorrows in alcohol, and…I guess things haven't changed much. But somehow I can't seem to drink as much as I used to. I have this pain in my stomach…my gut…What could it be? *Koff! Koff! Splurt!! Ugh*…blood?! What the…?! What's going on?!

I work at the Yuusari Post Office. Every day, I vomit *koff-ugh-sploosh*…I will review the circumstances of this *blarrrgh*…

■ HEAD BEE

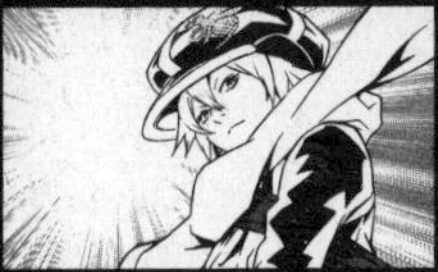

Ugh...I don't feel well. No, no, I don't want a doctor! No way! *Ugh*...my stomach hurts...

As Gauche explained in the first volume, the Head Bee is the top-ranking Letter Bee. It is the dream of all Bees, their hope, their goal. Even Lag, while pursuing Gauche, had the Head Bee position in his sights.

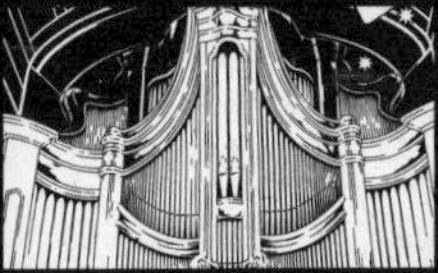

What's that? Oh, Junior's theory? Well...it's merely a theory, mind you. But I suppose...if I imagine it's true...it seems to make sense...or maybe not. But if it's correct, how awful for Lag! If I felt as sick as Lag would feel upset, what would cure me? A checkup? An endoscopy? Nooo! I had one of those through my nose a few years ago! Never again!

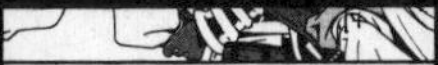

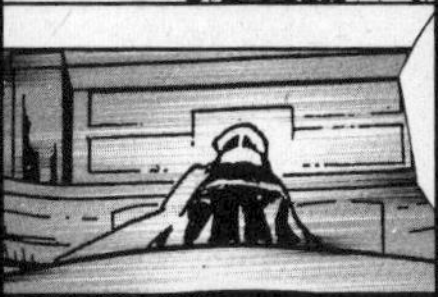

■ LETTER FROM ROSIE

How sad it is...as sad as my own physical decline. A mother working her fingers to the bone so her child can be happy. A child is the center of her parents' lives. Whether or not that's good for their child is the question. Rosie is no longer with us, but her mother will carry Rosie in her *heart* as long as she lives. It's the same way my body carries on my ailments...*sob*...

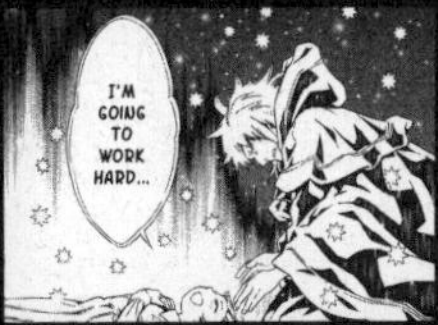
I'M GOING TO WORK HARD...

nb: "Rosie" / the 1980 debut song of the Japanese rock band The Roosters. The band members at the time were Shinya Ohe (vocals/guitar), Hiroyuki Hanada (guitar), Tomio Inoue (bass) and Jyunji Ikehata (drums).

■ PONTA AND SHIGETON'S ANIMAL TALE

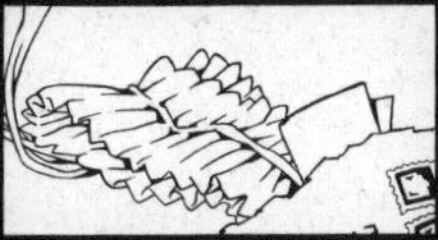

I'm so crazy about animals that I almost yelled, "Pontaaaa!" It looks like he had light spots as a newborn. He seems to be a capicaba, but I doubt anyone has seen one as large this. Could that have been caused by the artificial sun? It seems Ponta was born without front legs. Now that I think about it, Emil at Wuthering Heights was blind, and Lag...*hmm*...

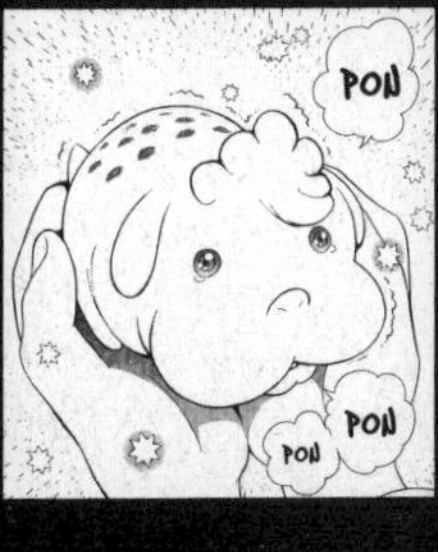
PON
PON
PON

But it looks like not only humans were affected by the Day of the Flicker. If there are plants and insects like that too, this could be trouble.

Oh no! What if there's mutant nest-eating *Helicobacter pylori* bacteria in my stomach? It might be better not to disturb them. *Sigh...*

So Lag and his friends need to find two more children born on the Day of the Flicker. I still think that minx in the wheelchair is a little suspicious.

■ CHICO NEIGE
The Beehive is desperate to hire new staff, so they're bound to get some questionable hires. And sure enough, this one is full of mystery! Chico is another "one who could not become spirit." She looks mostly human, but her ears and tail seem to be those of a rabbit. So now we have a Reverse agent in the Beehive! I guess there are the twins too. *Hm...*Did they infiltrate before anyone noticed? And what's infiltrated my body? *Argh...*I can't stand it! I need a drink!

nb: Neige / French for "snow."

■ REVERSE
And then there's Reverse! Their charismatic new leader, garnering the loyalty of Chico and hordes of other believers, is none other than Largo Lloyd, former Director of the Beehive! Looks like the reborn Reverse has finally started to move.

Lloyd acts like he knows everything. He keeps uncovering more and more of the truths hidden away by the Amberground government. I guess he wouldn't have been able to do all that if he'd remained on the government payroll. The way things are going, I don't think there's any turning back for him. What will I do if there's no turning back for me either?

■ GAICHUU SLEEPING WITHIN THE SUN (SPIRIT AMBER)
W-w-what?! Huh?! No, no! It can't be true! We must find out! Hurry! Get to Blue Notes Blues! Fast! I'm going too! As fast as I can! To the doctor! I must see a doctor! Oh no! Please hope and pray (for me)!

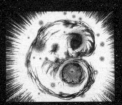

Route Map

Finally, I am including a map, indicating Lag's route since the last volume, created at Lonely Goatherd Map Station of Central Yuusari.

A: Akatsuki B: Yuusari C: Yodaka

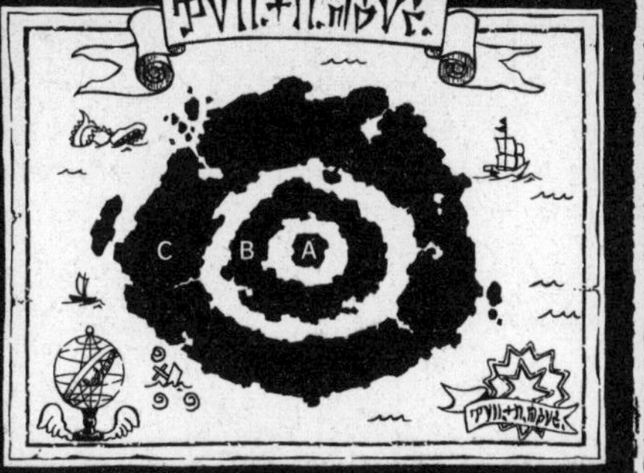
C
B
A

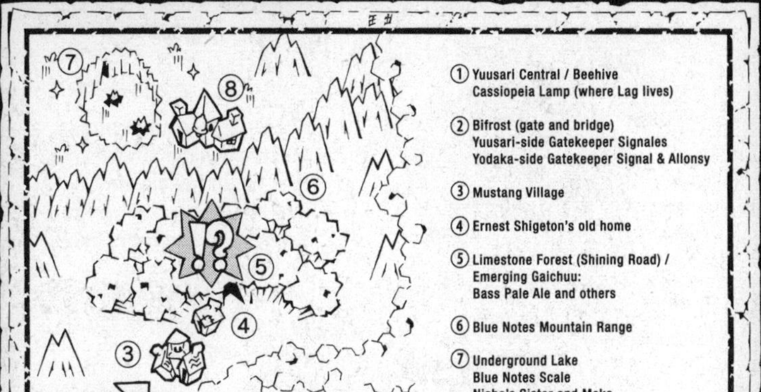
① Yuusari Central / Beehive
Cassiopeia Lamp (where Lag lives)
② Bifrost (gate and bridge)
Yuusari-side Gatekeeper Signales
Yodaka-side Gatekeeper Signal & Allonsy
③ Mustang Village
④ Ernest Shigeton's old home
⑤ Limestone Forest (Shining Road) /
Emerging Gaichuu:
Bass Pale Ale and others
⑥ Blue Notes Mountain Range
⑦ Underground Lake
Blue Notes Scale
Niche's Sister and Maka
⑧ Blue Notes Blues
Reverse + Largo Lloyd

You folks have given me the energy to go on living! I promise to see my doctor! I think I've forgotten how it feels to be healthy. Yes! I will regain my health for volume 18 and shout out loud! When do I get to make my appearance? My appearance, my appearance, my appearance (echo...).

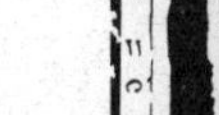

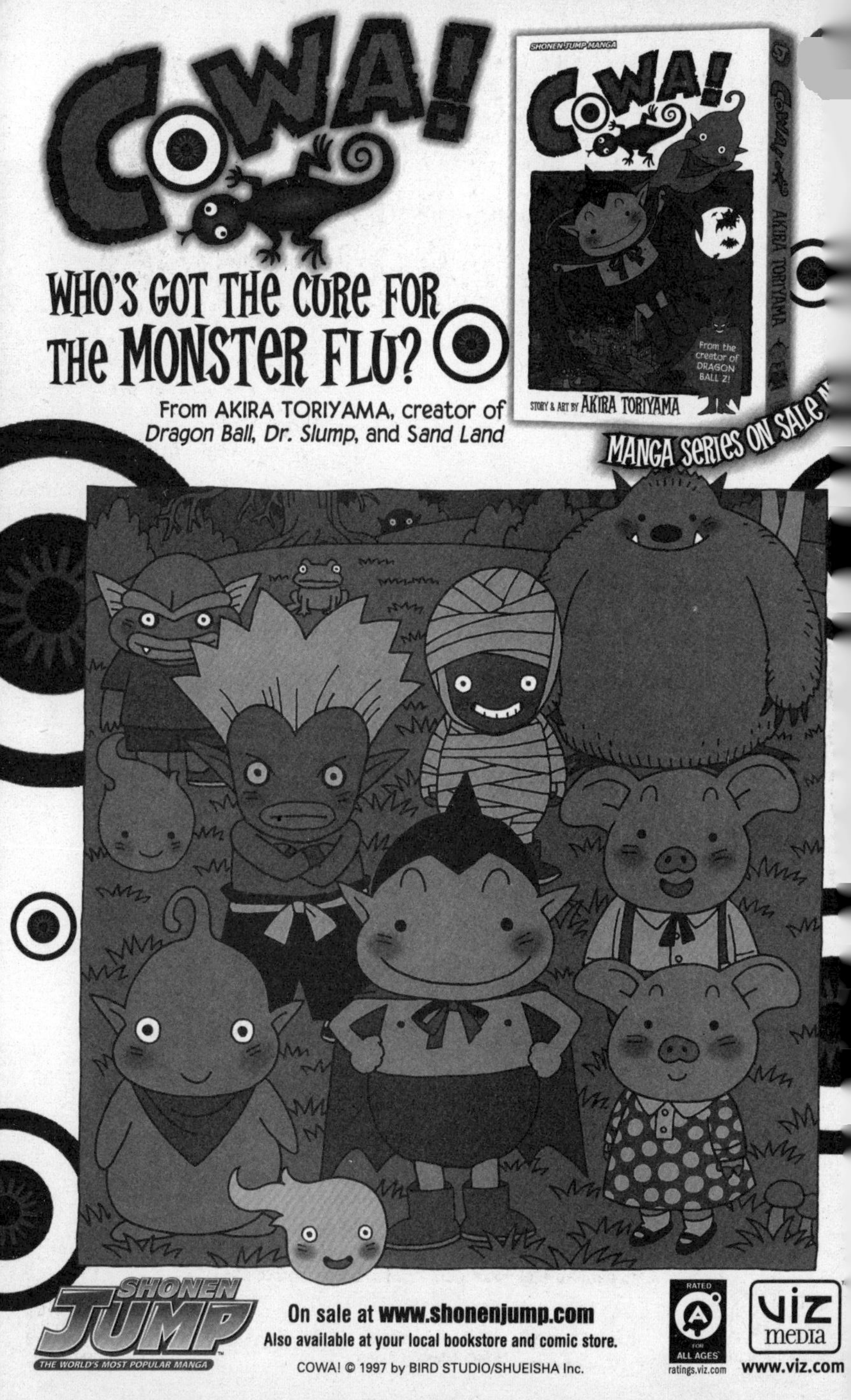
COWA!
WHO'S GOT THE CURE FOR THE MONSTER FLU?
From AKIRA TORIYAMA, creator of Dragon Ball, Dr. Slump, and Sand Land
SHONEN JUMP MANGA
COWA!
From the creator of DRAGON BALL Z!
STORY & ART BY AKIRA TORIYAMA
AKIRA TORIYAMA
MANGA SERIES ON SALE
SHONEN JUMP
THE WORLD'S MOST POPULAR MANGA
On sale at www.shonenjump.com
Also available at your local bookstore and comic store.
COWA! © 1997 by BIRD STUDIO/SHUEISHA Inc.
RATED A FOR ALL AGES
ratings.viz.com
VIZ media
www.viz.com

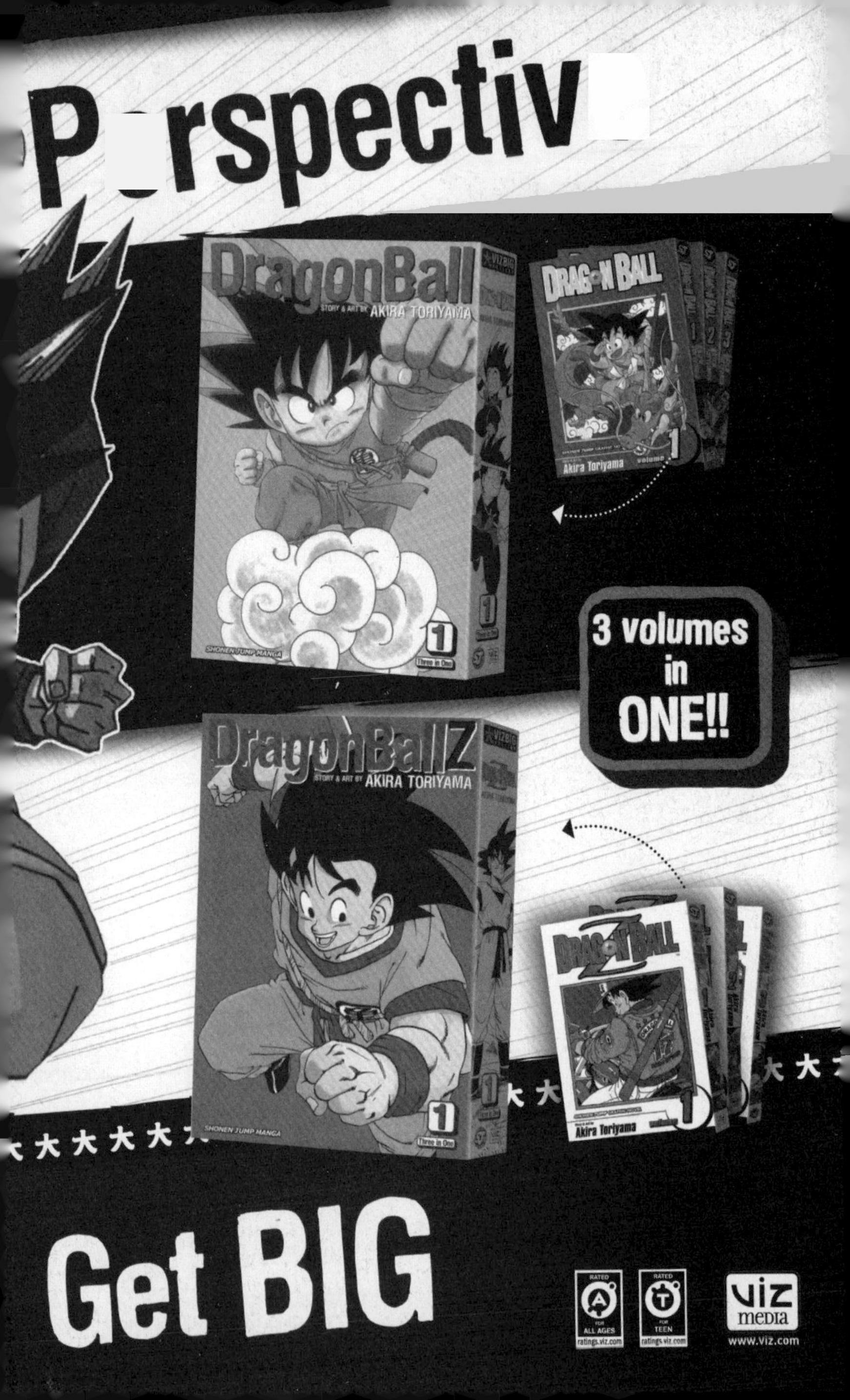

P rspectiv
DragonBall
STORY & ART BY AKIRA TORIYAMA
SHONEN JUMP MANGA
Three in One
DRAGON BALL
Akira Toriyama
3 volumes in ONE!!
DragonBall Z
STORY & ART BY AKIRA TORIYAMA
SHONEN JUMP MANGA
Three in One
DRAGON BALL Z
Akira Toriyama
Get BIG
RATED A FOR ALL AGES ratings.viz.com
RATED T FOR TEEN ratings.viz.com
viz media
www.viz.com

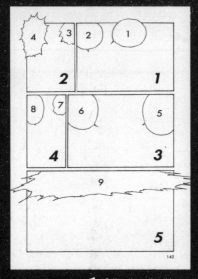

142

← Follow the action this way.

THIS IS THE LAST PAGE.

Tegami Bachi: Letter Bee has been printed in the original Japanese format in order to preserve the orientation of the original artwork.

Please turn it around and begin reading from right to left. Unlike English, Japanese is read right to left, so Japanese comics are read in reverse order from the way English comics are typically read. Have fun with it!